Roger and Patricia Jeffery's book is the result of extensive fieldwork in two villages in Bijnor District, western Uttar Pradesh in North India. In an accessible and sympathetic account, they examine the demographic processes in two castes – the Hindu Jats and the Muslim Sheikhs – and ask why there are higher levels of fertility among the Sheikhs. The authors conclude that explanations can be only partially attributed to narrowly economic concerns, to gender relationships or to religion. Rather, the different economic and political interests and positions of the two groups within the locality are the defining factors. Given their marginalization from the formal urban economy, the Sheikhs have little incentive, for example, to have small families or to invest in the education of their children. In contrast, the Jats – who are locally dominant – are using birth control and educating their children for as long as possible. In the final chapter, the authors demonstrate the significance of their analysis for a wider understanding of the problems of population and politics in India generally. The book will be invaluable to students of South Asia and to anyone interested in the demography of developing countries.

Contemporary South Asia

Population, gender and politics

Contemporary South Asia 3

Editorial board

Contemporary South Asia has been established to publish books on the politics, society and culture of South Asia since 1947. In accessible and comprehensive studies, authors who are already engaged in researching specific aspects of South Asian society explore a wide variety of broad-ranging and topical themes. The series will be of interest to anyone who is concerned with the study of South Asia and with the legacy of its colonial past.

Population, gender and politics

Demographic change in rural north India

Roger Jeffery
and
Patricia Jeffery
University of Edinburgh

CAMBRIDGE
UNIVERSITY PRESS

PUBLISHED BY THE PRESS SYNDICATE OF THE UNIVERSITY OF CAMBRIDGE
The Pitt Building, Trumpington Street, Cambridge CB2 1RP, United Kingdom

CAMBRIDGE UNIVERSITY PRESS
The Edinburgh Building, Cambridge CB2 2RU, United Kingdom
40 West 20th Street, New York, NY 10011–4211, USA
10 Stamford Road, Oakleigh, Melbourne 3166, Australia

First published 1997

Printed in the United Kingdom at the University Press, Cambridge

Typeset in Plantin 10/12pt

*A catalogue record for this book is available from the
British Library*

Library of Congress Cataloguing in Publication data applied for

ISBN 0 521 46116 2 hardback
ISBN 0 521 46653 9 paperback

CE

Contents

Tables

Preface and Acknowledgements

Since the early 1980s we have carried out three extended periods of fieldwork in Bijnor District, in the northern Indian state of Uttar Pradesh. Our Muslim research assistant, Swaleha Begum, had worked for us in 1982 and in 1985, and we were keen to have her work with us again when we arrived for our third trip in July 1990. But our research got off to a bad start, one which ominously foreshadowed the problems we had in completing this project. To begin with, students agitated against the reservation of places to members of the 'Other Backward Classes' and Swaleha was unable to complete her B.Ed. at the University of Rohtak in Haryana. When the university was closed for an unspecified period, she moved to Delhi in August and September, awaiting a call for her to take her final exams. She eventually joined us at the end of September.

By then we were working in Nangal, a village on the opposite side of Bijnor from Dharmnagri, the village where we were living. Every morning we set off, uncertain whether our route would be blocked by student demonstrators; furthermore, in Nangal we were interviewing Hindu Jats. Swaleha wore *shalwār qamīz,* the baggy trousers and loose-fitting shirts common to Muslims and to unmarried Jats, so her religious identity was not obvious. On several occasions, Jat women let forth diatribes against Muslims before (apparently unknowingly) asking Swaleha what *zat* (community or caste) she belonged to. After only a fortnight or so of work, Swaleha was clearly very uncomfortable with her position. Then rumours of violence, planned or actual, began to spread through the Bijnor countryside: on several days we abandoned fieldwork entirely because a curfew had been predicted in Bijnor town before nightfall. Nevertheless, on 20 October when we gave Swaleha a few days' holiday to attend a wedding in her home town of Nagina, 25 miles away, we did not expect that she would not work for us again before January 1991. In the interim, riots and police repression had convulsed Bijnor town, which was under curfew from 30 October to 10 November. Officially, 48 people were killed; many shops and houses were set alight

and looted. We had the luxury of escape, and spent much of November
and December discussing whether to abandon our research and return
to Edinburgh prematurely. Eventually we decided to complete an
uncomfortable year in India. In doing so we gained a new perspective on
population dynamics in north India. This book – very different from the
one we expected to write – is one of the fruits of that experience.

Although this book is based mostly on the material we collected in
1990–1, our understanding of the processes involved in recent demographic changes in north India is heavily dependent on our earlier
research as well. We are grateful for the funding we have received over
the years from the Economic and Social Research Council, the Overseas
Development Administration, and the Hayter Fund at the University of
Edinburgh. None of these, of course, bears any responsibility for what
we have written here. During our research in Bijnor we were helped by
Radha Rani Sharma and Swaleha Begum in 1982–3, 1985, and 1990–1,
by Savita Pandey in 1982, and by Zarin Ahmed, Chhaya Pandey and
Swatantra Tyagi in 1990–1. We are endlessly grateful for the care and
attention they brought to their work, in conditions that were often far
from pleasant. The material in this book comes from just two of the
villages where we have worked, Nangal (a caste Hindu and Scheduled
Caste village, with a small population of Muslims) and Qaziwala (a
Muslim village, with a small population drawn from Scheduled Castes).
Our thanks also go to Khurshid Ahmed, who helped us in 1982, and
from late 1990 worked with Roger for some three months, smoothing
our access to Qaziwala when the combination of the Ayodhya crisis, the
brewing Gulf War and Muslims' worries about the implications of the
national decennial census was threatening to derail our research again.

While we were based in Bijnor we relied upon many people for
hospitality, and for intellectual and moral support. In particular we
thank Meera Chatterjee and her family, Bina Agarwal, Loki Madan,
Walter Fernandez and others at the Indian Social Institute, Jennifer and
Robert Chambers, Carolyn Elliott, Kamlesh and John Mackrell, James
and Willi Barton, June Rollinson, and especially Kunwar Satya Vira and
his family.

Since completing our fieldwork we have exploited the patience and
good humour of friends and colleagues who have commented on all or
some of the manuscript, or discussed the general issues raised by our
writing. In particular we would like to thank our editor Marigold
Acland, Michael Anderson, Anthony Carter, Ben Crow, Tim Dyson,
Betsy Hartmann, and Jonathan Spencer for detailed comments. Others
have commented on versions of some of the material presented at
conferences and workshops since we returned to Edinburgh, especially

Alaka Basu. Eryn Starun gave valuable editorial assistance when our energy was flagging. We also thank our daughters Laura and Kirin, for putting up with their parents' workaholic lifestyles.

Without the co-operation of many people in Dharmnagri, Jhakri, Qaziwala, and Nangal, our research would have been impossible. So many of them went beyond co-operation, showing us warmth and kindness which we did all too little to deserve or to recompense. We cannot easily convey our gratitude to them all, and it would be invidious to pick out one or two for special comment. In writing about their lives, we hope we have expressed something of what we feel for them.

Glossary

alag	separate; a woman living in a household separate from her mother-in-law
āmdani	everyday income or expenses
āzādī	freedom; from *āzād*, free
bahū	bride, or daughter-in-law (*bahū mol-lenā* to pay money for a bride)
bāngar	high ground, well-drained land
chūlhā	cooking hearth; by extension, a household, the people who eat food cooked at the same hearth
Eid	a Muslim festival, especially those marking the breaking of the fast of Ramzān (Mīthi Eid) and commemorating Abraham's willingness to sacrifice Isaac, at which goats are slaughtered (Bakr Eid)
gaunā	cohabitation, the ceremonial bringing of a new bride to her husband's home, which symbolizes the start of her married life; cohabitation may take place at the same time as the marriage or some months later
ghī	a form of clarified butter
gur	crudely refined raw sugar product
hakīm	practitioner of Unani (Greek or Arabic) medicine; usually Muslim
imām	Islamic religious specialist, usually the leader of prayers at a mosque
izzat	prestige, family or personal standing or status
jāti	caste group, in the sense of a local kin network within which marriages are arranged; to be distinguished from *varna*, one of the four classes described in the classical texts
jawān	young adult; a girl who has reached puberty
jījā	elder sister's husband (eZH); by extension, the husband of a cousin (e.g. FeBDH)
kāshtkār	literally, tenant farmer; used to describe a substantial farmer

khādar	low alluvial land, suitable for rice, for example
khāndān	family, a group of relatives linked through the male side, a lineage
khāndsārī	private sugar processing plant, making semi-refined sugar
khetībārī	farming, agriculture
kisān	peasant, cultivator
kolhū	press, sugarcane mill, processing plant for *gur*
len-den	exchange relationships; literally, 'taking-giving'
madrasā	Islamic school or academy, taking children from about age five to eleven or twelve for girls, and to fifteen or sixteen for boys
mālik	master
maulvī	a learned man, teacher of Islamic law
mazdūr	labourer, usually on daily wages; *mazdūrī* labour, day-wages
panchāyat	village council, of five or more members
patwārī	registrar of village land records
rishtedār	relative, someone who is connected by blood or marriage
rotī	unleavened griddle-baked bread; by extension, daily food
sājhe	joint, in partnership; a woman sharing a cooking hearth, usually with her mother-in-law or daughter-in-law
tāwīz	amulet, charm
zamindār	landlord, person responsible for paying ground rent to the Government

Textual conventions

Transliteration

We have marked the Hindi long 'a' as 'ā', the long 'i' as 'ī', and the long 'u' as 'ū' to distinguish them from the short versions, and 'kh' (as in the Scottish 'loch') to distinguish from 'kh', an aspirated 'k'. An 'e' is pronounced like the 'é' in French. We have not distinguished different Hindi 'r', 't', and 'd' sounds but in most other respects have followed the transliteration schema in McGregor (1993).

Currency

The Indian Rupee now has 100 paisa. Prior to decimalization, there were sixty-four paisa and sixteen annas in one rupee. There were about thirty-three rupees to the US dollar in 1995, or about fifty rupees to the pound sterling.

Kinship terminology

Kin terms used in Bijnor by Hindus and Muslims conform to the structure discussed by Vatuk (1969). We have adopted the following notation:

M = Mother	F = Father
W = Wife	H = Husband
D = Daughter	S = Son
Z = Sister	B = Brother
e = elder	y = younger

These can be combined to describe the full range of kin relationships, as in 'HeBW' (a woman's husband's elder brother's wife). In north India the 'HBW' has very different rights and obligations from the 'HZ' (a woman's husband's sister) and from the 'BW' (brother's wife), though all three would be translated as 'sister-in-law' in English.

1   An island of peace?

When we were first looking for a research site, in 1982, one of the attractions of Bijnor District was its reputation for intercommunity and intercaste peace, and its freedom from organized crime, by comparison with some of the neighbouring districts. According to the national press, Bijnor was not involved in the violence which affected Hindu–Muslim relations in the late 1970s (unlike neighbouring Moradabad and Meerut). Nor was it affected by the *dakaitī* (armed burglary) which mushroomed in the early 1980s. Bijnor lies just below the foothills of the Himalayas, to the east of the River Ganges after it reaches the plains at Hardwar and flows through Uttar Pradesh, Bihar and Bengal to the sea. It seemed to be a backwater, out of the mainstream of national political life. The villages of Dharmnagri and Jhakri, five kilometres north-west of Bijnor town, were the sites of our research in 1982–3 and in 1985. Village residents, as well as our contacts in Bijnor town, used the events of Independence and Partition in 1947 to provide the clinching argument. Despite the presence there of large numbers of Muslims, Bijnor had remained free of trouble when Hindu–Muslim and Sikh–Muslim rioting and communal violence was widespread in Punjab (to the west) and in Bengal (to the east). That was as far back as local political memories went.

A modest amount of historical research, however, produced evidence to suggest that the district had experienced considerable violence in the nineteenth century, which had been interpreted by the British colonial Government as communalist in nature.[1] As in other parts of western UP, different landholding groups vied for local dominance, at least since Rohillas and Pathans, Muslim leaders of small armies, began to acquire land rights and move out of the district towns in the early eighteenth century (Bayly 1983:41–8). Some tensions came to the fore in the events

---

[1] In the Indian sub-continent, 'communal' and 'communalist' refer to acts or feelings of hostility and animosity between members of different groups (or communities) defined usually in terms of religion. The terms beg many questions, but are such an integral part of the discourse on violence and religion in India that we cannot avoid using them.

of 1857–8.[2] Muslims led the revolt against the British in the district, but apparently were easily diverted into attacking Hindu villages and petty nobles; Muslim artisans began to attack Hindu landlords and traders in the towns. Hindu Jats and Rajputs then retaliated against Muslims (thus acting in the British interest). Saiyid Ahmed Khan's view was that, 'Before this fighting there had never been a dispute, nor feelings of hostility nor even a religious altercation, between Hindus and Muslims of this District' but that after fighting in Sherkot in August 1857, 'the tree of Hindu-Muslim aversion ... became tall and too firmly rooted to be dug out' (Khan 1972: 40, 47; see also Bayly 1983: 365).[3]

None the less, whatever had happened in 1857 or since, local people were largely unaware of it, and collective amnesia fuelled a somewhat complacent belief that Bijnor was immune to the problems suffered elsewhere in India.[4] Relatively few Muslims went from Bijnor to Pakistan in 1947. Since then, some Sikhs from the western areas of Punjab that were allocated to Pakistan have settled part of the tarāī (the low-lying land at the foot at the Himalayas areas next to Garhwal in the north-east of the district); and some Bengali Hindu refugees from East Pakistan (now Bangladesh) were allotted land for four villages near the Ganges to the north-west of Bijnor town. Until 1990, we have no evidence that friction between these incomers and particular locals, between Muslims and Hindus, or between caste Hindus and members of the Scheduled Castes[5] had ever flared into mass lawlessness. Only in the late 1980s did the Bijnor Sikhs seem to pose a threat to public order,

[2] Pandey (1991) argues convincingly that, when it comes to issues of Hindu–Muslim disputes and differences, the Gazetteers tended to stress pre-British hostilities and the calming role of British rule. There is more than a whiff of this in the *Gazetteer* account of the events of 1857–8 in Bijnor. See also Bayly's summary of Sir Saiyid Ahmad Khan's account (Bayly 1983: 364–6). More detail on the Bijnor riots of 1990 can be found in R. Jeffery and P. Jeffery 1994 and Basu 1994.
[3] After the events of 1857–8, both communities had land confiscated by the British authorities, and curiously, others from the same communities were rewarded. The largest losers were Hindu Rajputs, then Muslim Pathans, Saiyids and Sheikhs; the largest winners were also Rajputs, then Hindu Brahmans, Tagas, Banias and Jats, followed by Pathans, Saiyids and Hindu Ahirs.
[4] Pandey (1991: 563) also notes how important it was to Muslims in Bhagalpur, in eastern UP, to deny any quarrel with Hindus and to claim that even in 1946–7 there was little trouble, though the Bhagalpur Riot Inquiry Commission into the rioting of 1989 cited communal clashes in 1924, 1936, 1946 and 1967, all in Bhagalpur town itself (Engineer 1995).
[5] Using 'Harijan' ('Children of God', the name used by M. K. Gandhi instead of 'Untouchable') is contentious; in many parts of India, members of the Scheduled Castes have adopted the name 'Dalit' (Depressed Classes) but we never heard this used in Bijnor; whatever the anomalies of using 'Harijan' or 'Scheduled Caste' we will continue to do so since they represent local usage.

as some were accused of harbouring – either willingly or under duress – terrorists from the Punjab.

Nobody could give us a satisfactory account of the relative absence of overt communal problems. One explanation we heard was an 'urban proportions' argument, in which urban communal relationships are said to be most hostile where two communities are evenly balanced electorally.[6] Bijnor District has three substantial towns: Bijnor itself, Nagina and Najibabad. Muslims make up 57 per cent of their combined population, with another 7.5 per cent being Scheduled Caste. Some people argued that urban caste Hindus – only one-third of the population – have accepted a subordinate political position. But in Bijnor town, the District headquarters – with all the district offices, banks, shops, hospitals and political prominence which goes with that status – the communal mix is 48 per cent Muslim, 8 per cent Scheduled Caste, and 42 per cent caste Hindu – not quite such a convincing picture of one-community dominance. Other accounts of the rise of communal violence have located the fracture points in the larger towns; or have seen it as a social and political consequence of uneven economic development (Engineer 1984; Saberwal and Hasan 1984). All the towns in Bijnor District are comparatively small. Bijnor town itself has a population of only 65,000 people. Until recently it has had relatively poor communications: only in 1984 did a barrage across the Ganges cut travelling time to Delhi by two hours, and make neighbouring Muzaffarnagar easily accessible for the first time. The Bijnor towns have been growing slowly, and have little in the way of large-scale or organized industry, so they may have escaped some of the tensions that often accompany rapid urban and industrial growth.

Hindus and Muslims on the whole occupy rather different economic niches in Bijnor town. The larger shopkeepers and market traders are Hindus. Most small fruit and vegetable stalls are owned by Muslims. Most of the white-collar jobs in the government administration and in the only substantial enterprise – the local sugar factory – are held by Hindus, while the skilled workers and labourers are mostly Muslim.

---

[6] Akbar (1988) and Engineer (ed.) (1984) note the role of comparative population proportions. For example, in Meerut the populations are evenly balanced and city council elections are a key issue (Banerjee 1990: 55); in Moradabad (not really suffering a communal riot in 1980, but a police attack on Muslims) 60 per cent of the population is Muslim. In Agra (with a relatively riot-free history) the worst rioting of December 1990 took place 'where there is a mixed population and the population is more or less at par' (*The Illustrated Weekly of India*, December 29–30, 1990: 5). Accounts of how neighbouring Saharanpur suffered its first major riots in March 1991 (*The Sunday Times of India* 23 December 1990: 13 and 7 April 1991: 15) also stressed the communal balance. The Hindu 'right' often interprets these correlations as 'there are only riots where there are many Muslims'.

None the less, economic interests have not hitherto fused with religious allegiance to intensify local disputes.

Other factors may have played a part in maintaining a semblance of peace. The state administration has often been implicated in South Asia in the origins of local riots, or in tacitly permitting them to emerge. There clearly have been incidents in Bijnor that generated intense feelings, but successive District Magistrates seem to have been willing and able to control potentially explosive events.[7] If we are to take Tambiah (1989) and Saberwal and Hasan (1984) literally when they argue that a history of riots itself contributes to further riots, then the absence of local riots, and people's belief in the exceptional character of Bijnor, may also have contributed to its on-going peace. Again, local newspapers have often been accused of intensifying hostility by exaggerating disputes and giving them a communal slant. Unusually, however, in the 1980s the Bijnor Urdu and Hindi newspapers were both run from the same office by men with strong secular backgrounds.[8]

Until 1990, local politicians, landowners and professionals also played a part in 'keeping the peace'. If there is a limited repertoire of collective actions played out by crowds, (Tilly 1986; Das 1990) so also is there a limited repertoire of 'practical secularism' as a means of keeping the peace. In Bijnor (as elsewhere) 'unity marches' – the joint touring of troubled areas by leaders from both communities – and other public shows of intercommunal amity have often been used to defuse potential troubles. One local Hindu politician with a record of such practical peace-keeping is Satya Vira, born in 1912, who lives in Dharmnagri, one of our research villages. We have been able to observe his actions over extended periods since 1982, and we describe his activities during the

---

[7] We visited the Bijnor District Magistrate on 13 September 1982 on other business; he revealed that he had spent the past few days dealing with communal 'incidents', now resolved, and that he had forbidden any reporting by the press. When riots do break out, the District Magistrate and Superintendent of Police are usually transferred, a move regarded as a punishment they would presumably wish to avoid. Thus we need to understand who, in the District administration, acts to encourage trouble, and with whose support ('politicians' of one kind or another are usually blamed).

[8] The *Bijnor Times* (Hindi) and *Rozānā Khabr Jadīd* (Urdu) were owned and managed by a man who decorated his office with pictures of Marx and photos of his own involvement in Indo-Soviet Friendship Committee events sponsored by the Communist Party of India (CPI). He edited the Hindi paper himself, but the Urdu paper was edited by a member of the CPI (Marxist). Neither communist party was strong locally, and many people took other north Indian papers, especially *Dainik Jāgran* and *Amar Ujālā* (Hindi), and *Qaumi Awāz* (Urdu). For discussions of the role of newspapers in encouraging intercommunal hostility, see *The Sunday Times of India*'s 'Media File' 23 December 1990; *India Today* 30 November 1990:62, 82; Ramaseshan 1990. The most notorious example – the totally unfounded claim that Muslim doctors in Aligarh Muslim University's Hospital had killed Hindu patients – is exposed in *The Illustrated Weekly of India* 15–16 December 1990: 1, and in Sofat 1991. See also Mody 1987.

1990 riots below. His older brother, Dharm Vira, has been Jawaharlal Nehru's secretary, Governor of Karnataka and West Bengal, and an Ambassador. Satya Vira was a member of the Indian Congress Party until 1975, when he resigned in protest against the suspension of democratic processes, and the authoritarian policies (including forced sterilizations) committed under cover of the Emergency of 1975–7. He joined the Janata Party and was a junior Education Minister in the UP Government in 1977–8.[9] Among many other economic interests the family trust runs schools and colleges in Bijnor. His political style has been resolutely 'secularist'; one of his sons says that his Hindu enemies regard him as an honorary Muslim (a term of abuse in the eyes of Hindu chauvinists), though Muslims still regard him as a Hindu. He and his family are very prosperous, but they are not regarded as personally corrupt, and (unusually for an Indian politician prominent since the 1970s) he is not accused of maintaining his position through support from 'criminal elements'.

In the area of Dharmnagri his peace-keeping efforts involved him in negotiating dispute settlements at *panchāyats* (i.e. in front of all the interested parties). He dealt mostly with domestic conflicts, and often took the line (on behalf of women who had run away from unhappy marriages, for example) of trying to ensure justice for the poor and weak. He also settled disputes across ethnic boundaries which threatened to precipitate much more serious unrest.[10] Villagers who otherwise objected to the low wages paid on his farms none the less admitted that a benefit of his presence was that he kept the police out of the area. He provided summary justice for petty offenders (thefts, for example) and punished directly, publicly slapping offenders himself, or in the worst cases, ordering a Balmiki (Sweeper) to do the job, which compounded the humiliation. Before the events of 1990, within the locality his rule was increasingly being criticized, as not tough enough on offenders. In his activities on a wider stage, he had become increasingly marginalized, and had failed to get a ticket as a candidate for any political party after 1980.

Satya Vira's political decline was symptomatic of more general trends. In western UP, the power of large landowners, able to influence a substantial area through their direct economic clout as employers and patrons, is steadily weakening. Since the 1950s, legislation has limited the amount of land that can be held by any one individual. Nehru, India's first Prime Minister, provided much of the impetus to forcing this legislation through. His socialist intentions were outwitted by many

[9] In 1995 he rejoined the Congress Party and became District President.
[10] For some examples, see P. Jeffery and R. Jeffery 1996.

landholders, who exploited a number of loopholes which they had lobbied to have inserted into the Acts. Now, though, many of the larger units that remained are being divided on inheritance. Rich peasants are unwilling to put their profits into buying more agricultural land, preferring urban and industrial investments that have less risk of being expropriated by the Government. Increasing commercialization is also changing the nature of wage employment on the remaining larger farms. For example, Satya Vira's large holding was maintained while he and his two brothers had it farmed collectively. In 1991, it was divided into three shares, and Dharm Vira's share was then farmed by an Indo-American joint venture for sunflower cultivation, under salaried management. The conditions for a change in Bijnor's dominant political style were thus already in place by the mid-1980s.

Threats to public order in Bijnor, 1990–1991

Almost immediately after we arrived in Bijnor in July 1990 we became aware that its relative political isolation was breaking down, as people responded to national political events in ways we had never experienced before. At this time, national politicians were making a series of attempts to mobilize political support along different fracture lines. In the first of these, the Deputy Prime Minister, Devi Lal, believing that he had been tricked into nominating V. P. Singh as Prime Minister in 1989, tried to undermine V. P. Singh's position and advance his own. Eventually, in July 1990, Devi Lal, a Jat farmer from the State of Haryana, was forced to resign. He immediately claimed that he was a victim of urban India's hostility to the rural masses. But his attempt to highlight a rural–urban divide had little impact in Bijnor, mainly because the Jat leaders in western UP (Ajit Singh, son of the late Charan Singh, and Mahender Singh Tikait) were, unusually, united in being unwilling to support Devi Lal. This brief skirmish passed over with little visible effect, but three further national events had much more significant effects on Bijnor. The first of these was the announcement by V. P. Singh of a new policy on job reservations. The second was growing manipulation of religious symbolism by the Bharatiya Janata Party and its allies, and the third was the Indian involvement in the Gulf War, closely followed by the elections of May–June 1991.

Competition for employment

Before Devi Lal could weld an alliance around his rural platform, V. P. Singh counter-attacked by announcing that he would implement the report of a Commission headed by B. P. Mandal, which in 1980 had advocated an extension of caste-based job reservations. Caste-based reservations were written into the Indian Constitution in 1951 to benefit the outcastes whose traditional occupations – leather-working or latrine cleaning, for example – had previously made them 'untouchable' by clean-caste Hindus, and confined them to poverty.[11] These castes were listed in a Schedule of the Constitution, and are now collectively known as the Scheduled Castes. Nationwide, a quota of all public-sector employment is reserved for members of these castes, who also receive educational priority and scholarships. As a result, there are now many Scheduled Caste civil servants (though proportionately more in the lower grades than in the higher ones). But it is not clear that the communities as a whole have benefited, rather than members of some families who have managed to take advantage of what are, after all, still a very small number of jobs in proportion to the total population. Galanter (1989:193) estimates that between 6 and at most 10 per cent of all Scheduled Caste families had benefited in the first 25 years of reservations. In response to the perceived failures of Government policy towards them, some members of the Scheduled Castes have embraced Buddhism, claiming that Hinduism still does not give them the dignity they deserve. Many members of the Scheduled Castes are active in political attempts to rectify continuing political, economic and social disadvantages. Many of them are in heavy debt, usually because of extortionate interest rates and fraud. From time to time they are the target of brutal violence from landholding dominant castes, for example if they demand their rights to land or the legal minimum wage.

The national reservation policy, then, has considerable limitations, but a deep-rooted symbolic significance for those who are included in the legislation. It also generates a strong sense of grievance among those (including Muslims) who are excluded from its benefits. These other groups have demanded similar protection, and some of the Indian States (mostly in south India) have developed an additional reservations policy to benefit groups that have come to be known as the Other Backward Castes (OBCs) or Backward Classes. Policies over which groups are included and to which benefits they are entitled vary considerably. In some cases the castes that benefited have been very similar to the Scheduled Castes; in other States, reservations have embraced a wide range of castes, in an attempt to limit the power of the small numbers of Brahmans or other high castes, who have historically dominated higher

---

[11] The relationship between caste and class is a complex one. Most members of the Scheduled Castes are still very poor, though there are also poor Brahmans (from the top of the caste hierarchy).

education or government employment. In some States, then, the main beneficiaries of reservations are relatively wealthy groups. The extension of reservations to Other Backward Castes tends to undermine some of the legitimacy of the reservations for Scheduled Castes, and carries 'the threat of expanding into a general regime of communal allotments' (Galanter 1989: 197).

Despite the scepticism over the benefits reaped by the Scheduled Castes, and even more uncertainty about the benefits of the additional reservations in individual States, the Mandal Committee recommended that there should be a national scheme of reservations for the OBCs, not just in those States that had already legislated, on the grounds that they were under-represented in education and official employment throughout the country. The Report was ignored for 10 years, although references to it often appeared in party manifestos (including the Communists, Congress and the Bharatiya Janata Party (BJP) – in other words, across the whole political spectrum). On 7 August 1990, V. P. Singh announced that he would act to implement the Report, but many commentators suggested that this was merely a cynical ploy to undermine his opponents, rather than the principled desire for social justice Singh claimed it was.[12]

There was little public response in most of south India, where battles against the extended reservations had already been fought and lost. But after a short delay, north Indian students began a high-profile campaign against the proposals. Access to professional and technical education in India is highly competitive. Admission to the better schools and colleges depends not only on grades but also on 'connections', and the families of students who fail to gain entry deeply resent the reservations for Scheduled Castes – especially those for medical and engineering colleges – and see them as back-door favours to less well-qualified (and thus less deserving) students. Upper-caste students saw the Mandal Report as a further blow to their educational and job prospects.[13]

In what appeared to be spontaneous gestures reflecting a sense of futility and despair, some students began attempting suicide. The first case – on 19 September 1990, when a Delhi University student called Rajiv Goswami set fire to himself in the middle of a demonstration – was widely publicized. In north India, according to one report, over 50 students set fire to themselves, and another 30 took poison in the next

[12] For more general sociological discussions of reservations, see Beteille 1992.

[13] In 1994, the Mandal reforms provoked further violent opposition in Uttarakhand, immediately north of Bijnor. In this part of UP there are very few members of the Other Backward Castes, and local people argued that the whole region was thus being discriminated against, despite being generally poor.

fortnight (*Illustrated Weekly of India* 7 October 1990, p.17). Committees of students sprang up, organizing rallies and marches, which frequently ended in roadblocks and attacks on public buses, the traditional target of agitating students. These committees ignored the student unions, which are dominated by mainstream political parties, themselves caught wrong-footed by the scale and intensity of the agitation, and too compromised to take a clear stand. V. P. Singh's Janata Party gradually organized members of the castes who would benefit from the new policy to take part in counter-demonstrations, but these were notable for their small numbers and lack of great enthusiasm. Congress and the 'left' parties were unable to take advantage of the student movement, since they were publicly committed to extending reservations. Even leaders from the BJP, which in general represents high-caste Hindus, were spurned when they tried to visit the bedsides of burned students, because their offer of support was undermined by their manifesto commitment to implement the Mandal Report.

Opponents of Mandal's proposals argued that access to the privileged positions of professional, managerial and high public sector jobs should depend solely on merit, ignoring the evidence of the role of elite schooling (often English-medium) in stacking the odds against the rural population and the poor (Beteille 1992). Employment opportunities are restricted, and conflicts are increasing because rising levels of schooling increase the intensity of competition.[14] Bijnor, as a local educational centre, received its share of disruption in late September when the anti-Mandal agitation was at its height. Students from the Bijnor degree colleges and a women's post-graduate college (teaching to MA level) blocked roads on several occasions. At this time we had to travel through Bijnor town every day. On one occasion, our way was blocked by students brandishing hockey sticks, and only swift thinking on the part of Radha (one of our Hindu assistants) managed to prevent them commandeering our jeep into a roadblock and possibly setting it alight like buses in Delhi. On another day, our journey to visit our children in school in Mussoorie was held up: the previous day, Delhi students had provoked the Dehra Dun students into action by sending them a gift of bracelets – accusing them of being weak like women – and in the rioting that followed, one student was killed in police firing. We had to wait on the outskirts of Dehra Dun for three hours while demonstrating students were cleared from the main road, and we eventually proceeded through the town behind a police jeep, watching trucks with broken windscreens come the other way. For several weeks we were never sure if our research

[14] We shall discuss how education and employment are linked locally in Chapter 6, when we consider the differential positions of Jats and Sheikhs in the local labour market.

assistants would feel it was safe to turn up. As events turned out, beyond the smashing of bus windows there was little violence in Bijnor, and no cases of self-immolation. But ominously, while Hindu traders observed a *bandh* (closing of all the shops in the *bazār*) called by the students, Muslim traders did not take part.

When we discussed V. P. Singh's proposals with villagers in Bijnor, we found little enthusiasm. To begin with, no-one knew exactly which Hindu castes would benefit. Even those who thought they might be included in the policy did not think they personally would ever benefit. Nor was it clear what effect it would have on members of the Scheduled Castes, who already had reservations. In general, the new policy cut across Bijnor's political alignments. In the 1989 national elections, the Bahujan Samaj Party (BSP) won the Bijnor seat in the Lok Sabha, the national Parliament. The BSP draws most of its support from the north Indian members of the Scheduled Castes; it won the Bijnor seat by attracting additional support from Muslims (who would not benefit from Mandal's proposals). An electoral pact with the Janata Party in the Lok Sabha in Delhi and in the UP State Assembly in Lucknow gave the BSP influence in both Janata Governments. The Mandal policy offered the BSP the chance to extend its support into new caste groups, but it was more important for the BSP in Bijnor to maintain its following of members of the Scheduled Castes – especially Chamars – and Muslims, which could give it an easy majority in the District. The Mandal proposals were more popular in eastern UP and Bihar, where the Other Backward Castes are much more significant electorally.

The Janata Party tried to persuade people that its support for the Mandal proposals was a general support for the idea of reservations. Most members of the Scheduled Castes we talked to were sceptical. Jats in Nangal (one of the two villages where we carried out research in 1990–1) also connected Mandal to the reservations for Scheduled Castes. When we discussed Mandal and job reservations with them, they immediately talked of the iniquity of the reservations for Scheduled Castes. In their view, Chamars (the largest local Scheduled Caste) were getting everything from the Government – brick houses, jobs, even land – while Jats could not get jobs, nor could they get labourers to work on their land, and so Jat crops were damaged. Several Jats asked us what was the point in their spending money on education since their children would no longer get 'service' (secure, public sector white-collar jobs) as a result of the reservation policy – but they talked of the Chamars getting the jobs, rather than the Other Backward Castes who were ostensibly to benefit from the Mandal Commission.

The agitation against the Mandal Commission report, then, forcefully reminded us of the desperation with which the urban middle and upper classes – including two of our own research assistants (who were Brahman) – were clinging to education as a lifeline to ensure their own or their children's futures. Those who believed they would be adversely affected – e.g. wealthier Jats in Nangal – were opposed to all such reservations, deploring the decline in the village-level dominance from which Jats had benefited in the past. But most villagers had no chance of a family member acquiring one of the relatively privileged positions covered by the proposals. Villagers in Bijnor were mostly bemused by the ferocity provoked among urban students by V. P. Singh's adoption of the report.

As the anti-Mandal agitation continued through late September, the resolve of the student leadership weakened. It became clear that they had little political clout, representing as they did only a part of the urban middle classes, in a country where electoral success still requires support from the rural areas, where 65 per cent of the population lives. The students negotiated with the political leaders for support. At a rally in Delhi, Mahender Singh Tikait (the main Jat leader from Western UP) failed to bring his rural supporters to their aid (as the students had hoped), instead calling on the students to burn the sons of Janata Party MPs as a form of protest. His speech demoralized the student leadership.

Hindu–Muslim conflicts over religious sites

By October, the media had turned their attention to the activities of the BJP and their allies, the Vishwa Hindu Parishad (World Hindu Union or VHP). The BJP party chairman, L. K. Advani, set out in a decorated minibus on a so-called *rath yātrā* or pilgrimage across north India, from Somnath in Gujarat, the site of a temple desecrated by Mahmud of Ghazni in 1026, and rebuilt during the British period, to Ayodhya in eastern UP, a journey of some 1,500 km. Ayodhya is believed by many Hindus to be the place where the God *Rām* was born, and VHP activists had waged a campaign of increasing intensity to remove the so-called Babri mosque in order to allow the building of a temple in its place, claiming that the mosque occupied the precise site of *Rām*'s birth.[15]

Advani's political pilgrimage was a response to the twin challenges posed by Devi Lal's resignation and by the anti-Mandal agitation. The BJP, the party identified with urban high-caste Hindus, had been unable to make political capital out of either issue. The BJP leadership needed

---

[15] For more details on the BJP and VHP campaigns, see van der Veer 1987, 1994; T. Basu et al. 1993; Gopal 1991, Engineer 1995, Mukhopadhyay 1994.

to redraw the political divisions. Its response was to throw its full weight behind the VHP campaign. As Advani's chariot moved across central India, it drew large crowds of supporters. In its wake, it left an increasing number of communal incidents. Janata Dal leaders in north India responded in turn by launching a campaign portraying themselves as 'secularists'. Throughout October, tension rose as Advani neared his destination. Volunteer supporters of the VHP's campaign began travelling towards Ayodhya from all directions, with the aim of pulling down the mosque and building the foundations for a temple. A massive police and army campaign was launched to stop them in their tracks, at bus and train stations, at State borders and at river crossings.

The rising communal tension stoked much warmer fires in Bijnor than did the anti-Mandal agitations. Bijnor District has a large Muslim population (about 40 per cent of the total in 1991) and some of the BJP's propaganda (such as the claim that Muslims were outbreeding Hindus in a conscious attempt to gain electoral superiority) had obvious resonances there.[16] The Ayodhya campaign offered Bijnor Hindus a means of redressing a political balance which they felt had shifted unwarrantedly towards the local Muslims. The 1989 elections for the chair of the town council had been won by a Muslim, Javed Aftab, who had made his reputation by defying the District administration over the funeral arrangements for some Muslims who died earlier that year. His election was resented by many of the town's predominantly Hindu traders and petty bourgeoisie. After the BSP won the Bijnor Lok Sabha seat later in 1989, the economically powerful Jats and urban Hindus were left out in the cold.

In the summer of 1990 the first communal issue to arise concerned an empty plot of land and a well behind a mosque in Bijnor town. Javed Aftab declared that the town council owned the land, over the objections of a local Hindu. On 25 August some Hindus started to erect a small shrine on the site.[17] Council officials tried to stop them, and this led to processions, stoning incidents, and some police firing. One elderly Muslim woman was hit, possibly by a ricocheting bullet, and died on the spot; one other Muslim died in hospital. Shops, schools and colleges were closed for four days.

[16] We shall discuss in detail in Chapter 6 the way in which comparative communal population figures have been used in political discourse in India, and some of the consequences of the social construction of a Muslim population 'problem'.

[17] This is a classic way of generating communal tension. If a temple is constructed behind the rear wall of a mosque, Muslims praying towards Mecca would be implicitly worshipping the Hindu deity placed directly in the way. In addition, the noise of the conch shell blown by the priest in charge would compete with the call to prayer of the muezzin.

Over the following few weeks, the student anti-Mandal agitation reclaimed the headlines. But in early October Bijnor was directly involved in the looming shadow of the conflict over Ayodhya between supporters of the BJP and those who were in favour of the Janata Dal. On 9 October the UP State Chief Minister, Mulayam Singh Yadav of the Janata Dal, visited the District. His nominal task was to open the new Bijnor Government hospital, but his wider stated agenda was to consolidate his political support. At his 'anticommunalism' rally in Bijnor he appealed to the Other Backward Castes because they would benefit from the job reservations policy; to Muslims by promising to protect the mosque in Ayodhya; and to the Scheduled Castes by defining the 'forward' castes as the enemy.[18] Bus-loads of supporters coming to the rally were seen as a provocation by his opponents, mostly supporters of the BJP. Some of those going to the rally attacked some villages as they passed through, and some buses were stoned.[19] In his speech, Mulayam Singh Yadav promised that his Government would protect Muslims and the Backward and Scheduled Castes from attacks; and that it would not be surprising if Muslims were to store arms against the threat of such attacks. BJP supporters claimed this was an incitement to minorities to break the law and to attack innocent Hindus.

In the days following Mulayam Singh Yadav's visit, about 30 shops were looted and set on fire; bomb-blasts were heard around the town; and the *bazār* remained closed for four days. The *Bijnor Times* reported that a mob (by implication, Muslim) attacked the detachment of Provincial Armed Constabulary (PAC) at the Clock Tower in the centre of town; with help from other paramilitary police, the crowd was thrown back. Three people died (two Hindu and one Muslim). The *Bijnor Times* also reported that religious slogans were now being raised – '*Allāh-O-Akbār*' (a Muslim rallying cry that 'God is Great') and '*Har, Har, Mahadev*' (a Hindu equivalent, referring to Shiva); Hindu shopkeepers in Muslim neighbourhoods (and vice versa) were emptying their shops and moving out. In Bijnor, as a precautionary measure, 95 people were arrested, mostly local leaders of the BJP and its associated organizations.

---

[18] For more on the 'anticommunalism' rallies and their effects see *Frontline* 13–26 October 1990, pp. 26–9. Ramaseshan (1990) argues, contra the press reports, that the link between the rallies and the rioting was not direct (people attending the rallies being encouraged to riot) but indirect (BJP workers shutting down markets and shopping areas and organising strikes and demonstrations in opposition to the rallies).

[19] One incident highlights the dangers of relying on press reporting: one man who died was reported by the *Bijnor Times* as a participant in the rally, but the *Dainik Jagrān* reported that he was attacked by participants going home from the rally. *Dainik Jagrān* was one of the newspapers censured by the Press Council of India for its 'gross irresponsibility and impropriety' in covering the events of 30 October; see Engineer 1991: 1263.

The District Bar Association claimed those among them who were advocates were all innocent and should be released immediately. A women's procession went to the police headquarters to demand the release of all 'majority community youngsters' and the lawyers; it was led by banners of a women's wing of the VHP called the *Durga Wahini* (the Army of the Goddess Durga, Shiva's wife). They raised a specific injustice: more Hindus (65) than Muslims (30) had been arrested. They claimed that this showed that 'the administration officials, police personnel and other leaders always follow a policy of appeasement of the minorities, the Indian Muslims in particular' (*Bijnor Times*, 13 October 1990, our translation from Hindi).

Bijnor, then, was primed to react to the tension which rose in the next few weeks throughout north India. Small incidents could act as triggers for more marked responses. One day when Satya Vira was absent from Dharmnagri, four Muslims were discovered playing cards in the local fields. This was regarded as a potential flash-point: young men at a loose end, engaged in immoral behaviour. One of them (from Bijnor) had a gun. A large crowd quickly gathered. The situation was diffused only when Sufi Akhtar (a Muslim and staunch Congress Party supporter from the neighbouring village of Chandpuri) was brought in to convene a meeting at Satya Vira's house. In front of the largely Hindu crowd he temporarily confiscated the gun, reprimanded the men and sent them packing.

The VHP had set a deadline of 30 October when they had threatened to begin the demolition of the Babri mosque in Ayodhya; Advani's plan was to arrive there that day. As 30 October approached, increasing numbers of volunteers (known as *kar sevaks*), who had set out for Ayodhya from further west in UP and from Simla and Ludhiana, were stopped at the bridges over the Ganges. Two of these bridges – the rail bridge at Balawali and the Madhya Ganga barrage – are close to Bijnor, and those arrested there were taken to Bijnor town. Local BJP and VHP leaders were also rearrested as a precautionary measure. A total of 637 were imprisoned in Bijnor, far outstripping the capacity of the local jail. They were housed in the nearby Girls' Intermediate College (which had already been closed for several weeks because of the Mandal problems). There they had no proper kitchen arrangements, and members of the VHP and BJP arranged for food to be sent for them from middle-class Hindu localities.

On 28 October demonstrations against the prisoners' conditions, and demands for their release, were only barely controlled without serious bloodshed. Satya Vira was physically attacked when he visited those arrested. The previous day he had made a statement calling for unity and respect for religion, quoting from poems which stressed the unity of humankind, and pointing out that most Muslims – and certainly those from Bijnor – had supported the idea of a secular India in 1947 and had not wanted India to be partitioned so that Pakistan could be created. The crowd outside the Girls' College asked him why he was not supporting the people from his own religion, and he was attacked when he said he thought the temple should be built in Ayodhya but the law should be observed. The next day, the prisoners rioted and were beaten with staves; after police firing three prisoners needed hospital treatment.

On 30 October itself, when the BBC reported that the VHP had raised its flag on the mosque in Ayodhya and started its destruction, *bhajans* (holy songs) were sung at a temple near the centre of Bijnor, and then a victorious thanksgiving procession set off. What happened next is unclear. The women in the march seem to have been stoned as they passed through streets where Muslims lived; Muslims told us the marchers were chanting anti-Muslim slogans such as: *Hindu, Rām kā bachchā, Musulmān harām kā bachchā* ('Hindus are the children of God *Rām*, Muslims are bastards'). As far as we can piece together what happened next, it seems that the women and children in the procession retreated and were kept in safety for several hours; meanwhile, the rest of the marchers threw stones back at their assailants, leading on to an interchange of shooting, then arson, the throwing of hand-bombs and looting. A well-known Muslim doctor, with a clinic on the main *bazār*, was one of the first to die, shot on his roof, possibly while he was stoning the processionists. Over the next three days, the local administration stated that forty people were killed in Bijnor town and eight in other parts of the District. Persistent rumours said this was an undercount, and that lorries had taken dozens of bodies to the Ganges and just tipped them in.[20]

Atrocities were reported from both sides of the communal divide, from bomb-blasts and armed attacks to stone-throwing. Much of this violence was gendered: from both sides we heard accusations of rape, and of women being captured, killed and disfigured, with rumours that Muslim women had been abducted by Hindu *sādhus* (ascetics), and Hindu women had had their breasts cut off by Muslim men. According to official reports, more Hindus apparently died in the early period and more Muslims later on. It was widely believed that many of the Muslims died at the hands of paramilitary forces (including the PAC), who contributed to the attacks on Muslim neighbourhoods and the looting of Muslim shops, instead of attempting to prevent them. One official said

---

[20] Basu 1994 provides a more detailed account of the violence in Bijnor.

that 342 people had been arrested, of whom 88 were Hindu and 254 were Muslim. Of 48 dead bodies, 12 were from one 'caste' (Hindu?) and 30 from the other 'caste' (Muslim?); 2 were unidentified and no information was provided on the remaining four deaths (*Rozānā Khabr Jadīd*, 15 November 1990). Four mosques in Bijnor town were damaged; there were no reports of damage to temples. On the fourth day, the city was handed over to units of the regular Army and there was little further bloodshed and arson. The 24–hour curfew imposed in the first few days was gradually relaxed, and after 10 days was removed altogether.

While this was going on, we remained in Dharmnagri, hearing the rumours that were circulating. Some said that fighting was also taking place in the rural areas of the District.[21] Some said that the PAC were spreading out from Bijnor and attacking Muslim villages. Some Hindus said that Hindus in Muslim majority villages were being killed or driven out (and some Muslims told us the reverse was also happening). Gangs of armed men were said to be roaming the countryside; or Hindu and Muslim men from different villages were said to be getting together to attack their neighbours. Whenever Roger joined a group of men on the main road in Dharmnagri during this period, someone would break up the meeting after a while by pointing out that observers might think an attack was being prepared. In addition, no-one knew if Section 144 of the Indian Penal Code, banning gatherings of more than 5 people and being enforced in Bijnor town, applied in the rural areas as well. The rumours gained most credence where there were pre-existing causes of tension. For example, we witnessed the actions of young men from villages of Bengali Hindus. Their families had fled from East Pakistan in the 1960s after they had experienced religious intolerance. They resented their enforced migration into a district with a substantial Muslim population, and were seeking revenge. We saw them busily cutting down and sharpening bamboo stakes to make spears, bows and arrows – the latter allegedly tipped with cyanide to make them more deadly. Young Bengali men spread rumours of impending attacks, and called for pre-emptive strikes.

Agricultural work practically ceased, making life very hard for house-holds which depended on selling milk, fruit or vegetables, or on daily wage labour. Satya Vira toured the surrounding villages, either on his own account or in response to calls from local leaders, to investigate

---

[21] If true, this would have been a further novelty; communal rioting in the post-Independence period has rarely moved out of the towns. But we were later told that trouble occurred in only two directions from Bijnor – to the south (Himpur) and to the north-east (Kiratpur)

claims of intercommunal outrages. In Dharmnagri itself, he calmed a potential flash-point by prompt action. A Sahni (Hindu) youth had attacked a Muslim Nai ('Barber'), riding past (quite legitimately) on a bicycle the Nai had borrowed from the youth's father. Satya Vira's solution was to slap the Hindu youth and send him home in disgrace. On another occasion, our (Hindu) cook was wrongly accused of planting 'bombs' (large fireworks); one night a 'dead body' (bundle of rags) was found in the orchard opposite our house; 'bomb-blasts' (or fireworks) were heard every night; a shot was heard between our village and the nearest Muslim village; and on one evening a great commotion started at about 10 p.m., explained the next day just as a period of 'confusion' set off by a drunkard. Satya Vira took in a Muslim youth who said he was injured by a sickle, despite rumours that he had been hurt while making bombs. Out of all these events, rumours, claims and accusations, only one turned out to have some substance: two Muslims riding a motorcycle on a road through a Hindu village were shot at, and one died later in hospital. The young men were taken to a nearby Muslim village, whose *pradhān* (village headman) called in Satya Vira, who walked into the village unarmed, accompanied only by his son, and managed to cool tempers and forestall further trouble.

More positive attempts were made to reinforce the previous patterns of intercommunal relationships. Meetings were held at Satya Vira's house with Sufi Akhtar and men from surrounding villages. At one of these meetings Satya Vira collected signatures for a letter to the District Magistrate asking for permission to establish a committee of village leaders who would tour the locality to reduce tension. A further public meeting was held in the village, possibly contravening the official ban. Village council leaders and representatives (mostly Sahnis and Sheikhs, but including a Bengali) from about 20 villages attended. Each leader stood up for a couple of minutes; all but one (rendered speechless by the occasion) said something about Hindu–Muslim brotherhood, the common themes in religious texts, the irrelevance of the happenings in distant Ayodhya, and the need for people to live together: 'we all come into and go out of this world in the same way, so we should live in peace and harmony'.

These almost ritualized statements were received with some cynicism. Several people told us afterwards that what these leaders said, and what they felt in their hearts, might have been very different. But the meeting helped to reduce tension, and more people went into Bijnor and discovered which of the rumours were true and which were unfounded. Shops began to reopen, and the demands of agriculture could no longer be ignored; all those who depended on daily wages returned to work in order to buy food, while others took fodder, milk or other agricultural produce to sell in Bijnor.

Tension was reawakened by outside visitors – like Rajiv Gandhi, who came with the Kashmiri Muslim politician Faruq Abdullah. Others (from more extreme Muslim and Hindu parties) tried to visit but were excluded. In an attempt to maintain the momentum of their movement, the VHP toured around UP with the ashes (*asthi kailash*) of those supposedly killed in police firing in Ayodhya. Police activity minimized the effects in Bijnor. The new Superintendent of Police had a reputation for dealing successfully with communal disputes, and he had brought two Muslim Deputies with him. The ashes were allowed into Bijnor only late at night, were kept in only one temple, and were sent out of the District the next day. By mid-December a casual observer might have thought that all was over, except for the obvious signs of burnt-out shops. Closer inspection would have revealed Muslims wandering around begging because they had lost everything in the riots; and people who were in the religious minority in villages and urban neighbourhoods looking around to find a safe haven among their co-religionists elsewhere.

The Gulf War and the 1991 elections

On the national stage, V. P. Singh's Government fell, and all sides in Delhi agreed to provide a breathing space to his successor, C. S. Chandrashekhar. The major international event of his Prime Ministership was the Gulf War, with India having to repatriate several hundred thousand Indians from Kuwait and Iraq, losing valuable foreign exchange income from their remittances in the process.[22] There was considerable, if muted, tension among Indian Muslims, directed at the Government (for its tacit support of the US-led attack on Iraq) and on foreigners from countries in the allied coalition. Both the Gulf War and the Indian national census operations of Spring 1991 illustrated for us the extent to which many Muslims distrusted the 'Hindu' Government.[23]

In the circumstances, Chandrashekhar's Government – with only 10 per cent (57) of the seats in the Lok Sabha – was remarkably successful, but it lasted only until March 1991. Rajiv Gandhi, the leader of the

---

[22] The foreign exchange position also worsened because of the decline in tourism – during the peak winter tourist season – caused by the reports of the communal violence.

[23] This distrust, also manifested in attitudes towards Government schooling and Government health and family planning facilities, represents one facet of why Jats and Sheikhs have such different demographic experiences – which we explore further in Chapter 6.

Congress Party, the largest party in Parliament, then withdrew his party's support on a technicality when he judged the time was right for new elections. Voting was delayed until May and June, in order to avoid holding elections in Ramzan, which would have offended many Muslims, but the electioneering was marred by violence, especially in Bihar and parts of UP. To complete one of the worst years for the Indian democratic process, at the tail end of the election campaign Rajiv was assassinated in Tamil Nadu, near Madras (probably by Tamil secessionists from Sri Lanka). But during the elections, and after the assassination of Rajiv Gandhi, there was no further serious trouble in Bijnor.

In the May elections, support for Congress and Janata Dal collapsed in most of western UP. In the Lok Sabha election for the Bijnor District seat there was no alliance against the BJP; the BSP, CPM (Communist Party of India, Marxist) and Congress divided 48 per cent of the vote between them, so the BJP won with 47 per cent of the total. In the State Assembly election for the seat of Bijnor town and its surroundings, a tacit anti-BJP strategy gave the BSP 41 per cent of the vote, but, with 53 per cent of the vote, the BJP won by a clear margin. The BJP seemed to have attracted support from new social groups, like the Jats of Nangal, for example, who defected from Congress before the election and supported the BJP in substantial numbers.[24] In Dharmnagri, Brahmans, Jats, and at least as far 'down' the caste hierarchy as the Sahnis voted for the BJP; in Jhakri, all the Muslims we knew waited anxiously for guidance on which of the anti-BJP candidates had the best chance of success.

Researching before and after communal violence

We had arrived in India in July 1990 with an intricate and detailed proposal for research on gender relationships, fertility and mortality in six villages. We had visited them all in 1982–3, and two of them featured in our previous book, *Labour Pains and Labour Power*. In 1982–3 we had managed to maintain the fiction that events outside the immediate area of our research villages could be put on one side. Even then, though, we had had to confront accusations that we were agents of the Government attempting to enforce family planning programmes in new, more subtle ways, and rumours spread that we were involved in plans to build a

---

[24] The Jats of Nangal left Congress well before the election. More than a dozen young Jat men had been arrested on 22 October 1990 as members of the Shiv Sena; and 18 Jats went into the local town to court arrest on 29 October. Of these youths (10 aged under 20, only 2 aged more than 24) who went to support the BJP, most (16) were middle or small peasants, expecting to inherit 4 acres or less; only 2 were from wealthier families. Three were married; the rest single. All but 2 had completed high school (8th class).

nuclear power station nearby on the River Ganges. But these problems had not really prepared us for the extent to which national politics would impinge directly on our research in 1990–1.

Several considerations had originally led us to Bijnor. We wanted to be in a Hindi- and Urdu-speaking area, since these are the only Indian languages we can speak. Two further reasons were (in juxtaposition and hindsight) somewhat ironic. Bijnor District has the highest proportion of *rural* Muslims in UP (over 30 per cent in 1981), and we wanted to be able to look at the effects of different Hindu and Muslim marriage patterns on child-bearing behaviour (very little, as it turned out). We also looked for a relatively peaceful district, since we were taking our 2-year-old daughter with us.

The national events of 1990–1, and their local ramifications, were frightening and appalling. Bijnor itself temporarily moved from being a backwater to being central to national politics. In proportion to its population, Bijnor was arguably the worst hit by the communal rioting which spread across many parts of north India in October and November 1990. In Bijnor, 'violence penetrated into spaces that had been considered relatively immune' and the riots may thus have been more traumatic than violence which has become routinized and repetitive (Das 1990: 11–12). While these riots may not say anything 'new' about Hindu–Muslim relations in India in the 1990s, they certainly made us much more aware of how communalism was part of everyday life, and had become inextricably bound up in the way official agencies went about their business. In our previous research, we had been continually made aware of negative ethnic stereotypes – in discussions of eating habits or marriage practices, for example.[25] But people did not use these stereotypes to justify violence against members of the 'other' group. In 1990, however, such stereotypes fuelled aggression and hostility in the villages as well as the towns, even if the loss of life and arson was largely confined to the urban areas.

We were in the District throughout this period. We never saw any of the violence (almost all urban), though our research assistants described what they had seen and we saw burnt-out shops and homes, mangled girders beside the roads, and shopkeepers decanting their goods and moving them to safety. Our fears for our own safety, for our children (in school four hours' drive away) and our friends and neighbours, as well as our research assistants, coupled with our ambiguous status as foreigners with research visas, disabled us from any action that might draw us to the attention of the authorities or of those actively engaged in

---

[25] See more on the everyday nature of communalism in P. Jeffery forthcoming.

the violence itself. When we talked to villagers we borrowed the Indian secularist discourse of stressing common humanity, respect for others as equals, and the need to live peacefully together. But on several occasions we had to confront people who supported the violence, and found it hard to know how to respond.[26] Because it would have reawakened painful memories, and been potentially provocative and possibly dangerous for us, we did not inquire closely into what had actually happened. We limited ourselves to noting the rumours, and reading the local papers, and we heard few eye-witness accounts, or accounts from survivors, of the kind so movingly analysed by Veena Das (Das 1990). Like most of those trying to come to terms with communal violence, then, we ended up being concerned more 'about context – about everything which happens around violence' (Pandey 1991: 559) than with the violence itself. We focused on attempting to complete our research and using our research grant responsibly. We tried to understand and explain what had happened, and to integrate those lessons into our interpretations of the material we were collecting, without losing sight of the issues of gender politics which had informed our original research proposal.

Thus the communalization of identities – people's heightened awareness of themselves and others as Hindu or Muslim, Jat or Chamar – set a context for our research. Until mid-October 1990 we managed to keep these concerns somewhat in the background; after the events of October–November, they occupied much more of our attention. At first, they seemed annoying distractions from our main work, but increasingly, we realized that they were themselves part of what we were trying to understand. They were not unwelcome noise, to be minimized or ignored, but intrinsically related to the substance of our research. Population and gender issues – how many babies are born, how many children survive into adulthood, who makes decisions about women's fertility and their reproductive health – were deeply affected by the social divisions around caste and religion which came to the surface in the second half of 1990.

Our research agenda was totally upset. We had expected to begin by rehiring two women, Swaleha Begum and Radha Rani Sharma, who had worked for us in 1982–3 and in 1985, who knew us and our research methods, and were known to the villagers of Dharmnagri and Jhakri, where we intended to start again. In addition to Swaleha's difficulties in

[26] On our first visit back to Nangal after the curfew had been lifted, we were closely questioned by Brahmans and Jats about who was to blame for the rioting. By refusing to endorse the Hindu chauvinist interpretation that the riots were caused by violent Muslims, we nearly lost our ability to complete our research in the village.

finishing her teacher training and joining us (see the Preface), Radha had not been able to work as regularly as we had expected, even before the events of October and November. The fears of curfews and street violence disrupted her work even more. As November neared, she fell ill. Not surprisingly, then, by mid-October we had fallen well behind schedule.

Furthermore, the events of October–November had undermined a major assumption of our work – that it was possible for us to take Hindu and Muslim research assistants into either Hindu or Muslim villages without any problem. We hired two extra Hindu assistants, and an extra Muslim woman to carry on the work, but they were all unwilling to work on their own. They had to work in pairs, with at least one married woman and either Patricia or one assistant from the 'right' religion in each team. As the elections of May 1991 drew nearer it was increasingly hard to maintain a good research team spirit. Electoral politics were a canker at the heart of our research, since our Hindu assistants were plainly intending to vote for the BJP, whereas our Muslim assistants planned to vote for whichever party they believed had the best chance of keeping the BJP out.

The first of our additional four villages was Nangal, a Jat-dominated village on the far side of Bijnor from Dharmnagri, where we were living, and we were in the midst of data collection there when the worst of the troubles broke out in October 1990. In mid-November, as we reconsidered our research strategy, we decided to drop the second additional village, Mundahla, from our sample. Mundahla is dominated by Muslims, but has a long-standing dispute with a nearby Jat-dominated village, Suaheri, which controls the main road and access to Mundahla. Suaheri was also the site of intercommunal violence in 1857 (Bayly 1983: 364) and in 1983 women from Mundahla had told us that they were unable to use the health clinic in Suaheri, because of abuse from Jats. We were therefore not altogether surprised to hear of trouble in Suaheri on 9 October, when Mulayam Singh Yadav addressed his supporters in Bijnor; of the discovery of 'rocket launchers' in Mundahla in early November; of the arrest of 30 men from Mundahla; or reports of a bridge on the road to Mundahla being destroyed, probably by Jats from Suaheri. We replaced Mundahla with Qaziwala, a Muslim village where we had a number of good contacts. Qaziwala had a peaceful reputation, and was more convenient to Dharmnagri. But we were working in Qaziwala in January–March 1991, during the period leading up to the Gulf War and the Indian Census, and while the mistrust and anxieties of the events of October and November were still fresh in people's memories. Despite being well known in the area, and being helped by

Jhakri friends with strong marriage connections in the village, we had to work very cautiously to avoid hostility from those who saw us as representatives of Britain, a country at war with their fellow Muslims, or as agents of a hostile Hindu Raj.[27] By this time it was clear that we could not hope to study two more villages, and we abandoned our plans to do so. The research reported here is thus based on detailed village studies of one caste group in each of Nangal and Qaziwala, supplemented by general understandings derived from our research in Dharmnagri and Jhakri.

In 1990–1, national and local political events required us to look more closely at Hindu–Muslim differences and relationships. For one thing, our research topic itself has had a high profile in the national debates about 'minorities' in India. We were collecting population data – through our censuses of Nangal and Qaziwala, and through the marital and birth histories of selected women in these villages, and this focus added to the problems of carrying out our research. Selected aspects of social demography have been politicized by the BJP, who have drawn attention to Muslim fertility rates (not to their overall levels of mortality, or to the evidence of relatively less discrimination against girls, leading to a more balanced sex ratio among Muslims, for example). According to the BJP, the Muslim population is growing rapidly in India to a level where Muslims could form an electoral majority in the foreseeable future. They claim that this is a conscious political strategy by Muslims, whereas Hindus are doing their national duty and adopting contraceptive practices. These claims have never been systematically challenged in the political arena, though they have been exposed as massive lies in more academic circles.[28] Despite the gaping flaws in the BJP argument, we have met well-educated Hindus – and even some Muslims – who remain convinced that Hindus will soon be in a minority in India. In fact, Muslims make up at most only 13 per cent of the national population and the Muslim population growth rate is only slightly more than that of Hindus. We return to these issues in more detail in Chapter 6.

Research design

When we originally planned this research project we targeted a set of issues from the general demographic literature. We wished to investigate whether, in a rural population where demographic change was generally

---

[27] We manipulated our own ethnic identities, using our 'Scottishness' to distance ourselves from the 'English' and the US Governments.

[28] These arguments are considered in more detail in Chapter 6.

slow, differences in gender relationships might be related to differences in fertility. We identified three factors which were thought to affect women, their relationships with men, and their fertility, and which we knew – from our earlier research – to be significant in Bijnor. Two of these factors are the most commonly discussed: girls' schooling and women's involvement in economically productive work. The third – the distance women move away from their natal kin when they marry – is particularly discussed in India, as a result of the work of Tim Dyson and Mick Moore (Dyson and Moore 1983; Vlassoff 1992). All three factors have been argued to affect fertility, mostly through their impact on women's autonomy. Educated women, those who have an independent source of income, and those who marry into familiar households and retain access to their parents after marriage, are thought to have more equal conjugal relationships, to want fewer children, and to be better able to limit their own fertility in the light of those preferences.

In each of the new villages, in addition to Dharmnagri and Jhakri, we planned to collect information from about 24 women, taking all the women from the same caste group but ensuring that they differed substantially on one of the factors listed above. Our material on Dharmnagri and Jhakri was to form a backdrop to what we collected from the other villages, because we had parallel and much more detailed information from these two villages as a result of our previous research trips. Since we eventually studied only two caste groups in two additional villages we have organized our account in terms of a comparison of the demographic regimes of Jats of Nangal and Sheikhs of Qaziwala. In doing so we consider far more than the factors we used to stratify the samples of couples for intensive study. Two of our decisions are somewhat unusual in demographic research, and need to be explained in more detail. The first is our decision to select caste groups for analysis, rather than the whole village or a sample of people from several villages. The second is how we chose couples from these castes for more intensive study.

Caste groups as social categories

Beyond the individual household, the most important forms of community organization in the Indian countryside are kin groups, villages and caste-based groupings. We selected caste groups as the basic unit for sampling purposes in Qaziwala and Nangal, but we need to justify this decision, since the nature of caste and its relevance as a social category have been heavily contested, and there are other notable candidates for choice. Why not, for example, take the village as a whole?

Most sample surveys in India assume that the village is an obvious basis for the selection of respondents, but the apparent 'naturalness' of the village as a political, social or demographic unit must be questioned. As Ursula Sharma has reminded us, the coherence of the village in north India is very much a male construction, since adult women normally move in on marriage and come and go regularly to their natal villages (Sharma 1981).[29] Village residents may share certain environmental characteristics, including features such as the accessibility of social and economic resources like canals, towns, or Government services like clinics and schools. But their ability to make use of these resources is conditioned by class and caste-group membership. Castes usually cut across class boundaries, but, none the less, in many villages, most of the land may well be held by members of only one or two castes, while another caste or castes provide most of the landless labourers. Both within the village and beyond, social networks – visiting patterns, gift-giving, lending and borrowing of small sums and exchanges of labour – tend to be organized predominantly within caste boundaries. In terms of social pressures to conform with local practice, the caste group – especially that part of it in which a household has intermarried in the recent past and expects to find brides or grooms in the near future – is in a stronger position to affect behaviour than village neighbours from different castes or religions. Caste groups also link networks of villages, and eventually provide much of the basis for modern party politics in India. Thus neighbouring households may be subject to quite different pressures, and respond very differently – in political, social, cultural and demographic terms – to the pressures they experience, despite their close proximity within a village. Even if caste group members are not all in similar economic positions, they may still be involved in very different demographic regimes from those of their physical neighbours from the same class (McNicoll 1992: 19). None the less, caste is a controversial category for social scientists analyzing Indian society.

The study of caste in India has gone through a number of phases. Before the period of British rule, European visitors to India showed no great interest in social variations amongst Hindus, except for the groups with whom they came into most contact – Brahman priests, Rajput kings

[29] By the same token, of course, bounding a caste group by village limits is not entirely defensible, since significant others in the same caste group may be in different villages. Our defence is pragmatic – there are no obvious boundaries if one traces marriage links, for example. Where caste groups are heavily represented in a village (as in both cases considered here), we can reasonably assume that those who share a village and caste membership do form real social groups, though more so for men than for women. Our concern with women's relationships with their natal kin is an attempt to reduce the significance of this.

and princes, and Bania traders. The British were drawn further into trying to make sense of social differentiation as they attempted to apply Hindu law, in particular to family issues, and were confronted with people who claimed that customary practice in some communities was very different from that laid down in the great legal texts. The full flowering of British attempts to codify castes came in the second half of the nineteenth century. A number of interests – in legal reform, in army recruitment, in taxation and land revenue policy – led to a series of texts that set out what the different castes were called, where they came in the overall hierarchy of castes, what their special ('racial') characteristics were, how many members they had, where they were located, what their kinship system was, and how they were governed in their relationships within and between caste groups.[30] By 1881 the Indian Census adopted caste as a major category for analytic purposes. The British Army developed theories about which of the different castes were suitable for military duties: these so-called 'martial races' were described and defined in printed handbooks, which were taken into the countryside by officers to help them select appropriate recruits. Similarly, land settlement officers pontificated on the innate farming abilities of different castes.

These various endeavours threw up several intellectual problems. How did the classic Sanskrit discussions of caste (or *varna*, colour) relate to the castes now being identified? The Sanskrit discussions of *varna* were really concerned only with four main categories: Brahmans (priests), Kshatriyas (warriors), Vaishyas (traders) and Sudras (workers). Outside and beneath these categories were the Untouchables, whose tasks were defined in terms of their role in removing ritual pollution. But many thousands of castes were identified in villages by the Census authorities. The favoured solution to the problem of how to reconcile the four basic *varnas* with the many thousand castes was to distinguish between *varna* and *jāti* (Srinivas 1962). Whereas *varna* refers to the all-India categories described in the classic texts, people identified themselves (or so it seemed) with *jāti*, much smaller groups of people with whom they shared a common status in a local region. These *jāti* formed marriage pools, had some political organization (for example to settle disputes among their members), and recognized a basic equality (for example, by sharing food without inhibitions). The *jāti* could locate themselves in terms of the *varna* classification, but locally there were often disputes about where an individual *jāti* might be placed.

Some of these issues were clarified when ethnographic village studies

---

[30] Much of this discussion was carried on using a racial terminology: see Robb (ed.) 1995.

were published, describing how *jāti* related to each other at the village level. The early classics *The Hindu Jajmāni System* and *Behind Mud Walls* (Wiser 1936; Wiser and Wiser 1971) were written in the 1930s, based on observations of Karimpur, 250 km or so south of Bijnor, in southern UP. The former book focused on the ways in which different castes were related to one another. According to the Wisers, the *jajmāni* system was a pattern of payments, usually in the form of grain, by landowners to a variety of castes who performed tasks for them during the year. Blacksmiths, potters, Brahmans, and sweepers all received a share of the crop, irrespective of the amount of work they had carried out in that year. The Wisers portrayed this as a largely harmonious system that worked to integrate the village, since in times of need the poor still received some of their basic food needs in this way. Other studies in the 1950s focused on the hierarchy of prestige and purity that emerged if people listed who was prepared to accept food of different kinds from whom within a village community, and how this related to more general concerns of purity and pollution. When Louis Dumont codified much of this discussion in his *Homo Hierarchicus* (Dumont 1970) there appeared to be some consensus about the ways in which people's everyday lives were organized in terms not only of local relationships but also the classic Sanskrit texts of Manu and others. Objections – that the *jajmāni* system seemed hardly systematic and, to some, appeared more exploitative than just, or that lower castes had a distinctly jaundiced view of the upper castes' claims to ritual purity as the basis for their privileges – were dismissed.[31]

Since 1970, however, this apparent consensus has crumbled. Dumont's summary has been criticized in several ways, of which the most important for our purposes here are the issues raised by the presence of caste-like forms of social organization among non-Hindus, and by the Subalternist historians' revisionist interpretations of European writing about caste.

The problem of castes among non-Hindus was raised in relation to Buddhists, Christians, Sikhs and Jains, as well as Muslims.[32] Muslims constitute some 30 per cent of the population of India, Pakistan and Bangladesh together, and they espouse a very different, arguably more egalitarian, set of religious beliefs from those of Hinduism. If, as Dumont argued, caste is a way of dealing with issues of purity and

---

[31] For classic discussions of the caste system, see Leach 1964; Beidelman 1959; Fuller 1989.

[32] There are very few Buddhists in mainland South Asia. Sikhism and Christianity, like Islam, profess the equality of all believers, yet Sikhs practise *jāti* endogamy and south Indian Christians do operate systems of caste-like ranking. Jains can for these purposes be seen as sects of Hindus. See Ahmed 1982; L. Caplan 1977.

pollution for Hindus, why do Muslims have *jāti*? In many ways these *jāti* seem to operate as Hindu castes, receiving annual payments, for example, or being located along with Untouchables in rankings of hierarchy in villages where they form a small proportion of the population. Sometimes the most obvious explanation is that many Muslim groups seem to have converted to Islam as whole *jāti*, and sometimes retained their original caste names or took on Islamic titles without changing many of their social practices. In pre-Partition Punjab, for example, there were Muslim, Sikh and Hindu Jats. Other groups, however, claimed to be descended from Muslim invaders, either from north-west India (Pathans) or from further west, even from Arabia (Qureshi, Saiyyid). Despite their Islamic origins, though, they followed a number of practices typical of Hindu *jāti*, particularly in arranging marriages solely within the *jāti* and having a basic status hierarchy (with those who claimed descent from the invaders, the *Ashraf*, having a nobility which they denied to those who were believed to be descendants of converts or from the trading classes, the *Ajlaf*). Neither caste endogamy nor status differentials have any sanction in Islamic law, which proclaims the spiritual equality of all believers, though some parallels can also be seen in Islamic practice in West Asia and North Africa.

While the heterogeneity of the Indian population has been ignored by many writers, on the grounds that Hinduism is dominant at the ideological level and thus a legitimate focus of attention, the Subalternist historical challenge to the nature of caste has to be taken more seriously, since it questions much of the material on which the orthodox social science views have been based. Following on from the critique posed by Edward Said in *Orientalism* (1978) and Benedict Anderson (1983), several writers have suggested that caste is largely a British colonial invention (Appadorai 1993; Inden 1990; see also Prakash 1992). It fits neatly with the European obsession with creating an Orient which consists of all that the Occident wished not to acknowledge in itself: irrational, superstitious, rigid, and concerned with hierarchy and innate characteristics rather than equality and achievement. In this reading, the British created fixed and immutable castes in their attempts to pin down the 'essential' Indian character, as much to portray themselves as to understand Indians. Whatever caste is today, or however it was described in the nineteenth century, it arguably has more to do with the social interests motivating the observers than with any social reality which predates those concerns.

This argument has some considerable plausibility. The Indian Army recruiting handbooks, for example, are full of caste stereotypes, and the whole British literature on the 'martial races' was obviously generated out of the events of 1857 and fear of their recurrence. Similarly, the Census and other attempts to define people as belonging to a limited set of castes was constantly being challenged by people who claimed to be of a different caste, or who began to change the names of the caste they were said to belong to (Cohn 1987; Inden 1990). Soon after the Census began its work on a nationally co-ordinated basis, in 1872, it generated political movements of members of caste groups which challenged the basis of their allocation to a particular position in the *varna* system (Pant 1987).

After Independence, the Indian Government took the view that caste had been exaggerated by the British as part of its policies of 'divide and rule', except for the case of the Untouchables. Following Gandhi's campaign to eradicate Untouchability, the Government granted preferential rights to those castes it listed in a Schedule to the Indian Constitution. But the Government attempted to draw a line at this point, arguing that no other caste identities should have any relevance. All other listing of caste-group membership was dropped from the Indian Census. No social analysis on the basis of caste can now be carried out through the use of official statistics, though this did not stop sample surveys from including caste in their analysis, for example, of fertility differentials (Misra 1982). The general attempt to root out caste-consciousness has failed, as is obvious from the decision to implement the Mandal Commission's recommendations in the 1990s, and the reactions to this decision outlined above.

In the light of these uncertainties – over the relationship of *jāti* to *varna* and issues of purity and pollution, over whether or not there is caste among Muslims, and over the reliability of historical and other reports about caste groups – we may seem perverse to base our research on such a social category. We would certainly want to distance ourselves from the racial and divisive reading of castes which characterized the early British colonial accounts. Similarly, we reject the view of many of the village studies of the 1950s, which tended to underplay economic issues and to stress caste (and religion) as 'Indian society's essence' (O'Hanlon and Washbrook 1992: 142). On the other hand, the colonial project concerning caste was internally contradictory and 'colonial bureaucratic operations did not necessarily transform practices and mentalities on the ground' (Appadorai 1993: 327). Caste identities certainly predate their partial transformations during the British period. But we agree with Kaviraj (cited in Chakrabarty 1995: 3376–7) that in the early nineteenth century people probably had a 'fuzzy' sense of caste, one which has been increasingly replaced by administrative categories of fixed identities. These have been assumed to be simple, homogeneous identities which can be counted, rather than fluid, negotiated ones which change, for example by discussing electoral politics in India as the outcome of 'vote banks' made up of caste and religious communities.

Religious identities have been subject to similar processes. As with caste, the British seem to have stressed the significance of 'community' (as religion is usually described in Indian discussions) and to have rigidified the distinctions between the different communities. These policies can be more clearly seen as attempts to divide and rule, particularly with respect to the introduction of special constituencies for members of different minority religions. But in addition, the British were prone to look for religious roots to conflicts which might be better understood in class terms or as expressions of nationalist sentiments (Pandey 1991). Partition, and the creation of Pakistan on the basis of religious identity, was the culmination of the dynamic set in motion in part by the mutually reinforcing effects of British communalist policies and of politicians who organized to strengthen people's sense of communal identity. After Independence, the Indian Government refused to accept arguments based on religious identity as the basis for discrimination or policy: the Sikhs in Punjab, for example, were unable to argue for a State in which they would be religiously dominant, but were conceded new boundaries for Punjab on the basis of those areas where Punjabi was spoken. Language and religion were fused, with Hindus in Punjab being urged to declare that they spoke Hindi, while Sikhs were told to declare their allegiance to Punjabi as a mother tongue. Such developments tended to polarize Hindu and Sikh Punjabis, despite the evidence that intermarriage was common, and indeed Hindu parents might rear one or more of their children as Sikhs, because of vows made at Sikh shrines. Thus despite official refusal to acknowledge the everyday significance of religious identities, political and social developments depended centrally on religious issues. Despite the Congress party's official commitment to secularism, indeed, its actions were continually challenged (by Hindu partisans as well as Muslim leaders) in terms of the benefits or advantages offered to members of different communities. As we shall argue in Chapter 6, even though people's behaviour may not follow directly from their doctrinal beliefs or the advice of their religious leaders, religion remains very important politically.

Caste and community, then, are two key categories by which Indians themselves construct an understanding of the world in which they live. Since before the British codified, recorded and counted caste or community identities, Indians were clear that caste and religion were significant social labels: 'On the appropriate occasion, every individual would use his cognitive apparatus to classify any single person he interacts with and place him quite exactly, and decide if he could eat with him, go on a journey, or arrange a marriage into his family' (Kaviraj 1989, cited in Chakrabarty 1995). Furthermore, even if they were imprecise and unclear at the edges, these caste and religious groups had recognizably different patterns of social organization.[33] Of course these differences can easily be stereotyped, as the British did, ignoring considerable internal variations and the extent to which social patterns overlapped and cross-cut caste and religious boundaries. But, at the very least, almost all marriages were and are still arranged by the couple's parents within *jāti*, not only in the rural areas but also for many urban social groups.[34] Precisely because they encapsulate kinship links, caste groups (and thereby religious groupings) are still key channels of political mobilization at the local level.

Since kinship and family relationships are very largely organized along caste lines, *jāti* are an obvious unit for demographic analysis. Although all *jāti* in one region may have fairly similar kinship systems, these can also differ between one *jāti* and the next. Some of the differences between a Hindu and a Muslim *jāti*, or between different *jāti* of the same religion, may be accounted for by the fact that different *jāti* tend to occupy different economic positions. But economic differences do not explain all the variations between *jāti*. Some of these variations appear to have no significance in demographic terms: differences in the observation of certain rituals, for example. Indeed, there may well be local variations within *jāti* on these scores. Mothers-in-law often told us that they needed to spend a lot of time with a new daughter-in-law to teach her how her new family marked births and deaths, or carried out religious ceremonies, because her natal family (in the same *jāti*) managed these affairs differently. In terms of our concerns, however, caste group membership can affect demographic behaviour in two main ways: differences amongst caste groups in aspects of social life which have a direct relevance to fertility; and those which operate indirectly.

Mandelbaum, in his survey of material on fertility differentials in India up to the early 1970s, singles out widow remarriage and the age at which girls are married as important ways in which groups might differ (Mandelbaum 1974: 33–41). Many high-caste Hindu *jāti* have banned the remarriage of widows, which could contribute to lower fertility rates,

---

[33] In carrying out our survey of women who had recently given birth in 1982, for example, we came across only one caste group – Gujjars – where young married women regularly worked on the family fields.

[34] We discuss the exceptions to this generalization in the two study populations in Chapter 4.

especially where women marry husbands several years older than themselves and substantial numbers of women may thus remain widowed through a considerable portion of their potential child-bearing years. Neither of the *jāti* we are concerned with here restricts widows from remarrying. Most young Sheikh widows are found new husbands by either their own kin or their husband's kin. Amongst the Jats, and sometimes amongst the Sheikhs, young widows may be expected to accept their husband's younger brother as their new husband. Indeed, as we carried out the census in Nangal, Roger visited one Jat household where a woman denied her late husband's younger brother's claim that she was now his wife. Age at marriage can be much more important as a direct factor in fertility decline, however, and we discuss the patterns which emerge for Sheikhs and Jats in Chapter 4.

Indirect effects of family systems on demographic variables could include any impact of marriage arrangements on gender relationships and on a woman's ability to determine her own fertility. For example, there are differences amongst *jāti* in the people who can be regarded as appropriate spouses for children, in the way in which spouses are chosen, in the relative ages of husband and wife, and in their attitudes towards schooling of boys and of girls. We take up all these issues in later chapters, dealing with marriage arrangements in Chapter 4, and · age at marriage and schooling in Chapter 5.

Women's schooling and marriage distance as stratifying variables

In both Nangal and Qaziwala we carried out a census of the whole village and then selected two *jāti* – Jats and Sheikhs – for more detailed study. In Nangal, Jats were the dominant political and economic *jāti* though there were more Chamars; in Qaziwala, Sheikhs dominated the village on all three factors. We collected basic information on child-bearing experiences (maternity histories) from all ever-married (currently married, divorced, widowed and separated) Jat and Sheikh women in order to provide some population estimates for demographic variables, and to ensure that we could accurately select the women we wanted to interview in more depth. For the Jats, we intended looking particularly at the effects of girls' schooling, and matched 12 couples where the wife had at least finished secondary schooling (8th class) with 12 couples where the wife had never been to school or was functionally illiterate.[35] For the Sheikhs, we chose marriage distance as the significant

[35] In our original proposal we had included two further villages: in one we would compare Rajput couples, 12 where the wife had had at least eight years of schooling and 12 where the wife had not been to school; in the fourth village we intended to compare Gujjar

variable, and selected 12 couples where the wife had been both born and married in Qaziwala and matched them to 12 couples where the wife could not reasonably visit her parents on a daily basis. Matching in both cases was on the basis of age and class.

These women were chosen systematically according to several additional criteria. All the women were aged 25–34, and had at least one living son. We expected these to be women for whom contraception might be a relevant issue. Younger women usually refuse to speculate on how many children they might like. Women with daughters but no son tend to refuse to consider family planning until they have a son. Older women are likely to have already decided on contraception, possibly some years before (and may thus not be reliable guides to how and why they decided to stop having children) or to feel that they are unlikely to have any more children. By selecting women only in the 25–34 age band and with one son we hoped to maximize the chance that differences would emerge in couples' views of appropriate family size. To guard against the possibility that our respondents were unusual in their maternity histories, we compared them on a number of variables (age at marriage, marriage distance and education) with all the women in the relevant caste group in the village.

Even after we had reduced our expectations in Autumn 1990, things did not run as smoothly as we had hoped. We had aimed to collect the views of a sample of 24 couples from each village, but in practice different numbers of men and women were willing to answer our questions. Since we drew up our sample on clear grounds, it was not always possible to find a suitable replacement for unwilling informants. We had also hoped to take things slowly, visiting men and women separately two or three times and leaving the more sensitive questions (on matters of family planning) till the end, when we expected to be able to ask them in a relaxed fashion, for example asking questions while women were working, and allowing the women's responses to guide the sequence of questioning. But as time pressed upon us, we decided that the interviews could not be done as we had originally planned. In practice we decided that one interview would normally have to cover all the topics in which we were interested, since we were not sure if we would be able to return (because of the communal uncertainties). All of the women had already met one of our interviewers already, when their maternity histories were collected. Even so, a small number of women refused to take part at all, or walked out in the middle of the interview and refused to agree to a time when the remainder of the questions

couples, 12 where the wife was actively engaged in agricultural work in the fields and 12 where the wife's work was restricted to the area immediately surrounding the house.

could be asked. Only a few women were interviewed more than once, and then because we had been unable to finish the interview on the first occasion. For some of the men, moreover, Roger's visit to arrange an interview was the first contact they had with the research, because some other member of their household had supplied their details for the census. Some men were elusive, either because their work took them away from the village at the times Roger could look for them, or because they were avoiding being interviewed. In two cases, then, we have material from only a husband, and in three others, from only a wife.

Despite these difficulties, many of our interviews did yield the full nuanced answers we had hoped for. In addition, we have been able to supplement our direct interview material with insights gained from our work in Dharmnagri and Jhakri (including with Jats and Sheikhs who had marriage links to their caste-fellows in Nangal and Qaziwala), and from more general fieldwork in Nangal and Qaziwala. One of our Hindu assistants – Chhaya Pandey – was a Brahman from Nangal, and she was able to flesh out some of the material we were gaining from our interviews. Some of the Qaziwala Sheikh sample were related to families we knew from Jhakri, and Swaleha and Radha were able to use their local knowledge to encourage women to relax and tell us more about their lives.

Our theoretical approach

At this point, purist social researchers may object that our data are too flawed by small numbers or by the context in which they were collected to offer any reliable or valid insights into social behaviour. Furthermore, our analysis is not restricted to the comparisons within caste groups which was the basis of our research strategy. We have moved away from our original plans for two main reasons. To begin with, as we rapidly realized, demographic differentials *between* the two caste groups were considerable, and were much more significant than differences *within* the groups. Secondly, as we demonstrate in Chapter 4, differences in women's positions in the two *jāti* make little contribution to an understanding of why Sheikhs have larger families than do Jats. Since gender relationships seemed to be less important than we expected, we considered alternative explanations for the demographic differences between the two *jāti*. In the maternity histories from all the ever-married Jat and Sheikh women in Nangal and Qaziwala respectively, we have sufficient data to show that the differences are not happenstance; and through our discussions with men and women in the key reproductive age groups, we have insights into their behaviour which are general enough to hold, despite the unusual way in which they were selected for interview. Finally, we are drawing on our experience over 10 years in conducting research among people in rural Bijnor. As with all social research, there are loose threads in the picture we will weave: none the less, we believe the broad outlines are sufficiently clear and robust.

Our experience, then, helped to extend and deepen our understanding that we should try to 'situate fertility, that is, to show how it makes sense given the sociocultural and political economic context in which it is embedded' (Greenhalgh 1995: 17). We have complemented the politics of gender, which is where we started our research, with a politics of class and community. We see this book helping to move social demography away from a concern solely with measurable features of individuals (age at marriage, desired family size etc.) towards a concern with relationships which link the decisions (or non-decisions) of individuals to the social collectivities of which they are a part. Within households, differences of gender, age and genealogical generation create competing and conflicting as well as common interests (Sen 1990). Gender relationships are crucial (both as cultural and political issues). Reproduction is 'enwrapped in gender relations, relations of difference and inequality in beliefs, resources and power' (Greenhalgh 1995: 14). But this concern with the internal dynamics of power within households must be balanced by an awareness of how, for some purposes, the behaviour of individuals and households cannot be understood except in the context of much wider social processes (McNicoll 1994). For McNicoll, history and location are crucial. Social institutions (including those which affect fertility) are what he calls 'path-dependent': they depend on past adjustments, and (especially through the role of expectations) affect how the future is envisaged and changed (McNicoll 1994: 7). For Greenhalgh, fertility transitions must be understood as the 'products of changes in class-specific opportunity structures in response to transformations of global and regional political economies' (Greenhalgh 1990: 21). In attempting to make these links between the demographic processes within households, and national or global economic and political changes, however, we must not lose sight of the ways these wider issues of political economy are themselves gendered.

For the *jāti* we consider here, the political economy of population is partly a matter of State policy, of the communalization of politics and the politicization of identity. It is also a politics and culture of patriarchy, in which opportunities for women are constrained by the imagery of 'woman' which enters into communal discourses. At the time of our research, there were national debates over Muslim Family Law (generated in 1986 by the case of Shah Bano, a divorced woman who demanded financial support from her ex-husband under the civil laws) and over Hindu approaches to *satī* (when a widow burns herself along with her husband's body), precipitated by the death of Roop Kanwar on her husband's funeral pyre in 1987. These debates had made political battlegrounds of the appropriate limits for Hindu and Muslim Indian women's agency. The events which temporarily transformed the lives of people in Bijnor in 1990–1 did not come out of the blue; and the consequences of those events remain of great significance, not only at the macro-level of State politics but at micro- and meso-levels of households and of intergroup relationships. In the rest of this book we flesh out this approach to demographic issues in contemporary India by reporting on the research which we did manage to complete, and by showing how the concerns of that research, and the difficulties we had in carrying it out, throw light on gender relationships, communal differences and their interaction in northern India in the early 1990s.

Chapter 2 provides a survey of overall population trends in India, locating Bijnor within that part of the country where fertility and mortality rates are highest. We then turn to a brief discussion of the major academic attempts at understanding and explaining regional variations in demographic regimes in India, and predicting change in mortality and fertility. We point to some weaknesses in those explanations of fertility that focus on individual economic, social and political characteristics. In Chapter 2 we also locate important aspects of the two villages – Qaziwala and Nangal – we studied in rural western UP, and introduce in more detail the two *jāti* (Sheikhs in Qaziwala, Jats in Nangal) whose demographic differences form the core problematic for this book. In Chapter 3 we consider demographic issues in the context of the agrarian system – agricultural technology, working practices, cropping patterns and land ownership patterns. We ask whether fertility differences can be satisfactorily explained by an economic rationality, derived from class position, in a narrow sense: do the poor want more children because they are poor, or the rich more because they are rich? Chapter 4 looks at gender politics and asks whether women have many children because they lack the autonomy to determine their own fertility. Are women ready to contracept, with unmet needs for fertility control, but unable to do so because they lack the ability to implement their views? Chapter 5 addresses issues of so-called 'ideational change', and women's empowerment through schooling, asking in particular whether schooling has an impact on fertility. We find all these approaches have limited explanatory power, and in Chapter 6 we offer an alternative explanation, based on the demographic effects of people's religious identities as members of politicized social categories. We conclude by drawing out the implications of these at the local level for Indian society at large.

2 Populating Bijnor

Any research or writing which touches on population issues in India is liable to be misinterpreted. For white western scholars like us, writing about two caste groups, one Muslim and one Hindu, with a special reference to issues of women's agency, is a hazardous enterprise. Here we explain why we selected this research topic, why we chose to study population issues in Bijnor and how any insights we gain might apply beyond the two villages where we collected most of the information on which our arguments are based.

Population issues in India: Malthus, Marx or reproductive rights?

The contentiousness of India's population dates from colonial times. The body of writing about India's demography and its population policy is voluminous and varied. Here we pick out three main strands of such writing – the Malthusian, neo-Marxist and feminist – in order to help locate our own position.

The British rulers of India, almost as soon as they established a presence in any part of the sub-continent, started to enumerate the population, as well as counting their crops, animals, and anything else that might be of interest. Much of this counting went way beyond what could ever have been of direct use, and contributed to a categorization of the Indian population by caste and religion, some of whose results can be seen in the anti-reservation and communal riots we described in the last chapter (Cohn 1987; Appadorai 1993). The census operations, increasingly centralized and co-ordinated from 1870 onwards, also provided the raw data to allow western observers to comment on whether India is 'overpopulated', and whether India's poverty is caused by its large population or its rapid population growth.[1]

India's population – estimated at about 850 million in 1991 – is the

---

[1] Cassen, 1978, provides a sophisticated account of discussions of India's population, also considering China, whose census operations have been irregular and partial.

second largest in the world, and is likely to exceed that of China before 2050 (Visaria and Visaria 1994). In the 1960s, when western access to China was severely restricted, India was a focus for westerners concerned about overpopulation. In an influential book, Paul Ehrlich graphically conveyed his sense of population pressure in the Old City in Delhi (Ehrlich 1968). He reinforced the conventional wisdom that the benefits of industrial growth and social development were being eaten away by the need to feed, house, school and employ ever-growing numbers of people. Until their recent displacement by sub-Saharan Africa, India and Bangladesh were the key sites of research and experiments, as development experts and aid agencies tried to limit fertility. More recently, such efforts have received an additional boost from those environmentalists who argue that over-population in countries like India has to be tackled in the interests of planetary survival (Hardin 1995).

Neo-Malthusians see population growth as the major threat to the future of the world as they know it, and argue for birth control programmes to be enacted on a war footing. In general, the major aid agencies – the World Bank in particular – and the Indian Government (with the partial exception of the Janata Government of 1977–9) have accepted these lines of argument. Within India, many members of the urban middle and upper classes often note with pride that theirs was the world's first official Government population programme, and they fully support the Government's attempts to lower the birth rate – or even argue for more forceful measures to be introduced (Ravindran 1993; Pai Panandikar and Umashankar 1994). Until 1964, the family planning programme was based on a network of urban clinics, offering little more than advice on the rhythm method, condoms and spermicidal foam tablets; very few sterilization operations were carried out. In the mid-1960s, the family planning programme was extended to rural areas. Sterilizations (originally of men, later mostly of women) and IUDs (intra-uterine devices, often known as the 'loop', 'coil', or, in the 1980s, the 'Copper-T') became the major methods offered.[2] The 1961 census results showed that the Indian population was growing much faster (over 2 per cent per year) than had previously been believed. This imparted a sense of urgency to the programme, which has subsequently combined threats, offers of monetary and other incentives, and propaganda to persuade people to limit the number of children they have. During the political Emergency of 1975–7, when democratic rights were suspended, Sanjay Gandhi, Prime Minister Indira Gandhi's son, was

[2] The contraceptive pill has not been prominent, and the introduction of injectable contraceptives was much later and slower in India than, for example, in Bangladesh.

given almost unlimited power and chose to implement a ruthless compulsory sterilization campaign (Kocher 1980). Outright physical force was used against the poor, in an attempt to speed up a shift to lower fertility rates. In India as a whole, between April 1975 and March 1977, more than 10 million people (mostly men, sometimes widowed or more than 40 years old) were pressured into being sterilized.[3]

These policies contributed to the defeat of Mrs Gandhi's Congress party in the 1977 elections. Despite this popular backlash, though, the Indian Government is still strongly committed to the goal of limiting India's population (Vicziany 1983; Narayana and Kantner 1993). Heavy-handed pressure, accompanied by financial incentives for very poor people, means that coercion and threats still underpin the Indian Government's approach to population issues, despite the formal abandonment of targets for workers to fulfil. The language of the programme attempts to disguise what, to many of its recipients and critics, are its real concerns. 'Family planning' has been renamed 'family welfare'. Incentives to people to be sterilized are called 'compensation payments' (supposedly to meet lost wages or to pay costs of medical treatment); staff are given 'targets' for 'motivating cases', rather than encouraged to find ways of meeting the needs of clients. Alone among Indian Government programmes, those who take advantage of family planning services receive a cash payment. In no other Department does the Government pay its staff cash incentives for reaching the targets they have been set in their normal course of work, nor threaten such penalties (dismissal, suspension, cutting of pay) for those who fail. The overriding demand to reduce the birth-rate also seems to justify the cavalier approach to patient safety employed by some of those who introduce new contraceptive technology in India. Ironically, the international agencies (like the World Bank, USAID and the Ford Foundation) who supported the introduction of contraceptive targets and heavy-handed motivational efforts are now trying to redirect Indian policy away from the more high pressure methods – less for ethical reasons than for concern about the effectiveness of the programme, and without abandoning their belief that 'population' is a major problem for India (Minkler 1977; World Bank 1989).

The stress on population control as the key to removing India's poverty has not, however, gone unchallenged. In all the mass of English

---

[3] In a fascinating paper, Tarlo (1995) has described the ways in which two policies of the time – forced resettlement of the poor on the then outskirts of Delhi, and the sterilization campaign – combined to involve the poor themselves in recruiting new candidates for sterilization. The Emergency is still referred to by many of these people as *nasbandī ka vaqt* (the time of sterilization). See also the Shah Commission Report (1978).

language writing about India's population, Mahmood Mamdani's *The Myth of Population Control* is by far the most widely read. Based on a course-paper for his Master's degree, it was published in 1972 and generated a substantial debate on the reasons for high fertility in rural India. The core of the book is a neo-Marxist critique of an early experimental rural family planning programme in Ludhiana District, in the Indian state of Punjab. From 1954 to 1960, as part of a research programme conducted by public health academics from Harvard University, villagers were offered foam contraceptives and condoms.[4] Ten years later, Mamdani visited Manupur – one of the villages which was a target of the campaign – and analyzed the records of the programme. He concluded that the programme displayed a class bias, reflecting the prejudices of a very small part of Indian society – the urban middle and upper classes, and those in rural India whose relatively affluent material circumstances have led them to limit their own fertility. This prevented the staff from understanding the values and behaviour of peasants, for whom the family labour force was crucial to their survival and prosperity. Family planning would, for agricultural labourers and middle peasants alike, be extremely irrational, and (he claimed) the research programme managers never understood this. He also claimed that the research managers had manipulated the results to disguise the extent to which the programme had failed.

On publication, Mamdani's book received enthusiastic reviews in general journals like *New Republic* ('What we really need at the moment is about one thousand Mamdanis') but was hardly noticed in the standard demographic journals. When *Population Studies* published a review in 1975, Pravin Visaria argued that Mamdani's book had received 'undue, and to some extent, undeserved, attention' and concluded that the book was 'facile and highly misleading'. Apart from the fact that it is short and lucidly written with extensive use of anecdotes, what accounts for the book's popularity? Clearly, Mamdani caught a political tide. He provided a credible picture of arrogant Western medical and social scientists being outmanoeuvred by diplomatic but rational peasants. He seemed to show that 'the population problem' was a Western, bourgeois invention which could be resolved by land reforms and socialist policies, not by population propaganda and contraception. At the height of the anti-Vietnam War agitations, students and a radicalized academia were attracted to a message that peasants are heroes and that 'development is the best contraceptive'. High fertility was a result of poverty, he argued, not a cause of poverty. Far from 'overpopulation' being the problem,

[4] The programme is fully described in *The Khanna Study* (Wyon and Gordon 1971) a book which has never received the same attention as Mamdani's critique.

Mamdani argued that the problem was inequality and poverty; he justified a class-based analysis of demographic issues (though his book devoted more space to caste than to class). Finally, perhaps, he provided an eloquent testimony to the value of the study of local-level demographic processes in understanding global population issues.

While Visaria pointed to several flaws in Mamdani's arguments, the most compelling criticism is provided by hindsight. Mamdani had concluded that for the majority of villagers, to 'practise contraception would have meant to wilfully court economic disaster' (Mamdani 1972: 21). He argued that partial mechanization of agriculture in the 1950s and 1960s had increased the demand for labour among farmers and labourers alike, and that there was little scope for further introduction of tractors (which might drastically cut the need for labour) because 85 per cent of farm holdings were too small. Yet almost before the ink was dry on his pages, and before tractorization could have had the results predicted by Mamdani, rural Punjab experienced both an economic boom and a relatively steep decline in fertility. By 1989 the use of contraception was higher in Punjab than in any other Indian State (Satia and Jejeebhoy 1991: 35). Dyson suggests that birth rates were in fact falling throughout the 1960s in Punjab (Dyson 1991) and in Ludhiana District itself total fertility probably dropped from a peak of about 7 in the 1930s to about 5.5 in the early 1950s and to just over 4 when Mamdani carried out his study in 1971 (Das Gupta 1995: 483). When Moni Nag and Neeraj Kak restudied Manupur in 1982 they discovered that many of those peasants who had told Mamdani that contraception would mean economic disaster had changed their minds and favoured small families. Of couples where the wife was of child-bearing age, half were using modern contraceptive methods (Nag and Kak 1984). Yet, despite the failure of its main prediction, *The Myth of Population Control* is still in print after more than 20 years, and regularly appears on student reading lists.[5]

Part of the legacy of Mamdani's book has been to sustain alternative views on the causes of, and solutions to, India's poverty. Some critics of the Malthusian approach believe that processes of social and economic change will generate the conditions in which it will become rational for people to have small families. Others argue that social groups at all levels (from the household to the world 'global village') will find ways of coping with a larger population, as they have in the past; or that attempts to speed up this adaptation should focus on encouraging development,

---

[5] In Britain, for example, the Open University's revised course on Third World Development includes a respectful summary and quotes extensively from it (Bernstein et al. 1992: 114–118).

since birth-control programmes cannot succeed on their own. Many social demographers – whether neo-Malthusian or not – have explicitly rejected futurology, and restricted themselves to exploring processes of economic and social change and their effects on fertility and mortality. In practice, of course, much of their work does contribute to policy discussions. For example, research which shows that educated women have smaller families is widely used to justify programmes to increase the number of girls in school.[6] But the most telling difference between Malthusians and their critics is in the way they approach the issues of demographic change. For Malthusians, population numbers or growth rates are at the core of the world's environmental, political and economic problems. For the rest (amongst whom we would count ourselves) the impact of larger numbers of people *per se* is less important than patterns of inequality in the consumption of resources; and the denial of citizens' rights, as well as women's reproductive and other rights cannot be justified by the arguments of those who would suspend those rights in the interest of population control (Bose 1991). Mamdani may be wrong on many specific points, then, but his approach remains instructive.

Issues of reproductive rights brought us to the study of population processes in Bijnor in 1990. In our research in 1982–3 we attempted to steer clear of issues of family planning and the Government population programme. Carrying out our work so soon after the Emergency, and fearing that we would be seen as sterilization workers, we were loath even to ask whether a woman was using contraception. We soon discovered, however, that the issue could not be avoided. Many people were convinced that our explicit (and real) interests in childbirth and how it was socially organized were merely a cover for a hidden contraceptive agenda. After their fears were set at rest, however, women often turned the tables on us by asking for family planning advice and contraceptive supplies. We became increasingly aware of the extent to which many women's reproductive needs were left untouched by either public or private initiatives. By the end of our stay in 1983 we could demonstrate how the local form of patriarchy, in combination with a Government maternal health programme deformed by its linkage to the population control programme, left women's needs during pregnancy, delivery and the post-partum period very poorly catered for (P. Jeffery et al. 1989).

Feminist-inspired writing on reproductive rights has attempted to recast the population debate in different, sometimes conflicting ways.[7]

---

[6] For an extended discussion of some of the issues raised by this argument, see Jeffery and Basu (eds.) 1996.
[7] For recent discussions see Dixon-Mueller 1993; Jackson 1993; Sen et al. 1994; Sen and Snow 1994.

Springing from concerns with human rights, some authors have identified physical reproduction as the defining feature of womanhood, and have sought to release women from outside control, whether by husbands, other kin, or the State. For many of them, issues of fertility should be decided by the woman alone, and environmentalist or Malthusian concerns are irrelevant and unimportant.[8] As a Women's Declaration on Population Policies expressed it, 'Women have the individual right and the social responsibility to decide whether, how and when to have children and how many to have; no woman can be compelled to bear a child or be prevented from doing so against her will'.[9] Some feminists argue for a wide definition of reproductive rights, to include issues of coerced sex, reproductive disorders like pelvic inflammatory diseases, and women's access to general health services. But in placing reproductive rights in a context of 'social and global welfare and limits' (Berer 1993: 9), some of these authors allow Malthusian concerns a role in setting limits to a woman's own freedom to choose. Other writers have been more modest in their aims, for example trying to ensure that principles of informed consent replace the coercive elements of population programmes, without making frontal attacks on patriarchal structures, whether in the State or in the household. In this latter camp we can place much of the recent discussion by Western donor agencies, who seem to use the language of women's reproductive rights as a way to enhance the efficiency of population control programmes. Population programmes are thus justified on the grounds that 100 million married women of reproductive age worldwide are at risk of unwanted pregnancy each year, and may resort to abortion (often illegal) and thus have unmet needs for contraception (Sen et al. 1994: 10). The current family planning orthodoxy attempts to include feminist concerns by advocating population policies which include commitments to ethics and human rights, as part of broader human development approaches, while giving priority to women's empowerment and sexual health services (Sen et al. 1994: 5–6). Potential conflicts between such policies and population control interests have been laid aside on the grounds that changing population programmes in these ways would also create the conditions for fertility decline.

Our own position on all of these issues, in brief, is to accept a

---

[8] Overall (1987: 170) discusses the arguments of those who put forward the 'strong version of the claim to a right to reproduce' in the context of surrogacy and fertility treatments. See also Hartmann 1987 and 1995; Bok 1994.

[9] This statement was prepared for the Cairo Population Conference in 1994 and is reproduced in Sen et al. 1994: 32.

sceptical, anti-Malthusian position, inspired by much of the debate in the 1980s and 1990s in feminist and other circles. India's many problems have not been created by its absolute population size, nor its growth in population since the 1920s; nor is current population growth a major barrier to solving those problems. Issues of overcrowding, pollution and poverty might be easier to solve with a smaller population, but focusing on population is usually a way of drawing attention away from the issues of dominance and inequality which remain acute in India. Understanding how women often suffer from these processes, and how improvements in their position may be brought about, is important in its own right. Among other things, such changes might reduce a woman's fertility, but this is a goal to be sought only insofar as it reflects a woman's own desires, set in the framework of what is possible for enhancing her own welfare as she defines it. But a woman's desires, and her views on her own welfare, emerge from the social contexts in which she must live: elucidating how women interpret their desires, and their best strategies for survival in those contexts is part of the task we have set ourselves. Thus when there is no form of social security for old age, for example, a woman's preference for sons is easily understood, but a social security system is a valuable goal in its own right, not merely as a means to reduce the birth-rate.

This perspective underpinned the research we proposed in 1990. The women we studied in 1982–3 had alerted us to the many ways in which they were constrained and limited in trying to reach their own fertility goals, but we were unhappy with an academic literature that suggested that such women had no freedom of action. We wanted to investigate sources of a woman's agency, through her work, her schooling or her kinship networks, and whether these would make a difference to her ability to influence her fertility. In attempting to understand fertility outcomes in a broader context, we recognized that these are not just matters for individuals or even couples on their own.

In research that assesses the relationships between women's agency and demographic outcomes, two main methods have been used. On the one hand are those who focus almost entirely on census figures and the results of very large sample surveys. This literature has produced a mass of detail about regional patterns of population change through time, and some basic data on correlations between various economic and social aspects of the population and rates of mortality and fertility. (For a recent example, see Murti et al. 1995.) On the other hand, and in line with our own preference, is small-scale field-based research, at household or village level. We believe that understanding social processes is much better advanced through engaging with the people who also have to make sense of these social processes for themselves. While none of these smaller studies, whether ethnographic or based on questionnaires, can claim to be representative or typical, together they have made considerable contributions to understanding local processes of change. The analysis of small-scale situations, with due concern for unusual features, can illuminate a much broader section of Indian society, since villages in India today are affected by and contribute towards regional and even national social processes.

In order to set some of the context for our research, we shall first establish how Bijnor's general demographic, social and economic conditions reflect its particular position in India as a whole, and then describe in more detail the two caste groups who are central to this book's analysis – the Sheikhs and Jats in Qaziwala and Nangal.

Regional variations in India's population

Because the Indian censuses, by comparison with those in most of the rest of the world, have been remarkably well-conducted, and because the population is so large, it has been possible to perform quite sophisticated analyses of their results. Here we shall not be concerned with the minute details – what is sometimes called decimal point demography – but with the overall features.

The results of the 1991 Census seemed to confirm for Malthusians a 'pessimistic' view of India's demographic situation. Between 1981 and 1991 India's population grew at over 2 per cent per annum, much as it did in the 1950s, the 1960s and the 1970s. At this rate, it doubles every 33 years. India's population is growing fast because its mortality rates are currently falling much faster than its fertility rates. Until around the beginning of the twentieth century, birth- and death-rates were both high and fluctuating, and the total population was roughly static. Death rates began to fall as famines were controlled, and some limited public health measures were introduced. After the massive mortality caused by the influenza pandemic of 1919–21, crude death-rates fell steadily, from around 49 per 1,000 population in the 1910s, to around 27 in the 1940s, and to about 10 in 1991. By contrast, crude birth-rates, which were also around 49 per 1,000 population in the 1910s, had dropped only to about 40 in the 1940s, and probably rose slightly in the 1950s before dropping slowly to about 30 in 1991 (Jeffery 1988; Satia and Jejeebhoy 1991). While demographers dispute whether growth in a particular decade was 2.1 per cent or 2.2 per cent (Dyson 1992), one simple conclusion is unavoidable: India's population growth rate in the 1990s is not likely to be very different from that of any of the last four decades. Because of the fall in child mortality in the past 40 years, India's population is relatively young. As the larger age-cohorts of children born in the 1960s and 1970s marry, even if they have only two children on average, India's population will continue to grow well into the twenty-first century.

The national picture disguises some considerable local variations. Table 2.1 summarizes a number of indicators for Bijnor, the State of Uttar Pradesh (UP) of which it is a part, the demographically similar four large north Indian (LNI) States of Bihar, Madhya Pradesh, Rajasthan and UP, the rest of India and India as a whole.[10] The four LNI States accounted for 335 million people in 1991, 40 per cent of India's total. Death rates in these four States are roughly 45 per cent above those in the rest of India. Birth rates in the four LNI States have dropped by about 15 per cent since the 1940s, whereas they have dropped by 30 per cent in the rest of India in the same period. In 1971 Total Fertility Rates (the best comparative indicators of the number of children a woman is likely to bear) were 6.0 for the four LNI States and 5.1 for the rest of India; they had dropped to 5.2 and 3.6 respectively by 1986 (Satia and Jejeebhoy 1991: 4). Demographic change (and some kinds of social and economic change) has been fastest in Kerala and Punjab, where in 1989–91 death rates were 6 and 8 respectively, birth rates were 19 and 28, and total fertility rates were nearly down to 2 (Satia and Jejeebhoy 1991; *Sample Registration Bulletin* 1993, Vol. 27, no. 1: 10, 12). Although the four LNI States might be expected to be growing faster than the rest of India, the effect of their higher fertility rates is reduced by the higher death rates and by migration out of the four LNI states to the metropolises of Calcutta, Bombay and Delhi, as well as to work in the more affluent areas of Punjab and Haryana. Therefore the share of the four LNI States in India's population is no higher now than it was in 1951. On the basis of these mortality, fertility and migration indicators, Ashish Bose (1991) classifies the four LNI States as the most 'Demographically Vulnerable' ones, closely followed by the eastern States of Orissa, Assam and West Bengal.

Dyson and Moore, in their classic 1983 article, attempted to go beyond a mere tabulation of figures like these and to put them into a coherent pattern. They argued that there are different 'demographic regimes' in India. They contrast northern and southern patterns. Compared to the southern regime, the northern model (most obviously visible in the four LNI States) has higher overall fertility, an earlier age at

---

[10] The term 'Bimaru', coined by Bose from the initial letters of Bihar, Madhya Pradesh, Rajasthan and Uttar Pradesh, suggests the Hindi word *bīmār*, meaning sick or unwell, which causes offence to some commentators, and we shall follow Satia and Jejeebhoy (1991) and use the acronym LNI (Large North Indian) states instead.

Table 2.1. Demographic indicators for Bijnor, UP, four large north Indian states, the rest of India and All-India, 1951–1991

		BIJNOR	UP	Four LNI states	Rest of India	ALL-INDIA
Total population (millions)	1951	0.98	63.2	148.6	213.3	361.9
	1991	2.44	138.8	335.1	508.8	843.9
Growth in total population						
in millions:	1951–1991	1.46	75.6	186.5	295.5	482.0
as an index:	1951=100	249	220	226	239	233
Crude Birth Rates: (per 1000)	1941–50	36	39	41	40	40
	1979–81	43	40	39	31	34
	1989–91	n. a.	36	35	27	30
Crude death rates: (per 1000)	1941–50	n. a.	27	29	26	27
	1979–81	n. a.	16	15	11	13
	1989–91	n. a.	12	12	9	10
Infant mortality rates	1941–50					183
	1980	120	130	122	111	115
	1989–91	n. a.	105	98	61	84
Literacy rates (of population aged 0+)						
Female:	1951	4	4	4	11	8
	1981	15	14	14	32	25
	1991	21	21	20	40	32
Male:	1951	18	17	18	32	27
	1981	37	39	38	52	47
	1991	42	45	45	58	53

Table 2.1. (cont.)

	BIJNOR	UP	Four LNI states	Rest of India	ALL-INDIA
Sex ratios (females per 1,000 males)					
1951	885	910	942	949	946
1981	863	885	915	944	934
1991	873	882	903	945	929

Sources: Bose 1991; Census of India 1989; Census of India 1988; Satia and Jejeebhoy 1991; Census of India 1951.
Note: The 1951 figures for the Four LNI states are for the States of Bihar, Rajasthan, Ajmer, Madhya Pradesh, Madhya Bharat and Uttar Pradesh, which are almost exactly coterminous with the current states of Bihar, Madhya Pradesh, Rajasthan and UP.

marriage, and higher levels of infant and child mortality (Dyson and Moore 1983: 42). In the four LNI States (but also in Haryana and Punjab), female mortality rates at most ages are much worse than those of males in the same regions. Child mortality rates for girls in the four LNI states were about 11 per cent above those for boys in 1981, whereas in the rest of India they were almost exactly the same (Jejeebhoy 1991: 135). Not surprisingly the sex ratio of the total population in the four LNI States (903 females per 1000 males) is more masculine than in India as a whole (929 females per 1000 males).[11] In other words, if one counts 'missing females' (compared to a notional normal or expected ratio of unity, or equal numbers of males and females) then the four LNI States contributed 17.4 million (55 per cent) of the 31.8 million 'missing females' in India in 1991, up from 5.4 million (41 per cent) of 13.4 million in 1961 (Agnihotri 1995).

Dyson and Moore's article has stimulated considerable debate, concerned especially with anomalies in their analysis: in particular, Punjab and West Bengal seem not to fit particularly well into this northern description, and in the south, differences between Kerala and Tamil Nadu are quite considerable. But as a picture of the core Gangetic plain, including Bijnor district, the characterization fits very well. Bijnor, indeed, could be said to be at the heart of the northern regime. The available data suggest that the birth rate there (at least in the last 20 years or so) is probably above that in other parts of UP, and death rates have been at or slightly below the UP level, generating more rapid population growth since 1951 than in other parts of UP. Bijnor's sex ratio has consistently been among the most masculine in north India.

Since the early 1940s, most attempts to understand regional differences such as these have been, essentially, in terms of modernization theories (Greenhalgh 1995). Death-rates and birth-rates are expected to fall as a population becomes more urbanized, wealthier, spends longer in formal schooling, and its adults are more likely to be employed in nonagricultural jobs – all taken as indices of 'modernization'. Although the sequence and speed of changes can vary considerably, the received demographic wisdom is that a 'modern' population will have low rates of both mortality and fertility, and will settle at an equilibrium level with the total population growing little if at all. There is some basic plausibility to such explanations of regional variations in birth- and

---

[11] As Agnihotri (1995: 2082) also points out, if the effects of migration are taken into account, the female–male ratio becomes even more masculine in the four LNI States, as well as in Punjab and Haryana, because they have net emigration of men to other parts of India. Thus the published sex-ratio figures probably understate the extent to which female life chances are worse than those of males in the four LNI States.

death-rates in India. By most accounts poverty and inequality are more extreme in the four LNI States than in other parts of India. Two indicators of poverty – the proportion of the total all-India population of Scheduled Castes and Scheduled Tribes – showed the four LNI States in 1991 with 43 per cent and 41 per cent respectively, compared with their overall population share of 40 per cent. The four LNI States (with Jammu and Kashmir and Orissa) have the lowest 1991–2 per capita incomes in India. Orissa and the four LNI States are also estimated to have the lowest 1991 Physical Quality of Life Index (based on infant mortality, literacy rates, and the percentage of population above the poverty line), the only States to be below the all-India average (EPW Research Foundation 1994: 1304, 1307). Not surprisingly, then, mortality (especially infant and child mortality) has dropped more slowly and later in these states than in the rest of India.

Furthermore, these states have the lowest literacy rates in India – 33 per cent of the total population is recorded as literate, compared to 49 per cent in the rest of India. Female literacy rates are lower still, with only 20 per cent of all females literate, compared to 40 per cent in the rest of India. The four LNI States are also less 'modernized' in their government services, with lower proportions of public expenditure on social services, out of State per capita incomes which are only 62 per cent of those in the rest of India – a proportion which declined between 1970 and 1985 (Satia and Jejeebhoy 1991: 10). Government anti-poverty programmes in these States have had the least success so far, and voluntary social change organizations are also weak. The four LNI states tend also to have lower proportions of their populations living in urban areas. In 1991 they contained 43 per cent of India's rural population, but only 30 per cent of its urban population. An exception to this picture of relative 'backwardness' is the evidence of economic change: some parts of the four LNI States (such as western UP, where Bijnor is located) have seen more technical change in agriculture than many parts of the rest of India (such as interior Orissa, or parts of Andhra Pradesh). But the general picture in the four LNI states is one in which social change is slow.

But 'modernization' in the narrow sense of economic and residential patterns turns out to be a poor explanation of demographic changes in south Asia. Kerala, Tamil Nadu and Punjab are the major anomalies in this account. The case of Kerala is the best known (Caldwell 1986; Jeffrey 1993). Kerala has moved rapidly from having relatively high birth rates in the 1940s to having the lowest rates in India by the 1960s. Yet Kerala is among the poorer Indian states, is less industrialized and has a lower urban proportion than much of the rest of the country. Attempts

to explain this have focused on a number of Kerala's special features. Some have argued that Kerala has a more equal income distribution than elsewhere in India, but the evidence for this is now regarded as equivocal at best (Nag 1982; Jeffrey 1993). Others have stressed Kerala's unusual residence patterns: with a high density and good communications, most Keralites share the benefits of urban residence even if they are not, for Census purposes, recorded as urban. More commonly, commentators have suggested that Kerala's women have historically enjoyed unusual rights and privileges which enable them to take up educational and employment opportunities more easily than women elsewhere in India, and which have led to a high age at marriage and high use of contraceptives. In addition, Kerala has had a long history of social welfare provisions, which have provided a degree of social security – including low infant and child mortality rates – unmatched elsewhere in India.[12] But there has been considerable dispute about the extent to which these sorts of explanations of Kerala's particular experience can also explain demographic changes (or lack of change) in other parts of the country.

Since about 1990, Tamil Nadu has been singled out for attention (Ravindran 1993). Dyson and Moore placed Tamil Nadu along with Kerala as representatives of a southern demographic regime, but in many key respects the two are very different. Although Tamil Nadu's literacy rates are high (at 63 per cent in 1991) they are well below those for Kerala (90 per cent). Life expectancy figures in Tamil Nadu are roughly equal to those in Kerala 10 years ago, and Tamil Nadu's infant mortality rates in 1991 in rural areas were 67 per 1000 live births, compared with Kerala's 17. In other respects as well – such as the age at which women marry, female literacy rates, or the sex ratio – Tamil Nadu is little different from several other states, such as Karnataka, Maharashtra, Gujarat, West Bengal or Punjab. Yet its Total Fertility Rate in 1988 was 2.5, close to Kerala's 2.0 and well below the 3.4 or more reported for the other states (EPW Research Foundation 1994: 1304, 1307). The Government of India has started to claim that the case of Tamil Nadu proves that comprehensive family planning provision by itself – without the changes in women's position, economic welfare or other factors which are generally seen to be part of 'modernization' – is sufficient to explain Tamil Nadu's 'success'. But others have pointed out that Tamil Nadu is relatively urbanized, with 34 per cent of the population living in towns, and have argued that this is more important

---

[12] Robin Jeffrey (1993) suggests that many of these historical arguments are not as persuasive as they sometimes seem; and Irudaya Rajan et al. (1996) produce evidence which suggests that Keralan women's relative autonomy has also been exaggerated.

in understanding the rapid decline in fertility in Tamil Nadu in the 1980s than Government family planning programmes or social sector expenditures (Savitri 1994).

The case of Punjab provides other anomalies. Punjab has the most commercialized agriculture of all the Indian States, and despite claims to the contrary by some Punjabi politicians, has a substantial industrial base as well. In some respects, it fits very closely with Dyson and Moore's 'North Indian' model, with a very adverse sex ratio (888 females per 1000 males in 1991, second only to Haryana among the major States) and marked female-male differentials in literacy, with under half of females over the age of 7 literate in 1991 (Bose 1991). Yet it has also seen very rapid declines in mortality, with an Infant Mortality Rate in 1991 below that of Tamil Nadu. Fertility has also declined, to a Total Fertility Rate in 1988 of 3.4, much more similar to those of Andhra Pradesh, Gujarat, Maharashtra or Karnataka than to Punjab's neighbours Haryana, Rajasthan or Uttar Pradesh. Punjab also has very high rates of contraceptive use. In 1987, according to survey results, two-thirds of all couples in the reproductive age groups were using a modern method of contraception, more than half of them having been sterilized (Narayana and Kantner 1992). This level of contraceptive use is matched only in Kerala.

At the level of generalizations about regional patterns of demographic change in India, then, several unanswered questions remain. None the less, many commentators agree that the area where demographic change has been slowest is the Jumna-Ganges basin, including Rajasthan on its western end and Madhya Pradesh to the south (Bose 1991; Satia and Jejeebhoy 1991). Bijnor, where we carried out our research, is clearly within this area, and shares many of its characteristics, while having some others (notably its reliance on sugarcane, and its relatively high level of commercialization) that set it apart.

Bijnor District: history and population

Bijnor's past does not emerge clearly from the mists of history: its records are partial and have many gaps, and they have not been subject to detailed study. Local people sometimes like to identify sites within the district, or in neighbouring districts, with scenes from the Sanskrit texts like the Mahabharata and Ramayana. A river to the north of Bijnor town, the Malin, is said to be the Malini of the dramatist Kalidasa, who locates part of the story of Shakuntala there (Nevill 1928). The documented history of the district starts with the invasions associated first with the Delhi Sultanate in the thirteenth century. Until the sixteenth century, centralized rule from Delhi was hard to maintain, because the region was apparently heavily wooded and somewhat remote, protected by the Ganges from intrusions from the west and south. The Mughal Emperor Humayun established more permanent control in the 1540s, and his son Akbar consolidated his rule – though not without a number of rebellions sweeping across the land. The *Aīn-ī-Akbarī*, the revenue records from the end of the sixteenth century, show that the dominant landholders in the district were Jats, Tagas and Brahmans, with some areas controlled by Rajputs and by Ahirs, all Hindus. Less is known about the subordinate classes, those who actually worked the land.

During and after Mughal rule, the balance of power in the countryside began to change. As the Mughal empire began to collapse, fighting over the Bijnor lands became more frequent, and supporters of the successful Rohillas (Muslim families who claimed Afghan descent) were rewarded with the *zamindārī* rights (rights to collect tax revenue) to Bijnor's villages. By the early eighteenth century a number of these Rohillas had settled in Bijnor and the region to the south, west and east, farming on their own account as well as collecting tax revenue. Probably at much the same time, or earlier, some of the subordinate classes converted to Islam, usually in groups of related people, or sub-castes. Some of these – such as the Telis (oil-pressers) Julahas (weavers) and Nai (barbers) – kept their Hindu occupational caste names. Some others seem to have taken respectable Muslim clan names – such as Sheikh.[13] Towards the end of the eighteenth century overall control passed into the hands of the Nawab of Oudh, based in Lucknow, and his revenue officials seem to have been excessively predatory. When the Nawab was nevertheless unable to pay his debts to the British East India Company in 1801, he was forced to cede the area known as Rohilkhand, including Bijnor.

Apart from its minor role in the events of 1857, Bijnor seems to have remained an obscure part of the British Empire, with little to distinguish it from its neighbours. Many of the changes that happened elsewhere passed Bijnor by. No canals were provided on the east bank of the Ganges to match those which revolutionized agriculture – and possibly caused epidemics of malaria – on the west bank, the *doāb* (the land between the two rivers of the Jumna and the Ganges) (Stone 1984). Bijnor had very poor road communications. Access to Delhi was restricted by the Ganges, which was impassable during the monsoon except by ferry and was hard to cross (by bridges of boats lashed together) the rest of the year. In the 1880s a main railway line (linking,

---

[13] In the first British Census to record religion, in 1872, Muslims formed one-third of the District's population.

eventually, Lahore and Calcutta) was constructed across the north of Bijnor District, with a bridge across the Ganges. The railway through Bijnor town was completed only in the 1930s. To this day, it offers a very limited service, one passenger train in each direction, both passing through Bijnor in the early hours of the morning, linking Bijnor to Delhi and Dehra Dun. One train a day also provides a direct connection to Lucknow, the UP State capital. Roads in the District – even the metalled ones – tended to be impassable during the monsoon until well after Independence. As British officials noted as late as the 1930s, the metalled roads linked various towns within the District but hardly connected the District to the rest of UP. The export of sugarcane and cane products, and the import of grain in periods of shortage, was handled by the railways. Nowadays, most goods and passenger traffic is handled by the roads, with trucks and buses providing transport of various degrees of comfort to those who want to travel. The direct route to Meerut, Muzaffarnagar and Delhi improved dramatically with the opening of the Madhya Ganga barrage and road across the Ganges in 1984. This relative isolation seems to have created a lack of interest among the academic community. When we first lived in Bijnor in 1982 we seemed to be the first people to have carried out systematic social research in the District, and few outside western UP are able to locate it properly.[14]

Bijnor's population history under the British was little different from that of the surrounding areas. After the first reasonably reliable census in 1872, the population dropped, following a famine in 1877–8. Considerable population growth in the 1880s was followed by a further famine in 1896–7 and another decline. Growth in the period to 1911 was followed by a decline, following the influenza epidemic of 1919. Only since 1921 has there been a consistent pattern of population growth, and, as Table 2.1 (see pages 48–9) shows, Bijnor District experienced faster growth between 1951 and 1991 than other parts of UP or of India in general. This seems to be the result of slightly higher birth rates, combined with death rates no higher than elsewhere in UP and perhaps with less out-migration, possibly as a result of Bijnor's relatively poor communications.

These demographic features cannot be explained by lack of economic change. As a part of western UP, it is in the relatively more 'developed' part of the State. On indicators like the value of crop output per hectare, the use of fertilizer per hectare, the level of electrification of its villages or

[14] The Census of India in 1961 carried out some village studies as part of its routine programme: one of these was of Raoli, eight kilometres to the north of Dharmnagri, where we were based for our fieldwork in 1982–3.

an index of economic development, Bijnor is above the UP average. But it scores below its westerly neighbours across the Ganges (Meerut, Muzaffarnagar and Saharanpur) on the same indicators, and its lower levels of use of bank credit and of industrial activity, in particular, suggest that processes of commercialization and capitalist development are less well established in Bijnor than in its neighbours to the west (CMIE 1985). None the less, agriculture in Bijnor is now relatively profitable, with a high proportion of land under sugarcane, as a result of public and private investment in tubewell irrigation in the 1960s and later. The major reasons for this economic buoyancy in the 1970s and 1980s relate, firstly, to a relatively egalitarian landholding pattern, and, secondly, to the use of relatively reliable irrigation sources to invest in sugar production.

Landholding in Bijnor

Land-ownership in Bijnor villages was not static under the British, nor is it today. We can be sure that 'development' of various kinds was taking place as far back as records exist. The further changes set in motion under the British, and accelerated since Independence in 1947, were deeply affected by the historical patterns of land-ownership and land tenure, and in turn have created the pattern of landholding today. The available printed historical sources do not provide a detailed picture of landholding relationships before or under the British. These sources tend to construct history as a series of events involving prominent, powerful men: the ordinary soldiers, and the effects of their fighting on those left behind, are hardly mentioned. When Saiyid Ahmad Khan, then a junior official in the British administration, described the events of 1857–8 in the District, he provided a snapshot (and a very partial one at that) of relationships among landholders. His account, along with that provided in the District Gazetteer of 1907–8 and the Settlement Reports produced every thirty years or so after the 1830s, allows certain elements of the situation in the nineteenth century to emerge.

One crucial feature is that the landholding class was not static. Rights to *zamīndārī* as well as to farm land had been bought and sold at least from the eighteenth century, as well as won in battle. The rewards and punishments handed out by the British to those who took part in the events of 1857 were merely the latest in a series of such transfers. The dominant caste groups in terms of *zamīndārī* they paid to the Government were Chauhans (Rajputs), Jats, Tagas, and Banias, all Hindu. Sheikhs were the only Muslim caste group with substantial *zamīndārī* holdings. The Banias (often urban traders and shopkeepers) increased their *zamindārī* holdings over the last half of the nineteenth century, at the expense of Jats and, to a lesser extent, Sheikhs and Muslim Pathans, by lending money against mortgages and then foreclosing when the landholders could not repay. The largest *zamindārs* in the District were a Jat family based in Sahanpur, on the outskirts of Najibabad: in 1903 they controlled the revenue from 153 villages in the District. The largest Chauhan *zamindārs* were based in Haldaur, immediately south of Nangal. Both these families received honorary titles from the British authorities.

Below the *zamindārs*, the population actually involved in cultivation was dominated by Jats and Rajputs, who, with Chauhans, farmed nearly half the land in the District at the end of the nineteenth century. The next most substantial farmers were Sainis, followed by Sheikhs and Chamars (a Harijan caste). They were formally tenants, but about half the land was held in fairly secure tenancies, with the other half held on leases which could be ended very rapidly by the *zamindārs*. In general, the higher castes – Jats and Chauhans, and (among Muslims) Saiyids and Sheikhs – had the more secure leases, but they were always vulnerable to losing that security if they fell into debt on their rents. Finally were those who had no rights in land, but were compelled to earn a living from agricultural or other kinds of labour. The least is known about them, though the 1881 Census recorded as many in the labouring classes as it did cultivators and landholders put together.

Rents and land revenues were revised many times from the earliest land settlement under the British (that of 1802) until the last, carried out in the 1930s. Historians have differed greatly over whether British land revenue policy led to impoverishment or gradual improvement in living standards, and these assessments differ for different periods in different parts of the country: no detailed accounts exist for Bijnor. But there is general agreement that under the British there was a steady transfer of landholdings away from traditional landholding castes and into the ownership of urban castes – especially Banias – as agriculture became more commercialized and failure to repay debts was followed by foreclosure. Failure to meet obligations to the Government led to forced sale of land, in which the urban traders were often able to make higher bids. Along with the division of landholdings and tenancies between sons, each usually entitled to an equal share, these processes led to a situation in which most holdings in Bijnor District were of less than 10 acres by the 1940s. In this category, 130,000 landholders held 58 per cent of the land, whereas only 2,200 landholdings were over 25 acres, holding 14 per cent of the land (UP Zamindari Abolition Committee Report 1948: 387–88). Compared to areas to the south and east, then, Bijnor had a relatively flat distribution of landholding, with the median farmer holding no more than about 6 acres, and relatively few very large farmers.

At Independence and the Partition of India, some Sheikhs, Pathans and Saiyids left Bijnor for Pakistan, but the main changes in land ownership came with the abolition of *zamindāri* in the 1950s. Many tenant farmers were in a position to take over the land as owners. Some of those in a weaker position – with smaller holdings, close to the *zamindār*'s own farm, with shorter tenancy agreements or indebted – were forced off the land by ex-*zamindārs* who maximized the amount of land they could retain by claiming that they were farming it themselves, rather than through tenants. The ex-*zamindārs* were helped by the long delay between the publication of the draft legislation and its final passage through the UP legislature, enabling them to exploit those loopholes that were left there by their allies in the Congress Party. Following the abolition of *zamindāri*, the Government of UP also passed land-ceiling legislation, limiting the maximum amount of land any one person could hold. Again, the effect of this legislation was limited, since land could be transferred to other members of the family, and certain categories of land (such as orchards) were exempt. Concurrently, throughout the period since 1950, landholdings have been consolidated, so that scattered holdings have been brought together in one place.

The newly secure ex-tenants became a major political force in UP, most noticeably represented by Choudhury Charan Singh, a Jat from Muzaffarnagar (the neighbouring District across the Ganges) who dominated the politics of UP from the early 1960s and was briefly Prime Minister of India at the end of the Janata Government of 1977–9 (Byres 1986). Some would argue that these 'bullock capitalists' (Rudolph and Rudolph 1989) are the dominant force in Indian politics today. Certainly, they were well placed to take advantage of the new sources of credit, new seeds, and new technology which became available, starting in the 1960s.

Irrigation and cropping

Until the late 1960s, agriculture in Bijnor had to rely on the winter rains and on the monsoon, which reaches this part of north India in late June. Bijnor land is relatively well-drained, but villages with low-lying land near the Ganges were subject to regular monsoon flooding until the Madhya Ganga barrage and its associated earthworks were completed. The closeness of the Himalayas guarantees more reliable rains in the winter and in the monsoon than in some other districts in western UP, and also provides cooling breezes to mitigate the worst heat in May and

June. None the less, agriculture in Bijnor was an uncertain occupation until the spread of private tubewells in the 1960s provided farmers with a reliable source of irrigation. So far, at least, Bijnor has not suffered from the environmental problems associated with an uncontrolled spread of private tubewells elsewhere in India. Because the Ganges is close, recharge of the watertable seems to have been maintained, and there has been no need to sink ever-deeper wells. Nor are there the signs of waterlogging and salination which have affected some tracts in Punjab. During the 1970s and 1980s, these secure water supplies placed Bijnor's agriculture on a sounder footing than it had ever been before.

The story of Bijnor agriculture since the middle of the nineteenth century is essentially one of increasing concentration on three main crops – wheat, rice and sugarcane (R. Jeffery et al. 1989). As late as 1930, a substantial proportion of the land was under barley (the main *rabī* or winter crop) with pulses and coarse grains the main *kharīf* or summer crops. Planting a broad spread of crops was probably a strategy to deal with the uncertainties of unreliable rains and the virtual absence of other forms of irrigation. In addition, since the market could not be relied on for subsistence purposes, most crops were grown for home consumption, and a range of crops helped to provide a variety of diet. Even so, by the end of the nineteenth century, sugarcane was already a prominent cash crop, despite its heavy use of water. In the first years of the twentieth century, less than 4 per cent of the land was irrigated: none the less, about 16 per cent of the land was under sugarcane in the monsoon season. By 1979, Bijnor had – at 70 per cent of the summer crops – one of the highest proportions of land under cane of all the western UP districts, with almost all the rest of the land under rice. The range of winter crops has also narrowed considerably. In 1902–6, over half the land was under barley, with the rest shared between wheat, gram (a kind of pulse) and some other minor crops. By 1979, nearly 95 per cent of the land was under wheat in winter. As transport conditions improved, and particularly since the tubewells became widespread, the cropping pattern has become much simpler: rotations of rice (planted in June/July and harvested in October/November), wheat (planted in November and harvested in May) and sugarcane (planted between February and June and harvested around 10 months later, between October and April/May) (R. Jeffery et al. 1989).

The importance of sugar

The most significant feature of agriculture in Bijnor is the extent to which the District grows sugarcane as its main cash crop. In order to understand the economic choices facing Bijnor farmers – and how far their situation may be unusual within north India – we must therefore look more closely at the special features of sugarcane as a crop and as a product. Cane has been widely grown in India for many centuries. In recent times it has been associated with three major areas, which Baru characterizes as follows: the dominant cane cultivators in western and southern India (Maharashtra, Gujarat and Andhra Pradesh in particular) are rich peasants and landlords; in eastern UP and Bihar they are small and medium peasants; and in western UP, Punjab and Haryana they are mostly rich peasants (Baru 1990: 2). As far as Bijnor is concerned, a minor caveat is in order. With so much cane being grown in a District where landholdings are relatively unconcentrated, middle peasants contribute more of the total production than in many other areas of western UP.

Cane can be turned into white sugar crystals in large mills; into a less pure form of sugar called *khandsārī* by two methods in intermediate or small-scale units; or into *gur* or *jāgrī* (solidified cane juice which still contains molasses) (de Haan 1988). There are three different kinds of large sugar mills, each of which tend to dominate in one part of India: private sector mills, some owned by major multinational concerns (such as Birla or Shriram), especially in eastern UP, and some by local industrial capitalists; government-owned mills, which are often bankrupt private sector mills that have been taken over by the Governments of UP and Bihar; and the co-operative sector, which tends to be dominated by the landlord and rich peasant growers, especially in Maharashtra and Gujarat (Attwood 1990).

Farmers who grow sugar are drawn directly into a highly complex and politicized market, which is a central feature of the political economy of modern India. As Mintz (1986) points out, sugar and its products have a significance in modern diets much larger than their share in food expenditure would suggest. The Indian Government's ability to provide a secure supply of subsidized sugar for the urban electorate is one of the issues on which its credibility is judged. On the other hand, its ability to provide a high purchase price to satisfy the demands of cane growers can make a material difference to its electoral success in large parts of India. The sugar mills are under pressure to ensure that high prices are paid for cane, but they are also forced to supply some of their output to the Government at low prices for the urban consumer. Not surprisingly, the mills have often lost out, requiring rescue with Government subsidies. Finally, waiting in the wings, but sometimes playing a significant part in the prices that are finally fixed, is the world market, which acts as a source of supply when Indian home production is insufficient, or as an outlet when there is a surplus for export. Thus world prices have an impact, albeit often indirect, on the price received by the peasant farmer in Bijnor. Relationships between cultivators of cane and the sugar mills are complicated by the large variations in supply, and the existence in most years of excess supply beyond what the sugar mills can process.[15] Fluctuations in supply result from the heavy demands on water made by cane, and on unstable prices. In a good crop year, canal and tubewell irrigation is supplemented by a good and timely monsoon, and high yields result. But if high production leads to a glut and the price falls in one year, farmers may take land out of cane and production falls.

Cane requires a regular supply of water, and it occupies the land for much longer than most crops. In Bijnor it is planted by chopping cane stalks into short lengths, and laying them lengthways along furrows, beginning in February and continuing until after the wheat harvest in April or May. Cane ripens and is ready for harvest over a period of six months or so from late October the same year until April or May the following year. If the roots are not removed after the cane is cut, a second crop can be had from the same root structure: occasionally a third crop is taken the same way. The benefit of these second and third crops is that they require less labour and mature more rapidly; the cost is that yields fall off in the second and third years. After the second or third crop of cane has been taken, the land is reploughed and given over to a new crop or left fallow for a season. Most farmers have at least some cane in each stage of this sequence at any time.

After the mid-1960s, the arrival of secure sources of irrigation led to a dramatic increase in the amount of land sown with cane. By the late 1970s, Bijnor was the third largest producer of cane in UP (Singh 1987: 163; CMIE 1985). In the 1980s, between 25 and 30 per cent of gross cropped area in the District was under cane, which placed it in the same league as the Districts on the other side of the Ganges – Meerut, Muzaffarnagar and Saharanpur (Government of UP 1990). The District's reliance on cane has usually been profitable: between 1950–3 and 1976–9, the value of Bijnor's agricultural output per hectare rose by 140 per cent at constant prices, the fastest growth in the whole of UP, where the average was only 65 per cent (Singh 1987: 127–9)

Bijnor cane growers have a variety of outlets for their crop. Sugar mills are large investments and they require continuous supplies of good quality cane to run efficiently. They have been given the right to collect cane from designated areas surrounding the factory, and in return they

[15] Baru (1990: 184–5) quotes figures showing fluctuations from 39 million tonnes of sugar in 1979–80 to 84 million tonnes in 1981–2, down to 59 million tonnes in 1983–4 and back to 85 million tonnes in 1986–7.

are obliged to pay producers the minimum supply price which is set every year by the Government of India, and often enhanced by the UP State Government as well. In Bijnor District, there are five mills. The three oldest, in Bijnor town, Seohara and Dhampur, were founded in the private sector in the 1930s, after sugar imports into India were controlled and sugar production became more commercially rewarding. The Bijnor mill was taken over by the UP State Sugar Corporation after a long period of continuous losses. A fourth mill, in Chandpur, also State Government owned, started crushing in the 1977–8 season (de Haan 1988: 57); the fifth, near Najibabad, opened in 1991. These mills rarely have the capacity to take all the cane that farmers could grow, but there are usually alternative local cane processors who will step in and buy cane.[16] The smallest (known as *kolhūs*) make only *gur*; larger units (*khandsārī*) make inferior qualities of sugar, with more impurities than in the sugar made in the mills, which fetch lower prices in the market. *Kolhūs* and *khandsārīs* are permitted to pay a market price for cane. When cane production is low, the market price may go well above the official minimum prices; when supply is abundant, the *kolhūs* and *khandsārīs* will usually pay below the official price, though they may sometimes still be preferred because they offer cash payment in hand, whereas the mills take longer to pay. The proportion of cane in the reserved area around the Bijnor mill that was actually crushed by the mill has varied dramatically, for example from 7.4 per cent in 1976–7 to 22.7 per cent in 1980–1 (de Haan 1988: 134). Sometimes this is a result of production difficulties at the mill; more often the share going to the mills drops when there is a shortage of cane, and higher prices can be earned on the open market. Farmers cannot take cane very far (using buffalo carts or tractor-trolleys) before transport costs become prohibitive, and losses through the cane drying out begin to exceed the benefits of any higher prices.

In Bijnor, farmers do not deal directly with the large Government mills, but through an intermediary, the District Cane Co-operative Society, established in the 1940s to prevent exploitation by a monopoly purchaser. The Cane Society contracts with the mill to supply cane on a regular basis, and members of the society are allocated a fixed number of 'passes', which entitle them to send a specified quantity of cane to the mill or to collecting stations near their village. Every week during the crushing season a local employee of the Cane Society brings passes to the village, setting out how many cartloads of cane each member is to supply the following week. The Cane Society attempts to ensure the

---

[16] This is not true in Maharashtra, where nearly all the cane is crushed by the co-operative factories.

loyalty of its members when market prices are above mill prices by fixing a farmer's entitlement as a percentage of the amount he has supplied in the previous season. Cautious farmers tend to supply their quota to the mills even in years when they could earn a higher price from the free market. The Cane Society offers other benefits to its members, including loans at preferential rates. These loans are given in the form of bags of fertilizer to enhance cane production, but the fertilizer can be used for other crops, or sold on if cash is needed for other purposes.

Sugar production makes Bijnor different from a number of other settings where population processes have been studied in north India. Bijnor's economy is very unlike that of Punjab, for example, where wheat (and summer rice) were the mainstay of the Green Revolution (Das Gupta 1987). Even in Moradabad, immediately to the south, cane is not a major crop (Bliss and Stern 1982). Because of the possibility of windfall profits from sugar, the relatively high labour demand, and a relatively egalitarian land-ownership in the District, the commercialization of the 1970s and 1980s probably did not lead to as much pauperization there as has sometimes been reported from other parts of north India that were affected by the Green Revolution. As in Meerut, the incomes of landless as well as poor peasant households have probably risen in real terms, and distress sales of land are uncommon (Sharma and Poleman 1993).

Nangal and Qaziwala

Nangal and Qaziwala look like many other villages in the plains of western UP: slightly elevated above the surrounding land, with narrow lanes passing between mud-covered walls and buildings made of sun-baked brick with thatched roofs, used by humans and animals alike, or newer, kiln-brick housing for humans, sometimes two-storeyed and with separate animal quarters. In Muzaffarnagar and Saharanpur to the west, there are more signs of relative affluence such as fewer adobe huts and more brick and two-storeyed buildings. Further to the east and south in UP, villages look poorer.

Qaziwala

Most travellers to Qaziwala take the metalled road north-west from Bijnor to Begawala. The main road is straight and well-engineered, dating from the time when it carried a lot of traffic to a bridge of boats at Raoli across the river Ganges. As a result of the new road across the Madhya Ganga barrage, motorized traffic through Begawala has

Table 2.2. *Population by caste, Qaziwala and Nangal, 1990–1*

Religion and caste	Nangal		Qaziwala	
	Number	%	Number	%
Hindu	3,592	86	282	10
Brahman	130	3	0	0
Jat	1,199	28	0	0
Middle Castes	371	9	21	1
Chamar or Jatab	1,787	43	205	7
Other Scheduled Castes	105	3	56	2
Muslim	568	14	2,642	90
Sheikh	18	1	1,494	51
Qasai, Fakir etc.	550	13	1,148	39
All religions/castes	4,160	100%	2,924	100%

Source: Village censuses carried out by the authors, September 1990 (Nangal) and February 1991 (Qaziwala).

declined. No buses now ply this old road, but cycle-rickshaws and horse-drawn carts take passengers the 6 km from Bijnor as far as Begawala. A new road through the outskirts of Qaziwala may entice some rickshaws and horse-carts to add the final kilometre to the trip: in 1991, however, most passengers had to walk the last part of their journey. Begawala, because of its nodal position, has a large weekly market on a Wednesday, shops and stalls for tailors, doctors, barbers and tubewell mechanics. A *madrasā* (Islamic school) serves Qaziwala and about 20 other villages.

Qaziwala is a much bigger village than Begawala, however, and has other facilities of its own, including two mosques. There is a large pond, which is rented out each year by the *panchāyat* (village council) for the fish and water chestnut harvests. Access to Qaziwala's main street in the centre of the village is via narrow winding alleys. Tea stalls, tailors' workshops and small shops are dotted around the village, and one man with a qualification in Unani medicine operates a small clinic, where he mostly offers 'Western' treatments. There is one government facility in the village – a health sub-centre, easily missed, since it is almost never open. Outside the village proper – equidistant from Qaziwala, Begawala and a third village, Burhanuddinpur – is a two-roomed government primary school.

The main castes occupied fairly distinct sectors of the village until recently, but the village is expanding beyond its old boundary and the new expansion is more mixed. Apart from Sheikhs, the dominant caste in terms of numbers and landholdings, there are Muslim Qasais (butchers, most of whom trade in cattle), Faqirs, and Nais (barbers). Most of the Hindus are Harijans: Chamars (leather-workers, sometimes calling themselves Jatabs) and Balmikis (sweepers, sometimes called Bhangis). A small number of caste Hindus – Banias (traders) and Barhi (carpenters) – complete the picture.

Nangal

Nangal is further from Bijnor than Qaziwala, 15 km to the south-east, but it enjoys faster and cheaper transport connections to Bijnor and to Nehtaur and Haldaur, further to the east and south. The Bijnor-Nehtaur road has been metalled since about 1970 and half-hourly bus services ply along it. The Nangal village square is the scene of a weekly Tuesday market; tea stalls and shops line the main road near the bus stop, and more can be found on main paths through the village. Economic activities are visible and active in Nangal, with six cycle repairers, six flour mills, two shoe-menders, a cement and fertilizer store, three electricians, a dozen tailors, a pharmacist, and a shop selling locally brewed spirits. On the outskirts of Nangal there is a woodyard, and also one large and two small sugar factories, owned by Jats from the village, with some of the wage labourers seasonal migrants from eastern UP and Bihar.

The State Bank of India has a branch in Nangal, renting premises from the richest Jat land-owner, who lives above the bank. A health sub-centre in the same building is regularly attended by an Auxiliary Nurse-Midwife (ANM) who travels daily from Bijnor. Nangal has two Government primary schools, on a common plot to the north of the main road; two private primary schools; and a private secondary school. The temple on the village square is in a run-down condition, and houses a destitute old man. Other small shrines round the village are in better condition, but only one – a kilometre outside the village on the Bijnor road – has a part-time *pujārī* (priest). There is one mosque, which houses an Islamic school when the local Muslims can find a *maulvī* (Islamic scholar) willing to stay there.

Like Qaziwala, Nangal has a complex caste and class structure. The Jats own most of the land, but the largest in numbers are the Harijan Chamars. The village Brahmans farm some land, own shops and run two medical clinics, one offering Western medicines, and the other, Ayurvedic medicines only. Other prominent castes include Hindu Barhis (carpenters), and Kumhars (potters); other Harijans include Balmikis (sweepers), most of whom continue their caste occupations. There are also Muslims in the village: Telis (oil-pressers), Sheikhs and

Dhobis (clothes-washers). Jats dominate the core of the village, in the sectors nearest the main road, where there are many large two-storeyed houses, several with tractors in the yard. Most of the landless still live in adobe houses; the middle-ranking castes generally have single-storey brick houses, but the animals may still have only thatched huts.

Nangal and Qaziwala: typical or not?

In both villages, then, most land is owned by members of one *jāti*, who dominate the village politically as well. The other *jātis* hold subordinate positions, especially those from the minority religion in each case. While such one-caste and one-religion dominance seems to be the most common pattern in rural Bijnor, it is not the only one. In Chandpuri, for example, lying between Dharmnagri and Qaziwala, there are substantial Sheikh and Jat landholders, with many Muslim and Hindu families among the lower castes, and we came across some other villages where the communal balance was fairly even during our survey in 1982. After the events of 1990, we heard many stories of the minority groups in unbalanced villages trying to move out, if they could, to villages where they would be in the majority.

Both Qaziwala and Nangal, with about 3,000 and 4,000 people respectively in 1991, are larger than average for the District, where most villages have populations between 500 and 2,000: only about 5 per cent of Bijnor's villages have more than 2,500 residents. This was an inevitable result of our sampling strategy, since we chose villages with large populations in the selected *jāti*, so that we would have a sufficient pool of couples from whom to select those who met our research criteria. Thus, compared with other villages in Bijnor District, Nangal and Qaziwala have more public facilities and are much more closely linked to Government services and commercial centres, in Bijnor or elsewhere.

Although Nangal and Qaziwala offer more variation in their social organization, and are more closely linked to the towns than are many other Bijnor villages, these factors do not make them unreliable sources of evidence of more general patterns of social change. Differences are a matter of degree, not kind. The coming and going between villages is considerable, not least because they are linked by marriage networks. Most of the women married into Nangal and Qaziwala come from smaller, less well-connected villages in the District. Economic changes – new seeds, or fertilizer, for example – take no more than a few years to reach even the smallest villages.[17] Nangal and Qaziwala are not typical

[17] Political activities are, however, more intense in the larger, more accessible villages. We will return to this point in Chapter 6.

of Bijnor villages, then, and we have been very circumspect about generalizing about our findings with regard to villages in Bijnor as a whole. But nor are these villages unusual in ways which might make this study completely unrepresentative of wider social processes. We shall discuss this more fully in Chapter 6.

Basic demographic profiles of Qaziwala and Nangal

Population growth rates in Qaziwala and Nangal were different between 1951 and 1991, with Qaziwala growing much more than Nangal (and more than the rural population of Bijnor in general). The timing of the fastest growth spurts in these villages was also different (see Table 2.3). More importantly, for predicting future rates of growth, the Sheikh population of Qaziwala is much younger than that of the Jats of Nangal (see Table 2.4). The Sheikhs are likely to experience rapid population growth in the next decade because nearly half their population is under the age of 15. As these young people marry and start families population growth among the Sheikhs is inevitable, even if each couple has only one or two children. The Jats of Nangal, with only 30 per cent of their population under 15, are almost certain to have a much lower crude birth rate just because of this difference in their age distributions.[18] The child–woman ratios (which give one general indicator of recent levels of fertility) are more than twice as high for the Sheikhs as for the Jats. The relatively larger numbers of middle-aged and old Jats reflect the lower mortality levels among the Jats than among the Sheikhs. Finally, the sex ratios are more unfavourable to females among the Jats than among the Sheikhs.[19]

In both villages, mortality has fallen faster than fertility; indeed, fertility may have risen in the 1950s and 1960s as marriages lasted longer because mortality was falling, and women were better nourished than they had been. We have only indirect indicators of changes in mortality rates since 1951, derived from the maternity histories of the Sheikh and Jat women alive in 1990–91. These suggest that child mortality (deaths of children under the age of 5 per 1,000 live births) has dropped from over 300 in the 1950s to under 200 in the 1980s. Most of that drop took place between the 1950s and 1970; the rate of decline between then and 1990 was much slower. Until the mid-1980s, mortality rates among the

---

[18] Of course, the net effects of mortality, fertility and the age structure on population growth in the two villages will also depend on the balance of emigration and immigration.
[19] We discuss how these sex ratios relate to gender relationships in the two castes in Chapter 6.

Table 2.3. *Population sizes and annual population growth rates in Qaziwala, Nangal and Bijnor (rural).*

	Total population			Annual growth rates		
	1951	1971	1991	1951–71	1971–91	1951–91
Qaziwala	1,026	1,800	2,918	2.9%	2.4%	2.7%
Nangal	2,023	2,795	4,160	1.6%	2.0%	1.8%
Bijnor (Rural)	747,535	995,079	1,829,186	1.4%	3.1%	2.3%

Sources: 1951 and 1971 figures from the Census of those years; 1991 figures from village census conducted by the authors, except for the Bijnor (rural) figure which was provided by Census authorities in Bijnor.

Table 2.4. *Population by age and sex, and child–woman ratios, for Qaziwala and Nangal, 1990–1*

Age and sex:	Qaziwala Sheikhs	Nangal Jats
1. Girls aged 0–14	312 (20.9%)	142 (11.8%)
2. Boys aged 0–14	415 (27.8%)	220 (18.3%)
3. Children aged 0–14	727 (48.7%)	362 (30.2%)
4. Women aged 15–49	278 (18.6%)	293 (24.4%)
5. Men aged 15–49	335 (22.4%)	366 (30.5%)
6. Women aged 50+	69 (4.6%)	74 (6.2%)
7. Men aged 50+	85 (5.7%)	104 (8.7%)
8. All ages (N)	1,494 (100%)	1,199 (100%)
9. Sex ratio (females per 1,000 males)	789	738
10. Child–woman ratio (Row 3/Row 4)	2.61	1.24

Source: Village censuses carried out by the authors, September 1990 (Nangal) and February 1991 (Qaziwala)

Sheikhs of Qaziwala were much higher than those for the Jats of Nangal (see Table 2.5). But even the Jat rates were still very high in comparative terms: in the early 1990s, three or four children were dying every year among the Jats of Nangal, about twelve among the Sheikhs of Qaziwala.

Fertility changes can be assessed slightly more directly. Table 2.5 shows the age-specific fertility rates for the 76 Sheikh women and 93 Jat women born in 1945 or before, who have mostly ceased child-bearing and for whom we have reliable maternity histories. The age-specific fertility rates are calculated separately on the basis of all years from age 15 onwards (giving the total fertility rate), and for only the years after women have started cohabiting and before widowhood (giving the

Table 2.5. *Age-specific fertility rates and age-specific marital fertility rates for women born 1945 and before, Qaziwala Sheikhs and Nangal Jats, 1990–1*

	Age-specific fertility		Age-specific marital fertility	
Age of woman	Sheikhs	Jats	Sheikhs	Jats
15–19	0.157	0.097	0.185	0.208
20–24	0.368	0.297	0.397	0.306
25–29	0.335	0.335	0.344	0.341
30–34	0.343	0.286	0.363	0.290
35–39	0.270	0.185	0.311	0.191
40–44	0.186	0.075	0.212	0.080
Number of women	76	93	76	93
Number of full-term pregnancies	625	593	625	593
Number of years 'at risk'	2280	2790	2070	2512
Total fertility rate	8.30	6.38	9.06	7.08

Table 2.6. *Total fertility rates for Sheikh women in Qaziwala and Jat women in Nangal, born up to 1965*

	Women born pre-1946	Women born 1946–1955	Women born 1956–1965
Sheikhs			
Total fertility rate, 15–24	2.63	2.57	3.00
Number of years 'at risk'	760	540	800
Total fertility rate, 15–34	6.02	6.31	–
Number of years 'at risk'	1520	1080	
Total fertility rate, 15–44	8.30		
Number of years 'at risk'	2280		
Number of mothers	76	54	80
Jats			
Total fertility rate, 15–24	1.97	2.31	1.76
Number of years 'at risk'	930	610	720
Total fertility rate, 15–34	5.08	4.28	
Number of years 'at risk'	1860	1220	
Total fertility rate, 15–44	6.38		
Number of years 'at risk'	2790		
Number of mothers	93	61	72

marital fertility rate).[20] Overall, these older Sheikh women had a total fertility rate of 8.30 children, almost two children more than the Jat figure for comparable women of 6.38. The figures for marital fertility rates show that some of these differences were the result of an earlier age at marriage among the Sheikhs. These Sheikh women were married at an average age of 14.6 years, and started cohabiting on average 11 months later, whereas the comparable Jat women's mean marriage age was 16.25 years, and they started cohabiting on average 13 months later.[21] Age-specific marital fertility rates allow us to see the effects of this difference, and Table 2.5 shows that marital fertility among these Jat and Sheikh women was virtually the same up to the age of 35. Sheikh women were, however, much more likely to have children from the age of 35 until their late 40s, whereas Jat women were stopping at earlier ages. Widowhood was fairly common. Thirteen Jat and 12 Sheikh women had been widowed or divorced before the age of 50, and had not remarried. But the marital fertility rates show that widowhood accounts for only a small part of the differences. Some of the Jat couples were using contraception of one kind or another, probably reducing the frequency of intercourse (though we have no direct evidence of this), for example, or using other methods (eight of the Jat women and the husbands of a further five had been sterilized). These differences in numbers of live- and still-births are larger than the differences in completed family sizes, however, because the Sheikhs had seen one-third of their children die (2.6 per woman) whereas only just over one-quarter of the Jat children had died (1.6 per woman). Table 2.7 shows that the effect of higher child mortality rates among the Sheikhs continues in the younger age cohorts of women.

In the rest of the book we are most concerned with understanding differences in fertility within marriage, and we focus on couples in three cohorts: those where the wife was born before 1946 (the women discussed above), those where the wife was born in 1946–1955, and

---

[20] Two ceremonies mark the transition to married status: the marriage itself, and a *gaunā* (ceremonial bringing of a wife from her father's to her husband's home), after which the couple begin living together. In the 1950s, it was not uncommon for women to be married before puberty but only to begin cohabiting when they reached the age of 15 or 16. In the 1990s, the two ceremonies are often carried out together (especially amongst the poor, who wish to avoid the expenses of two sets of celebrations) or are separated by a maximum of one year. We collected women's estimates of their ages when they began to cohabit – ages which we were sometimes able to establish more closely by talking to the woman's mother, or by reference to the ages of the woman's children or her siblings, or to a public event such as Indian Independence. Because the gap between marriage and *gaunā* was, in the 1950s and 1960s in particular, often several years in length, we have used the date at cohabitation for calculations of length of marriage.

[21] Both sets of estimates must be treated with caution: Jats in particular may be prone to exaggerate the ages, in the light of current views about appropriate ages at marriage.

Table 2.7. *Total marital fertility rates for Sheikh women in Qaziwala and Jat women in Nangal, born up to 1965*

	Women born pre-1946	Women born 1946–1955	Women born 1956–1965
Sheikhs			
Total marital fertility rate, 15–24	2.91	3.27	3.78
Number of years 'at risk'	666	425	625
Total marital fertility rate, 15–34	6.45	7.07	
Number of years 'at risk'	1481	965	
Total marital fertility rate, 15–44	9.06		
Number of years 'at risk'	2070		
Number of mothers	76	54	80
Jats			
Total marital fertility rate, 15–24	2.76	3.10	2.61
Number of years 'at risk'	662	455	472
Total marital fertility rate, 15–34	6.01	4.97	
Number of years 'at risk'	1572	1055	
Total marital fertility rate, 15–44	7.08		
Number of years 'at risk'	2512		
Number of mothers	93	61	72

Table 2.8. *Total fertility rates, and percentage of children born before 1986 and surviving to the age of five, for Sheikh women in Qaziwala and Jat women in Nangal, born up to 1965*

	Women born pre-1946		Women born 1946–1955		Women born 1956–1965	
	Sheikhs	Jats	Sheikhs	Jats	Sheikhs	Jats
Total fertility rate, 15–24	2.63	1.97	2.57	2.31	3.00	1.76
Survivors to age 5	1.65	1.41	1.85	1.80	1.78	1.09
Survival (%)	65%	71%	72%	78%	78%	80%
Number of births	194	183	139	141	127	99
Total fertility rate, 15–34	6.02	5.08	6.31	4.39		
Survivors to age 5	4.19	3.81	4.24	3.72		
Survival (%)	73%	74%	74%	85%		
Number of births	445	472	324	255		
Total fertility rate, 15–44	8.30	6.38				
Survivors to age 5	5.70	4.81				
Survival (%)	69%	75%				
Number of births	625	593				
Number of mothers	76	93	54	61	80	72

Note: These survival figures include only children born before 1986, because some children born in 1986 or after might have died before their 5th birthday but after we completed our study.

those where the wife was born in 1956–1965. In order to control for the effects of the different ages of women within these cohorts we shall use age-specific fertility rates and ignore the most recent births of women born towards the beginning of the cohort. Thus we shall compare age-specific fertility of women aged 15–44 in the first cohort, 15–34 in the second cohort, and 15–24 in the third cohort.[22] Women in the two younger cohorts, who started to cohabit in the 1960s, 1970s and 1980s, may not yet have completed their child-bearing, and in principle fertility differentials could change in either direction. But, as we shall see, many younger Jat women have been sterilized, whereas very few Sheikh women have been. Thus the total fertility differences between Sheikh and Jat women born in 1946–1955 (1.9 children) and 1956–1965 (1.2 children) are more likely to widen than to shrink.

The figures in Tables 2.5, 2.6 and 2.7 make it clear, then, that by the 1980s the demographic regime of the Jats of Nangal had moved from one of high fertility and high child mortality to one of relatively low fertility and low mortality, by contrast with other Hindu and Muslim caste groups in Bijnor District.[23] The Sheikhs of Qaziwala had not experienced such a shift: their child mortality rates had only recently fallen to levels reached among the Jats ten years previously, and their fertility levels showed an increase.

Conclusion

Bijnor, then, provides a suitable site to look at population processes in a part of the heartland of the north Indian demographic regime. Far from all groups showing similar demographic experiences, however, we have described two very different demographic regimes, in two caste groups in villages less than 30 km apart, in a relatively well-off District. In the following four chapters, we consider four possible explanations for these differences: that they reflect the different economic rationalities of those two caste groups; that they are a result of differences in the gender politics of the households in the two castes; that they reflect differences in the extent of empowerment of the women through schooling; or that they can only be understood as a result of the way in which the two castes are placed in a local political economy – a political economy which has ramifications far beyond the boundaries of Bijnor District itself.

[22] Very few Jat or Sheikh women aged over 44 have given birth, and to allow comparisons with other studies, we have calculated fertility rates for the first cohort up to the age of 44, accepting that this may very slightly underestimate the true rates.
[23] Our data from Dharmnagri and Jhakri support this conclusion.

3 'In these expensive times'

One of Mamdani's central claims was that almost all rural Punjabis were acting with economic rationality in having large numbers of children.[1] In particular, he argued that a farm labourer's income 'will depend upon the amount of work his family can contract during the busy season. A larger family means a greater income during the busy season and higher savings for the slow season' (Mamdani 1972: 95). For small and medium landowners, sons can bring in wages from a young age; as they get older their work can enable their fathers to avoid hiring labourers to work on family farms, and to generate a surplus which allows them to buy more land. Only for large landowners who had enough access to capital to purchase tractors, was there an economic incentive to have small families (Mamdani 1972: 87). On a similar basis John Caldwell has developed a much more sophisticated general economic analysis of demographic transitions (Caldwell 1982). Before a transition from high and fluctuating to low and stable mortality and fertility rates, he argued, wealth flows from the young to the elderly. Couples have many children when their investment in rearing children is small relative to the income that the child can generate for the parents. When the costs of rearing children rise (especially with compulsory education, and when women can no longer combine their own paid work with child care) or when children's employment opportunities fall, the relationship shifts. Wealth then flows predominantly from parents to children, and women's fertility generally drops. Both Mamdani and Caldwell assume that economic rationality is central in fertility behaviour: couples seem to be responding to economic stimuli, even if they do not themselves explain their behaviour in economic terms.

Attempting to quantify the variables involved in these analyses has stimulated a considerable body of research and debate.[2] Problems

---

[1] Mamdani 1972 has sometimes, wrongly, been read as claiming that all peasants in all situations are economically rational in wanting large families.

[2] For a fuller discussion of the South Asian data in a wider international context, see Dyson 1991 and Vlassoff 1991.

emerge most acutely in trying to assess the 'real' value of a child's labour in comparison with the costs of raising him or her. In most of South Asia, young children do not earn very much; indeed, parents have to wait until children are seven or eight years old before any benefit becomes apparent. In one classic study in Bangladesh, Mead Cain estimated that boys regularly earn more than their keep only after they are 11 or 12. By the time they are 15, boys might have paid off the costs of their upbringing (Cain 1980: 246). For some people – especially the poor – a couple may benefit from the wages of their sons only during the few years before they marry. In rural India, sons of poor parents usually set up independent households quite quickly and may refuse to support their parents. Girls – who are paid much less for their work – can rarely pay off the costs of their upbringing. In north India, in nearly all classes and castes, daughters move away on marriage, and in many castes, their parents must also provide a substantial dowry if they are to be married well. It is shameful for parents to receive any support from them. As Robert Cassen showed, on a strictly financial calculation, children may not be a very good investment. None the less, children may still be a better and safer investment than anything else available to the poor, though the rich may be able to find alternative forms of investment (Cassen 1978: 63–76).

Further problems are raised if people's views of the value of child labour are considered. An outside observer might calculate a financial benefit when local people see only costs, or not see financial calculations as having anything to do with how many children they have. In rural India, until the 1960s, very few couples actually did make calculations of this kind: the Punjabi farmers (all but one, Sikh Jats) studied by Mamdani may have been unusual in adopting a calculating approach to the benefits and costs of large and small families, a point we return to in Chapter 6. More commonly, people in north India seem to have felt that they had little control over the number of children they had, how many were girls (and possibly seen as economic liabilities) and how many were boys (and normally seen, in the long run, as economic benefits). Further, people recognized that they were not able to control how many boys and girls survived to maturity (see, e.g., P. Jeffery et al. 1989). If children survived, then they may have been put to work to help with their keep – but this may have been their parents' *response* to having a large number of children, not the *reason* why they had a large family in the first place (Dyson 1991).

Fundamental problems also arise in calculating the economic benefits of children, because people in different agrarian settings and class positions usually have several options open to them (Jodha and Singh

1991). For example, the simple Mamdani model assumes that the children of medium landholders can earn a wage or save their parents from having to pay wages to someone else. First of all, this argument assumes that labour-saving technologies do not provide a low-cost alternative means of production with less need for either family or wage labour. But furthermore, with a given set of tools, farmers with few sons can cultivate the same crops with less labour (for example, weeding less often, or sowing rice broadcast rather than transplanting it) and, in a context of uncertainty over monsoon rains, pest attacks and so on, they will never know what difference this may have made to their yields. Farmers can also alter their cropping patterns to match their family labour availability, choosing to cultivate crops with lower labour demands if they have fewer family workers to help out on the land. Crop yields also depend heavily on differences in soil fertility and the suitability of different fields for different crops, as well as the use of different kinds of fertilizer. Only rarely may farmers be able to judge if they would have a higher income if they had more children. Little is known about how much farmers switch among different crops and techniques, let alone how much more income a farmer could get with more abundant family labour, or indeed if they have ever made such calculations. The argument thus requires couples to act in economically rational ways even if they are unaware of the benefits and costs involved. This is by no means an unrealistic assumption: people are rarely fully aware of their reasons for acting in a particular way at a particular time, or they may be unwilling to admit to economic motives in relation to private and apparently emotional decisions such as when or who to marry, or whether to have an additional child. But in a situation where the benefits of extra children are distant and unpredictable, we are justified in being sceptical of the general argument that economic rationality is an adequate explanation for high fertility.

While the benefits of large families are uncertain, the farmers we talked to in Bijnor knew that a growing family involved immediate and tangible costs: children were described as 'eating', and more children need more food, clothing and general maintenance. And in the long-run, couples pointed out, a farming family's prosperity depended on the productivity and amount of land each adult man is able to farm. Nobody doubted that, in the medium-term future (after 20 years or so), the more sons who lived to maturity, the smaller the share of land each would inherit. If the whole family was not to suffer downward social mobility, fathers of several sons knew thay had to raise yields dramatically, or purchase additional land (in a highly competitive land market), or hope that several of their sons would obtain alternative sources of off-farm employment. In other words, when landowners feel prosperous and labour is in short supply, farmers and labourers alike might welcome the idea of several sons. With labour-saving technologies and a shortage of off-farm jobs, they might wish they had only one or two. To match the success stories of men with several sons (stressed by Mamdani), we should also note the families he mentions who were 'the living victims of the process of land fragmentation' (Mamdani 1972: 76). By contrast, singleton sons were secure in the inheritance of their father's entire estate, while those families to whom 'fate' had given a surplus of daughters faced many years of struggle to provide them with dowries.

North India in the 1990s has some similarities to the situation described by Chayanov in Russia in the early twentieth century (see Chaianov 1966; Durrenburger 1984). On the one hand, many farmers are peasants whose economic decision-making cannot be understood solely in terms of profit-maximization, as one of their prime concerns is to meet their household's demand for basic foodstuffs (wheat, and often rice as well). A larger household needs more food. In the classic Chayanov model, as soon as the young people become useful labourers, the household looks for more land in order to use their labour to produce more food, as well as a surplus for sale. When the household contracts as sons establish independent households, land must be sold, or rented out, or divided among the sons. Since wages are not paid within peasant households, it is hard for a peasant to frame decisions in terms of household profitability. The crucial issue is not profit but the continuation of the household enterprise. But unlike nineteenth century Russia, rural north India does not have a land frontier which allows peasant farmers with large families much opportunity to buy or lease more land, or to clear marginal land and bring it into production. The more common response is to farm land more intensively, or to shift to higher value crops (like sugarcane). Furthermore, north Indian agriculture does have a labour market, with fairly standardized wages, and farmers are well aware of the price of wheat and rice in the market.

Farmers, then, cannot easily buy or lease extra land to ensure their young adult sons can earn their keep. Nor can they be sure that the future will be much like the present, or change in predictable ways. The strategies of different classes within the village can change key relationships quite significantly within a generation. Thus, if landlords and rich peasants invest in labour-saving technology to reduce their need for family or hired labour, middle peasants with large families may find that they too need less family labour because they can hire tractors for ploughing or grain threshers at reasonable prices. If middle peasants have large families so that they can replace wage labour by family labour, and if small peasants have too little land to need hired labour except in the very busiest season, labourers who invest in large families may find that the amount of work available for their mature sons and the wage rates paid have declined (Das Gupta 1978). The short-term narrowly economic benefits of children are uncertain, then, as some of the Manupur men reinterviewed by Nag and Kak in 1982 acknowledged (Nag and Kak 1984). Thus they may have, in the 1960s, been making 'rational' calculations about family size, but after the event they felt they had been mistaken about the benefits which would accrue.

Moreover, farmers in Qaziwala and Nangal were aware that a family with only one son was in a risky situation, since that son might die or turn out to be unreliable. They could, then, have been economically rational in having large numbers of children because sons are expected to provide long-term security for the parents in their old-age. Here what is crucial are the chances of a son surviving to the old-age of his parents and the social mechanisms which ensure that at least one son will indeed support his parents when the time comes.[3] In the north Indian countryside, there are few old-age pensions or other collective arrangements. Sons are expected to provide for their parents and, whenever possible, daughters should not do so. In the absence of any mechanisms to determine the sex of live babies in advance, couples who say they need 'at least two sons' would need to have four children even if child mortality were zero.[4] If people cannot be sure that their child will survive, there could be a tendency to play safe and have more children than they might 'really' want or need. Under certain assumptions, particularly those of the high levels of child mortality typical in India in the mid-1960s, an average woman would need to give birth to 6 or 7 children for her husband to have a 95 per cent chance of a son to look after him when he reaches the age of 65 (May and Heer 1968).[5] If and when child mortality declines, and people become aware of this change, fertility should also come down, after a lag of time sufficient for young couples to be confident about the survival chances of their children.

Of course, to argue that the need for old-age security provides a motive for high fertility is to assume, firstly, that older people do 'retire',

---

[3] Whether that is normally a son or a daughter may have other implications for sex-specific mortality.

[4] Attempts to control the sex of the foetus range from indigenous treatments (discussed in P. Jeffery et al. 1989) to ultrasound, amniocentesis and other new technologies which allow sex-typing and are often associated, in the Indian sub-continent, with the selective abortion of female foetuses.

[5] The calculations were based on the husband's chances of having a son to look after him, the assumption being that his views would dominate those of his wife. At the time, the total fertility rate in India was indeed between six and seven; in 1988 it was four.

and, secondly, that they see their children as the main source of support when they do so. In Maharashtra in the 1970s, neither was particularly the case; most men worked until they dropped, and had very short periods of illness or disability before dying. Ownership of economic resources gave the few retired old middle or rich peasant men security; without this source of control, poor peasant or landless men could rarely rely on their sons (Vlassoff and Vlassoff 1980). Because they have so few opportunities for paid work, and cannot farm on their own, widows need sons in a way which widowers often do not. As Cain (1981, 1988) points out, fertility is highest in those parts of South Asia where the fate of a widow without a mature son is worst. Old men as well as old women tend to live close to their sons; at the very least, this suggests that sons provide some emotional security for their parents. People are generally very aware of the unfortunate condition of the elderly without a son to support them (Datta and Nugent 1984). Therefore, despite caveats about 'retirement', and the differences between the positions of the landed and the landless, and of men and women, we would accept that long-term security enters into a couple's assessment of the desirability of having children at all, and having a son in particular. Whether or not security enters into decisions (and non-decisions) about total family size is much less well established.

Mead Cain has argued that what counts are not just the risks of child mortality or of adult children refusing to support their parents, but the relative risks of different aspects of the environments (social, political economic and physical) in which people live (Cain 1981). Where natural disasters are common and social arrangements are unreliable or even hostile to vulnerable groups like widows (as in Bangladesh, particularly in the 1970s), children may be seen as a major source of insurance against other kinds of risks. When those external risks are reduced (as in Maharashtra, where 'food for work' schemes have cushioned the results of crop failure, and a minimal old-age pension has been introduced) fertility is much lower. Maharashtra may be a very unusual case, however, for no other Indian state has yet provided the same degree of coverage and reliability of pension arrangements. Elsewhere (including, perhaps, Bangladesh) poverty may be undercutting the potential role even of children in insuring against risk. Children are a heavy burden to rear, and are unlikely to return those costs in later life, either because of their own unemployment or a refusal to honour the debts of their own upbringing.[6] In some circumstances, then, increasing feelings of

---

[6] The case of Bangladesh has recently been the subject of considerable controversy, in part because the risks most couples face are still very much as Cain described them. Some authors see the recent fertility decline as a success story for the family planning

insecurity might lead couples to have fewer children, or to delay births. We will explore this possibility in Chapter 6.

All these arguments about the links between economic rationality and decision-making require some unrealistic assumptions. In agriculture, not all the elements in a calculation are known, knowable or predictable (Simon 1976). In the face of uncertainty, much intensive peasant farming is better understood as 'risk-averse'. Farmers act to minimize risks where they can be controlled, by planting a mix of crops, or using seeds which will give a reasonable crop even if the rains fail (Jodha and Singh 1991). Only when supplies of water, fertilizer, pesticides and bank credit are proven reliable do farmers switch fully to crops which are inherently more productive in good conditions, but might be more vulnerable in bad ones. By the same token, when child mortality rates are high, and social security schemes weak or non-existent, people's behaviour might also be risk-averse. In terms of narrow short-term economic calculations it might be rational for couples in particular settings to have small families, although they may still want several sons to reduce the risk of having to rely on the market or on the charity of their relatives if they are unable to earn for themselves.

The rationality arguments also assume a *conscious* decision-making procedure in a *unified* household, in which the interests of all those involved in fertility decision-making are the same, or, at the very least, that differences among the members are negotiated in co-operative ways (Sen 1990). We return to this issue in Chapter 4, in so far as it relates to gender issues within households. Crucially, also, 'rationality' arguments assume not merely the calculation of economic benefits but also a situation in which couples (or men) can act on their own in pursuit of economic interest. But individual households rarely make fertility decisions in isolation from social groups which specify what 'respectable' families are like, and create a kind of social or collective rationality. In other words, what is economically rational can be culturally very specific.[7]

Narrowly economic theories provide only weak explanations for high fertility in contemporary South Asia.[8] The benefits from the labour of

programme (Cleland 1993; Cleland et al. 1996), while others see a desperation-led fertility decline (Thomas 1991, 1993; Kabeer 1995).

[7] High fertility among Sicilian labourers between the two World Wars, for example, may be best explained not as cultural determinism or as economically irrational, but as a consequence of life-circumstances which led to the interdependent reproduction of labourers and gentry, and a *machismo* value system in which pregnancy for the wives of labourers affirmed the masculinity of their otherwise quite powerless husbands (Schneider and Schneider 1995). The general issue of the interaction between culture and economic rationality is discussed further in Binswanger et al. 1980 and in Hammel 1995.

[8] Narrow economic explanations have also been questioned when applied to other parts of

small children are rarely high enough to overcome the costs of feeding and clothing them. The evidence for the role of old-age security in fertility decision-making is also insufficient. Furthermore, there are enough cases where couples seem to act in defiance of economic rationality (as defined by outside, usually western, observers) that economic motives cannot be accepted as an adequate general explanation for fertility behaviour. However, it is still possible that the economic value of adult sons could be a significant reason for high fertility among landed households, and that changing economic circumstances (such as the introduction of new technology) might be important grounds for fertility decline. The economic theories might also help to explain high fertility if economic factors are understood as part of much broader environments of risk experienced by different groups. The job opportunities outside agriculture available to each caste group may also be important, as well as an alternative argument – that differences in the economic circumstances can be caused partly by differences in demographic patterns. These are questions we return to in Chapter 6.

Here we confine ourselves to the narrower question of the relationships between the demographic regimes of the Jats and Sheikhs and their landholdings, farming practices, and notions of economic rationality. To examine these issues we need to consider the historical processes that have led to the current patterns of landholding and cropping, as well as the kinds of calculations made by farmers in different class positions when they decide what crops to grow now. We must also ask whether couples recognize for themselves any economic considerations in having many or few children. If economic factors alone are central in fertility patterns, we would expect peasants from the same class – whether Jats or Sheikhs – to share greater similarities in demographic profiles than they share with people from the same caste group but in different classes. In this chapter, then, we explore family labour use, off-farm employment and attitudes towards family size for couples in different class positions.

Land-ownership and class structure in Qaziwala and Nangal

The various changes in land tenure in Bijnor outlined in Chapter 2 have all had direct effects in Qaziwala and Nangal, but the one most mentioned by farmers was that the abolition of *zamindāri* benefited

the world as well, of course: see Simmons 1988: 123–4. Much of this criticism has been prompted by the results of the Princeton European Fertility Project, which demonstrated the difficulty of coming to any simple conclusions about relationships between economic conditions and demographic change.

them because they no longer had to pay land revenue to the *zamindār*. It is now paid direct to the government, and the rate has been raised by only about 25 per cent in cash terms since the mid-1950s. Also, they said, the *kisān* (peasant) became the *mālik* (master); he was free, and it raised his sense of self-respect.

Qaziwala had four *zamindārs* in the 1920s: three were Hindu Banias, including the two holding the largest amounts of land, and the fourth was a Muslim. Only Mungo Lala Seth, the largest *zamindār*, farmed any land directly in the village. After *zamindārī* abolition in 1952, all the land of the other *zamindārs* was transferred to their larger tenants, but Mungo Lala Seth was able to avoid this forced sale. He soon sold all his land in the village, however, to five Sheikh men, mostly now dead or in their 70s and 80s, whose descendants form the core of the most substantial farmers in the village. These men had been tenants of relatively large farms, which they owned as a result of the 1952 Act, and they were also able to make enough surplus to buy additional land around this time. But none of them had more than twenty acres or so in 1952. Thus the early land-ceiling legislation, implemented from the 1960s onwards and fixing limits to the amount each person could own, had no effect in Qaziwala, because there were no farmers with landholdings above the limit. When the limit was reduced to 12.5 acres, landholdings had already been divided through inheritance. Today, most of the Qaziwala land is owned by Sheikhs from the village: but some of the village land is owned by outsiders, including some Jats from Mandauli to the north; some Qaziwala men also own land in other villages.

In the early twentieth century there were three *zamindārs* with land in Nangal. The largest was Rajah Harbans Singh Riasat, a member of the very powerful Chauhan family of *zamindārs* from Haldaur, though he controlled only about 25 per cent of the Nangal land. The second was Murari Lal, a Bania, also from Haldaur, who had just less than this. The third share – about one-fifth of the land – was owned by a member of the Tajpur family of *zamindārs*, who received a hereditary title from the British, converted to Christianity and steadily lost his land through indebtedness. In 1922 he sold his *zamindārī* in two sections. One half was bought by five Jat men, the grandfathers of seven wealthy Jat farmers alive in 1990. The other half was bought in the names of the two widows of Jehangir Singh, only one of whom had any children, all daughters. One of these daughters stayed in Nangal after she was married, and had three sons. One of her sons – Mahavir Singh – held about 150 acres in *zamindārī* in 1952. Mahavir Singh in his turn had only daughters. One of these daughters now lives elsewhere in the district with her husband, and is the only substantial absentee landlord in the village; the land inherited by the other two daughters was sold. Jehangir Singh's two other grandsons had one son each in their turn: these men are also substantial farmers in Nangal. None of the other *zamindārs* had farmed directly in Nangal, nor had they bought any land with their compensation money, so there are no remnants of the *zamindār* families in the village. Some of the substantial Jat farmers lost some land when the land-ceiling legislation placed limits on what each person could own. When the land-ceiling was fixed at 12.5 acres per person, about forty acres was surrendered to the government, mostly by five descendants of the men who had purchased *zamindārī* rights in 1922: the rest of the larger landowners were able to avoid the effects of the legislation by transferring land into the names of their relatives, or by declaring it as orchard land.

In both Nangal and Qaziwala, the predominant activity is agriculture, and most households can be classified in relationship to their ownership of land (see Table 3.1). We have two sources of landholding data: what people told us they owned when we took a census of each village; and what the land records show. Here we shall use summary figures derived from our own census, cross-checked where possible from the land records.[9] Where holdings were farmed together, we have combined the holdings of men and their sons (and, occasionally, of mothers and sons).[10] (The only women who are recorded as owning land, or are locally regarded as landowners, are women who were widowed when their children were still young, and the wealthy non-resident woman mentioned above.)[11] Our census and the land records agree that the dominant caste in both villages (Jats in Nangal, Sheikhs in Qaziwala) own more than 80 per cent of the land owned by residents in the village. All the large landholdings (those with twelve acres or more) belong to members of these castes. Very few Jat or Sheikh households own no land, or cannot expect to inherit land.

But here the similarities end. According to our census, the Jats in Nangal own three times as much land between them (1,540 acres) as do the Sheikhs in Qaziwala (500 acres) (see Table 3.1). Out of roughly the

[9] It proved impossible to track down all the people listed in the landholding registers. The man who maintains the land records (the *patwārī*) may have been bribed to alter them; or some men may have owned land in village registers we were unable to consult. But most men were willing to give us a precise figure for their holdings, and where we could check these out, they were corroborated by the records. Only some men with very large landholdings were reticent about the extent of their holdings, probably because the combined totals exceeded the land-ceiling legislation, and in their cases we have supplemented the *patwārī's* records with estimates provided by other villagers.

[10] The alternative solution – treating all landholders as independent – can give a clearer picture of likely land-ownership after inheritance and fragmentation of holdings, but underestimates the degree of land concentration at one point in time.

[11] Agarwal (1994) discusses the general position of women and land-ownership in India.

Table 3.1. *Landholdings of Nangal and Qaziwala residents by caste*

Caste	Total land (in acres)	Percentage of total land	Number of production units	
		Nangal		
Jats: of whom	1,586	81.9	171	
Landless	0	0		7
up to 1 acre	4	0.3		4
1 but < 2 acres	11	0.7		7
2 but < 4 acres	83	5.2		29
4 but < 8 acres	272	17.1		49
8 but < 12 acres	354	22.3		37
12 acres or more	862	54.4		38
Chamars	160	8.3		
Brahmans	80	4.1		
Others	111	5.7		
Total	**1,937**	**100.0**		
		Qaziwala		
Sheikhs: of whom	503	83.7	161	
Landless	0	0		18
up to 1 acre	18	3.6		39
1 but < 2 acres	50	9.9		34
2 but < 4 acres	73	14.5		26
4 but < 8 acres	164	32.6		31
8 but < 12 acres	55	10.9		6
12 acres or more	143	28.4		7
Qasai	57	9.5		
Chamar	14	2.4		
Other	27	4.4		
Total	**601**	**100.0**		

Source: Village censuses, October 1990 and March 1991.

same total number of production units in the two caste groups, there are only seven landholdings over twelve acres in Qaziwala, but thirty-eight in Nangal. The median land holding is 3.4 acres in Qaziwala but 7.4 acres in Nangal. These crude figures allow only a limited comparison, since they make no allowance for the fertility of the soil or whether or not it is irrigated. Furthermore, landholdings support very varying numbers of people. It is therefore more useful to classify households (grouped, if necessary) by their relationship to the land.[12] Here we use a system of classification based essentially on a combination of land-ownership and work.

Labourers get their living from *mazdūrī* (manual employment). Some

---

[12] See Patnaik (1976) for a discussion of this system of classification.

government land and land confiscated from the larger landholders under land-ceiling legislation has been given out in plots (usually one acre or less), mostly to Scheduled Caste households. This land is often of very poor quality (for example, sandy, or located far from irrigation sources), is not cultivable, or provides only a very small yield, and occupies the men of these households for only a few days a year. No landless Jats or Sheikhs received any small parcels of land in this way. Nine Jat men and sixty-nine Sheikh men have to earn their livelihoods entirely through wage labour for others; no Jat or Sheikh women earned a wage income in their own right or as heads of households.

Poor peasants own more land, which is generally more productive, but they need to supplement their incomes by working for others most of the time. Men in this class describe themselves as doing *mazdūrī* and also some *khetībārī* (farming) on their own land. Middle peasants own or rent sufficient land to keep busy most of the year, and they rarely work for others. Middle peasants may employ others, but only in periods of extreme pressure – usually for harvesting, and also for transplanting rice. They may occasionally work on other people's land, more often for a share of the crop or on an exchange basis than for a cash wage. They describe themselves as doing *khetībārī*. Rich peasants and landlords have enough land to be able to restrict their farm work largely to the supervision and management of the work of others. The main difference between the last two categories is that rich peasants may drive a tractor or engage in other work themselves, whereas landlords hire others to do it all for them. Non-resident landlords usually delegate the supervision and management to employees as well. They may describe themselves as *kāshtkār*, roughly translatable as 'gentry'.

Allocating people to a class position is not, however, straightforward. For many purposes, the social unit with most significance in everyday life is the group of people who eat from the same *chūlhā* or cooking hearth (we call these households). Most middle-aged couples, especially those with land, would prefer to maintain a single household with their unmarried children, their married sons and daughters-in-law, and any grandchildren. This ideal is rarely followed through in a strict form, however. It is common for married sons to continue living with their parents until two or more sons are married, at which time at least one son and his wife may establish a separate household. Where the father owns land, he and his sons normally still retain a common economic pool for much longer than this, until all the sons and daughters are married or until the father has died. If young men and their wives argue with the husband's father, mother or brothers, they may set up a separate cooking hearth and start running their household expenses separately. If the sons still work on the land, the crops may be divided, or, for a while, if a young man is excluded from his father's land, he may have to support his own household by working as a labourer. The exclusion of young men is more common when there is barely enough land to support the whole family, but sometimes also happens with the sons of middle or rich peasants. We should not regard excluded men and their households as landless. If they are making decisions about fertility on economic grounds, they presumably have a longer term perspective in view. Thus, since they normally inherit their share of the land when their father dies, we have included such couples as part of the production unit with the man's father, even if they are working separately. In passing, we should note one of the consequences of looking at couples in this way. Mamdani (and many other writers) assumes that couples are economic and fertility decision-makers. Our data suggest, by contrast, that a sizeable minority of young men are still subject to their fathers and joint with their brothers in economic matters, at the very time they and their wives are most likely to be involved in family-building. They are unlikely to be calculating the value of child labour to themselves in the short term, since their children will be contributing to a much larger pool of labour. Couples might, of course, look forward many years, to when they might have to rely on the labour of their own adult sons, and on the land they expect to inherit or be able to buy (although their calculations about the longer term must be much more uncertain).

Table 3.2 shows the economic classifications of the Jats and Sheikhs which result from allocating production units to a class position. The main message of the table bears out that of the previous one, that the Qaziwala Sheikhs are in a much less advantageous position than the Jats of Nangal, with proportionately far fewer men in rich peasant and landlord households (4 per cent of Sheikhs compared to 22 per cent of Jats) and far more poor peasants and labourers (64 per cent of Sheikhs compared to 21 per cent of Jats). Indeed, because the distributions are skewed in such different ways, it is hard to make detailed comparisons of landlords, rich peasants, poor peasants and labourers from the two communities, because there are so few Sheikhs in the richer classes in Qaziwala, and so few Jats in the poorer classes in Nangal. The most reliable comparisons, in what follows, can be made between middle peasants in the two caste groups.

Occupational structures

With such large and differentiated villages, there was already considerable occupational specialization before the economic changes of the

Table 3.2. *Production units by class, for Jats in Nangal and Sheikhs in Qaziwala*

Class:	Nangal Jats		Qaziwala Sheikhs	
	Production units	Men aged 21+	Production units	Men aged 21+
1 Landlords	5 (3%)	13 (4%)	0	0
2 Rich peasants	25 (14%)	62 (18%)	4 (2%)	13 (4%)
3 Middle peasants	113 (62%)	210 (61%)	60 (31%)	101 (32%)
4 Poor peasants	31 (17%)	52 (15%)	69 (36%)	131 (42%)
5 Labourers	7 (4%)	9 (3%)	59 (31%)	69 (22%)
Total	**181 (100%)**	**346 (100%)**	**192 (100%)**	**314 (100%)**

Source: Village censuses, October 1990 and March 1991.

period after about 1965. Most specialized labour in the past, however, was handled by the caste system. In both Nangal and Qaziwala, for example, Hindu carpenters – all from the Barhi caste – still provide a service to farmers which is repaid in grain twice a year rather than by cash payments. Both villages also have Scheduled Caste Balmikis (sweepers) whose men and women separately provide simple sanitation services on the same basis. Since the 1940s or so, however, occupational differentiation has increased within most caste groups. Growing and substantial minorities of adult Jat and Sheikh men are not farmers. Landed households could afford to school their children, especially when schooling was uncommon, and their sons were able to dominate the new positions within the village that required a school certificate of some kind. In Qaziwala, all the *maulvīs* (Islamic scholars, employed by the mosques or the Islamic school in Begawala) are Sheikh, while two of the teachers in Nangal are Jats (the remainder are Brahman). Each village has some other state employees – for example, the postmasters (a Barhi in Qaziwala and a Brahman in Nangal). Other opportunities have arisen from the growing incomes in the villages. All of Qaziwala's shopkeepers and traders are Sheikh: three tea stall-holders, two tailors (three more Sheikh men are tailors in Begawala), five shopkeepers and two medical practitioners. In Nangal, by contrast, relatively few traders are Jats. Jats provide only one of the fifteen tailors, for example, one of the six tea stalls, one of the six cycle repair stalls, and one of the eleven general stores. Two of the eight men who provide medical services are Jats.

No Jat or Sheikh women are regarded as having any occupation other than that of managing the home, bearing and rearing children, processing

Table 3.3. *Primary and secondary occupations of resident adult males, Nangal Jats and Qaziwala Sheikhs*

Occupations	Nangal Jats Primary	Secondary	Qaziwala Sheikhs Primary	Secondary
Agriculture				
management of land and other	5	0	0	0
farming	283	7	184	24
labour	12	8	114	21
Farm-related				
butchers/cattle trade	0	0	4	1
others	0	2	0	2
Services				
shop-keeping; cloth sale; tea stall	12	1	7	1
flour mill	1	1	1	1
teachers	5	1	2	2
medicine	1	0	2	0
Urban employment				
non-manual	8	0	4	0
manual	8	0	30	0
Retired: with pension	5	2	0	0
without pension	28	1	14	0
Students	44	0	16	0
Ill, unemployed	10	4	6	2
Total	**422**	**27**	**384**	**54**

Source: Village censuses, October 1990 and March 1991.

crops for home consumption and occasionally helping with sowing or harvest in the fields. Of course, this seriously fails to account for the range and significance of the work that women do. In some cases (as with the feeding, milking and general care of milk cattle) women may have almost sole responsibility, but they receive no cash payments for this work. Nor do they necessarily receive the payments when (as among the Sheikhs) milk is sold for urban consumption. Women may also help with running the stalls owned by their husbands. But these activities are in almost all cases regarded as secondary to a woman's primary responsibilities within and around the domestic space.

Both Nangal and Qaziwala include some men who are still regarded as part of the village although they work too far away to commute to work on a daily basis, and so live outside. Some castes have caste-specific emigration around existing links, sometimes linked to their traditional occupations. For example, some Muslim Nais (barbers) from Qaziwala are now working as barbers in Kashmir and Delhi; and from both villages Balmiki (sweeper) men are working as cleaners in Dehra

Dun and further afield. These castes have higher proportions outside than do the Sheikhs and the Jats. One Sheikh man and one Jat man are in the army. Both groups have men living outside who work as shopkeepers, teachers and semi-skilled mechanics. Two Sheikh men are working as *maulvīs* in mosques away from Qaziwala. Seven Jat and two Sheikh men have jobs in government service. In total, twenty-four Jats and nineteen Sheikhs (about 5 per cent of adult men, in each case) were identified as 'men of the village' who were currently away, some of them for ten or more years, others on a much more temporary basis (e.g. as students). No women are away from the village on a similar basis, though in both villages, most daughters of the village migrate away on marriage.

In addition to those who have moved out to look for work, there has been a limited amount of male in-migration. In Nangal, two households of Jats moved into the village in the recent past; in Qaziwala, all the Sheikhs could trace their residence in the village at least as far as their grandparental generation. Temporary in-migrants (to work in sugar-factories, for example) and longer term migrants are members of other castes. The low numbers of men from eastern UP or from the Himalayas is in contrast to the position in Punjab or Haryana, or even in the UP Districts across the Ganges to the west, and this low level of in-migration of labour is a further indicator of Bijnor's relatively less commercialized economy. But men from both villages commute on a daily basis to work in neighbouring towns, mostly in Bijnor. Some Sheikh men labour in the Bijnor sugar mill; others carry produce for traders in the Bijnor market. One Sheikh man in Qaziwala is a building contractor, employing varying numbers of his kinsmen and others depending on the business he has managed to attract, and several others work occasionally as itinerant mechanics, drilling and repairing tubewells. Jat men who commute mostly do so for white-collar work, as clerks, as minor civil servants, or as lawyers.

Jats and Sheikhs, then, have experienced relatively low levels of male migration. But they are neither isolated from the external influences that come from working outside the village, nor so involved in urban economic activities that an analysis of their position in the village economy would be meaningless.[13]

Patterns of female migration are very different. Most women migrate only on marriage. Clearly they are also workers, so it is debatable whether it is appropriate to distinguish them from 'economic migrants',

---

[13] Breman (1985) has argued that the concept of the village as a bounded economic unit is often questionable, as in the situation he described in south Gujarat, where emigration is the normal pattern of life for large numbers of the landless.

as most discussions do. Women marrying into a village are mostly compensated for by equal flows of women of the village who migrate away on the same basis. There are two significant exceptions. Some thirty-two Jat men (and two Sheikh men) have 'bought' women, who have come from long distances (often from the UP hills, or from eastern UP) as brides. These men have found it impossible to attract a local wife in the normal way. We shall discuss the effect on women of their marriage migration in Chapter 4, when we will also deal with the other exception – women who do not leave their home village on marriage.

Following from the differences in land-owning, far more Sheikh men (35 per cent) than Jat men (5 per cent) describe themselves as labourers, or have to supplement their own-account farming by working as labourers on other people's land. Furthermore, off-farm employment by Sheikhs is more likely to be in manual jobs than 'in service' as clerks or white-collar workers. This pattern has continued for many years: there are no men in Qaziwala described as 'retired' and receiving a pension from the police or other white-collar employment, but seven Jat men are in this position. By both kinds of indicators of social class – landholding and occupation – Sheikhs are distinctly worse off than Jats.

Ownership of land and class position based on agricultural labour tell us only part of the story about the economics of household labour. To understand the possible role of economic rationality in fertility decision-making we must take account of the crops grown, and the labour needed to grow them.

Cropping patterns in Qaziwala and Nangal

As elsewhere in Bijnor, the key issue in Qaziwala's recent agrarian history has been access to reliable water. Until the 1960s, if the monsoon failed, so would most rice and other summer crops. Much land was regularly left fallow in the summer, with only a small amount being irrigated from the large pond on the outskirts of the village. A wide variety of crops was grown, including pulses, coarse grains like barley, and cotton. Little wheat was grown, because it was vulnerable to pest attacks, and many farmers in Qaziwala grew coarse rice and corn for flour. Some men bought low-lying land near the Ganges, despite its proneness to waterlogging and its distance from Qaziwala, because the opportunities on Qaziwala land were so poor. Until about 1960, indeed, most fields only produced one crop annually, and very little land was under sugarcane. The village lands were unable to support the village population and many men – including some from landed families – had to look outside for labouring work. With the arrival of electricity in the mid-1960s, rich peasants drilled tubewells, paid for an electric power supply to their fields, and grew rice and sugarcane on the newly irrigated land. Medium and small farmers followed. In the mid-1970s two government tubewells were introduced and output grew dramatically. By 1990, all the Sheikh land was irrigated, but the electricity supply was much more irregular than previously and most farmers used diesel engines (or took a drive from a tractor) to power their pumping sets for at least part of the year. Now wheat, rice and cane are grown in complex crop rotations, and other crops – for example for fodder – play a very small part.

Qaziwala farmers have ready access to the sugar mill in Bijnor town, as they just have to transport the cut cane to a collection station at Begawala. A private mill (owned by a Punjabi Sikh) was opened in Begawala in the 1960s, but it failed after 10 years or so and closed down. The Sheikhs have managed to retain a large number of mill passes, and in 1990–91 almost all their cane was sent to the Bijnor mill. This gives a secure income, since the government price is very stable, and tends to move up by two or three rupees a quintal (100 kg) every year. But this strategy has drawbacks. When the national crop is poor, market prices for cane may be above the government fixed price, yet Qaziwala farmers may continue selling their cane to the government mills in order to protect their access to guaranteed prices when market prices are lower. Secondly, because so much cane from Qaziwala goes to the government mill, there is no scope for investment in private sugar mills in the locality. No local rich peasant or landlord can make additional income in this way, nor can labourers easily find this kind of work. When there is a surplus of sugarcane for sale, Qaziwala farmers must turn to small factories owned by Hindus in villages 5 km or more away.

Similarly in Nangal, prior to the mid-1960s, there were only two main crops – wheat and rice – and the rice depended on the monsoon. People also grew some pulses and some coarse grains on the higher land. The land is mostly smooth and sandy loam, which gives a very good crop, especially for wheat, but it tends to drain too fast for cane, unless the water supply is plentiful. Three government tubewells were drilled in the 1920s, and another one has since been added. The first three tubewells had a relatively small command area, and one was closed and a larger one was opened elsewhere. For those whose land could not be irrigated from the government tubewells, there was no water other than the rain – no Persian wheels or other systems were in use. As in Qaziwala, private tubewells were established in 1963–4, after electricity was brought to the village. In the 1960s electricity was supplied 24 hours a day. By 1990, this had fallen to only 8 hours at best, and farmers complained that the charges (of Rs 25 per month per installed Horse Power) had to be paid whether electricity came or not. Now 65 per cent of land is under cane. The other crops are wheat, rice and fodder crops grown mostly for household use; only a few small farmers inter-plant pulses, cotton, mustard and so on.

Marketing cane outside Nangal was difficult until the late 1970s, when the new government sugar mill was opened in Chandpur, 22 km to the south. From the late 1980s farmers in Nangal could also supply cane to the Dhampur mill, 22 km to the east, which had expanded dramatically to become one of the largest in India. But most cane from Nangal is still processed locally, because the mills do not have sufficient capacity. The first private cane-crushers (*khandsārīs*) were opened in 1966 by two Jat brothers from the village. Others have opened and shut, depending on the ability of their owners to manage them properly. In 1990–91 two were running (one of the original factories and one more recently opened), as well as three small *kolhūs*, all serving Nangal and some of the surrounding villages.

Farmers use different kinds of strategies to decide what crops to plant, depending on the qualities of their land, and on how much land they own. In each village, land is described in terms which capture the particular mix of clay and sand, and whether it is liable to flood in the monsoon. The higher, more sandy land, *bāngar*, was less valuable before irrigation. The lower-lying alluvial land, called *khādar*, benefits from a high water table, but unseasonal flooding can destroy crops in the fields. Neither village suffers from a dropping water table, nor are there problems of salinity. None the less, individual plots of land can vary considerably in their fertility, and farmers work out their crop cycles separately for each field.

If farmers have only small holdings, they usually try to grow enough wheat and rice to meet the subsistence needs of the household, and supplement this by working as casual labourers.[14] More rarely, if they have regular employment and a cash income, they may put all the land down to cane and wheat and buy rice from the market; very few choose to buy their wheat. Farmers with larger holdings normally keep enough land under wheat, rice and fodder crops to meet the daily needs of their family and the household cattle, and they put the rest of their land under sugarcane. Rich peasants and landlords still grow their own staples but may also diversify away from the main crops, putting land under orchards of mango or guava, partly in order to avoid the land-ceiling legislation. But very few middle or poor peasants sell or buy wheat or

[14] For more detail on production strategies of Bijnor farmers, see Lyon 1988.

rice, despite the government support schemes to ensure fair prices. All farmers prefer to avoid buying their staple diet, arguing that it is impossible to be sure of the quality of wheat and rice in the market. From one year to the next, farmers may adjust the balance of crops in the light of changing circumstances: for example, if a wedding is in the offing, some land may be put under fine varieties of rice like Hans Raj or even Basmati, so that the wedding parties can be given appropriate hospitality. Usually, a range of high yielding varieties of both wheat and rice is sown. Most farmers try to spread their risks by planting several varieties, as well as by matching different varieties to the characteristics of different plots of land.

Labour demand and supply

Since the arrival of assured water supplies in the mid-1960s and the increasingly intensive patterns of cultivation, labour demand at some times of the year has risen. In November, rice is harvested, winnowed and threshed, and the sugarcane harvest has also started. Once land is cleared of rice or cane it may then need to be rapidly prepared for sowing wheat or new cane. A second peak of labour demand is in April–May, when cane is still being harvested, the wheat ripens and it must be harvested, winnowed and threshed, and land must be prepared for rice or cane.

The arrival of new farm machinery has not led to widespread mechanization and a loss of demand for human labour power – though as elsewhere in India, when a task is mechanized it is done by men, even if the tasks were previously done by women. In Nangal – the wealthier village – Jats own 22 tractors; Sheikhs in Qaziwala own 8. The most widespread machines, however, are pumping sets (an engine, either diesel or electric, with a pump and necessary piping to operate a tube-well): a total of 129 owned by Jats and 67 owned by Sheikhs. Electric engines are more expensive to establish, but cheaper to run, and able to water more land: in 1990 there were 93 in Nangal and 16 in Qaziwala. Water can also be pumped by taking a drive from a tractor, or moving a diesel engine to the site of the tubewell. Both kinds of engine are vulnerable to problems of power supply: the electricity connections are unreliable and can be cut off, and the supply of diesel to the local petrol stations is often delayed, so that long lines of customers build up when new supplies come in.

Many tasks are still not mechanized at all. For example, wheat, rice and cane are all still cut by hand, usually by hired labourers. Combine harvesters have been introduced to cut wheat elsewhere in western UP, but they have been used only by the very largest landowners in Bijnor, often as part of a campaign to try to discipline unruly labourers. Most other farmers say that they dislike the combine, because it does not leave any wheat straw for their animals; but in any case, their fields are also usually too small and too dispersed for combines to be a feasible option. Sugarcane is entirely cut by hand, by farmers themselves, or by contract hired male and female labour on a cash basis. A popular alternative is for labourers to be paid in kind with the cane tops that can be added to the feed for their animals. Other tasks are carried out both with and without machinery, so that mechanization provides an alternative option which can be considered by farmers in the light of their own situations. Winnowing may be done entirely by hand or with the help of mechanical fans. Wheat threshing is almost entirely mechanized; but rice is often still threshed by hand. For wheat and rice alike, further processing of the crop – drying, cleaning and storing – is nearly always done by female family labour, though rice husking and wheat milling are now almost fully mechanized.

The preparation of land is increasingly mechanized. Households with tractors will plough, harrow and prepare all their own land. Some make an additional income by hiring the tractor out to work on other people's land. In one hour, one acre can be ploughed, harrowed or levelled by tractor for Rs 50 to Rs 75. This is much the same as the price of hiring a ploughing team with oxen or buffaloes to do the same work, but the ploughing team would take all day. Wheat and cane can also be sown with the help of the tractor: wheat in seed drills, and cane by teams walking behind the tractor and sowing in the furrows before the tractor levels the land again afterwards. But middle peasants also sow cane behind a single plough pulled by oxen, or groups of men and children may plant cane in furrows dug by spade (which is reckoned locally to provide the highest yields). Rice can also be sown broadcast in land prepared by tractors; but in flooded fields buffaloes are less likely than tractors to be bogged down or to compact the soil when preparing land for transplanting rice, which gives much higher yields. The great disadvantage of not owning a tractor – as with not owning a boring and pump-set – is less the cost of hiring than the problem of timing. Tractor-owners plough their own land at their own convenience; tubewell-owners water their own crops first. Others have to hire a tubewell, and wait, fearing that they will not be able to sow their crops in time.

Thus farmers can reduce any problems of a labour shortage by using less labour-intensive methods, or choosing not to grow rice (relatively more demanding of labour). Since there is still a large pool of landless labourers, wages are not regarded as too onerous, except in the peak periods, when even farmers with several sons may need extra hands. In addition, farmers can rely on exchange relationships to deal with labour shortages; and households may stay in joint production relationships longer if they foresee a shortage of labour. Machinery is sometimes held jointly (almost always with households of cousins or brothers).

Jat and Sheikh farmers in the same class showed relatively few differences in their economic behaviour. Proportionately more tractors and tubewells were owned jointly in Qaziwala than in Nangal. Common ownership reflected the attempts (often, from the outside, looking increasingly desperate) to stave off the effects of land fragmentation, which has gone much further among the Sheikhs than among the Jats. In this way, farmers whose landholdings are not big enough to justify individual ownership can still benefit from mechanization, as long as disputes do not threaten the management of the joint resource. Farmers are very aware of how acting together in joint farm management is better than separation.

These complexities emerge clearly by outlining three individual cases from our sample couples, a rich, a middle and a poor peasant. The figures involved are rough estimates, since none of the men had kept detailed written accounts, and exclude the value of fodder for the animals and fuel (mainly dung-cakes) for cooking. It also proved very difficult to make reasonable estimates for animal products consumed in the house, or for depreciation on agricultural machinery.

Mahavir – a rich peasant

Mahavir was born in Nangal in 1965, and married in 1985. In 1990 his household consisted of his father, his father's unmarried younger brother (who limps as a result of childhood polio, cannot do farm work and teaches in the junior high school), Mahavir's wife and son, his younger brother Narendra (who is setting up a bookshop in Bijnor, in a building owned by Mahavir's father-in-law) and Narendra's wife and son, and an unmarried sister. They own about twenty-five acres, and have a 50 per cent share in a tractor and thresher with a neighbouring household. One man is employed as a labourer on an annual basis, mostly to work in the fields but he also does most of the work for the five ploughing animals, seven milk animals and two calves. He is paid Rs 500 a month plus food and some payments in grain and semi-processed sugar. The women divide the housework between them, and do no work which gives them an independent source of income.

Mahavir's father has had a tubewell since 1975. In 1990 they had 3.6 acres under wheat, which was sown with the help of four labourers over

Example A.

INCOME		EXPENDITURE	
Source	Value (Rs)	Outlay	Value (Rs)
Wheat	5,000	Annual labourer: in cash	6,000
Rice	2,000	in kind	2,000
Cane	87,750	Daily wage labourers	9,850
		Fertilizer	8,000
		Electricity for tube-well	4,200
		Maintenance of equipment	4,500
		Diesel for tractor	5,000
TOTAL	94,750		39,550

two days. The annual labourer, Mahavir and his father, controlled weeds by hand and spread fertilizer, not only manure from the animals but also bags of urea and NPK (Nitrogen, Phosphate and Potassium). The harvesting was contracted out, with the contractor taking five bundles of harvested wheat in every 100 cut. Threshing was done by Mahavir's own machine. Only one acre had been under rice; that had also been transplanted by hiring in labourers, four people for five days at Rs 20 per day. Weeding was done when necessary by hired daily labour, and the harvesting was by contract paid at 150 kg of paddy per acre. Unusually for households in this class position, they had grown twice as much grain as they needed for the year, and sold half for a total income of Rs 7,000.

About 14 acres of land was under sugarcane. Four acres were freshly planted with cane, while 10 acres had cane allowed to grow again from roots left from previous years. Additional labour was hired to plant the new cane, taking 20 man-days of labour (costing Rs 400) and another Rs 1,000 was spent on weeding etc. The cane was cut under a contract of Rs 2.50 per quintal (100 kg); with a total of about 3,150 quintals (225 quintals per acre) this cost nearly Rs 8,000. The family had passes allowing them to sell 750 quintals to the government mill, at Rs 37 per quintal; the remaining 2,400 quintals were sold to a crusher for an average of about Rs 25 per quintal, giving a total gross income on cane for the year of about Rs 87,750. Their annual budget for the year looks approximately as shown in example A.

The household thus had a net cash income of about Rs 55,000 in the year, excluding the salary of Mahavir's unmarried uncle – about Rs 5,000, plus a small amount from tuition fees. This calculation does not include the value of grain consumed in the household (worth about Rs 7,000) nor the costs of feeding the animals and the household consumption of milk and *ghī*, none of it sold, from their seven milk animals. Nor does it allow for depreciation on the animals, the tractor or the tubewell, but gives some idea of the kind of return possible for a rich peasant: ignoring the animal products, about Rs 2,500 per acre.[15]

Nasim – a middle peasant

Nasim's mother had four sons, but Nasim (born in Qaziwala in 1964 and married in 1986) is the only one still alive. He lives with his parents, his wife and two sons. Nasim's mother looks after the animals – a ploughing team, three buffalo cows, two calves, and a goat – while Nasim's wife Nur Jahan is responsible for most of the housework, and occasionally spins cotton. Nasim and his father own 3 acres of land. They can water all their land from the borings and diesel engine owned jointly with Nasim's two uncles. Nasim and his father planted wheat on 1 acre themselves, using their own ox and plough, and buying in two different kinds of seed. The wheat was given 15 cartloads of manure (said to be for the benefit of the sugarcane which would be planted on the same land after the wheat was harvested) as well as five bags of urea and a half bag of NPK. They paid Rs 100 to have five men take a day to prepare the land for sowing. The harvesting was also done by labourers, who received six bundles for every hundred cut. Nasim and his father also paid 12 kg per quintal of wheat to have it threshed. The net yield to Nasim and his family was 12 quintals of wheat: enough to feed the family, and pay the 1.25 quintals in customary payments to the *madrasā* (Muslim school at Begawala), mosque, barber, sweeper, clothes-washers and to the carpenter who looks after their plough.

Only 0.4 acre was planted with rice, using seed kept back from the previous year. One bag of urea was used. All the work was done by family labour, except for the harvest, when they paid 10 kg for every quintal of paddy harvested. The net yield was 10 quintals of paddy, with an estimated six quintals of grain once it had been husked. No rice or wheat was bought or sold, and 0.2 acre was left fallow.

Of the rest of the land, half (1.2 acres) was under new cane and the other half was cane allowed to grow from the previous year's roots. Twenty-four cartloads of manure were spread on the land where the new cane was to be planted, as well as 6 bags of urea and 1 bag of NPK. Some of the land preparation was done by Nasim and his father, but they became short of time and paid Rs 360 for two tractors to finish the

---

[15] Further income might have been earned from renting the tractor out, but their and their partners' needs kept it busy for much of the time. Renting out also increases the rate of depreciation.

Example B.

INCOME		EXPENDITURE	
Source	Value (Rs)	Outlay	Value (Rs)
Wheat	0	Daily wage labourers: in cash	1,540
Rice	0	in wheat	470
Cane	16,500	in rice	220
		Tractor hire	360
		Fertilizer	2,300
		Diesel for tube-well	800
		Maintenance of equipment	1,500
Total	**16,500**	**Total**	**7,190**

job. Weeding and other cultivation was done by labourers, also for Rs 360. On the cane from the previous year's roots, only 6 bags of urea were spread as fertilizer, but Nasim and his father hired labourers to weed and prepare the land, at a total cost of Rs 1,080. All the cane harvesting was done by Nasim and his father. The yield was reasonable, at about 185 quintals per acre on average. All but 40 quintals was sold to the government mill: Nasim and his father had spare passes for cane to be sold to the mill. These passes were given to neighbours and relatives, as part of informal long-term reciprocal relationships. Their farm budget is shown in Example B.

If we include the value of the grain consumed within the household, about 17 quintals at a market value of Rs 200 per quintal, the total income is about Rs 12,750, or Rs 4,250 per acre (as against Mahavir's on the same basis of Rs 2,500). Most of this difference results from the higher prices of cane in 1990–91 at the Bijnor mill than at the cane crushers in Nangal, giving Nasim 33 per cent higher prices on average than Mahavir. If the price differentials reversed, Mahavir would probably earn a higher income per acre. The remaining difference between Mahavir and Nasim is accounted for by the cost of hiring labour and the higher costs of maintenance of the tractor. Nasim and his father have been able to buy land recently: one of their three acres was purchased in 1989, from their own resources and borrowings from neighbours. Their major additional expenditure has been through a court case over a small piece of land, which has so far cost Rs 20,000 on legal fees.

Om Pal – a poor peasant

Om Pal lives in Nangal with his widowed mother, his wife and their four living children (two boys, two girls). Om Pal owns about 0.7 acre of

Example C.

INCOME		EXPENDITURE	
Source	Value (Rs)	Outlay	Value (Rs)
Cane	1,300	Water	180
		Seed	640
		Tractor hire	200
		Fertilizer	220
TOTAL	1,300	TOTAL	1,240

land, all under sugarcane. All the ploughing and preparation was done by tractor, for Rs 200. He bought water from a neighbouring tubewell for Rs 180, and spent Rs 640 on cane for seed. The planting was done by Om Pal and his twelve-year-old son, with the help of a relative, who did not demand payment: otherwise he would have had to pay Rs 45 to hire a man and ploughing team, since Om Pal owns no draft animals or equipment himself. He spread two bags of urea as fertilizer, at Rs 220, and did all the other labour himself. The land is sandy, and he had trouble with the water supply, so his crop was poor – about 95 quintals per acre. As a new grower, he could not get any passes for the mill. There is a shortage of passes in Nangal so none was available for him. All 65 quintals went to a *khandsārī*, at Rs 19–20 per quintal. His farm budget is shown in Example C.

His net income from the land was at most Rs 60, (or Rs 90 per acre), though he would have made Rs 1,200 or so if he had cane society passes. Perhaps as a result of his lack of success with cane, he was planning to plant wheat in the next season. Fortunately for him, he has steady work for 6–7 months in the year, labouring at a brickworks for Rs 30 per day, or about Rs 800 per month. This is enough for him to buy food – he needs about 9 quintals (costing Rs 1,800) of grain a year, for example, for his household. In addition, by 1990 Om Pal had paid back the loan of Rs 5,000 at 4 per cent per month, which he had used to buy half an acre of land in 1988. Om Pal's wife, Omkari, and his mother look after the cattle, as well as doing all the housework. They own one milk buffalo, with one calf. A second calf was being raised on a sharecropping basis: Omkari and her mother-in-law feed and look after the calf, and when it is old enough to be sold, they expect to receive half the sale price, with the rest going to the owner of the calf's mother. They sell milk when they can. Neither of the women helps with the farmwork.

These examples are by no means complete. We have left milk animals out of the reckoning, for example, because none of the households kept detailed accounts of milk yields, nor how much was sold. This would tend to underestimate the relative cash incomes of the Sheikhs, since middle and rich peasant Jats made it a matter of pride not to sell milk or milk products, whereas some Sheikh families regularly sold up to two litres of milk a day. Even without these additional potential sources of income, however, the complexity of peasant farm finances makes it all but impossible to generalize about the economic rationality which might make children a sensible investment for any particular peasant household in its individual situation. Mahavir's father, for example, could have saved about Rs 8,000 a year by bringing Mahavir's brother back from the shop in Bijnor to do some of the labouring work on the farm, and he may yet have to do so if the shop fails. When Mahavir's son is big enough to help, he could replace the annual labourer, but the household has hopes that he will get some urban employment. Certainly, Mahavir and his father see the annual labourer not as an unwanted drain on their resources, but as a relief from some of the more burdensome work around the farm. For Nasim and his father, extra household labour would not have saved much of the wages for daily labourers, because they were needed only at the busiest season of the year, when time was the limiting factor. Nasim did not see any benefits of more family labour for the rest of the year, but he wanted one son to help him out as he himself grew older and his father became weaker. Neither Nasim nor Mahavir spoke in terms of extra output if the land could be farmed more intensively, and both wanted better for their children than the position of wage labourers on someone else's farm or in town. Om Pal, similarly, is aware that his land provides only a very basic minimum long-term security, and feeding his household is only just possible on his income from his hard physical labour at the brickworks.

Generalizations about the potential economic rationality of farmers in Nangal and Qaziwala are difficult because very few farmers can draw up detailed profit and loss accounts for their activities.[16] Early in our research in Nangal, Roger sat down with a group of peasants (Brahmans as well as Jats) and asked about the costs involved in cultivating an acre of land with cane, if labourers were used for all tasks. The men rapidly understood what he was doing, and provided figures which were discussed and accepted as appropriate. But it became clear that they had never done this kind of calculation themselves, although some of them

---

[16] As we have pointed out earlier in this chapter, even if people cannot articulate an economic rationality for their actions they may still be responding to economic stimuli. But in discussing this issue, farmers in Bijnor rarely suggested that there were good economic reasons for large families, either now or in their parents' generation.

had studied agriculture and economics in high school or college.[17] For several days afterwards, men asked Roger about the outcome of the calculation, and were interested in the results. But they all said that farmers never thought in terms of an overall balance during a year, or from a particular crop on one field. Instead, they saw the benefits of sugarcane because they made several small payments out (and they made not even a notional charge for their own time and labour), whereas the income came in a small number of substantial receipts. Wheat and rice were crops for which a cash calculation was even less likely, since they were grown mainly for consumption and to provide high quality food which could not be guaranteed by buying in the marketplace. Thus, even when someone in the household had a regular cash income, all middle and rich peasant households in the sample made production decisions that ensured that they had enough land under wheat and rice to feed all household members throughout the year. Only land surplus to this basic requirement would be put under a cash crop (most often, cane). Households wanting to maximize their cash income would thus find additional children (boys and girls, while young and when they grew up) a burden, since their food demands would reduce the land available for cash cropping. These perspectives were strengthened by the farmers' own experience of the reasons for economic success and failure over the past 20 years or so. Apart from crop failure (which is rare now locally, because of secure access to irrigation) the dominant cause of farming success was a high price for cane. In 1979–80, and 1980–81, for example, cane prices were up to twice those of previous years. With windfall profits like this, farmers saw the quantity of cane they could grow and the cane price as the major determinants of whether they would prosper or not.

Middle and rich peasant farmers saw the security of water supplies and the quantity and quality of their land, not labour costs, as a major barrier to raising profits. The use of manure and the need to use expensive chemical fertilizers loomed much larger in their calculations than the price of labour. They also calculated the benefits of managing land as a single joint operation, against the costs of splitting it into

[17] Stone 1984 makes a similar point about late-nineteenth-century peasant rationality in UP Districts with canal irrigation, west of the Ganges: 'The profit and loss accounting framework the officials continued to apply to peasant decision-making to justify their decisions and recommendations on prices had little relevance to the peasant cultivator. Just as the latter frequently paid an "uneconomic rent" for an extra field because it allowed better utilisation of his resources – in particular his fixed stock of labour – in relation to his family's needs, so the realignment of irrigation charges was likely to be seen within the context of the peasant producer-consumer unit, and not simply in terms of a particular crop's profitability' (p. 191).

smaller plots. Men frequently argued that operating land jointly was more productive than farming separately, using the analogy of a clenched fist, which is much more powerful than the five fingers could ever be separately. As far as our economic data can be trusted on this, they were probably correct to reason in this way – especially with respect to the most common joint resources, tubewells and (to a lesser extent) tractors. But large numbers of children put a strain on maintaining joint operations with other hearths, leading to pressures for more rapid division of farming operations as brothers squabbled over the costs of raising their nephews and nieces. For the landless and poor peasants, wage rates and opportunities in agriculture were not very desirable, and Jats and Sheikhs seeking wage labour had to compete with men from many other castes (regarded as their social inferiors).

The demand for labour is highly seasonal. Middle and rich peasants might experience only a few weeks in the year when the overlapping pressures of harvesting, processing, preparing the land and sowing a new crop make labour shortages a serious concern. Even middle peasants with large families could hardly avoid hiring labour at these times: for the rest of the year, most such farmers could work steadily within their own labour resources, or with the help of brothers and cousins on an exchange basis. Seasonality also limits the opportunities available to labourers, though these problems are mitigated by the good wages that can be earned at peak periods. None the less, most labourers need non-agricultural employment to earn an annual income sufficient to see them through the year.

The use of family labour has costs in terms of social prestige. Nasim and his father, like other men in the sample, could have done more tasks themselves, but they chose to hire labourers to complete them. Peasants often said that their lives involved hard work, with no holidays and an obligation to spend long hours in dirty conditions, in rain or shine, and even sometimes at night. They drew clear contrasts with the office jobs many hoped their sons would obtain if they were successful in school and college. For no farmer was the labour of their young children (under 14 or 15 years of age) regarded as significant: work such as grazing family animals had no priority in men's calculations, and was very poorly paid when done for others.

Similarly, men chose not to ask their wives, mothers and daughters to work in the fields, even though most were physically capable of helping at times of peak labour demand, such as the wheat and rice harvests. Men are inconsistent in their views on the work done by the women in their households. On the one hand, men say that 'women don't do any work' and they deride women who claim to be exhausted by a long day's work. On the other hand, a man is often very unwilling to allow his wife to visit her parents, on the grounds that he cannot manage without her. Women themselves point out how much work they do in crop processing and animal management, as well as their domestic work of cooking, cleaning, child-rearing, washing, and so on. Rich, middle and poor peasant Sheikh and Jat men explained their unwillingness to take women from their own households to help with the harvest in status terms, rather than because their wives and daughters-in-law are already overburdened. It was not that 'farm work' was unrespectable. Indeed, women were usually heavily involved in animal husbandry and crop processing, but these tasks could be done close to the house. In the nineteenth century, Jat women were praised by colonial ethnographers for their sturdiness and the help they gave their husbands in farming (Chowdhry 1994: 59), but we found no significant differences between Sheikh and Jat women's labour use, holding class constant. Both castes proclaim that it is best if women do not work in public spaces where their safety and honour might be compromised.[18] We do not have detailed information about the non-cash contributions that children make to household incomes, for example by carrying out tasks (such as child- or animal-care) that might release an adult for gainful employment. Although this might reduce the burden of work for the woman involved, this is not likely to have made much difference to the cash incomes in either Sheikh or Jat households, since no women earned wages on a regular basis, and hand spinning or sewing provided very small incomes. Among the poor peasants and landless, women might be drafted in to help a man harvesting grain or cutting cane on a contract basis, when their other commitments allowed them to do so, but even this was less common among the Jats and Sheikhs than among some of the other castes in the area.

There is, then, relatively little evidence to support an argument that 'economic rationality' would favour large families for Jats or Sheikhs in any class position. This generalization holds whether we adopt some kind of objective, externalist account (valuing labour in ways which couples themselves do not, or making profit/loss calculations which they do not) or if we restrict ourselves to the perceptions of the couples themselves. Bijnor might, of course, be different from areas where claims about rationality have been advanced. Firstly, the strength of economic incentives for high fertility may be heavily dependent on crop opportunities. Cane, as a 10-month crop, increases the seasonality of labour demands. Its high value also makes farmers want to maximize the

---

[18] We will discuss the implications of this further in Chapter 4.

land under cane, and to limit household consumption needs for wheat and rice. Secondly, Bijnor has reached a level of mechanization which allows even those with landholdings too small for outright purchase of equipment to be able to hire tractors, threshers and pump-sets, all of which tend to offer low cost labour-saving alternatives to hiring labour, at least for some tasks. None the less, it is still possible that couples in different class positions would see demographic issues differently.

Class and demography in Nangal and Qaziwala

Our analysis so far has suggested no obvious reasons why couples in a particular class position would choose to have larger families than those in any other. One might expect poorer households to have had more children die, and this might lead them to have more children. To check for this possibility, Tables 3.4, 3.5 and 3.6 show fertility and the experience of child mortality by class within the two populations, taking the woman's year of birth and (in the tables of marital fertility) age at cohabitation into account. The tables show that in both castes, middle and poor peasants and landless couples usually have had more children than rich peasants and landlords. But there is one exception: for Sheikh women born 1946–1955, the class gradient goes the other way, with rich and middle peasant women having had more children than poor peasant and landless women. As one would expect, for most cohorts of women, women in the poorest households in both caste groups have also had more children die than women in the higher class categories; but, again, women born between 1946 and 1955 are exceptions, since for the Sheikhs (combining the small number of rich peasant women with the middle peasants) and for the Jats the child death rates seem to be hardly affected at all by class.[19] The class differentials are most marked among the older Sheikhs, those women born before 1946, and the younger Jats: for the other cohorts the class differences are small. Overall, when child mortality is taken into account, the class differentials are considerably reduced, but the differences between the caste groups are maintained.

In almost all comparisons of couples from the same class, and married for the same length of time, the Sheikhs have had at least one more child than equivalent Jats. The number of middle peasant women in each caste are sufficient for meaningful comparison, particularly if we take women born before 1946, who have completed their child-bearing. The 55 Jat middle peasant women aged 45 or over had a total of 354 live

---

[19] Among the Qaziwala Sheikh mothers who started cohabiting in 1970–9, it is not clear why the poor peasant and landless couples have had fewer children die than middle peasant couples.

Table 3.4. *Total marital fertility rates for Jat women in Nangal and Sheikh women in Qaziwala by age at birth and class*

	Sheikhs			Jats		
	Class 1, 2	Class 3	Class 4, 5	Class 1, 2	Class 3	Class 4, 5
Women born pre-1946						
Total marital fertility rate, 15–44	8.70	9.35	9.49	6.63	7.11	7.81
N of years at risk	131	744	1195	623	1498	391
N of mothers	7	27	42	23	55	15
Women born 1946–1955						
Total marital fertility rate, 15–34	8.95	7.51	6.74	3.44	5.11	5.76
N of years at risk	38	301	626	186	730	139
N of mothers	2	17	35	11	42	8
Women born 1956–1965						
Total marital fertility rate, 15–24	2.22	3.66	3.95	2.73	2.52	2.75
N of years at risk	27	197	401	88	282	102
N of mothers	4	26	50	17	42	13

Source: Maternity histories collected by the authors, Nangal, October 1990 and Qaziwala, March 1991.

births (mean 6.44); the 27 Sheikh women had 232 live births (mean 8.59). Total marital fertility rates (TMFRs) take into account the differences in age at marriage and the effects of divorce and widowhood, and so reduce the size of the differences. As Table 3.4 shows, the differences in TMFR for women of the same class and cohort are as small as one child or less only for poor peasant and landless women born 1946–1955, and for women from all classes born 1956–1965. Some of the cell sizes are very small, but eight of the nine comparisons point in the same direction, and are not the result of differences in the length of cohabitation.

The Sheikh women have also had more children die, both absolutely and as a percentage of the number of children they have had, than Jat women who started cohabiting around the same time (see Table 3.5). Again, some cell sizes are very small, and are based on very small numbers of child deaths, but some cautious suggestions can be made. If we compare the two caste-groups as a whole, the relative poverty of the Sheikhs probably helps to account for the higher levels of child mortality, especially in the two earlier cohorts. But if we compare couples in approximately the same class positions, in the first two cohorts Sheikh mortality rates are higher in thirteen of the fifteen comparisons, with

Table 3.5. *Child mortality by class and age of mother, Jats in Nangal and Sheikhs in Qaziwala, children born up to 1985*

	Women born pre-1946					
Child death rate	Sheikhs			Jats		
	Class 1, 2	Class 3	Class 4, 5	Class 1, 2	Class 3	Class 4, 5
Mothers aged 15–24	40%	35%	39%	30%	26%	37%
N of children	10	66	117	43	110	30
Mothers aged 15–34	25%	31%	31%	27%	22%	32%
N of children	24	150	271	109	283	79
Mothers aged 15–44	26%	33%	32%	25%	24%	28%
N of children	38	209	378	137	354	102
N of mothers	7	26	43	23	55	15

	Women born 1946–55					
Child death rate	Sheikhs			Jats		
	Class 1, 2	Class 3	Class 4, 5	Class 1, 2	Class 3	Class 4, 5
Mothers aged 15–24	56%	25%	27%	22%	17%	20%
N of children	9	44	86	18	96	20
Mothers aged 15–34	40%	25%	25%	16%	15%	15%
N of children	15	108	201	31	185	39
N of mothers	2	17	35	11	42	8

	Women born 1956–65					
Child death rate	Sheikhs			Jats		
	Class 1, 2	Class 3	Class 4, 5	Class 1, 2	Class 3	Class 4, 5
Mothers aged 15–24	20%	22%	22%	11%	19%	26%
N of children	5	65	138	18	67	27
N of mothers	4	26	50	17	42	13

Source: Maternity histories collected by the authors, Nangal, October 1990 and Qaziwala, March 1991, excluding children born in 1986 or after.

only poor peasant and landless Jat women born 1956–1965 showing a markedly higher child mortality rate than comparable Sheikh women. Although the Sheikh women were in general poorer than the Jat women, this alone is unlikely to account for the higher number of children they have had, nor their higher experience of child mortality.

There is, however, one further complication to consider here. All the women in these tables have been classified by their current class position. This is clearly appropriate for the younger women, since this is also their class while they are having children and making decisions about their fertility. For older women, however, this may not be the case. If having large families was economically rational, those with large numbers of children may have been able to raise their class position between when they married and 1990–91. If, on the other hand, large families were economically irrational, those with large families are more likely to be in a worse class position now than when they started having children. A priori it looks as if it was not rational to have large families, since those with more children (the Sheikhs) are also poorer. But it is more difficult to show clearly whether they were poorer to start with, or became poorer because they had more children.

One indicator of the likely processes at work is the evidence about land transfers in the two villages. In Qaziwala, only small plots of land have changed hands recently. Ten of the twenty production units in our sample said that they had neither bought nor sold land. Five had bought house plots, or less than half an acre for cultivation, and five had sold similar amounts of land. The most recent case of land sales affecting Qaziwala was the sale of land by a landlord who lived in Bijnor but owned land in a village adjoining Qaziwala. When he decided that he could no longer manage the land himself, and as he had no son prepared to take over the management, he sold most of his holdings between 1989 and 1991. Some Qaziwala Sheikh farmers managed to buy some of this land. About half of the Nangal sample had bought land since 1965. Details about these purchases are difficult to establish, because of the unreliability of the *patwārī*'s records and the men's unwillingness to be specific. Almost all other land transfers in both villages represented sons dividing their inheritance, sometimes immediately and sometimes several years after a man's death.[20] There is, then, little evidence in the land records of men with large families buying more land. Since we do not have a clear picture of landholdings thirty years ago, we cannot be sure. We will return to this point in Chapter 6.

Class and family size preferences

The final question for this chapter is whether or not young couples in the two villages perceive an economic value to having children. Do people in different classes express different views? Can the differences between Sheikh and Jat fertility be explained by different perceptions of economic value? In this section we draw on the views of the sample couples we interviewed. We stratified the samples differently in the two

---

[20] A landholding mobility matrix, showing gains and losses of land by class position at inheritance, of the kind generated by Cain (1981, 1990), would show virtually no changes for Sheikhs in Qaziwala, but steady moves up for middle peasant Jats in Nangal.

villages, and in neither case was class the crucial stratifying variable. None the less, we included couples from the complete range of economic positions within each category (in Qaziwala, of women married close and far away, and in Nangal, of women with little or a lot of schooling). Despite the differences in sample design, the patterns that emerge reflect differences in orientation towards family size between the two castes. This view derives not only from the interviews, but also from discussions we held with other men and women not from the samples. In neither caste group, nor in any of the different classes, did *anyone* argue that large families were economically rational.[21] In view of the marked differences between the Jats and the Sheikhs in other respects, however, we will deal with them separately.

Jat views of family size

Two boys and a girl are good, because they will mean fewer expenses. You should consider a girl and boy equal. And someone must have daughters. Otherwise, who could get married? One or two children are also OK, but the most important thing is to have a small family. I don't want them all to be doing farming. I'm only doing it myself out of necessity. We have less land because the population is growing. (Surinder, h/o Sudha, J11, 12 years of schooling, middle peasant, farms 12 acres with his father and two married brothers, two sons and one daughter.)

I myself wanted three children, because there are boys and also a girl. And in these times, what would we be doing having more children? Prices are going up all the time. For the schooling for three children, clothes and also for marriages, a lot of money is needed. If these children become suitable for anything at all, that would be an achievement. (Sudha, w/o Surinder, J11, no schooling, middle peasant, joint household with her mother-in-law and two younger sisters-in-law.)

These statements, from a middle peasant man and his wife, are typical of the responses of Jats to questions about how many children they desire. Jats of all classes mention the costs of education, upbringing and marriage as reasons why small families are better: and 'small', in this context, means two or three children. But couples also point to other expenses. Clothing, feeding and housing costs rise when children have to be made presentable for school. And very few Jat children are earning and contributing to their keep before the age of 16 or 17. For Jat couples with young children, the costs of extra children loom large, and any possible benefits they may supply when they are adults are a long way in the future. In most cases, those benefits themselves are contingent on

---

[21] The views expressed by the Sheikhs and Jats also largely replicate the views of Sheikhs in Jhakri and members of middle Hindu castes in Dharmnagri. For more detailed discussion of their views, see P. Jeffery et al. 1989, Ch. 8.

sons' gaining off-farm employment, for the problems of land fragmentation are clearly in the forefront in people's minds when they talk about desirable family sizes.

I don't want any more children, my two boys are enough. I've always thought that. I'll educate them as far as possible. If they get service that's fine. If not, they can open a shop or something. I'd like it if they didn't do farming – the work is too heavy and there's not much benefit. (Anil, h/o Anita, J10, 9 years of schooling, middle peasant, farms 20 acres with his brother, his father and two married uncles, two sons.)

I want only two children. The expenses of two children are met with difficulty, so how would it be with more children? With few children we can look after them properly and bring them up right. That's why I want only two children. I am taking pills to stop having more. For as long as the pills do the work, that's all right. If not, then I will have to be sterilized. (Anita w/o Anil, J10, 8 years of schooling, middle peasant, lives with her husband's two aunts and a cousin's wife, two sons.)

Among the Jats, if a family has more than two children, the couple generally explain that they wanted sons and had extra daughters; or that they had only sons and wanted a daughter. If a couple has only one son, they may be tempted to have another child in the hope of having a second, but they are all aware that in trying for a son, who knows how many girls might be born?

I wanted just two children, one boy and one girl. But since I didn't have a girl what could I do? Two children are correct. If, in waiting for a girl, I had a third boy, then what would we do? There isn't that much land. If with two children one is a girl that would have been fine. No girl was born, but even so it is all right. (Kelo, w/o Kapil, J14, middle peasant, separate from mother-in-law, uneducated, two sons.)

I wanted only two children from the start. The land is going to be divided into small pieces, and many children make for worries. I don't want my sons to do farming, because there isn't going to be enough land. They'll only get just over one acre each. (Kapil, h/o Kelo, J14, middle peasant, farms 13 acres owned jointly with father, three married and one unmarried brother, and the widow of a fifth brother, 8 years of schooling, two sons.)

Three households in our sample had four children, but none had more than that. In the case of Om Pal and Omkari, the fourth child had been a mistake:

I myself wanted to have three children. But the younger girl was born in ignorance, and now I have four children. After the younger girl was born, I had a Copper-T. But before that I hadn't used any contraceptive. After my third child, my father-in-law said that I should be sterilized, but I was frightened by what my mother-in-law, my husband's sister and some neighbouring women said. So in fear I didn't have the [sterilization] operation done. For as long as the Copper-T stops children, for that long it's all right. If not, then I'll have the operation done. Four children are a lot in these times. A lot of money is needed for children's education, feeding and their weddings, and we don't have so very much. (Omkari, w/o Om Pal, J17, poor peasant, no schooling, joint household with mother-in-law, two sons and two daughters.)

In addition to concerns about expense, a woman's illness may be grounds for having few children. For Shanti, J18, her two sons and two daughters were more than she had wanted: she complained of being continually ill. She had an abortion, and was sterilized in 1990. Sometimes, the desirability of a small family can overcome a hesitancy about stopping at one son. In the case of Som Pal and Shivani, even their one son's weak leg did not prevent Shivani being sterilized while under the anaesthetic after a stillborn child was born by Caesarean operation:

Two or three, that's enough. My wife had the [sterilization] operation after she had a stillborn child, because we were scared she might have the same trouble if she had more children. It's good to have a small family for educating them. There's also less day-to-day expense. A small family needs a smaller plot of land to live. If I had a large family we wouldn't have enough land. Then my sons would have a bad fate. They would have to do labouring work or set up a shop of their own. My own son has had polio and has a weak leg. Even so, I don't want more sons. (Som Pal, h/o Shivani, J12, poor peasant, runs a small shop and farms 1.4 acres, 10 years schooling, one son and one daughter.)

I myself do not want many children, two or three, because there is little land and the expenses would be great. And also these days people shouldn't have many children. I never made any contraceptive arrangements. The thing is this, that I have two children, a boy and a girl and the boy has polio in his leg, so I wanted to have another boy. (Shivani, w/o Som Pal, J12, poor peasant, mother-in-law dead, no schooling.)

Only among the richest peasants and landlords might several sons be regarded with relatively little concern. These farmers have a substantial surplus from their land and other interests, which can be ploughed back into new economic enterprises. Their sons can realistically be educated to at least a professional level and set up as lawyers or doctors. But even here, small families are considered best, and young couples talk of the costs of education and upbringing. In some cases, they were paying large sums to have their children educated in private schools in Bijnor or further afield. Even so, the financial costs may not be as important as the effort that must go into supervising homework and arranging for extra tuition, as this husband and wife agree:

I want only two children, because with more children you cannot pay proper attention to them. With few, that is two, children you can look after their upbringing properly. And for two children, their schooling and clothing can be fulfilled according to one's wishes. You can clothe them well and you can feed them well. With more children, all this is very difficult, in these expensive times. And also, we have one boy and one girl, so what's the point in making a third child? (Shamo w/o Shiv Singh, Ji, MA, landlord, living separately from her mother-in-law.)

We don't want any more children. With these two we can make sure they grow up properly. They'll get a good education and inherit the property. Also, it's what the Government wants, and we want it too. (Shiv Singh, h/o Shamo, Ji, MA, landlord, farming about 40 acres with his father, and managing small private sugar crusher.)

Examples of other prominent families in Nangal encouraged this kind of calculation. Khushi Ram was one of the largest landholders in the village in the 1930s, at one time owning 180 acres. Shyam Singh, one of Khushi Ram's grandsons, told us about how his own family had come down in the world. Khushi Ram had four sons, the eldest of whom (Maharaj Singh, the father of Shyam Singh) in turn had four sons. When Maharaj Singh inherited 40 acres in 1947 he did not have enough surplus from his everyday expenses to be able to invest in *kolhūs*, like his brothers did. Shyam Singh and his three brothers inherited only 10 acres each, and each of them had three sons, who would thus inherit little more than 3 acres. Shyam Singh compared himself with his cousins, now owning substantial sugar factories, and the family of Kedar Nath, another large landholder from the 1930s, whose son and grandson were only sons. Shyam Singh explicitly explained the differences between their current situations in terms of being an only son or having few uncles. The differences between the situations of these households could be seen as a result of the working out of 'fate' in the past, he said, but now, with family planning, landholding households all understood the benefits of having no more than two children.

Most Jats would agree that it might be risky to stop at one son. As Charan Singh, a middle peasant with three sons put it, 'One son is not enough – he might turn out bad; two sons would be right; three is too many.' Given the extra costs of having a girl (with dowries believed to be escalating) it is perhaps surprising how many couples had gone on to have another child if they had two sons. Other chance factors may leave a couple with more than two children. For example, Ajay's first wife died of cancer when her son was 4 years old and her daughter only 4 months. Ajay married again, and has two more children:

I have four children, which are enough. I have so many only because I married twice and my second wife wanted children of her own. That's all we're going to have. Full stop. It's my own view. I haven't been swayed by government propaganda about how many people there are in the country and so on. It's all a question of how to get them educated and look after them properly.

ROGER: What about having enough sons so that you wouldn't need to employ labourers on your farm?

AJAY: Farming is very heavy work. It's all right, but not what I want for my children, so that's not a reason to have more sons. There are better ways to earn your daily bread. (Ajay, h/o Asha, J5, rich peasant, farms 25 acres by himself, 11 years schooling, two sons and two daughters.)

Among the Jats, then, there is a clear perception of the costs of large families, and little wish to have more sons to help with the farm work. Given the centrality of sons to people's perceptions of family size, the best comparisons of fertility behaviour can be made amongst couples who already have at least one living son: no couple could countenance stopping having children without at least one living son. Very few couples who began cohabiting in the 1950s had used contraception; most of those who began cohabiting in the 1980s were too early in their marital careers for contraception to be a serious consideration. Of the 112 couples who began cohabiting between 1960 and 1979, 107 had at least one son in 1990, and 56 of them were taking steps to avoid having more children. While some women were frightened of the sterilization operation, particularly if carried out by government doctors, there was a wide knowledge of other methods. The most common form of contraception was female sterilization (forty-one women), followed by the Copper-T (seven women), vasectomy (seven men), and one woman was using the contraceptive pill. Those who began cohabiting in the 1960s and were contracepting in 1990 had had 4.5 children on average, but those who began cohabiting in the 1970s had had on average only three children by the time they began to contracept. Of the fifty-six who were not contracepting in 1990, five had no son; seventeen had only one son, and a further twenty-four had two sons. Only ten women with more than two living sons were not contracepting.

Crucially, however, there is no discernible variation according to class position, as Table 3.6 shows. Couples from all social classes are behaving in much the same way, which is unlikely if there were class-specific economic rationalities in favour of large families. Despite facing very different class-related economic opportunities, Jats from all classes seem to be agreed about the virtues of small families. There is some evidence that the rich peasants and landlords moved fastest to use contraception to limit their families: such couples who began cohabiting between 1960 and 1969 stopped at three children on average, while middle peasants and landless couples went on to an average of 4.5 children each (though

Table 3.6. *Number of living children of couples who began cohabiting between 1960 and 1989, by contraceptive status and social class, Jats, Nangal, 1990*

Cohabitation year	Contraceptive status	Class			
		Landlords and rich peasants	Middle peasants	Poor peasants and landless	All
1960–69	Contracepting	3.0 (N=5)	4.6 (N=15)	5.1 (N=9)	4.5 (N=29)
	Not contracepting	2.7 (N=6)	4.0 (N=19)	4.0 (N=3)	3.8 (N=33)
1970–79	Contracepting	3.0 (N=2)	2.9 (N=18)	3.0 (N=7)	3.0 (N=27)
	Not contracepting	2.4 (N=5)	2.7 (N=12)	2.8 (N=5)	2.7 (N=23)
1980–89	Contracepting	2.5 (N=6)	2.4 (N=9)	2.0 (N=1)	2.4 (N=16)
	Not contracepting	1.3 (N=15)	1.2 (N=46)	1.3 (N=10)	1.3 (N=72)

Source: Maternity histories collected by the authors, Nangal, October 1990.

our numbers for rich peasants and landless are small). But all couples who began to cohabit between 1970 and 1979 – from whatever class – seem to have made similar decisions on contraception, with those who are contracepting having three children on average. Most of the twenty-three couples from this cohort who are not contracepting can best be understood as following approximately same strategies as those who are contracepting. That is, they are trying for a family of two sons and a daughter, but have had daughters, or sons who died, and therefore have not yet reached their minimum requirement. Of these twenty-three couples, four have no son and nine have only one son; eight have two sons and only two couples have three sons. Thus, middle peasant households, most affected by the need to hire labour at peak periods, and less able to resort to the use of major labour-saving equipment such as tractors, are behaving in essentially the same way as rich peasants and landlords, who are already using tractors and other equipment as far as possible. Although the poor peasants and landless were slower to limit their family sizes than their wealthier neighbours, they are now limiting their family sizes to a degree not paralleled by other comparable groups in western UP, such as the Chamars.[22] Among the Jats, then, the similarities between the classes are much more striking than their differences.

Family size preferences among the Sheikhs

We've had no benefits in the last ten years. We still have as many shortages. I still have to work as a labourer to buy half our household food. We can cover only

---

[22] Other middle-class and caste groups in Dharmnagri – such as Sahnis and Dhimars – are not using contraception as widely as are the Jats of Nangal.

half our expenses from the land. The children increase as fast as we get any
benefits from new crops and higher prices. We were three brothers. Now twenty-
one people have to be fed from the same land. (Sultan, h/o Sabra, S17, poor
peasant, farms 1.6 acres with two married brothers and father, does labouring
when available, uneducated.)

Do you have any medicine to close my 'factory'? I have so many children that by
evening I am dizzy with having shouted at them all day. And the children need to
be looked to. There should be land, so that your offspring can't say 'our parents
have done nothing for us'. I don't want more children for this reason. Three are
a lot. One must also look to one's body. It is not a question of dividing the land.
The question of land is this, when the children get big they must earn to eat.
(Sabra, w/o Sultan, S17, lives separately from her two sisters-in-law, mother-in-
law dead, no schooling, two sons and one daughter.)

Many Sheikh men and women in Qaziwala were willing to talk about
the costs of large families. In this minimal sense at least, they may make
economic calculations when considering desirable family sizes. For men,
and a few women, the effect on land fragmentation was most often
mentioned.

ROGER: You and your brothers have 13 children, and they'll inherit only a half
　　　acre each. How are they going to manage? What will this lad here do?
RIAZ: Labouring. Is it like that in your country? Or do they all have sterilization
　　　after two children?
ROGER: No, not often. People are more likely to use condoms, or pills, or
　　　Copper-T.
RIAZ: I've heard that some Jats – not all – had one child and, whether son or
　　　daughter, then were sterilized.
ROGER: That's very rare.
RIAZ: But it happens. They don't mind if their name ends or not.
ROGER: Your name could go on with a girl.
RIAZ: That's right, if you have a son your land would go to him. If you have a
　　　daughter you could bring her to live with you after her marriage and the
　　　land would go to her. If you have no children the land would go to your
　　　brothers.
ROGER: How many children are enough?
RIAZ: Four. You mustn't go for sterilization, but after four you should do
　　　something to stop. Lots of people are beginning to say that. And the
　　　women are always complaining that they have so much worry with the
　　　children that they want to stop. (Riaz, h/o Rasheeda, S16, middle peasant,
　　　farming 5 acres, owns a tractor with his father and three brothers, educated
　　　in Urdu for five years, one son and two daughters.)

I want no more children. These are more than enough. What would we do with
more? I have three children and we can spend what we like on them. If there
were more, they'd snatch from only a small portion and that wouldn't be enough
for them all. My mother is already meeting the expenses for the older girl. My
husband thinks, 'let them be born, however many there are. What worries do

you have?' But I'm worried with three and I can see others around me gone mad with their five or six. If I have more, won't I become mad too? (Rasheeda, w/o Riaz, middle peasant, living separately from her mother-in-law and three sisters-in-law, can read the Qur'an, one son and two daughters.)

Along with these concerns about the expense and other difficulties associated with many children, however, were statements that God will provide, that the number of children is up to Him, and that sterilization was a sin for Muslims.[23]

My husband says nothing about having more children, nor have I asked his opinion. This is a matter of God's orders. I have also not thought about it. Children are the gift of God, no matter how many he gives. You aren't going to stop our children are you? (Usmana, w/o Usman, S19, uneducated, middle peasant, lives separately from her five sisters-in-law, mother-in-law dead, five sons and two daughters.)

In the last 10 years, all the improvements have gone in extra expenses. My grandfather says that there are now 50 people to be fed from the land. They are eating all the benefits of higher prices and better yields from the tractor and our diesel engine. Also wedding expenses have risen. We can't afford to buy more land at Rs 75,000 per acre, and we haven't done so in the last 10 years. All we've managed to do is to build some new brick housing. (Usman, h/o Usmana, middle peasant, farming 25 acres with his five brothers, five years of schooling, five sons and two daughters.)

I want no more children but it isn't in my hands. My husband also doesn't want more children. But the operation is a sin for Muslims. We two don't want more children voluntarily, and it's also a matter of land division. The children's upbringing would also be able to be good. That's why I want no more children. (Naima w/o Nizamuddin, S13, middle peasant, joint household with mother-in-law, uneducated, one son and two daughters.)

Many Sheikh couples express complex feelings, and husbands and wives may contradict each other. As good Muslims, most feel they should leave matters in the hands of God. But many perceive the economic costs of doing so. Even where their husbands acknowledge the economic problems of large families, women are inhibited from taking action. Some couples described an ideal family size of four children, if at least two of them are sons, and said that, since they had reached that position, they would like to take steps to avoid having more children. Of our sample of twenty women who answered this question, thirteen said they wanted no more children, and two more answered that it was a matter for God but they themselves wanted no more children. Three would say no more than that it was a matter for God. The two women

---

[23] This is only one of the Islamic views on contraception: we discuss this more fully in Chapter 6.

who said they wanted more children each had only one son but two daughters.

The Sheikhs in our sample, then, clearly expressed the costs of large families. None, from any class, talked about the economic (or any other) benefits of large families. Given the relatively small plots of land owned by middle peasants (and the very small numbers of rich peasants), it is not surprising that no couple talked about the benefits of extra sons to help with working the land. Similarly, no small peasants and landless labourers described the benefits of extra hands to bring in an income, preferring instead to stress their own problems in keeping jobs which paid wages barely sufficient to keep their families alive.

The almost universal condemnation of sterilization as unIslamic, however, and the wariness about alternative contraceptive methods which might be in opposition to what they believed to be the tenets of Islam, have led to very low levels of contraceptive use. Of the 114 couples who began cohabiting in the 1960s and 1970s, only 3 (2.6 per cent) told us in 1991 that they were practising some form of modern contraception at the time. Only 21 couples had fewer than two living sons, 28 had two, and 65 had more than two. Of these 114 couples, 93 had four or more children. We suspect that some couples are using condoms, and other women may have had abortions or Copper-Ts inserted, but did not tell us. We could not ask about coitus interruptus, nor about the avoidance of sexual intercourse as couples grew older: such questioning would have jeopardized people's willingness to answer our other questions. Only one woman in this age group has been sterilized, and she had little say in the matter: her husband and his family believe that she is mentally subnormal. Her first four sons all died, and she refused to grieve for them. After four more boys and a girl were born, her husband took her to Bijnor to be sterilized. She was allowed to resume a normal social life only when her other in-laws decided that she was not at fault for being sterilized. Apparently, no blame was attached to the husband for his actions. One of our sample women had a Copper-T inserted on medical grounds, after her fifth delivery; one other reported sporadic use of contraceptive pills, and eleven women either asked us to get them medicines or said they planned to take pills in the near future.

Conclusion

Fertility differences between Jats and Sheikhs cannot be explained by economic arguments which stress the differences in class locations of the two groups. Holding class constant, the fertility differentials remain.

Furthermore, there is no evidence that having many children was regarded as economically rational by any class in either group. Sheikh and Jat couples alike were aware of the cost implications of extra children, and were sceptical that the benefits would outweigh the costs, either in the short or the long term. Rearing children 'properly' (with good schooling paramount here) was expensive. Among the Jats, these perceptions have led to a very small preferred family size – two or three children, as long as at least one is a son – and the consistent use of effective contraception means that most Jat couples who started to cohabit in the 1970s and 1980s have stopped at that number. Exceptions are rare. Among the Sheikhs, the preferred family size is larger – a four child family would be regarded as small – and few couples seem to have successfully limited their families to reach these goals. Sheikhs experienced higher child mortality than the Jats, in all classes except the highest, but the differences in current family size remain even after mortality effects have been taken into account. We now turn to one possible explanation: that Sheikh women are less able to act on their wishes for fewer children because they have less freedom of action than Jat women.

4 Women's agency and fertility

In cities, big people ask a girl before making an engagement, but no one asks a girl in a village. The girl doesn't even know which boy she is being married to. (Janistha w/o Jabir, S8, landless, no schooling)

My parents didn't look for a boy anywhere else than Nangal – though if they had done so what would I know, where do men tell these things inside the house? Men generally go outside and they do not tell outside matters inside the house. No opinion was sought from me about my marriage. (Lalita's sister-in-law)

Who used to ask girls' opinions previously? Even if a girl was thrown in a well, she couldn't say anything. (Lalita w/o Lokender, J9, landlord, 8th class pass)

Narrow class-based theories of demographic change have been subjected to several powerful criticisms. For example, the so-called 'new household economics', associated with the work of Gary Becker (1960) has been accused of failing to take into account the possibility of gender- and age-based conflicts of interest within the household.[1] Until the 1980s, most discussions failed to recognize that men's and women's views might be different, and affected by the structured inequalities between them (as Cain et al. 1979 and Basu 1991, point out). Asok Mitra (1978) was one of the first writers to stress the possibility that the 'status of women' might play a major role in understanding demographic change in India. Since then, demographic orthodoxy (following the work of Karen Mason 1984) includes variables on women's status in its model-making. But the discussion of how women, their views and their actions might be significant in understanding demographic change, has remained curiously detached from the theorizing of gender issues, whether feminist or not (Greenhalgh 1995). Essentially, three kinds of perspective can be distinguished: one is concerned with indicators of women's role or status; a second considers the key issue to be women's 'autonomy'; and the third is concerned to capture aspects of women's agency.

The literature on the status (or role) of women assumes that it is

[1] See also de Tray 1980; for a critique, see Folbre 1988.

possible to sum up 'the position of women' by means of relatively few variables (Cleland and Hobcraft 1985; for a critique see Watkins 1993). So far as the explanation of demographic change is concerned, a woman's schooling, her economic roles, and her position in the household, are considered to be powerful predictors of whether or not she is able to reduce the extent of male control, and become economically less dependent (Anker et al. 1982; Mason 1984). More variables can be added in: thus a woman is believed to have a higher 'status' the later she marries, and if her age at marriage is close to the age of her husband (Dyson and Moore 1983). Alternatively, as in a study in eastern UP, women's status can be classified as 'low', 'medium' or 'high' based on a series of indicators, ranging from her husband's education and income to her own contribution to decision-making and access to mass media (Yadava 1995).

A major problem with these approaches is that they treat individual characteristics as the main causes of differences between men and women in societies, ignoring the wider context of inequalities in social institutions and social processes which affect all women in a society. Furthermore, the meanings of the indicators for the women themselves are rarely addressed, but are assumed to be self-evident, usually on the basis of European or North American experience. An implicit modernization theory lurks behind these indicators: an assumption that progress towards the higher levels of schooling, women's greater participation in the workforce, and improved husband–wife communication which are presumed to be characteristic of industrial countries, is the future for the world as a whole. There is also a tendency to ignore the issues of power and conflict – on the basis of age as well as gender hierarchies – that have been shown to be at the heart of family relationships (Greenhalgh 1995). The 'status of women' literature thus often uses indicators which bear only a very loose relationship to the concepts they are supposed to be measuring.

The work of Dyson and Moore is a sophisticated attempt to go beyond this literature and explain why indicators of women's status and demographic outcomes vary in India. They use additional indicators, particularly ones derived from kinship systems, to approach issues of women's autonomy, which they define as 'the capacity to manipulate one's personal environment' (Dyson and Moore 1983: 45).[2] They

[2] Greenhalgh 1995: 24 dismisses Dyson and Moore's use of female autonomy as subject to the same criticisms as those levelled against women's status. Although Dyson and Moore's discussion now looks dated, it does clearly attempt to embed the discussion of female autonomy in at least some aspects of gender relationships, including (for example) the ability of females to control property and their own sexuality, and refers to 'equality of autonomy between the sexes' (p. 45).

explain the different north and south Indian demographic regimes (see Chapter 2) by showing how north Indian women are materially disadvantaged by the workings of aspects of their kinship system. They face more controls over their sexuality, through arranged marriages to strangers and norms of veiling and avoidance; they are more likely to share a residence with their parents-in-law, at greater distances from their natal homes; they are less likely to be involved in waged labour outside the home; and they have far weaker property rights than south Indian women. In most cases in north India, a woman cannot be married to anyone from her natal kin group. The terms by which kin are addressed, and everyday avoidance practices, reinforce distinctions between a woman's natal kin and the men to whom she may be married (Vatuk 1967). She is likely to be married more than walking distance away from her parents' home, to an unrelated man, and to experience conflict in a difficult relationship with her mother-in-law. However much her parents love her, she is seen as a drain on their resources: parents should not allow her to work outside any family enterprise before her marriage, nor should they ever receive economic support from her afterwards. At the time of marriage she is 'given', with a dowry, to her in-laws. In these circumstances, a woman has little say in most aspects of her life. After puberty and before she is married she cannot move around easily in her natal village, for fear of getting a 'loose' reputation which might damage her marriage chances. Once married she is even more constrained in her marital village and it may be many years before she is able to work, shop or market goods in 'public space' like the local town.

North Indian women also have more children than do south Indian women, and more of their children (particularly, more of their daughters) die. Dyson and Moore consider that these demographic outcomes reflect differences in women's autonomy. The more autonomous the woman, the more she is likely to be able to affect her own fertility and to ensure that she and her children (and especially her daughters) receive better medical care. Other writers applying a gender perspective to these issues have also tended to accept the general premises of Dyson and Moore's work, usually, however, without applying their concerns with the material consequences of kinship systems. Thus Sen (1995) uses female literacy and the proportion of women engaged in work (as paid or family labour) as indicators of women's autonomy, and explains rapid fertility decline in Kerala in the same terms.

Dyson and Moore's article has been extremely influential, but several problems are raised by recent research. According to their approach,

Keralan women might be expected to have the most autonomy of any women in the Indian sub-continent, but on a number of indicators, they show no more autonomy than, for example, women in Gujarat (Visaria 1996; Rajan et al. 1996). Although indicators of women's schooling (length of schooling, literacy rates) do correlate well with the demographic indicators (fertility and mortality rates), both at the individual level and in the regional or inter-district comparisons (Murthi et al. 1995), more direct indicators of women's behaviour (their freedom of movement or their contribution to household decision-making, for example) do not always do so (R. Jeffery and A. Basu 1996). Furthermore, the answers to direct questions – such as whether a woman can visit a nearby town on their own, or choose a sari – may not be good indicators of autonomy. We still do not know enough about what these actions mean to the women themselves. Are they seen as positive markers of valued areas of personal space, or as unwanted obligations which connote a loss of prestige, that could be avoided if they had more caring in-laws or were in a better economic position? If we do accept survey answers as good indicators of autonomy, we are faced with ambiguous and inconsistent findings. In some places, women who have more schooling have more apparent freedom of action, but in other places no differences emerge (R. Jeffery and A. Basu 1996). In a rare study of changes through time, Carol Vlassoff (1992; 1996) showed that as girls' schooling became more common in a Maharashtrian village, women's autonomy seemed to decline. Furthermore, processes of economic change do not necessarily lead to improvements in women's autonomy, as measured in these ways. For example, in more affluent groups in Punjab, on a number of indicators such as mobility outside the home or comparative child mortality rates, 'economic development' seems to have worsened women's position relative to men (Basu 1988; Das Gupta 1987; Sharma 1980).

We have additional reasons for unease over Dyson and Moore's perspective. To begin with, by the very nature of their approach, Dyson and Moore deal with quite large units – Districts with populations from 30,000 to 4 million – as do Murthi et al. (1995). But it is not clear that the variables which differentiate these large units also make a difference to the individual women within them. For example, do women who marry into familiar households (more common in south India), or move only short distances on marriage, actually have any more autonomy than those who marry more distantly in the same region? Indeed, in a personal communication, Dyson has suggested that he would not expect them to do so. But this inevitably raises questions about the appropriateness of the regional indicators of women's autonomy.

More problematic still is how differences in autonomy arise. The two most commonly cited indicators – women's work outside the home, and their schooling experience – do correlate well with lowered fertility, holding other things constant. But there is a tendency to leap straight from these correlations to assume a simple causative chain: that a woman schooled beyond primary level, or working outside the home, has more freedom of action, is better able to achieve her own goals, and can therefore achieve better care for her children as well as fewer births (Cain 1984). But there is remarkably little evidence about how women use schooling or waged work to change the quality of their domestic relationships in the predicted ways.

We began our own research in Bijnor in 1990 expecting to look for autonomy, as defined above: the parameters of our study were, in a general sense, set by Dyson and Moore's perspective. None of the women in our sample is employed outside the home except as part of the household enterprise, which gave us no basis for exploring the difference this might make to their everyday lives; we consider the implications of the much more varied schooling experiences of the Jat and Sheikh couples in our sample in Chapter 5. In Bijnor there are also major differences in kinship systems: Sheikhs (like other Muslim *jāti*) do not forbid marriages within the village or to related men, whereas Jats do. Sheikh marriage distances are also much shorter, on average, than are Jat marriage distances. There are also differences in age at marriage, and in the relative ages of husbands and wives. In the course of exploring these differences, however, we have become increasingly aware of the limitations of the 'autonomy' approach, though we do not deny its advance over previous discussions. We have begun to consider alternative ways of understanding what affects women's ability to act, and have explored this through the notion of 'agency', and its meaning for the women of rural Bijnor.

'Agency' is a much more elusive and inclusive concept than 'autonomy'. Nita Kumar (1994: 19–22) in an insightful discussion, points out that though men may be politically dominant, alternative discourses exist, in which women create some spaces for their own action, and challenge the dominant meanings through song, speech and action in ways that are hard to perceive. Agency in this sense emerges not only from direct actions or challenges to the status quo, but also through resistance, negotiated and partial – a resistance which is potentially available to all women, whether 'autonomous' or not. Demographers have yet to take on board feminist concerns with gender as a structural factor which (with class and ethnicity, for example) underlies social relationships and both provides and limits opportunities for women's agency. Susan Greenhalgh (1995: 24–6), for example, argues forcefully that demographers need to accept that gender permeates all aspects of social life, not just reproduction, and affects relationships among men and among women, as well as relationships between men and women. Men may be dominant, but their dominance is never complete, and although women may be 'victims' they should not be seen as passive in the face of wider social processes. Women enter into patriarchal bargains, which may lead to them sustaining a status quo which disadvantages them in some respects, but gives them protection and rewards in others (Kandiyoti 1988; see also Hart 1991; P. Jeffery and R. Jeffery 1996). They may resist and find strategies which can mitigate the effects of systems that oppress them, even if they seem quite powerless and lacking in autonomy according to accepted indicators.

The concern with agency can help us to avoid one problem with the concept of autonomy, often presented as an absolute value, which can increase without any necessary effects on other people (Basu 1996). A foregrounding of gender can also draw our attention to the ways in which processes of so-called 'development' may not lead to improvements in women's lives. Furthermore, since women are not homogeneous, social change affects women often in contradictory and ambiguous ways. Thus, women could have the freedom to move further and unchaperoned; to read more, see more television, choose their own saris as well as their own shoes, etc., without reducing other people's 'autonomy'. But this is an entirely individualistic perspective. Looking at agency forces us to consider the effects of actions on others: women might gain freedom of action only at the cost of the freedom of action of others, whether their children, parents-in-law or husbands. The enhanced agency of older women (as mothers and mothers-in-law) may be at the expense of limited or even reduced agency for their daughters and daughters-in-law. While confrontation and overt demands for freedom may not often be resorted to by Indian women, this does not exhaust their ability to influence what happens around them. Crucially, schooling or waged work would have to be used as resources by women in their everyday lives, as part of complex and shifting negotiations, if there is to be any correlation (let alone any causal connection) between schooling or employment indicators and outcomes such as the expansion of a woman's personal space. Yet this does not seem to be a necessary outcome. In western Kenya, for example, rising levels of schooling and increased work outside the family enterprise do not, apparently, protect women from domestic violence (Bradley 1995).[3]

---

[3] For a longer discussion of the definitional issues using Indian material, see P. Jeffery and

Another major problem with many discussions of autonomy is that they use a relatively simple model of decision-making (see, for example, Sen 1995). But household dynamics are still remarkably little understood: households are fairly opaque, and studying how their members make decisions has not yet been very fruitful. We do know, however, that decisions are very rarely 'made' in a straightforward way and on a specific occasion. They emerge out of a series of interactions, over a period of time, and may be subsequently refined and amended.[4] As Lukes (1972) has argued, seeing how issues are kept off the agenda for discussion may be more important than understanding how decisions are made about issues that are allowed to be discussed. As a result, we rarely get very far simply by asking questions about 'who made decision X?' This problem is compounded when (as in our research) interviews cannot be held in private, out of the hearing of others who may have a different view or more power. And without interviewing all significant participants in a household, it is hard to know what value to give to one person's account. Reproductive behaviour is particularly sensitive and personal, and in India the topic has been politicized to such an extent that evasion is the most likely strategy when people feel forced to give an answer. Furthermore, our data support the suggestion that couples rarely 'decide' to have a large family; rather, they 'fail to decide' to have a small one (Dyson 1991).

We are, then, left in something of a dilemma. While we are unhappy with Dyson and Moore's conclusion that most women in north India are 'socially almost powerless' (1983: 46), we have found it difficult to obtain access to the very sites where the women in our sample are able to exercise agency. Faced with evidence of restrictions on a young married woman's mobility, her veiling in front of her husband's elder relatives and so on, it is easy to conclude that there are serious barriers to her exercising much direct and visible power (see also Mandelbaum 1988). We do not wish to underplay the significance of these controls, and we specify some of them in this chapter. But we need also to be aware that women in such circumstances are not mere 'victims', or passive pawns in other people's activities.[5] Tactics are available to such women to try

R. Jeffery 1994, 1996; Basu 1996; Sen 1995, and several of the chapters in R. Jeffery and Basu (eds.) 1996.
[4] Carter 1995 analyzes some of our earlier work to stress the contingent, reflexively monitored and diverse flows of conduct which lead to reproductive outcomes. See also Caldwell et al. 1988 for more discussions of the ways in which a 'contraceptive decision' may be presented as one made by the woman when she has been pressured into accepting responsibility for something she might otherwise have preferred not to do.
[5] There is an extensive discussion of these issues. See for example Mani 1990; Abu-Lughod 1990; Rajan 1993; Thompson 1985; P. Jeffery and R. Jeffery 1994, 1996; Okely 1991; Sen 1990; Kandiyoti 1988; Jeffery 1979.

to work the system to their 'minimum disadvantage' (Hobsbawm 1973). As one of us has argued elsewhere (Jeffery 1979: 161), we should expect to find a 'complex mixture of deep-rooted commitment and reluctant compliance, of accepting things as they are and of undermining them through their questions and evasions'. We have found it useful to employ Scott's analysis of the extent to which dominated sections of society are prepared to accept the ideology that they should be powerless. He describes how 'the ordinary weapons of relatively power-less groups: foot dragging, dissimulation, false compliance, pilfering, feigned ignorance, slander, arson, sabotage and so forth . . . require little or no co-ordination or planning; they often represent a form of individual self-help; and they typically avoid any direct symbolic confrontation with authority' (Scott 1990: 29). Despite the direct references to Scott's work in the two chapters on rather exceptional women in a recent book on 'everyday resistance' in South Asia (Haynes and Prakash 1991), few authors have actually tried to see how this perspective might help us to understand 'ordinary' women's strategies. Yet north Indian women clearly possess the ability to invert the orthodox hierarchy when they are together singing wedding or childbirth songs which ridicule their husbands' families and praise their own; or parody male sexuality (Raheja 1994; Gold 1994).

In terms of how we might investigate women's agency, there are several strengths to an approach which recognizes that women have to employ the 'weapons of the weak'. These women are politically and socially weak: as we have seen in Chapter 3, their work is not seen as important or valuable, despite being long and arduous, and often involving some direct inputs into producing and processing milk and other agricultural products, for both domestic use and for sale. Women have no legal control over productive resources. In these respects, all rural women in Bijnor are vulnerable: in Sen's terms, if their marriage were to break down, they would be poorer, more likely to lose the family home, etc., than their husbands would be (Sen 1990). The work done by young married women in rural Bijnor does vary in *content*, particularly reflecting their class and the composition of the households in which they live (P. Jeffery et al. 1989). But these differences seem to generate little variation in the *control* women can exert over household resources. This might suggest there is little room for leverage over differences in women's agency. We have chosen to look at aspects of women's lives on which there is variability – access to a woman's natal kin, household structures, and, (in the next chapter), schooling experiences – to see whether they give women differential scope for agency (see also Jeffery et al. 1988; Carter 1995).

Women's agency is not only an outcome of how husbands and wives are expected to behave towards each other.[6] Women themselves emphasize their relationships with their mothers-in-law, but also talk about how much support they receive from their own parents. It might be expected that Sheikh women married close to their natal homes or to relatives would be better able to use their access to their parents as a resource in negotiating over key aspects of their lives; and that Jat women with more schooling might be significantly more 'autonomous' than their unschooled neighbours. Some of these differences might emerge through consideration of key transitions in women's lives: in the choice of a husband, or in the tussles which lead to the separation of households. The household itself is a major site where women's *āzādī* (freedom) is contested and must be negotiated, and we look at the influence of household structures and dynamics on women's freedom of action. In sum, women in rural Bijnor are not identically placed, despite many surface similarities. Those with more scope for exerting their agency directly may also be able to limit their fertility. In this chapter we attempt to answer the following questions. How far can young married women be active agents in their lives in general, and, in particular, in their reproductive lives, their marriages, their day-to-day living arrangements, and their access to economic resources? Are there variations in agency among and between Jat and Sheikh women, and can these be related to different fertility outcomes?

Marriage arrangement for Jats and Sheikhs

In Bijnor, marriages are almost always arranged by the couple's parents within *jāti* (we discuss some exceptions below), and there is the potential for differences in family and gender systems between one *jāti* and the next. Equally, however, *jāti* of similar social standing share some common features. A few basic moral rules influence marriage choices in almost all caste groups. In Bijnor, Jats and Sheikhs prefer the groom to be taller, better educated and older than the bride. Similarly, young couples are expected to start their married life sharing a residence and pooling economic resources with the groom's parents and unmarried siblings; and it is desirable for this state to continue for as long as possible. In particular, there should always be at least one son prepared to provide his ageing parents with a home to live in; and if there is any land owned by the father, it should not be divided until after his death.

[6] Adams and Castle 1994 discuss the influence of power, within and between genders, and relationships inside and outwith households, on women's autonomy and control over reproduction, using West African material.

Table 4.1. *Differences between ages at marriage of husbands and wives, for all couples who started cohabiting between 1950 and 1989, Nangal Jats and Qaziwala Sheikhs*

Age difference	Nangal Jats		Qaziwala Sheikhs	
	N. of couples	Percentage	N. of couples	Percentage
Husband 11 or more years older	16	6.7	8	3.4
Husband 6–10 years older	34	14.2	35	15.0
Husband 1–5 years older	161	67.1	176	75.5
Husband and wife same age	16	6.7	7	3.0
Wife older	12	5.0	6	2.6
Missing	1	0.4	1	0.4
Total	**240**	**100.0**	**233**	**100.0**
Mean difference	3.9 years		3.8 years	

These general principles do not, of course, mean that all marriages follow these rules in full.[7] Among Sheikhs and Jats alike, girls are married at relatively young ages, often under the legal minimum age of 18. But some are married to men much the same age as themselves, while others are married to men two or even considerably more years older than them (see Table 4.1).[8] Of the 240 Jat women in Nangal who began cohabiting between 1950 and 1989, fifty were married to men more than five years their senior, compared to only sixteen women who were the same age and twelve who were older than their husbands. The women with more than eight years of schooling were, on average only 2.4 years younger than their husbands, whereas the unschooled women were 4.5 years younger.[9] In Qaziwala, forty-three Sheikh women who began cohabiting between 1950 and 1989 were married to men more than five years their senior, compared to only seven whose husband was the same age, and six who were older than their husbands. There were no differences between those who had Qur'anic schooling and those who were unschooled, both sets of wives being on average 3.8 years younger than their husbands. Nor were there differences between women married within Qaziwala and its surrounding villages, and those women married more than 10 km away. In both villages, age differences

---

[7] We did not measure heights, and cannot comment on that comparison between husbands and wives.

[8] These figures should be treated cautiously, however. Many women seem to have guessed that they were two years younger than their husbands, and even after considerable cross-checking we sometimes could do no better than accept this estimate.

[9] The differences in marriage ages for the unschooled women were highly skewed, with nineteen of these women coming from more than 80 km away, from the UP hills or from eastern UP (see further below). These women were on average more than nine years younger than their husbands, with the largest difference we estimated at over 30 years.

between husband and wife probably added to the limits on most women's ability to negotiate within the marriage, but this was not a question we pursued any further.

Beyond the common features of Jat and Sheikh marriage patterns, however, there are differences, some seemingly trivial demographically but perhaps with unintended consequences. For example, the onus of beginning the negotiations for a new match falls on the bride's parents among the Jats, but on the groom's parents among the Sheikhs. Among the Jats, the parents of a girl must mobilize kin and sometimes other village personnel such as the family barber (usually regarded as a good source of news, since they travel between villages in the course of their work and attend marriages). By contrast, the Sheikhs expect the parents of the boy to make the first move. This has implications for dowry demands. Among the Jats, parents must be prepared to assess the likely level of expectations of the groom's parents while making their selection; and they remain in a state of some trepidation until the marriage is successfully completed and their daughter is happily settled. Jat men who are poor or have other disabilities may never receive an offer of a bride, and may eventually resort to other means to get one. By contrast, among the Sheikhs, because the groom's parents make the first move, most parents of girls feel less pressure to provide very substantial dowries, arguing that the groom's parents will have made their enquiries about the financial position of the girl's parents before they make an offer, and will then find it harder to withdraw if the dowry is unsatisfactory. Cash payments are almost unknown among the Sheikhs. Among the Jats of Nangal, the families of girls are in effect bidding in auctions of attractive grooms, and we heard of one payment of Rs 100,000 for the hand of a doctor. Among the Sheikhs, then, it is the parents of poor or unattractive girls who have to wait anxiously for an offer for their daughter. While dowry issues are increasingly seen as a problem for Sheikh families as well, Jats (like other middle-class Hindu *jāti*) face a more developed system.[10]

Because the Sheikhs can arrange marriages within the village and with people in much closer kin categories, many Sheikh women join familiar households when they are married, and then have more easy access to their natal kin than do Jat women. We might expect that this would also reduce the significance of dowry demands, and give them more scope for negotiating more tolerable day-to-day household arrangements. In

---

[10] People's feelings about dowry in rural Bijnor are explored more fully in P. Jeffery and R. Jeffery 1996. Although the evidence is scarce, most commentators see dowry-related beatings, aggravated suicides and murder as features largely of urban middle class (and clean-caste) families. See Kumari 1989.

combination, young Sheikh women married a short distance from their natal homes, possibly to relatives, and without the burden of high dowry expectations hanging over them, could be better placed than young Jat women, married into strange distant households and vulnerable to dowry demands. How far do normal and unusual forms of marriage affect women's agency?

Marriage distance and women's involvement in marriage arrangements

All the Jat women in Nangal were married at some distance, with only one able to walk home in less than an hour. In general, in arranging their marriages, their parents had avoided households where there was a previous relationship, so we cannot show any effects on a woman of her being married 'close', either geographically or genealogically.[11] None the less, when arranging their daughter's marriage, the fathers of some of the women in our sample had taken into account the ease with which their daughters could come back to see them after marriage. Several women reported that their fathers felt that Nangal's good transport facilities (on a main road, with regular bus services) were an attraction of arranging a marriage there. But all the Jat women would have to use at least one bus in order to return to their parents, though none had to travel for more than three or four hours. In these circumstances it is difficult to make meaningful distinctions of marriage distance for them.

Of the Qaziwala women who began to cohabit between 1950 and 1989, however, thirty-nine had been married within the village, ninety-five were married 1–3 km away, and ninety-nine had travelled more than 3 km on marriage. Our sample of Sheikh women was selected to focus on the extremes, with a view to exploring the implications of marriage distance for a woman's autonomy. Of the sample women, eleven were married within Qaziwala itself and eleven came from more than 20 km away. Furthermore, three of our sample (two married close and one married distantly) were married to first cousins. Women married 'close' (either geographically or in kinship terms) might be expected to have a greater say in who they married than those married distantly, since they would have more chance of having seen or met their future husband, or of hearing about their personal characteristics. But we have no evidence that the Sheikh women who were married within Qaziwala, or those married to close kin, played any more part in the decisions about their marriage than women married distantly.

---

[11] The rare exceptions were when two sisters were married into the same or adjacent households; or when a woman was married to the widower of her deceased elder sister.

Nobody asks a girl's opinion, and mine certainly wasn't asked. Even if a girl is given in marriage to a deaf-mute, she can't say anything in the face of her parents' wishes. (Buri w/o Bundu, S2, born and married within Qaziwala)

Since I have no brothers my parents wouldn't marry any of us five sisters far away. Without a brother there would be no-one to fetch us back, and if she is far away a woman has to be fetched. My parents did not search for a boy for me. They didn't ask my opinion. Would they seek it? In many places parents do take their daughter's opinion, but they don't do so with us, no matter what is found. Whatever is the parents' wish, is our wish too. With us we can't say we don't like a match. Our parents can pour (*dalnā*) us anywhere at all. (Farmudan w/o Fida Husain, S3, born and married within Qaziwala)

Indeed, Farmudan had known little about what her parents had decided. Once the marriage was settled, she stopped attending the *madrasā* in case she met her future husband on the way. 'And did you ever see him?' interjected Fida Husain's second cousin. Farmudan said she had, several times, but without realizing who he was at the time.

Childhood engagements

Although not the normal mode of arranging marriages, the 'childhood betrothal' (*bachpan-kā-mang*) among Muslims is a form of agreement that is not paralleled among the Jats.[12] Childhood betrothals are settled while the parties to them are infants or small children (and, clearly, highly unlikely to be able to speak up effectively). Muslims may look first amongst their kin for an appropriate bride for their son. A girl's aunt (particularly her father's sister or her mother's sister) or uncle (usually the father's brother rather than the mother's brother) may indeed speak up while both children are small. The girl's parents may be loathe to settle anything so soon, for a better proposal might come for their girl later – but they may also find it hard to refuse the request.

My parents decided my marriage. Since my childhood my uncle [FeB] had insistently said I would be married to his son. I was 15–16 when I was married. My uncle owned the same amount of land as us. They're our own people. That's why my parents didn't consider anyone else. My father's sister was the go-between. She organized the engagement when I was a child – that was why there were no other proposals for me. Since my uncle's son was all right, what was the need to consider any other boy? If a marriage is arranged in childhood, but the boy turns out bad, his habits are not good or he does not earn properly, then a childhood arrangement can be broken. People don't marry their girls to bad boys. The girl's opinion is not asked, though. And, in the face of her parents'

---

[12] One Jat woman – Omkari, J17 – was married at the age of nine, but this was not a long betrothal: she and her brother were both married quickly because her mother was seriously ill.

wishes, a girl can't say anything. (Farzana w/o Fiazuddin, S4, born and married within Qaziwala)

When I was 3–4 years old, my mother-in-law [also her FBW] asked for me, in my childhood itself. That's why no proposals came from anywhere else at all. The decision was made by my father's brothers, since my mother-in-law asked for me so persistently. With us, the parents don't decide a match, the uncles do. And they just looked among the black and the yellow [both bad colours, implying ugly]. My opinion wasn't asked. If it had been I wouldn't have been married here! I would have refused. I wanted to be married into a good place, where I wouldn't have had to cut sugarcane or bring back the cane tops for fuel. (Amna w/o Ali, S1, born and married within Qaziwala)

Childhood betrothals may take place at some distance, though there was none among the Qaziwala women in the sample. But we know of instances from Qaziwala and from Jhakri (where we had worked previously) of childhood betrothals taking place between a boy and girl in different villages, generally the children of two sisters or of a brother and sister. Occasionally, too, a childhood betrothal takes place within the village between people who have no prior close kinship:

When I was born, my mother-in-law said, 'This girl is mine, if she lives.' She told my parents that she needed me. But then she died a week before her oldest son was married, and to fulfil her wish I was married to the second son. That was the only proposal, because the matter was settled in my childhood and everyone knew that it had already been decided. Mine was a childhood decision. (Hasina w/o Hasan, S6, born and married within Qaziwala)

Even where there was no childhood betrothal, though, women born and married within Qaziwala all reported having had no more say in the decisions about whom they would marry and how far away from their natal home they would live out their adult lives than did their neighbours married at a distance. As we indicate below, however, marriage distance does seem to have a bearing on women's lives after marriage.

Making a second marriage: the bought bride

Men with some inadequacy – especially when not offset by wealth – may be able to marry only if they purchase a bride (*bahū mol-lenā*). Two of our sample women – one each from Nangal and Qaziwala – had been bought. Each woman had been married before. Sabra's husband, Sultan was a widower, and Muni's husband, Munesh, was 45 and still single.[13] These two women are typical of others we know in such a marriage.[14]

[13] We discuss the reasons for older Jat men remaining unmarried in Chapter 6.
[14] For more examples of the effects of being a bought bride, see P. Jeffery et al. 1989; P. Jeffery and R. Jeffery 1996.

They had no more control over their destiny than other married women: in each case, a go-between decided the match, received the payment, and transferred the woman to her new husband.

Sabra is from Bihar and was first married when she was 13 or 14 to a husband selected for her in her childhood. He died three or four years later, and Sabra's first daughter was born shortly after he died. Sabra stayed with her parents for more than a year, and found her life there more and more difficult, frequently getting into arguments with her parents. Then her cousin (FBS) said he knew of a potential husband. Sultan arrived at Sabra's house with five or six men, paid the cousin who was acting as go-between Rs 1,000, and took Sabra away with him three days later. Sabra did not object, because she was pleased to be free from the fight with her parents.

Muni's case – perhaps an extreme one – demonstrates how hard it is for a woman to sustain an attempt to be an independent agent in sexual matters, even if she is prepared to leave an unsatisfactory marriage. Muni came from a poor peasant family, and went only briefly to the local school. When she was about 18 her father married her some 30 km away, with a very difficult journey to reach her natal village. Muni was very unhappy because her mother-in-law and her husband used to beat her without any reason apparent to her. Eventually she ran away. She could not get to her parents' house because it was too distant, so she walked to the house where one of her cousins had been married. Her cousin's husband took her in, but within a few days he was visited by Munesh from Nangal. They started talking about Muni, and Munesh offered to pay Rs 2,000 for her. Muni was sent straight off with Munesh. Despite her act of defiance, she had been unable to decide her own future:

I absolutely did not want this to happen. I said my *jījā* [cousin's husband] should tell my parents, but he didn't listen to a single thing I said. He just compelled me to go with this man. It was only 3–4 days after I'd arrived at my *jījā's* house. My husband's younger brother was married long ago. My husband himself was very old and I'm much younger than him. I'm younger even than my husband's younger brother's wife! Her children are plenty big enough and one of her girls has already been married. When my parents found out, they were very angry with my *jījā* and my mother came to meet me here. (Muni w/o Munesh, J21, uneducated, middle peasant)

Shame and exclusion from marriage decisions

There are several difficulties in the way of women having a meaningful say in the arrangement of their marriages. The first is the consequences they would face if they did try to speak up. Women are afraid of the shame and embarrassment they would feel if they took a direct interest in such an explicitly sexual matter. Amongst the Jats, Sheela (J23) said that she was totally tongue-tied on the subject, and Pushpa (J13) said she was too embarrassed even to be involved in choosing the dowry clothes and jewellery. Parents may feel very strongly that their daughter's silence is a sign both of her good upbringing and her faith in their judgement.

More generally, a girl fears that her reputation will be so badly affected by any mistake she makes during the marriage arrangements, that she might just make matters worse.

If any girl even said that she didn't like the boy, then people in the village would say she's bad, she's speaking up herself, she has a bad character, she must have set eyes on some other boy and that's why she's refusing to do as her parents have decided. (Hasina w/o Hasan, S6, Islamic schooling, born and married in Qaziwala)

My opinion wasn't asked, and I won't ask my own children either. I didn't know when my marriage was arranged but when they talked about it in the house I began to hear and that's how I knew. (Naima w/o Nizamuddin, S13, no schooling, married 42 km from her natal village)

NEIGHBOUR: 'If a girl's opinion is sought, people will say that this girl is likely to run away!'

Even if a girl wants to influence her marriage, she may only learn that a marriage is being negotiated when it is too late to withdraw without a scandal. Several women, including some educated ones, had been unaware that their marriage was being arranged: the men of the household had not mentioned it in the girl's earshot. Indeed, some women reported that their mother had no more say in what was arranged than they had. Young women (and also most young men) can easily be excluded from the decision, if they do not know that the matter is being discussed, and several women said that their father (or whoever was making the arrangements) would not say anything about it when he came home, until everything was agreed. Even then, many women were not given many details about their future husbands, or when they were to be married, but had to gather what was in store for them from chance overheard discussions.

Marriage arrangements and the role of other kin

Marriage arrangement is certainly not a matter for the bride and groom; it is not necessarily just a matter for their parents, though normally it is their task to arrange their children's marriages. The wider community – the village, the lineage (_khāndān_) or other kin (_rishtedār_) also have rights which can over-rule the wishes of a girl and her parents. A father's illness may mean that other relatives deputize, an elderly grandparent may pressurize parents into arranging an early marriage for their children or the constraints of a large joint family may remove decisions from the girl's parents:

When I was in the 10th class at school I was already 18 or 19 years old, and people in villages think that is old enough. Also my grandfather wanted me to marry, and he was the oldest in the house, so his wishes had to be observed. In any case, my father had lost both legs in a train accident some years before, so he wasn't capable of arranging my marriage. (Asha w/o Ajay, J5, 10th class schooling, married 55 km from her natal village)

Buri's mother explained how Buri's marriage was arranged:

My daughter's marriage was arranged by my brother-in-law (HyB). I didn't want her married in Qaziwala, I wanted to accept an offer from Burhanuddinpur. But nobody listened to me and my brother-in-law's opinion prevailed.
(Q: Did your husband not say anything?)
He said nothing at all, he just does his farming and doesn't know anything else, he doesn't say anything about any other matter. He is very straightforward. We were still living jointly with my brothers-in-law when Gulshan was married, and the younger one did all the arrangements. (Buri w/o Bundu, S3, Qur'anic schooling, born and married in Qaziwala)

My parents wanted a boy from a small family and they wanted someone handsome for me. But it wasn't like that. My father's father forced them to do this marriage – even though my father and brother had seen the boy and didn't like him [his face is pock-marked]. My grandfather said that he'd given his word to the boy's people and he couldn't break it. He told my father that he could get my sisters married as he liked, but that I had to be married here. (Kelo w/o Kapil, J14, no schooling, married 9 km from her natal village)

Sometimes a girl's father even takes the decision over the objections of those whose advice he is expected to heed – like that of his brothers or parents, who might know about the character or situation of the potential groom or his family.

The decision was my father's. He didn't listen to anything my mother said to him. My father is very moody and does whatever comes into his mind. He doesn't listen to anyone at all. He had other offers for me from Qaziwala, as well as ones from elsewhere. My uncles [FeB and FyB] all objected to me being married here, because they knew my mother-in-law's character. That was why they wouldn't agree. But my father took no notice of anyone's comments. Would he have listened to my mother, if he wouldn't even listen to my grandmother? (Gulshan w/o Ghalib, S5, born and married in Qaziwala)

The decision about my marriage was done by both my parents. There was no previous relationship and I don't know who the go-between was . . . My father is very straightforward. Having given his word he went home and said he'd arranged my marriage. Then for a while all his relatives ostracized him, because he had made the engagement without telling them, and I wasn't to be married to a relative. All my other sisters have been married within our kin group (*rishtedāri*). (Yasmin w/o Yusuf, S22, married 25 km from her natal village)

Despite differences in the ways in which Jats and Sheikhs arrange the marriages of their children, then, all the women were excluded from taking a role in the selection of their own spouse. At most they might make a small input into the timing of the marriage. In exceptional circumstances a girl might be able to express her opinion – though to little avail.

My father did not want to get me married because I had TB in my neck and seeing this illness he refused to have me married. But he also used to think, what would happen to me if he died? One offer came from Soojru – that house was very good, there was land and animals, but my father did not do the marriage because I was weak and ill and I would not have been able to do so much work. No other offers came because no one wanted to arrange a marriage with me because of my illness. Then a neighbour was a go-between for an offer from my husband. She told my father that he had said that he would not make me work hard, so my father found the offer acceptable. When the marriage date was being settled and a ring was being sent to the boy, I cried a lot, I was very troubled by my illness. I asked my father not to arrange my marriage and said I would stay at home and look after my parents. But my father said 'Daughter, after I die, who will there be of yours? You have one brother and he will be tied to his wife and children, so you (Mehsar) where will you run around begging something to eat?' (Mehsar w/o Mahmud, S11, landless, no schooling, mother-in-law dead)

We have little evidence that young women had any significant opportunity to make a more substantial input into their own marriage negotiations. Basically, it is not for a daughter to question the decision either before or after the marriage.

Post-marital residential arrangements

For a married woman, the most important influence on her everyday existence after marriage is the household in which she lives. A woman's role in managing economic resources is determined within the household, as is her workload. Both of these are often regarded as central indices of a woman's autonomy. But to understand how a woman's fertility is limited or not, and her ability to influence this, we need to understand how a woman comes to control household finances, and under what constraints, and what work she does, within the wider context in which she lives. The key difference in household structure (from a woman's point of view) is whether she is living in a joint household (*sājhe*) with her mother-in-law or if she and her husband live separately (*alag*). (A third possibility – that her mother-in-law is dead – is in some respects similar to living separately. We discuss this situation briefly below.[15]) Within different kinds of households, control over economic resources is a key issue. Two questions then arise. What factors affect a woman's chances of being in either kind of household. Does her class or her access to her natal kin give a woman more say over her household composition, especially over whether she and her husband live separately from her parents-in-law? The second question is whether, whatever the kind of household she is living in, there is any evidence of systematic differences in women's influence over the use of economic resources, or in fertility limitation.

Living jointly

With a joint household there is this advantage, that the house continues to be built up, its progress continues. A house should only be joint. But the damage of being joint is that I cannot buy anything for my children when I want to. Every little matter and every single thing has to be told to the elders. That's all that is a bit difficult. (Anjali w/o Anil, J10, joint with her husband's aunts, rich peasant)

Being joint is good because there is no responsibility. If something is to be bought, I don't have to think about anything. Being separate brings troubles over coming and going, but there are none when you are joint. My mother-in-law does all the accounting. Whether I get to choose cloth or my mother-in-law chooses for me, she buys it all and gives it to me. (Naima w/o Nizamuddin, S13, joint with mother-in-law, poor peasant)

Most married couples expect to begin their lives together in a household shared with the husband's parents, one or more of his married brothers and their wives, and any unmarried brothers and sisters. As his younger brothers marry in their turn, and children are born, the household may grow to include twenty or more adults and children. If people cook and eat together in a joint household, they must share at least some basic interests in common. Further, the experience of collective action tends to strengthen common interests. But individual members of the household also have competing and conflicting interests, depending on their age and sex. When a woman is married, her father (or brother) ceases to control and be responsible for her; her affinal kin, especially her husband and mother-in-law take over. Because a man cannot easily monitor his wife's behaviour (he spends little time in and around the house) the older women police the behaviour of the younger. Mothers-in-law and husband's elder brothers' wives expect to be

---

[15] Patterns of residence in Bijnor are discussed more fully in P. Jeffery et al. 1989: 48–56.

obeyed. Through their marriages to hierarchically ranked men, women's interests are potentially in conflict. The newly married woman has to start at the bottom. Eventually, when she has children of her own, she will command a measure of respect; when she has a daughter-in-law of her own, she will have another married woman over whom she can exercise authority. A woman's interests are bound up with those of her husband; she has little time or incentive to be 'sisterly' with new brides as they come into her household, or those of her husband's brothers and cousins.

Young brides do not always find that their mother-in-law is the ogre she is portrayed as in myth and song, but many young women can add their own mite to the folklore. Older women often told us of being beaten by their mothers-in-law, and younger women mentioned that their husband's violence towards them was encouraged by his mother. To call a woman *susrī* (mother-in-law) is an insult. If the mother-in-law is not around, other women will police the daughter-in-law's behaviour. She is watched, and cannot do or say anything unusual without fearing that at some point it will be reported to her domestic authorities. Her female neighbours may store up examples of unacceptable behaviour, and taunt her in-laws if she is not beaten. A man who does not beat his wife is said to have let her 'sit on his head'. Only if there is a threat to life or limb might women rally round and protect an errant wife. Most of a woman's friendships created in childhood are broken when women are married, move away, and contact is curtailed. In her marital village, a young woman's movements are limited. She has little chance of finding sympathetic women and building a relationship, and the women in the marital village rarely provide strong emotional support to each other.[16]

A mother-in-law expects the new bride to help her. She may also distrust the training the bride has received from her parents, and so she teaches her (for example) how food is to be cooked and festivals celebrated. Thus, the newly married daughter-in-law usually has to negotiate her workload with her husband's mother. In a joint household, the women share a cooking-hearth and divide up the labour of cooking, cleaning, animal-work and farm-work between them. The daughter-in-law may be given mostly 'inside-' or housework, and may help to feed and water any animals; she may also help to clear up the cattle-dung and make dung-cakes for use as fuel. (In wealthier households, the picture is complicated by the use of servants.) Other 'outside-work' is mostly done by the mother-in-law and her unmarried daughters, who collect fodder and take food to the fields. But the

[16] Some women in Rajasthan maintain close contacts with other women from their natal village and married into the same village; see Lambert 1994.

outcome is not clear-cut, and some young married women do a considerable amount of outside-work, while others may not even have to do the animal-work.

In a joint household, then, a young married woman does only some of the necessary women's work. The cost to her is that she must accept her mother-in-law's authority. She has a limited scope for negotiating what she does, and she often feels that her mother-in-law and her sisters-in-law (HZ) have less, or less onerous work to do. When two women remain joint for a long period, this is usually because the younger one is willing to act the part of a demure underling, and the older woman does not abuse her authority; such households may last until broken by the death of the older woman.

Becoming separate

I lived jointly for seven years and then tensions were born and we moved here. The old house was small, we just had rush matting to divide up the rooms. My mother-in-law was very dangerous. My father-in-law refused to make the separation, but those who have no married daughter of their own do not know how to live with a daughter-in-law or understand her sorrows and pleasures. Their daughter was small then or else they would have understood about separation. We could not live together so my father-in-law had to agree. (Parveen w/o Parvez, S14, separate household, poor peasant)

I lived with my mother-in-law for five years, then my father-in-law made us separate. This was because he had taken my jewellery for my brother-in-law's wedding and then he didn't give it back, so my husband and I got very angry and we separated. My parents-in-law haven't divided the jewellery fairly between their daughters-in-law. Some have jewellery and some have nothing at all. That's not right. (Kelo w/o Kapil, J14, separate household, middle peasant)

Households easily outgrow the available physical space, or tensions within the household increase. It becomes more difficult to manage the relationships as the workload increases. Commonly, the older brothers establish separate households and their wives begin to cook separately; this may involve a physical move, but sometimes a wife will merely build a new hearth in one corner of the common courtyard. Usually, the wife of the youngest brother will continue living jointly with her mother-in-law longest, but if the wife of an elder brother has a better relationship with her mother-in-law, they may cook together. Particularly amongst the poor, where a father does not have the power that comes from his ownership of land, all the sons may move out, leaving their parents to manage on their own. When the father becomes unable to work, the sons may supply money or food. Most husbands die before their wives, and their widows may then move into a daughter-in-law's household. But overall, joint households are much less common among the poor.

Other factors may affect the length of time a woman lives in a joint household. Most obviously, if her mother-in-law is already dead, a young woman may establish a separate household as soon as she is married, or may only ever be joint with a sister-in-law. Sometimes a woman never moves to her husband's village, but stays with her own parents (usually because she has no brother to take over the land). At the other extreme, a woman who marries an only son may feel she has to remain the subordinate woman in a joint household through most of her married life. But there are also elements of choice; women can influence their residential arrangements (and are often blamed by their husbands for the collapse of a joint household).

The process of separation usually begins when another son is married. The problems of managing the collective enterprise multiply. Children's expenses – clothing, feeding and medical costs, for example – place strains on the ability of the elders to ensure equity and harmony. The younger couples begin to resent the demands made by the older ones for the costs of schooling or of marrying a nephew or niece. Usually, the first step is that the women's work is divided but the men continue to work jointly. This arrangement may last for years, but more often, especially if the father dies or is too old or poor to insist on the obedience of his sons, men's work also separates.

Whatever other factors may have been important, when the men continue to operate the land together, the outside world is generally told that disputes amongst the women made the households separate. People talk about a daughter-in-law being caught between her husband and her mother-in-law like grain being pounded between a large pestle (*masal*) and a hollowed stone in the ground used as a mortar (*okhlī*). Her best chance of escape is to establish a separate household. She may complain to her husband about his mother's treatment and ask him to press for separation. But she needs his support if she is to become separate:

My brothers-in-law beat up my husband and then we separated from my in-laws and made our house in a different place. Now my husband never criticizes me. Since we have been separate, my mother and brother come to visit me: previously, no-one at all came. Now I am separate I have freedom (*āzādī*), there is less work and I can come and go, and my parents help me. And my husband is fine, now no one incites him, and he doesn't beat me anymore. (Gulshan w/o Ghalib, S5, born and married in Qaziwala, separate household, landless)

Separations are rarely managed without hostility. The wives of brothers may fight about who is to receive which house-plots and which animals for their own use; the mother-in-law's interventions are often seen as an expression of her favouritism among her several daughters-in-law. Collaboration is also threatened because the women's interests are those of their husbands, who are themselves caught between their collective and conflicting interests. In the separation process, all the remembered or imagined examples of aggression or treachery may be made public. In rare cases, separation is achieved smoothly.

However it is managed, it may be a rapid or a long drawn-out process, with complex implications for a young married woman's work. If women's work is largely housework, the division may be simple and quick and the daughter-in-law may be freed from having to cook and clean for such large numbers. If animals are involved, however, separation may take longer and women's work will evolve slowly to a new situation. The animal-work for jointly owned draught and milk animals may be organized in common for many years, before a couple get their own milk animals. The work for draught animals may not become separate until the men's work is separated. In this kind of household division, a daughter-in-law may find that her workload is now more diverse, since she has to provide her own labour for some kinds of outside-work, and can no longer expect other women to do it for her.

Separation is not, however, simply a question of content and quantity of work: it also marks a change in relationships of power and authority, mostly to a young married woman's benefit. When she is separate, she cannot necessarily avoid her mother-in-law's criticisms but she can say, 'What's it to do with her, now we are separate?' Such a woman has more scope to negotiate aspects of her everyday life. As Parveen (S14) put it: 'Being separate gives me freedom – I can get up in the morning and go to bed when I like.' Her mother-in-law may still watch her comings and goings, but she can now come and go without needing to seek permission at every turn. Her cooking is now determined only by the preferences of her husband and children, not those of his relatives.

On the other hand, separation also brings some costs. The daughter-in-law who is separate is now the only adult woman in her household and is entirely responsible for her work. In a crisis, the position of a woman who separated under a cloud is much worse than that of a woman whose separation was amicable. A mother-in-law is by far the most likely source of emergency help for a young married woman. Even in less dramatic situations, for example when a woman wants to visit her parents, her mother-in-law is the most likely person to be willing to take over animal-work and the feeding of her husband. But even a friendly mother-in-law will not tolerate excessive requests for leave. Other women have their own work and cannot be expected to rally round. Once a woman is separate, then, she may not only lose potential help with her work on a daily basis, but she also cannot so easily find the help she needs if she is to visit her own kin. The benefits of reducing the significance of her mother-in-law's discipline have to be weighed against the strengthening of the ties which bind her to her in-laws' village.

Household types among the Jats and the Sheikhs

These processes of household formation and dissolution create a fairly limited range of household structures in north Indian villages, and allow for a number of generalizations. Table 4.2 shows the results of a 'woman-centred' classification of households. For women who have been cohabiting more than 20 years, the picture is complicated by the fact that women increasingly have daughters-in-law of their own, so we have excluded them from the analysis that follows. If we consider women who began cohabiting between 1970 and 1989 in the two populations we can see that far fewer Sheikh women are living jointly with their mother-in-law: 34 per cent overall, compared with 55 per cent of the Jat women.

The picture changes somewhat if we control for length of marriage and for class. Thus 44 per cent of the younger Sheikh women (beginning cohabitation between 1980 and 1989), but 66 per cent of the younger Jat women are 'joint'. Most of this difference can be understood as a result of the different class structures among the two populations. Class is important in both villages: as we would expect, women married into wealthier households are more likely to live in a joint household. Holding class constant, the differences between the women in the two populations reduce: 45 per cent of rich and middle peasant Sheikhs are in joint households, compared with 58 per cent of similar Jats; and 29 per cent of poor peasant and landless Sheikhs, compared with 39 per cent of similar Jats. The mothers-in-law of the poorer Jat women are also more likely to have died: 48 per cent of the poorer women are 'alone', compared with 19 per cent of the wealthier women. No such differences show up for the Sheikhs, though in both populations the proportion of women 'alone' is, not surprisingly, higher for those who started cohabiting in the 1970s than for those who started in the 1980s.

Access to the natal kin

A married woman has few chances to get help from her parents, and must find her own ways of making out within her marital home. But her links with her natal kin are not entirely cut off. Her parents may be able to offer a space for her to act out of the control of her in-laws. They may

Table 4.2. *Household patterns in 1990–1 amongst Jat women in Nangal and Sheikh women in Qaziwala beginning to cohabit between 1970 and 1989*

		Household type				
		Joint	Separate	Alone	Other	N
Jat women						
Class:	Upper	58%	12%	19%	10%	115
	Lower	39%	13%	48%	0%	23
Cohabitation year:	1970–79	36%	22%	34%	8%	50
	1980–89	66%	7%	18%	9%	88
Marriage distance:	Near	62%	8%	20%	10%	71
	Rest	48%	16%	28%	7%	67
All:		55%	12%	24%	9%	138
Sheikh women						
Class:	Upper	45%	14%	29%	13%	56
	Lower	29%	39%	24%	8%	108
Cohabitation year:	1970–79	23%	32%	34%	10%	77
	1980–89	44%	29%	18%	9%	87
Marriage distance:	Near	32%	34%	20%	14%	74
	Rest	36%	28%	30%	7%	90
All:		34%	30%	26%	10%	164

Note: 'Upper class' includes landlords, rich peasants, and middle peasants; 'lower class' consists of poor peasants and landless households. 'Near marriages' were less than 25 km distant for Jat women, and less than 3 km distant for Sheikh women. 'Joint' households are ones where the woman shares cooking arrangements with her mother-in-law. If a woman has separate cooking facilities from her mother-in-law she is classified as 'separate'; and if her mother-in-law is dead she is classified as 'alone'. Most 'other' women are sharing cooking arrangements with a sister-in-law (HBW).

intervene with support in her disputes with her husband or parents-in-law. More often, if they can afford it, they may provide economic support, either through major loans for house-building or agricultural purposes, or through a supply of subsistence goods – wheat and rice after the harvests, or small sums of cash which may be all that a woman can regard as her own. To what extent does good access to her parents give a woman more say in her everyday life?

Post-marital relationships between a woman and her natal and her affinal kin are highly structured. Jat and Sheikh women alike should observe a variety of modesty practices with respect to their husband's male elder kin (his father, elder brothers, uncles and older cousins) whereas they can behave with much more freedom in the presence of their own kin. The easiest way to handle this is for both sets of kin to be separate, so a young woman has one kind of behaviour in her natal village – relative freedom of movement and action – and another when she is at her home with her in-laws. A woman in her affinal village is under the scrutiny of her affinal kin; her behaviour in her natal village is normally very different. For Jats, indeed, the two sets of kin should be completely separate. By contrast, Sheikh women for whom their natal village and affinal village are the same experience considerable difficulty in working out ways to behave.

In Dyson and Moore's analysis of female autonomy, the north Indian woman's difficulties in accessing her natal kin are seen as an important subsidiary contribution to her low ability to act independently. The more frequent the contacts between a woman and her natal kin, the more chances she has to use their support in cases of dispute with her affinal kin. Seclusion practices and the control over a woman's mobility by her affinal kin can limit a woman's access to her natal kin and leave her to the mercy of her husband and his relatives. In such a system of marriage and kinship, with control over household resources firmly in the hands of men (and, to a much lesser extent, older women), a young married woman does not have direct access to these resources; since her work may receive little recognition either, she may appear to have little opportunity to be an active agent.

Yet a woman is reckoned to have the right (in certain circumstances) to visit her natal kin, even though there may be tensions over when she can go, and how long she may stay.[17] A young married woman needs permission from her husband and (usually) her mother-in-law before she can undertake any trip outside her marital village. In negotiating visits to her parents' home, her position is strengthened if some relative (normally her brother) has come to fetch her, and if there are life-cycle ceremonies (a wedding, the celebrations for a new baby, or a death) for her to attend. A young Jat woman is also likely to be allowed to visit her parents at the celebration of Tīj, held mid-way through the monsoon each year. Physical distance is an important consideration. If a Sheikh woman's parents live in the same village, visits may be made on a daily basis without prior permission. If the parents live within a half hour walk, a young woman may only need a chaperon to be able to visit and return within the day. But these are not visits by inalienable right: we came across some women married within Qaziwala and into related households who had been prevented from visiting their natal kin for long periods of time.

A woman can use her access to her natal kin as a weapon to further her interests as she sees them. Private space, social and psychological support, or gifts and loans from her parents can all help her in these

---

[17] We have discussed these issues elsewhere in more detail: see P. Jeffery et al. 1988a, 1989.

strategies. But sometimes, her in-laws may treat a woman like a pawn, since she can be seen as a hostage whose safety may be conditional on her parents' meeting financial demands from her in-laws. But a woman's parents have some moral authority as well, and a man usually tries to keep his in-laws in the dark about domestic disputes in order to avoid being called to task for his behaviour, which might threaten his access to financial resources. A woman's parents are often the first place a couple will turn to if they have some kinds of exceptional expenditure – such as medical expenses for the wife or children, or for schooling, or to take advantage of an opportunity to buy some land. The woman herself rarely acts as more than a conduit for such transfers, but clearly, her access to her parents gives a potential for at least defensive action on her part, as well as space for doing in private what is forbidden in her in-laws' home, where she is rarely out of their sight.

A woman is, then, potentially able to exploit her contacts with her natal kin. She does not stop being a daughter once she is someone's bride or daughter-in-law. But there are strong limits on how far her parents can help her. The hegemony of ideas about a wife's proper behaviour clearly restricts women's options. A woman's parents may support the more lenient aspects of these ideas because of their fondness for their daughter, but they may want to apply harsher views to their own daughters-in-law. Thus a woman's parents may make only a limited contribution to her freedom of action, and she is still dependent on others to help her rather than able to act on her own account. As we will see in what follows, relationships with natal kin are not clear cut in their consequences.

Her natal kin are potentially available to (almost) every woman, though there are variations. In addition to the issue of whether her parents are still alive, physical distance intervenes, though 'distance' means somewhat different things to women in different classes and household structures.[18] In north India, Muslim women have the most varied experiences, because some are married within their natal village, while others are married much more distantly; and some women are married to a cousin, while others are married into unfamiliar house-holds. In what follows, then, we have made particular comparisons among the Sheikhs, though we also consider the significance of marriage distance for the Jats, and the cases of women who are described as 'bought brides'.

Jat women are almost all married too far away for easy daily visiting to take place, but even so some of them are able to call upon substantial funds from their parents.

---

[18] Some of these differences are explored in P. Jeffery and R. Jeffery 1996.

When I go to my parents they give me clothes for the children and a sari and they also give Rs 100–200. . . They give me the money because the children's education costs a lot and our income is not enough. (Vinod w/o Vijay, J16, separate household, middle peasant, married 22 km away)

These gifts began as an attempt to protect Vinod from possible serious trouble with her in-laws over her illnesses after her marriage:

After I was married, I began to suffer from possession (*kuch ūpar*) and some people in my in-laws' village began saying that he [Vijay] would make another marriage. Several people at my parents' home, especially my oldest brother's wife, said that I was entitled to a share there and so I should be helped. My father and brother also thought that if he abandoned me, all the expenses of my marriage and the dowry would have been wasted and my life would have been spoilt too. So, fearing that, my parents paid out Rs 2,000–3,000 on my illness. I had become so weak that my first child was born only after seven or eight years. My mother was still paying for my treatment when I was pregnant for the first time. I was very weak and she said she would feed me up but the doctor said that I had to have treatment, so my mother paid for that. Every month, Rs 100 of medicines came for me. My mother-in-law is very miserly, so when my first son was born, my people did not send many gifts. They were angry with my husband's parents because they had been taunting me about my illness and then about my treatment. My brother asked why they should give much and said that he would help only me in future. While I was joint with my mother-in-law, all the things from my parents remained with her, but now that I'm separate I keep everything myself. (Vinod w/o Vijay, J16, uneducated, middle peasant)

Jats never arrange marriages within the village, then, nor do they routinely build upon existing kinship links. Even so, the possibility of reasonably easy access is one consideration which Jat fathers take into account. In general, however, when Jat women do visit their natal villages they are able to escape the surveillance of their in-laws almost completely. For the wealthier Jat women, their access to their parents can be turned to good account in situations of crisis, but their parents cannot be available to them in a routine way.

Many Sheikhs are ambivalent about close marriages, ones within the village or in a neighbouring village. Matters are seen slightly differently by men and by women. For women, some benefits of a close marriage are clear: it is possible to keep up regular contact with their parents and brothers (and sisters, if they have also been married close). News of births, illnesses and deaths travels fast. A woman can visit her own family and be back the same day, giving her husband no cause to complain of missed meals or other domestic comforts. She can be visited even by her mother and sisters, who have no problems travelling within a village or only a short distance away. Indeed, on several occasions, we interviewed within-village married women at their mother's house, having failed to find them at their marital home. In cases of trouble (illness, or accidents to children etc.) a woman can quickly get help from her father, mother or brothers.

But women also see drawbacks to being close at hand. Being too close can mean that marital disputes spread and cause unhappiness to a woman's parents. The norms against a woman's parents' intervening may be very strong:

If I have any fight with my in-laws, no-one from my natal home can say anything. If they ever get to hear that I am fighting with my sister-in-law (HeBW) they don't even walk past my house. My sisters don't come to visit. My cousin (FeBS) was married in Qaziwala and there was fighting every day in the alleys of that part of the village, because the girl's parents used to speak up. But that's the work of dishonourable people, to fight like that. (Hasina w/o Hasan, S6, born and married within Qaziwala)

Furthermore, a woman may find it difficult ever to go and stay at her parents' house, to get some rest from her everyday responsibilities, since she can be called back easily by her husband. A married woman going some distance to see her parents gets treated very well, since she comes so rarely; a woman who goes every other day rarely even gets a meal from her parents. These problems are compounded the nearer a woman's parents are. In particular, a woman married within the village has to cope with the contrasting expectations about how she should behave, having to decide whether she can come and go freely, or must show extra respect to older men and women she has known since infancy, perhaps as kin. In practice, she is likely to lose much of the freedom of behaviour she was used to, if her natal village is also her marital village. Thus women often say they prefer to be married a little distance away, rather than within their natal village itself.

For most men, the benefits from a distant marriage normally outweigh the disadvantages. The benefits are cast in terms of a man being able to rule over his wife in his own way, without having to worry about how his parents-in-law might react. By contrast, the benefits of a marriage within the village are few. A man appreciates the financial advantages of easy access to his in-laws: help with illness expenses, regular gifts of grain, and possibly help over work, and going to see them is quick and cheap. But the drawbacks are much greater. He no longer receives the respect of his in-laws when he visits them, since it is an everyday affair. More importantly, he feels that his in-laws are potentially watching how he treats his wife, and he would prefer the freedom to deal with her without such constraints.

Sheikh women in our sample who were married within Qaziwala are certainly happy to have the benefits of immediate access to their parents and other natal kin. In general, they stress the emotional benefits of being regularly in touch with the news from their parents, and being easily able to come and go. Some of them also derive financial benefits. In times of financial stress, natal kin can easily lend or give money to a woman. Gulshan (S5) was prevented from visiting her parents while she was joint with her mother-in-law, but now they are separate she goes every day and brings whatever she needs from there. Buri (S2) spends most of her time with her mother, and even gets her dung-cakes for cooking fuel from her mother. And when Mehsar (S11) said she thought marriages ought to be arranged more distantly, her mother pointed out that she was stupid in ignoring the benefits: her children often eat at their grandmother's, and Mehsar herself comes whenever she likes and always gets something tasty to eat. Others go less frequently, and if they have no need for help they may be given no more than the token amounts handed out on festivals. Too frequent visits can raise the jealousy of a woman's brothers' wives.

Although financial support from the wife's parents is welcome, it is also slightly embarrassing, since the husband should be in a position to look after all the expenses of his household.

(BURI): I get the appropriate gifts on Eid, as well as grain from my parents every harvest.

(BURI'S MOTHER): When Buri's house was being built I also gave her Rs 2,000. We're helping Buri because she has shortages. My husband's brother also used to give grain every year, because he arranged her marriage, but it's a long time ago now so he's stopped. One time when Buri was pregnant she was very ill. She became unconscious after a penicillin injection and she went out of her mind. She was ill for six months, she was shown to doctors and also got *tāwīz* (amulets) . . . When we got treatment from the *hakīm* (Unani doctor) in Inampura, it cost Rs 6,000 and all of this expense was met by Buri's brother. Later her husband gave the money back. (Buri w/o Bundu, S2, born in Qaziwala, separate household, landless peasant)

There is also ambivalence by daughters over asking for financial help. Although 'dowry demands' are less common among the Sheikhs than among the Jats, women were quick to deny that there was any 'demand' from their in-laws that they ask their parents for money. Hasina (S6) married within Qaziwala, listed all the various gifts which came to her at festivals, on the births of her children and when her brother was married, and then said, 'All this is given by my parents according to their capability. No one makes any demands. If my mother wants to give, then she gives, but if not she doesn't give. We married sisters can't ask for anything.'

But in any case, the money coming from her natal kin cannot give a woman any long-term economic independence in rural Bijnor. A woman's access to her parents' financial help is normally only available while her father is alive. She has no effective rights to long-term benefits that might come from land-ownership, unless she has no brothers. She may be asked by her brothers to renounce her formal, legal claims in her father's land, but normally she is never asked: by the time the land is divided she will be seen as part of her husband's household, having no claims on that of her parents. Although a woman's kin offer some resources in the invisible world of negotiations about the balance of power within the household, this does not seem sufficient to outweigh either her long-term economic dependence on her husband or her day-to-day subordination to the financial power wielded by the elders in a joint household. We now turn to see whether the amorphous resources provided by her parents have any impact on a woman's ability to control her everyday living arrangements, or her fertility.

There are some differences in household structure between women married closely and those married at a distance. Of Jat women who began cohabiting between 1970 and 1989, 62 per cent of those married less than 25 km from their parents, but only 48 per cent of those married further away, were 'joint'. Among the Sheikhs, 32 per cent of those married less than 3 km from their parents, and 36 per cent of those married further away, were joint with their mother-in-law. Taking class into account, and considering only the women in the richer households (middle peasants and above), in both populations women married closer to their natal homes are *more* likely to be living jointly. For Nangal, the figures are 62 per cent of those married less than 25 km, and 54 per cent for those married further from their natal home. In Qaziwala, of those married less than 3 km from their natal homes, 54 per cent are in joint households, compared with only 36 per cent of those married further away.[19] There are too few Jats in poor peasant and landless households for comparisons to be worthwhile, but among the Sheikhs, the pattern is reversed: 20 per cent of those married closely (less than 3 km) are in joint households, compared to 36 per cent of those married more distantly. However, the women in this category show a very skewed age distribution, and the differences for those who began cohabiting in the 1980s are much smaller – 35 per cent of those married closely are in joint households, and 42 per cent of those married more distantly.

On the face of it, then, women married close amongst the Sheikhs are slightly more likely to be living in a joint household than women married further away among the rich and middle peasant households, but the

---

[19] We consider the differences between schooled and unschooled women in the next chapter.

reverse is the case for women in poor peasant and landless households. Jat patterns among the wealthier households are like those among wealthier Sheikh households. We can do no more than speculate about possible reasons for these patterns. It may be that women whose parents are accessible are better able to negotiate living and working conditions in joint households than those women who have less support from their parents. Such an interpretation would take account of the reverse situation among the poor, where a woman's parents are less likely to be able to use financial aid to assist their daughter, no matter how closely they are married. But it would be foolish to read too much into these differences, since small numbers of women are involved. It would be more reasonable to conclude that we have no evidence that Sheikh women married close to their natal homes – the women who we would have predicted to have more 'autonomy' – show any significant differences in living patterns from those married further away, once class and length of marriage have been taken into account.

Control over economic resources

Not one of the married women we interviewed was employed – they were all family workers, for the most part concentrating their work efforts in the house, and possibly around the cattle byre. None of them had any formal title to land or other property. What room, if any, do such women have for controlling the household's resources? If they do not control resources, how far can they be said to manage them, or do they merely implement subsistence budgetary strategies?[20] As with so many other aspects of a young married woman's life, a key element is the structure of the household (*chūlhā*, or hearth) in which the woman lives. Other key constraints on gender relationships include class, and the role played by gifts from the woman's natal kin.

When a young married woman lives in a household with an older woman or women (generally her mother-in-law, and sometimes another woman such as her husband's older brother's wife), the senior man normally takes charge of the agricultural activities and the senior woman normally takes charge of the domestic financial matters. If milk or *ghī* are sold by the household, for example, the income is controlled by the older woman. She also organizes the household's exchange (*len-den*) relationships when weddings and births take place, and she ensures that food and clothing for the immediate household are bought when necessary. The farming income is organized by the menfolk (her own

[20] For a discussion of the differences between these concepts in the Indian context, see Standing 1991.

husband and/or her son) and even the older women may have to ask the men for spending money for routine expenses and for other expenditures incurred (as when a marriage takes place).

Young women in such households regard only the items they receive from their own parents as their own income (*āmdanī*), and even there, their control is not necessarily absolute. Generally, the daughter-in-law hands over foodstuffs and earmarked items of clothing to the mother-in-law who uses the food in the household at large and passes on the clothing to the individuals designated. The daughter-in-law retains the cash and clothing – a sari or two, maybe Rs 10 or Rs 50 – that her parents have presented specifically to her. What remains with the younger woman is clearly incapable of providing her with economic independence. She would normally need to ask her husband or other members of her household for money over and above what her parents provide. If loans or larger gifts are given by her parents the young woman may help in the negotiations but does not control the transfer of resources or their expenditure.

There is only one mother-in-law and my husband is an only son. He has no older or younger brothers and his father is also dead. So from whom could I become separate? If there were sisters-in-law (HBW) then we'd see. I don't have any income of my own. When there is spare milk, we sell milk or *ghī* and that income remains in my mother-in-law's pocket alone. Since she's still alive, she keeps the income. Mother and son keep all the income and they alone make the expenditures. I have no involvement (*matlab*), whatever they do. I give the money that comes from my parents to my husband. The things that are for eating and drinking just get consumed in the house. (Ujala w/o Uday, J4, 10th class pass, middle peasant, joint household)

I have no special income of my own. My mother-in-law sells *ghī* and that income remains in her pocket. Whatever money comes from my parents, that alone is my income. The clothes and the money from my parents remain with me. When I bring foodstuffs from my parents' house, I just put them in the house and they get eaten up. My mother-in-law organizes the *len-den* for the house. My husband has also set up a flour mill separately from his father and its income and expenses are his. (Shalu w/o Sher Singh, J22, uneducated, middle peasant, joint household)

I have no income. Any money remains in my mother-in-law's hands. If I have any need, I get money from my mother-in-law or my husband. My husband runs a flour mill separately, he runs it at night. But he also helps with the farming. (Farmudan w/o Fida Husain, S3, middle peasant, joint household)

Once in a household in which she is the oldest or only adult woman (because her mother-in-law has died, or because the households have become separate at least for consumption purposes), a woman can gain somewhat more control over the domestic finances. If milk or *ghī* are sold, she will usually manage the income. If she spins cotton, she will keep the payments. But all these are fairly trivial sources of income. Spinning in particular involves a great deal of work for very little return.

I used to spin, but not these days. I do it for the cloth, not for the money – if I get cloth, it seems as though it's free. My husband puts all his money into my hands. Whether I use it rightly or wrongly [black or white], whether I spend it all or not, he never says anything. (Buri w/o Bundu, S2, landless, separate household)

I spin and I also sell cow-dung cakes, and I sell half the milk from our buffalo and keep half for my children. All the money comes into my hands. Whatever work he gets, what he earns also comes to me. I do all the accounts, he's got no head for figures. He even asks me for money for *bīrī* (country cigarettes). He is a straightforward man – even if he gives me nine rupees and I make one hundred rupees, or he gives me a hundred rupees and I make nine, he doesn't complain. (Kausar w/o Khurshid, S9, landless, separate household)

I have no worries about money. I sell milk from my buffalo once a day and the other time we keep it for the house. All the money remains in my pocket. If I ever spin, my husband becomes angry and forbids me, saying 'What's the need for you to do this work? There's no need for so much effort. What, is there a shortage of money? You should pick up the spinning wheel and throw it away!' (Farzana w/o Fiazuddin, S4, middle peasant, mother-in-law dead)

The money that belongs to my husband and me is all kept in the same place. My husband gives me the money he gets from farming and whoever needs it goes and spends it. My husband has opened an account in his own name in Bijnor. (Sheela w/o Sushil, J 23, middle peasant, mother-in-law dead)

A woman in a separate household organizes the exchange relationships and retains control over virtually everything that she receives from her parents. But this situation should not be read as one in which she has much economic independence. The incomes that she handles are small and the bulk of the household finances will probably still rest with her husband. The farming income is normally managed by him. Small sums may be stored in the house for safekeeping, but that does not permit the woman to spend it freely. Large sums will probably be deposited in the bank, in the husband's name. Generally, he deals with larger-scale financial matters (payment of school fees, agricultural equipment) and she requests spending money for smaller-scale purchases of foodstuffs. Her position as supplicant is compounded by the need to spend these sums wisely, on goods for the benefit of the household as a whole. Most women still rely on their parents to provide some of their clothing (at the Holi and Tījo festivals for Jats, and at the Eid festivals for Sheikhs) and would not normally spend much household money on buying clothing for themselves. Nevertheless, women in such households generally consider that they can influence financial matters in ways that are denied them in joint households, since they have to express their priorities and negotiate their wants only with their husband, not with his male elders or his mother as well.

My mother-in-law died when my husband was still a child, so at first I lived jointly with his older brother's wife. I became separate three years later. That was my decision, because I had to do all the work and my sister-in-law fought with me a lot. So to escape the fighting I became separate. He didn't want to become separate but on my say-so we did. I don't sell milk, but if there's more *ghī* than we need, I sell that and keep the income. My husband also keeps the income from the land and grain with me. All the things that come from my parents remain with me and I do the exchanges for the house. After we became separate, my father sent me an American [sic] cow for our own use. When we were joint, I had to do all the work for my sister-in-law's entire family – that was a lot of people and a lot of work. And I wasn't able to save up any money for ourselves separately. Now we're separate and we're saving for our own future – that will be useful for our children. (Dholi w/o Dharmpal, J20, uneducated, middle peasant, separate household)

We have no evidence that women with better access to their natal kin (in the sense of being married more closely or into a familiar household) have more control over economic resources, or are better able to influence major economic decisions, than are other women. Distance seems to be less important than the particular circumstances of need (on the part of the daughter or sister and her husband's family) and ability to contribute (on the part of her father or brothers). If these two mesh, then considerations of distance or pre-existing kin links become secondary. Though help from a woman's kin is legitimately offered when needed, a household will prefer to do without it. Support from the natal kin may be very useful to a woman trying to affect how money is spent or whether or not to separate her household, but it seems unlikely that marriage distance *per se* is a major contributor to her ability to influence events within her marital household.

Reproductive choice

Many authors have argued that, if women neither own property nor control significant sources of income, they must have a very low level of autonomy. Yet despite this, and those demographers who would see a link between female autonomy and fertility, these Jat and Sheikh women have very different fertility experiences, with Jat fertility much lower than Sheikh fertility. A priori there is a case that, since Jat women have fewer children, this may be because they have been able to act to limit their fertility. But do their maternity histories really suggest that they have been 'autonomous' in fertility matters? Here we want to investigate further the opportunities for women to exercise agency in their fertility behaviour, beginning with the Jats.

Contraceptive decision-making among the Jats

In our sample of 23 women, all were in the age band 25–34 and all had at least one living son. Only two of the women (both uneducated) had as many as four children; four had three children, thirteen had two children, and four had one child. Six (five of them uneducated) had already been sterilized and a further seven (two uneducated) were using the contraceptive pill or an IUCD.

As we have already suggested, asking 'who made the decision to contracept?' is not likely to lead to a clear and reliable answer. Nevertheless, a cautious reading of our discussions with the Nangal women indicates that they rarely decided to contracept by themselves. Just one woman (Sudha, J11, uneducated, living in a middle peasant joint household with her mother-in-law and two sisters-in-law) said that she was sterilized without consulting her in-laws. She had three children and had taken pills for several years after her second delivery. She again took pills after the third child but became pregnant. She obtained an abortion and was sterilized at the same time. She said she was often unwell and wanted no more children. Her mother-in-law, however, had wanted her to have more children and her husband had opposed sterilization because he was afraid of the operation itself. When she suffered no adverse symptoms, he accepted the situation, saying that two boys and a girl were right, as he was worried about rising costs and did not have enough land for more children. Another woman (Madho, J6, educated to 10th class, living in a rich peasant joint household with her mother-in-law), reported using the Copper-T for a while. When she found it did not suit her, she then resorted to pills, which she had stopped taking when we interviewed her, partly because she felt they had disrupted her menstruation. She wanted a second child – after which she would be sterilized – but her husband and parents-in-law wanted her to stop at the one son she already had.

By contrast, Shivani (J12), whose case we reported in Chapter 3, had been sterilized while under the anaesthetic after a Caesarean delivery of a stillborn girl. According to her sister-in-law, Shivani had narrowly escaped death during the labour. Having seen her problems, Shivani's husband had willingly agreed to the operation, although he and Shivani had not previously discussed the matter and their only son had polio in one leg.

Far more common, however, is for the husband and wife to report reaching the decision about family planning together, sometimes even in the face of opposition from their elders.

I have a Copper-T but would like to have the operation. That's what my husband also thinks. But his mother will never agree – she wants me to continue having children. But we'll get the operation done. She'll be angry for a few days and then she'll be silent. I wanted the operation when I gave birth the second time but the doctor said that I was weak and should wait for a couple of years. (Shalu w/o Sher Singh, J22, uneducated, joint with mother-in-law, middle peasant)

My husband would have liked a girl, but the healer who has been treating me for possession said there was no girl in my destiny. When my husband heard that he asked what was the point in having any more children and he had my operation done. His mother did not want that but we did not listen to her. When my mother found out, she was very angry. She said that my uncle would be upset, and that we should have one girl at least. She said we shouldn't have had the operation done after only two children. (Vinod w/o Vijay, J16, uneducated, separate household, middle peasant)

Between the two children, I used various methods, sometimes condoms, sometimes pills. I did not have a Copper-T. Since the second child I've also been using condoms and pills. I haven't had the operation and nor am I going to. None of us want that, not myself or my husband, nor his parents. You see, no one knows what God's intentions may be from one second to the next. And if a child dies, what then? Because of that fear, I haven't had the operation, but I'm making other arrangements to stop having children and that is something decided by my husband and me alone. (Shamo w/o Shiv Singh, J1, MA, joint household, rich peasant)

Between the boy and the girl I'd had a stillborn boy so my husband wanted to have another son. But then I had another girl. So I had the operation done at the time I gave birth. I'd had a Copper-T after my first girl but that didn't suit so I had it taken out. The two of us took the decision about the Copper-T and the operation – we didn't ask anyone's advice. (Nirdosh w/o Navid, J3, 10th class, mother-in-law dead, middle peasant)

All these couples have decided that two or three children are enough, as long as one (and preferably two) are boys. In most instances, this was with the support of the man's parents. One of the two exceptions – the women with four children – would have preferred to stop at three. Both women are using modern contraception. Shanti (J18) has been sterilized. Omkari (J17) has a Copper-T, and, as we have seen (pp. 108–9), was insistent that her fourth child was unwanted.

Nearly all the women who were not currently contracepting planned to do so soon. The couples apparently hesitating about actively limiting their families were those with only one child: Muni (J21) whose husband refuses to allow her to be sterilized (apparently believing the operation would be a threat to her health); and Ujala (J4) who believes she is infertile because she has not conceived for so long. Only one woman (Jagvati, J15) said that it was up to God if she was to have more children, but she too wanted to stop at the three she had, and said that she would be sterilized when her husband said so.

What we know about the decision-making surrounding family limitation among the Jats of Nangal, then, gives no support to the argument that they decided by themselves to limit their fertility. Women's accounts of contraceptive decision-making reinforce our view that the husband was the active partner in the events surrounding contraception, particularly when it comes to sterilization. Jat women were able to take advantage of their husbands' desire for small families, but were rarely able to act in opposition to their husbands' views.

Sheikh fertility and non-decision-making

We have nine children and all are alive. There is no way to stop children except by sterilization and we cannot have that operation because we would not be able to say our prayers.

(SWALEHA:) But there are other ways, and if you go to the hospital, a doctor will tell you about them.

Whatever poverty there is in Qaziwala it is due to having too many children; however much one may earn, that too is too little. But in our Qur'an Sharīf the operation has been said to be bad and as we cannot say our prayers so we cannot have the operation. (Parvez h/o Parveen, S14, poor peasant)

However many children Allah gives, we'll take that many. My husband also thinks that however many there may be, that many is correct. When Allah gives, we want to take. We will not do the operation, and nor will I take pills. It is useless to 'take the blood' of children [i.e. kill by preventing them being born]. (Nur Jahan w/o Nasim, S12, two sons, poor peasant)

Many Sheikh women present themselves as having no choice in the matter of contraception, because they believe that the only method on offer – sterilization – is forbidden to them on pain of exclusion from Paradise when they die. Hostility to sterilization is nearly universal, but for many women, other methods do not attract the same moral condemnation. Thus Nur Jahan's interpretation of the Qur'anic ruling is shared with others, but they do not feel that this requires a ban on temporary methods of birth control. Parveen (S14), for example, had visited a hakīm (practitioner of Islamic medicine) to get treatment to stop her from having any more children. Another woman said:

The number of children we have is Allah's command. However much fruit He will give, that only will come. We're frightened of the operation, but pills are another matter. If you give me some, I'll take them. I want the children to be brought up properly, there's a lot of expense just in educating them. However much fruit is in our destiny will come, but the gaps can be lengthened. Muslims fear doing the operation because it's forbidden. We're not going to live here [in this world] for ever, we have to go to Allah's house. I haven't talked to my husband but he wouldn't object to pills. I'll ask my husband's advice and then go to the government dispensary in Dharmnagri. (Yasmin w/o Yusuf, S22, born 25 km away, four boys and two girls, mother-in-law dead, landless)

I have six children and I want no more, but sterilization isn't right, it's a sin. I'll take some medicine. Will you get me some? Taking medicine is easy, and my husband won't say anything. (Buri w/o Bundu, S2, married within Qaziwala, three boys and three girls, living separately from mother-in-law, landless)

What emerges from our interviews, then, is widespread willingness to consider using any methods of fertility control other than sterilization, but little ability to access them or use them consistently.

I have two boys and two girls, these are enough. I don't want any more. My husband won't let me have the operation and he says that I should take pills. After Eid [in about a week] I'll visit my sister in Jhakri and stay one or two days and get some medicine. I simply don't need any more children. You get me some medicine! (Mehsar w/o Mahmud, S11, mother-in-law dead, landless)

(KAUSAR): I don't want more children. I have four boys and one died. There's two and-a-half years between the children. In a few days I'll come to Dharmnagri and get some medicine from the doctor. I haven't taken any medicine previously. These very children are enough for labouring people like us, for feeding and clothing them is a heavy problem.
(KAUSAR'S MOTHER): Will you be sterilized?
(KAUSAR): No, I'll take medicine. My husband has no sense. I have nothing to ask him about family planning. What would he tell me? I myself will come according to my own wish and he won't say anything. (Kausar w/o Khurshid, S9, born and married within Qaziwala, living separately from her mother-in-law, landless)

Despite our presence in the dispensary compound in Dharmnagri, however, and the stimulus offered by our questioning, none of these women to our knowledge actually came to the clinic. Nor did they pursue their requests to be given medicines to stop having children. Nor did we actively offer oral pills, since we were doing our best to avoid being associated with the family planning programme. We suspect that the answers given by some of these women – that they wanted to limit their families – were a way of avoiding any presumed conflict with us, and not reflective of any determination on their part to act. Similarly, their requests for contraception may have been designed to test whether our proclaimed distance from the government programmes was genuine or not. But in the light of their maternity histories, it seems that they were indeed making little use of contraception, whether because they feared their husbands or agreed with them, or feared for their own positions in the eyes of God.

For the Sheikh women and the Jat women alike, then, evidence for women using their scope for manoeuvre to be active agents on their own account in affecting their own fertility is slim. Certainly, Jat women are apparently as constrained by their husbands' views as are Sheikh women. Furthermore, Sheikh women's inability to use contraception is arguably as much a result of the inadequacies of the Government family planning programme as it is of their own lack of agency – a point we will return to in Chapter 6.

In this chapter we have discussed several different aspects of women's scope for action. Of these, we only have evidence of variations among women in terms of their marriage distance (and that too, only for the Sheikhs) and current household type (for Jats and Sheikhs). What effect does marriage distance have on fertility among the Sheikhs? In a population (such as the Sheikhs) where a demographic transition has yet to take place, fertility differentials which arise can usually be understood in terms of unintended differences in behaviour which have the result of limiting fertility in some groups by comparison with other groups. In Qaziwala, the Sheikh women married further from their natal villages seem to have fewer children than those married more closely. Table 4.3 shows that in each of three age-cohorts, age-specific marital fertility rates are lower for women married three kilometres or more away from their natal homes. The largest differences are for women born between 1946 and 1955. Another contrast is that those married further away have had fewer children die, though the differences are small. In combination, these two processes mean that the women married close and those married distantly have much less divergent numbers of children still alive (see Table 4.4).

Both these results are surprising. In terms of the literature which guided our original research design, better access to the natal kin should give a woman more chance to affect her day-to-day existence in limiting her own fertility and protecting the health of her own children. This seems to be what is happening in the villages in Maharashtra studied by Vlassoff (1991). But in Qaziwala, the reverse seems to be the case. It seems highly unlikely that women married more distantly have more scope to negotiate over fertility and children's health because they are distant from their parents. Furthermore, they are no more likely to be living in separate households, with greater day-to-day opportunities to avoid the direct control of their parents-in-law, who may wish them to

Table 4.3. *Total marital fertility rates by year of birth and marriage distance, Sheikhs in Qaziwala*

Year of birth of mother	Mother's age at birth	Marriage distance		All women
		Less than 3 km	3 km or more	
Pre-1946	15–44	9.33	8.35	9.06
Number of women		54	22	76
Number of years at risk		1488	582	2070
1946–1955	15–34	7.41	6.67	7.07
Number of women		29	25	54
Number of years at risk		521	444	965
1956–1965	15–24	4.10	3.51	3.78
Number of women		39	41	80
Number of years at risk		288	337	625

Source: Maternity histories collected by the authors, February–March, 1991.

Table 4.4. *Survival rates to age five of children born up to 1985, and mean number of children surviving, Sheikh women, Qaziwala, by marriage distance and year of birth of mother*

Year of birth of mother	Mother's age at birth	Marriage distance		All children
		Less than 3 km	3 km or over	
Pre-1946	15–44	69%	71%	69%
Mean number of children surviving		5.89	5.23	5.70
Number of children		463	162	625
1946–1955	15–34	73%	75%	74%
Mean number of children surviving		4.55	4.28	4.43
Number of children		181	143	324
1956–65	15–24	75%	80%	78%
Mean number of children surviving		2.00	1.98	1.99
Number of children		104	104	208

Source: Maternity histories collected by the authors, February–March 1991.

have more children. The most likely reason for the differences in fertility is that women married more than an half an hour's walking distance from their parents spend longer periods every year staying with them. (The women married more than 50 km away, however, rarely visit their parents because long-distance travel was too expensive and dangerous to be done regularly.) For example, the mother-in-law of Qamar Jahan, S15, complained vehemently to us that Qamar Jahan was always going off to her parents and usually stayed away longer than she said she would. By contrast, women married within Qaziwala rarely stayed overnight in their parents' home, except at times of weddings or if there was a serious quarrel between a woman and her in-laws. While staying with her parents, a woman does not normally have a sexual relationship with her husband. No woman talked about the implications of this restraint, nor did they suggest that they consciously employed visiting their parents as a means of reducing the likelihood of conceiving. Older women sometimes said that because 'men won't "leave" their wives these days' the gaps between children were shorter than they used to be.[21] Over the course of a marriage, a reduction in the frequency of intercourse might lead to slightly longer gaps between children, and lower fertility overall.[22] But such effects are likely to be small for this population, since the visits are irregular and not very frequent.

We have some evidence to support the suggestion that distant marriage increases birth intervals, at least for women who began cohabiting in the 1960s and 1970s. In that period, women married more than 2 km away on average took more than 7 months longer to give birth for the first time (34 months) than those married within Qaziwala or in a neighbouring hamlet (27 months). But for women who began cohabiting in the 1980s the relationship is reversed: women married closely took longer (25 months) to give birth for the first time than did women married more distantly (22 months). There is also some anecdotal evidence that a shift in marital behaviour has taken place, and that young married men were now unwilling to let their wives go back home as frequently as in earlier generations. The women interpreted this as a sign of young men's greater 'heat' (in this case, sexual passion) brought about in part by the effect of chemical fertilizers (which make wheat 'hotter' than before) and the increased use of tea and other modern drinks, all 'heating' in their effects. Thus if there was any 'protection' offered by longer marriage distances in the past, its effect seems likely to be dying out.

For women married more than 10 years ago, the longer gaps between children of the more distantly married may be the reason for the lower mortality of the children born to these women. Certainly, women who have longer birth intervals are usually better able to maintain their own health, and that of their children, because their physical reserves are not so rapidly depleted. Our data are not detailed enough to investigate this

---

[21] We did not realize that such women had fewer children, until we analysed the figures after leaving the field, too late to return and ask more questions.

[22] Since women will try to avoid travelling while they are menstruating, they might not actually reduce the time when they are sexually 'available' by visiting their parents for two weeks or so.

Table 4.5. *Total marital fertility rates by household type, Jats in Nangal and Sheikhs in Qaziwala, by woman's year of birth*

Year of birth of mother	Mother's age at birth	Household type				
		Alone	Separate	Joint with mother-in-law	Other	All
Jat women						
1946–1955	15–34	5.15	4.25	5.31	4.62	4.97
N. of women		30	7	12	12	61
N. of years at risk		528	127	192	208	1055
1956–1965	15–24	2.87	2.62	2.37	3.20	2.61
N. of women		19	15	33	5	72
N. of years at risk		129	103	215	25	472
Sheikh women						
1946–1955	15–34	7.26	6.47	6.84	7.35	7.07
N. of women		23	10	9	12	54
Years at risk		419	173	158	215	965
1956–1965	15–24	3.66	4.03	3.65	3.58	3.78
N. of women		25	27	21	7	80
Years at risk		183	222	167	53	625

Source: Maternity histories collected by authors, September–December 1990 and February–March, 1991.

possibility any further: we cannot rely on our information on the gaps preceding the births of the relatively small number of children who died before their fifth birthday. We can only note the absence of supporting evidence: our figures show little difference in the gaps before children who die than before children who survive.

Do women who have established separate households have different fertility experiences, in either Nangal or Qaziwala? As an indicator of her ability to control her own fertility, a woman's *current* household position may be misleading, since it tells us very little about her situation at crucial periods (for example, for Jat women, the time at which contraceptive decisions were made). This is particularly problematic for older women, almost all of whom are now residing with a daughter-in-law of their own, so we have excluded them from the analysis that follows. For the younger women, we have assumed that the creation of a separate household might be a proxy for greater agency. Table 4.5 shows the age-specific marital fertility rates for the two younger cohorts of Jat and Sheikh women. In three of the four comparisons, women living in separate households have given birth to fewer children than those in the other types of households. In the fourth case, Sheikh women born between 1956 and 1965, women in separate households have the highest

Table 4.6. *Survival rates to age five of children born up to 1985 to Jat women, Nangal, and Sheikh women, Qaziwala, by household type and year of birth of mother*

| Year of birth of mother | Mother's age at birth | Household type | | | | |
		Alone	Separate	Joint with mother-in-law	Other	All
Jat women						
1946–1955	15–34	81%	96%	78%	87%	85%
Mean number of surviving children		3.60	3.57	3.33	3.33	3.72
N. of children		132	26	51	46	255
1956–1965	15–24	71%	80%	84%	86%	79%
Mean number of surviving children		1.32	1.33	1.15	1.2	1.24
N. of children		35	25	45	7	112
Sheikh women						
1946–1955	15–34	74%	82%	67%	73%	74%
Mean number of surviving children		4.61	4.10	3.67	4.83	4.24
N. of children		144	50	49	80	324
1956–1965	15–24	77%	64%	85%	94%	76%
Mean number of surviving children		2.16	1.59	2.24	2.14	1.99
N. of children		70	67	55	16	208

Source: Maternity histories collected by authors, September–December 1990 and February–March, 1991.

fertility rate. But this difference disappears when child mortality is taken into consideration (see Table 4.6). Mortality rates reduce the differentials in current family sizes between women in different household types, in general. Among the Jats, the combination of low fertility and low child mortality for women in separate households results in their having, with those who are alone, the most children surviving to age five. Among the Sheikhs, the very high mortality experience of children of Sheikh women born 1946–1955 and living in joint households, and those born 1956–65 and living in separate households, change the patterns for children surviving to the age of five. Among those women born in 1946–55, women living in joint households have the lowest numbers of surviving children, whereas among women born in 1956–1965, those in separate households have the smallest numbers of surviving children. Given the small numbers of women in some of the cells, and since we have no information on the length of time a woman has been in different kinds of household, we are not willing to push the analysis any further.

Conclusion

By any simple accounts of these women's lives, none of them has much freedom of action, at least, not of an officially sanctioned sort. Rather, they have great difficulty when they attempt to influence key aspects of their situations. The prime reasons have to do with their structural powerlessness: they have no independent earning power nor do they own any productive property. As young married women in their husband's homes, they were all at the bottom of a hierarchy of women and men, so we should not be surprised to find so little variation among them. The main sources of variation were the social class of the woman's household, and the amount of personal space a woman was able to create, but these different elements do not necessarily vary together. Thus the women in wealthier households were more able to afford to travel to visit their parents, and more likely to receive substantial economic support. But these women were also more likely to be living in joint households. This meant that their travel might be easier to arrange (though still subject to their mother-in-law's approval) but the cost was that their everyday lives were more subject to surveillance and control, and their ability to make economic decisions was likely to be lower than women in separate households. The ambiguities of their situations thus make it hard to see what women can do to enhance their opportunities to exert their agency.

As we have argued in more detail elsewhere (P. Jeffery and R. Jeffery 1994, 1996) this does not mean that women are incapable of seeing the undesirable features of their situation or that they never resist the structures within which they are required to live. None of the women had much space for legitimately acting to assert themselves, and women who attempt to bring in their parents too frequently may be given very little more licence than neighbours who cannot call upon their parents so easily. In other words, women's ability to draw on their support from their natal kin, or subterfuge and secrecy, were fairly limited.

Women's resistance to their subordinate position is also constrained by the extent to which a ruling ideology controls their consciousness. That control over consciousness may not be total, but nor it is totally lacking. Haynes and Prakash argue that subordinates make but partial critiques of the situation in which they find themselves. Both at the level of the individual and the social group we can observe 'omnipresent tension and contradictions between hegemony and autonomy in consciousness, between submission and resistance in practice' (Haynes and Prakash 1991: 10–13). It might clarify what we mean by 'cultural hegemony' if, for instance, we consider the connotations of the Hindi words that seem comparable to 'agency'. In English, the term 'agency' generally has a positive aura: it is considered desirable and appropriate for people to be able to make decisions about their lives and act upon them. But the Hindi terms are often rather ambivalent, if not downright pejorative, especially for women.

Perhaps the most neutral term that came up in discussions with women in the villages where we have worked is *mukhtiyār* (and other words connected with it, such as *mukhtiyārī, ikhtiyār, ikhtiyārī*). *Mukhtiyār* implies someone who is in control of their situation, someone who has authority to act as a free agent. Frequently, when we asked young married women about control over household finances, they would introduce the word in their adamant denials that they have such control, often seeming to be surprised that we thought it was possible. The word *āzād* (free, independent) may have a positive resonance – for instance, in reference to a nation state – but it generally takes on a rather different colour when applied to women, when it is often used in the same breath as *besharm* (immodest, shameless). And the word *zimmedār* (responsible) was generally used by women commenting on the drawbacks and risks of being in a separate household or in other positions that involved making decisions for which one would be held liable. In other words, that which we might want to call 'agency' may not be valorized by women because it seems unattractive and frightening.

This emerges from women's discussions of marriage arrangements as well as in their views on household structures after marriage. When discussing how marriages are arranged, women will say that a marriageable girl who voices an opinion on her future marriage knows she is playing with fire. In the face of the potential wrath of her entire family, silence is prudent. But more commonly, women endorse the ideas of family honour, of the shamelessness of displaying an interest in one's marriage (and by implication, one's sexuality), and of the appropriateness of leaving the whole business to their elders. Stepping out of line is dangerous, but not something that most women seek to do in any case. The small number of women who did assert their will became the focus of scandal and the objects of gossip in which other women were the key players. For example, in Dharmnagri, a Jat woman from Bijnor (with a BA) had made a 'love marriage'. She was rumoured by neighbouring women to have had a previous affair with a Muslim, and was said to have made her husband's three brothers 'happy' (by implication, sexually) before being admitted to his house to live. She is now socially virtually isolated (except for one of her three sisters-in-law) and plans to move back to Bijnor, ostensibly to oversee the children's education. In this and other cases of pre- and post-marital affairs, the women's gossip hardly touched on the men involved.

For most women, then, the fact that parents choose a spouse for them is not a matter of complaint. They trust their parents to do the best they can. 'When parents are looking for a good house, what is the need for girls to speak?' Any girl who knows anything about whether a boy is suitable or not is showing evidence of bad character. These views are common to Jats and Sheikhs alike.

The same is true of women's views about household life. Some women clearly find it rather irksome to live in a household with their mother-in-law or others from their older affinal kin. Young women in such households may need to ask permission (normally of the mother-in-law) to go on journeys or make any purchases, for example. But several other women expressed countervailing views and emphasized what they considered to be advantages of living in the joint household. A particularly common refrain was that living jointly enabled them to escape the responsibilities (*zimmedārī*) that they would acquire if they were to live separately. In part this reflects women's weak positions, for if their judgement seems faulty and things go wrong, they are very vulnerable. To take a clear position is to enter unknown and perilous territory, and many women are unwilling to take such a step lightly.

In any case, women need an independent source of income if they are to have any kind of freedom to make their own decisions about expenditures. Here too we can see a coexistence of structures of subordination with a reluctance of women to seek to act in ways which expose them to charges of irresponsibility or immodesty. On the one hand, a woman without employment outside the home cannot manage substantial economic resources unless she is permitted to do so by her domestic authorities. On the other, there is widespread disapproval among women themselves of the employment of women outside the home, even for women whose educational level might make them employable in a range of respectable white-collar jobs. Their proper place is as family workers based in their husbands' homes, engaged in a wide range of domestic labour, investing time in their children's education, household decoration and improvements and sewing, knitting and crocheting items for the home and their family. In that, women are hard to distinguish, at least Jats and Sheikhs in the same class position.

Even in separate households, then, the husband still controls major expenditures, whether or not a woman is allowed to budget the daily distribution of subsistence spending. Unless the husband seriously abuses his position and he fails to provide properly for his wife and children, this arrangement is not the object of general disapproval by women. On the contrary, women perceive their interests to be best served by binding their own with those of their husbands. The very idea that husband and wife should organize their finances separately from one another and that women should spend money unilaterally is seen as a contravention of the ideal unity of the married couple.

My husband alone meets all my expenses and he also gives me money when I need it. He says, 'What would the two of us do keeping our money separately?' What, are we separate from one another (*alag*)? The matter is one only. (Shalu w/o Sher Singh, J22, uneducated, middle peasant, separate household)

5   Modern mindsets or empowered women?

The idea that 'modern' people can not only ensure that their children live to maturity, but can also act 'rationally' to limit the number of children they have, is at the source of the modern discipline of demography in the disputes between Malthus and Condorcet at the end of the eighteenth century. Whereas Malthus was sceptical of the possible role of 'moral restraint', Condorcet believed that the abolition of prejudice and superstition, encouraged by the spread of education (particularly of women) would lead people to choose small families voluntarily (Sen 1995). Thus the idea that economic and social changes – urbanization and industrialization in particular – would bring new ways of thinking and understanding in their wake has a long pedigree. It was taken up most thoroughly in the 1960s, when the sociology of social and economic change was heavily influenced by the work of Talcott Parsons and Wilbert Moore. One of the most extended pieces of research in this perspective was organized at Harvard, and involved questionnaires administered to men (but not women) in countries in Africa, Latin America and Asia (including Pakistan). It was published under the title *Becoming Modern* (Inkeles and Smith 1974). Within sociology, work in this genre has been heavily criticized for its value-laden evolutionary schema in which contemporary US small-town society was treated as the archetype of the 'modern'. Writers using this approach have failed to take seriously differences in historical, cultural and economic context, have often used teleological arguments, and have made naive and often ethnocentric assumptions about the inevitability of 'progress'.[1] Modernization theorists often assumed that 'tradition' was static, whereas much anthropological work stresses the fluidity and change to be found in all contemporary and historic societies.

---

[1] Prominent representatives of the 'modernization' approach include David Lerner and Walt W. Rostow (see Lerner 1967; Rostow 1963). An early critical attack can be found in Frank 1967. Accessible recent critiques include Kiely 1995 and Webster 1990.

Somewhat surprisingly, despite these severe criticisms of modernization theory, some demographers have returned to a very similar approach under the title of 'ideational change' (Cleland and Wilson 1987; Cleland 1993). They argue that more 'traditional' views tend to be associated with religious support for large families, for example, and with a fatalistic acceptance of the numbers of children who are born or die. These arguments are not restricted to the modernization demographers, however. For example, Mamdani (among others) cites the need of a Hindu man for a son to light his funeral pyre, and the pressures on women to establish their position in 'traditional' families by bearing a large number of sons (Mamdani 1972: 128–142; Mandelbaum 1974: 21–22). As a Marxist, Mamdani was careful to argue that these cultural forces are not independent: if the economic rationality of large families evaporates, he suggests, the culture will change also, and new sayings and habits will arise to justify and support the new patterns of behaviour. For Cleland, by contrast, cultural forces (in his case, attitudes towards birth control, or 'tastes' concerning desirable family sizes) act with a degree of independence.

Classic modernization theories saw development less as a matter of increasing wealth or economic opportunities, and more as the spread of a set of attitudes. These new attitudes are usually thought to be conveyed through formal schooling, in which the curriculum is set by bureaucratic procedures and oriented towards science and ideals of national development. Implicitly or explicitly, non-formal means of socialization and 'traditional' (often religious) schooling are seen as inculcating fatalistic attitudes. Less often, modern attitudes may be seen to be spreading through personal experience of employment in 'modern' settings (particularly in factories and offices), or through visiting and living in urban areas, or through the surrogate access to these 'modern' influences which is provided by the mass media. Qaziwala and Nangal are roughly comparable in size and in their accessibility to small towns, and so we shall focus mostly on schooling.[2]

Schooling has increasingly been seen as the key feature of modernization which might change rural, agricultural people's views of the world (broadly speaking, their 'culture'). Schooling is, in effect, presented as a panacea for the failure of many developing economies – India included –

---

[2] Access to the mass media was not something we assessed directly. In both villages, most middle peasants and those above had access to TV, but watching was irregular because of frequent power cuts. Listening to the radio was more widespread, but batteries were expensive: most listening was to film music. More newspapers were read in Nangal than in Qaziwala, though in both villages an individual copy would be read by many people, sometimes out loud to the non-literate.

to deal with their problems of poverty.[3] Some writers on social and economic development – including many writing on the significance of the 1994 Cairo Population Conference – see schooling (especially of women) as more important than industrial development or land reforms. Like many demographers, they see schooling as necessary for the decline of fertility and infant mortality, but they also claim that other desirable changes (ranging from good governance to fitting people for dealing with the information economies of the future) are likely to flow from increased investment in schooling.[4] In the general modernization literature, boys are expected to use their schooling to gain urban or industrial employment, which will reinforce pressures towards 'modern' mindsets for them (Inkeles 1974, but see also Caldwell et al. 1988). Demographers, however, have rarely given the schooling of boys much attention. The statistical relationships between a boy's schooling and the number of children his wife will bear, or the chances of them surviving to adulthood, are much weaker than those between a girl's schooling and the number of children she bears and their chances of staying alive, whether or not she has ever been in paid employment. Demographers recognize that girls' schooling may lead to their employment, but much more demographic analysis has been concerned with the effects of women's employment or their employability on their domestic relationships. Early discussions within the 'new household economics' tradition stressed the opportunity cost to a couple if the wife was unable to work because of her child-care responsibilities: this opportunity cost increased with the greater earning power of educated women, and this was regarded (in industrial countries at least) as a plausible reason for the lower fertility of educated women. But these arguments held little weight in other parts of the world, where child care might be compatible with many forms of income generation by women, and where other members of their kin group might take over responsibility if mothers wanted or needed to work.

Since the mid-1970s, most discussions of the effects of girls' schooling on fertility and child mortality have moved beyond the spread of 'modern' ideas, to a concern with schooling's effects on the 'status' of women and on gender politics, within and outwith the household – in other words, what schooling might do to a young married woman's ability to influence her everyday life, *vis-à-vis* her husband and his

[3] Weiner 1991, Kanbargi 1991 and Sen 1995 all attach great importance to the failure of the Indian state to meet its goal – set out in the Constitution – of universal primary schooling. While we accept the desirability of this goal, we are much more cautious in our assessment of the effects universal schooling can be expected to have.

[4] See, for example, from a World Bank perspective, Summers 1993; for the viewpoint of some feminists preparing for the Cairo Conference in 1994, see G. Sen et al. (eds.) 1994.

family.[5] David Mandelbaum provides an early example of such reasoning: 'An educated woman is usually less closely confined, physically and psychologically, within her husband's family ... a young wife who has been to high school or college is not as duly submissive to her mother-in-law as is a less educated daughter-in-law' (Mandelbaum 1974: 54–55).[6] He goes on to argue that a schooled woman will have less belief in 'fate', feel more secure about the future and be more able to ensure that her children live to maturity. Female schooling may be associated with lower fertility, then, not because schooling provides knowledge about contraception or makes people more 'modern' in their attitudes, but because it enhances a woman's autonomy and increases the chances that others will take her views seriously.

Thus a new orthodoxy has arisen to explain high fertility, one which sees most women wanting to use contraception but prevented by their lack of power. Schooling is viewed as a means of empowering women and therefore of causing a fall in birth rates. In this chapter, then, we look in detail at local understandings of women's schooling, and address the question of how the lives of schooled women can be said to differ from those of unschooled women. We also consider the effects of the schooling a woman's husband has received. Before we present the material from Nangal and Qaziwala, however, we need to locate our approach within the two main approaches to discussing the relationships between schooling and fertility. On the one hand are those who use schooling as a proxy for education, and are content to carry out statistical analyses of linkages between schooling and other social variables. On the other hand are those, like us, who want to look much more closely at the meaning of schooling to those who participate in it.

Modernizing men, empowering women?

The basic assumptions of demographic approaches that apply modernization theories can be readily set out. 'Traditional' people are seen as fatalistic, bound into kinship networks, self-sufficient and slow to change. By contrast, 'modern' people assume that they can control their environments. They are more individualized, and are linked into an increasingly complex division of labour. Thus they relate more readily to 'modern' institutions (such as factories, health services, schools, political

---

[5] The literature is voluminous. For typical examples, see Caldwell 1979, 1982; Cochrane 1979; Safilios-Rothschild 1982; Dyson and Moore 1983; Mason 1984; Lockwood and Collier 1988; Sathar et al. 1988; Federici et al. 1993; King and Hill (eds.) 1993; Mahmud and Johnson 1994. For critical discussion of the South Asian material, see R. Jeffery and A. Basu (eds.) 1996.

[6] For other discussions of similar points, see LeVine 1991; Easterlin 1983.

parties or the state) to meet their needs, and they take advantage of new technologies in many spheres of their lives (Inkeles 1971). In a modernizing society, town-dwellers, people employed in factories and offices, and educated men, and more particularly, educated women, tend to want smaller families, and are more prepared to try to control the number of children they have through the use of contraception. The more 'modern' individuals end up with fewer children and, because of their greater acceptance of cosmopolitan medicine, fewer of their children die.

This model is susceptible to the same criticisms that we have already made of modernization theories in general. It tends to give too much weight to the free-floating role of ideas, assuming that they are the major barriers to social change, and to ignore structural factors grounded in local contexts and specific histories. It has no clear understanding of what 'culture' means: cultural factors are what is left over when economic or social characteristics fail to 'explain' changes. Thus, modernization theories tend to assume that 'modern' institutions (such as towns, schools, bureaucracies) have the same meanings wherever they are created, and will always be associated with the same kinds of attitudes in those whose lives are lived in their ambience. But this may not be the case: there may be no dynamic that tends to push societies along similar lines. And when demographic processes seem to bear little relationship to urbanization or education (for example), 'culture' is brought in to save the day (Carter 1995). In general, demographic writing has remained cut off from the mainstream of social theory, failing to take seriously globalization and localization which dominate recent debates about the post-modern or post-industrial world order (Kumar 1995; Harvey 1989).

As Cleland and Jejeebhoy note, 'Of all the indicators of socio-economic status, schooling has been most widely used by demographers' (1996: 72). Indeed in the 1960s and 1970s, men's schooling was seen as a proxy for socio-economic position, partly because it was uncontentious to ask men how many years they had attended school, when questions about income might provoke a hostile or evasive response. But it may be better to regard schooling as an intermediate variable, and look for more satisfactory explanations by 'taking a step backward' to ask why parents send children to school at all, and which children are sent to which schools, and for how long (Caldwell et al. 1988: Ch. 7).

Two separate issues arise here. First, what are the statistical relationships between indicators of 'education' (usually narrowly interpreted as number of years of schooling, or literacy at the time of interview) and fertility?[7] Second, what do these correlations mean, and what explana-tory models make sense of them? Cleland and Jejeebhoy (1996) provide an analysis of the results of decennial census data, and of special demographic surveys (such as the World Fertility Survey, and various Demographic and Health Surveys), with special reference to South Asian material. As with most recent reviews, they focus on female schooling and literacy. Cleland and Jejeebhoy describe three variants of schooling transitions, all from situations of low levels of schooling and high levels of fertility and child mortality, to ones of high levels of schooling and low levels of fertility and child mortality. In all three variants, for most levels of schooling, women who spent more years in school have fewer children.

The first variant applies to much of Africa and Asia. In these countries, at the beginning of the transition, women who have been to school have higher fertility: they tend to breast-feed for shorter periods, and they may have intercourse more frequently and sooner after childbirth, ignoring (for example) 'traditional' taboos on post-partum sexual relationships. Furthermore, their children are more likely to survive, so their completed family sizes can be considerably larger than those of unschooled women. But as female schooling becomes better established, the fertility rates of women who have been to school for longer periods tend to fall faster than those of women who have been to school for only a few years, or not at all. Women with more schooling marry later, and stop having children at younger ages. At the far end of this variant of transition, when almost all girls receive eight or more years of schooling, the inverse relationship between schooling and fertility tends to weaken again.

The other two variants are less common. In variant two, in some parts of west Asia, high fertility is combined with relatively high levels of female schooling. In variant three, in some parts of south-east Asia (and, recently, Bangladesh) fertility and child mortality have fallen despite the absence of widespread female schooling. In all three variants, a threshold can sometimes be observed: a small amount of schooling (up to about six years) seems to have little relationship to later fertility. But the general picture is well established, and Cleland and Jejeebhoy sum-marize several Indian studies which affirm the strong statistical relation-ship between female schooling and lower fertility.[8] Not only do women

---

[7] For classic discussions of the fallacy of equating schooling and education, see Freire 1962; Illich 1974.

[8] Murti et al. 1995, using district-level data from 1981, also show that the only strong correlations with fertility are provided by measures of female schooling and of women's employment outside the home.

who have been to school have fewer children, they also say they want fewer children and they are more likely to be users of contraception than women who have not been to school.

The statistical correlations may be clear, but interpretation is much more problematic. Despite the strength of the orthodox position, we remain sceptical. It is very hard to specify the causal chains by which schooling can plausibly have the results claimed for it. How do schooled and unschooled people differ? Is it the content of what children are taught in school (Mandelbaum 1974: 102–5)? This would be surprising, given the sustained criticisms which have been levelled at the curricula and teaching methods employed in most Indian schools (Dyer 1995). Is it what people can learn from reading outside the curriculum and after formal schooling ends? This again would be surprising, given how little literature is available to most rural residents. Is it the attitudes and behaviour inculcated by regular school attendance, the hidden curriculum of controlling bodies and disciplining minds rather than the content of the schooling, as LeVine (1980) and Lindenbaum (1991) argue? How much is it schooling *per se*, and how much do the fertility differences just reflect the fact that only certain kinds of families are able and prepared to make the sacrifices to ensure their children attend school regularly and for a full 8 or 10 years? Or is it possible that the families who choose brides who have several years of schooling for their sons are pursuing further strategies (like wanting their grandchildren to be schooled for urban employment), so that the new couple is under pressure to have a small family?

Two channels of influence can be identified in discussions of the effects of female schooling on fertility and child mortality (Mason 1984, 1993). On the one hand are the unintended consequences of longer schooling. If girls are not married until they have stopped going to school or college, their age at marriage is likely to be several years higher than that of their unschooled peers. This in itself is likely to reduce fertility, and protects a young woman from giving birth before she is fully mature, when she and her child tend to be at enhanced risk. But these effects may be neither intended nor perceived by the woman's parents, her in-laws or the woman herself.

The second influence Mason discusses is the possible effect of schooling on a young woman's self-confidence. Women who have been to school are assumed to be better able to confront doctors and minor government health workers, and to deal with shopping and transport, for example. Similarly, if a woman marries at a later age, she is thought to arrive in her in-laws' house more self-assured and more able to manage relationships with her parents-in-law and her husband. The empirical basis for these assertions turns out to be extremely weak. We know of only one piece of work in South Asia which systematically compared schooled and unschooled women in these terms. Focusing on child health, Shirley Lindenbaum explored the differences schooling makes to women's actual behaviour. Instead of assuming that the 'meaning' of schooling was clear or universal, Lindenbaum treated schooling as an 'empty category', with a variety of meanings for her respondents in Bangladesh. She argued that a Bangladeshi woman's education was 'a rapidly moving social counter' which 'defines a new aspect of her status at the time of marriage' (Lindenbaum 1990: 358). Lindenbaum accepted that schooling for her sample did have some psychological effects on women. Locally, a woman who had been to school was said to be able to depend upon herself, be braver, and more open in discussions within her new family, and some schooled women did individually display some of these characteristics. Schooling leads to 'the genesis of manners and the emergence of a sense of companionship in marriage' (Lindenbaum 1990: 360). In Bangladesh, women who had spent longer in school were also economically more valuable: educated women could manage household finances, tutor their children (saving tuition fees) and were seen as potential earners. Educated women seemed more willing to travel to use Western medicines for their children, and to be concerned about household hygiene and preventive care, but they did not seem to operate with different notions of disease causation from women with less schooling. The greater self-esteem and relative freedom from dependency and constraint of schooled women can be summed up as saying that schooling is a form of 'assertiveness training', and that ' "Education" is an index of membership in a class culture that extends beyond the boundaries of the local village and a key to acquiring resources in newly forming systems of distribution' rather than 'an information "handout", a body of knowledge that transforms the mind and the behaviour of the recipient along predictable lines' (Lindenbaum 1990: 363, 368; see also LeVine 1980).

This important account is unique, and draws attention to different strategies and meanings of education, and to some of the factors which might be important in helping to produce these particular outcomes. For example, Lindenbaum notes one strategy in which a first-born girl is educated almost like a son, and is possibly expected to use her education to help pay for the upbringing of her siblings. Furthermore, the value of schooling in marriage negotiations is significant. It cost these Bangladeshi parents less to get schooled daughters married and, while divorce and separation are increasingly common experiences for unschooled women, schooled women seem to be at a lower risk of marriage breakdown. Matters are very different in Bijnor. As in Punjab (Das Gupta 1987), a girl's schooling normally *increases* the amount of dowry required to get her married. Schooling is not seen as a way of enhancing a woman's economic potential, but of improving her position in the competition for desirable grooms. We explore this point further in Chapter 6, when we investigate female (and male) schooling as a reflection of membership in a class and caste culture. Here it is sufficient to note that we need to ask how schooled women differ from unschooled ones of similar ages and in similar class positions, in the ways they talk about and act in key areas of their everyday lives.

Lindenbaum and Cleland and Jejeebhoy differ on the causal significance of schooling, and their underlying theoretical models. Cleland and Jejeebhoy talk in terms of 'traditional' kinship structures, and introduce 'cultural conditions' to explain variations in the statistical relationships between schooling and fertility. But in common with Lindenbaum they stress the need to locate any emergent statistical relationships in a detailed local setting, with specific reference to patterns of gender stratification (Cleland and Jejeebhoy 1996). We need, therefore, to place female schooling in Bijnor – in Cleland and Jejeebhoy's terms, one of the 'more gender-stratified settings' – in a wider context, not only of male schooling (as we do in this chapter) and in the context of other aspects of gender relationships in the household (which we began in the last chapter), but also in the context of a political economy of fertility and mortality (as we do in the next chapter).

Schooling in Bijnor

In 1845, when the District authorities made their first enquiries into schooling in Bijnor, they found 278 schools, mostly teaching Persian, the language of government at the time, or Hindi, the language of commerce. It took a further ten years before any government schools were established, and their progress was immediately affected by the events of 1857, which (according to the Gazetteer) 'did much harm to education, especially in Bijnor, where the development of rancorous hatred between Hindus and Mussulmans accentuated the difficulty that had already been experienced in smoothing down differences of religion and caste so as to admit all classes to any school' (Nevill 1928: 173). Soon afterwards, American Methodist missionaries opened a school in Bijnor, and a Government High School dates from 1863. Over the following eighty years, schooling spread slowly, and literacy increased very gradually, first in the towns and then in the more substantial villages and among the wealthier classes. In the 1872 Census, only 1.4 per cent of males were recorded as being able to read and write; no females apparently had these skills. By 1951, 18 per cent of males were recorded as literate, but only 4 per cent of females.

A major feature of the community development programmes of the 1950s was the attempt to spread primary schools to villages that were able to offer a site and provide some contribution to the buildings. In the competition for schools, village councils with wealthy, well-connected landholding groups were at an advantage in the land and other support they could offer government officials. Government schooling was still prized in the 1990s, even though most people we talked to in Bijnor said that state schools now offered an inferior education to that available from private schools, especially those where English was taught. Unfortunately for the poor and rural students, additional tuition, before or after normal school hours, was usually considered essential for getting good grades. Stories abound of teachers who do little teaching in class and help only the children who pay them for private tuition. In Bijnor in 1990–91, tuition for children aged 11–13 might cost some Rs 50 per month; for older children, tuition could cost that much for each of several school subjects. None the less, good schools are still a key resource promised by rising politicians and are often demanded when government officials gather information on what villagers want in the way of social infrastructure.

Government schooling in Qaziwala and Nangal

Primary schools (classes 1 to 5) are still totally inadequate for the number of children they are expected to serve. By 1971 Bijnor had one school per 2,000 rural population (or about one for over 300 children aged 5–9). By 1991 the figure had dropped only to one per 1,600 (one school for 250 children). Since many of these schools had only one or two teachers, the goal of universal primary education (enshrined in the Constitution of India in 1950 and supposed to be achieved by 1965) was clearly still far from being realized in Bijnor.

These general patterns of schooling in Bijnor are reflected in the experiences of children in Qaziwala and Nangal. In Qaziwala, the nearest government primary school (with two rooms and two Hindu teachers) was sited on land equidistant between Qaziwala, Burhanuddinpur and Begawala, three mixed Muslim/Harijan villages with a total population in 1991 of about 3,600, of which Muslims were the overwhelming majority. In the Qaziwala primary school, from an age-cohort of 500 or so in the three villages it served, fewer than 100 were

Table 5.1. *Schooling by age, sex and caste, Nangal and Qaziwala, 1990–1*

Nangal Jats	In school (%)	Not in school (%)	Total
Aged 5–9: Boys (%)	56 (89%)	7 (11%)	**63**
Girls (%)	36 (90%)	4 (10%)	**40**
Aged 10–16: Boys (%)	101 (80%)	26 (20%)	**127**
Girls (%)	45 (63%)	27 (37%)	**72**

Qaziwala Sheikhs:	In school	In Islamic education	Not in schooling	Total
Aged 5–9: Boys (%)	13 (11%)	40 (35%)	62 (54%)	**115**
Girls (%)	2 (2%)	38 (44%)	46 (53%)	**86**
Aged 10–16: Boys (%)	10 (7%)	47 (34%)	81 (59%)	**138**
Girls %)	0	65 (58%)	47 (42%)	**112**

Source: Census carried out by the authors, 1990–1.

enrolled in 1991. Of the boys at the school, 48 were Muslim (most from Burhanuddinpur) and 32 were Harijan (mostly Chamar); all 14 girls were Harijan. Amongst the Qaziwala Muslims, not surprisingly, the school was known as the 'Chamar school'. Of the almost 400 Muslim boys in Qaziwala aged 5–15, only 7 attended state schools; of the 300 or so girls, just one attended a state school.[9]

A government junior secondary school (classes 6 to 8) was expected to serve a much larger area, so very few villages have one. Qaziwala students could go to the schools in Mandauli, a Jat-dominated village to the north, to Tikkupur to the south-east, or to the Dharmnagri school to the south-west. The distribution of students in the secondary schools reflected the primary schools which fed them: all had a very small number of Muslim boys, and no Muslim girls. In 1991, no Qaziwala Muslims – neither boys nor girls – attended the government junior secondary schools in Dharmnagri or Mandauli; just two Sheikh boys attended the Tikkupur school.

In Nangal, the first government primary school was established on land in the Jat and Brahman section of the village; the government girls' primary school which followed began life in the courtyard of a disused temple in the same section. Both were later shifted to the north-west corner of the village, farthest from the Muslim and Harijan sections. These two schools, with a total of eight teachers, served a population of

[9] She stays with her mother's parents in Chandigarh, the state capital of Haryana and Punjab.

around 4,000 in Nangal and some neighbouring villages. By 1990, both schools were co-educational, and just under half the age-cohort of 600 or so Nangal children aged 5–9 attended: 174 boys (68 of them Harijan) and 98 girls (31 Harijan). Five of the 50 Muslim boys aged 5–9 in Nangal attended government schools; no Muslim girls did. Nangal had no government junior secondary school: pupils had to travel at least five km in one of three directions – to Jhalu, Nehtaur, or (most commonly) to Haldaur.

The higher secondary schools (known as inter-colleges in UP, serving classes 9 to 12) were all sited in towns. Bijnor and Haldaur towns had government Boys' Inter-Colleges and Girls' Inter-Colleges. Negotiating access to these colleges depended in part on success in the examinations for the previous year, and in part on links to those who could influence admissions. The colleges drew students not only from the town but also from the surrounding villages.

Muslims in general, and Muslim girls in particular, were under-represented at all levels of the state school system. The siting of schools often made it hard for members of minority or subordinated groups, particularly girls, to attend. Boys and girls found their movements into 'foreign' territory (outside their own neighbourhoods) threatening. The low use by Muslims of the lower levels of schooling further reduced their potential presence in junior and higher secondary schools, themselves usually sited in areas that could be dominated by high- or middle-caste Hindu students (P. Jeffery and R. Jeffery forthcoming).

Responses to the inadequacies of state schooling

For many villagers, then, accessibility to government schools was limited. Furthermore, the quality of government schooling was questioned by many people, because there were so few teachers (who were also often irregular in attendance) and very poor physical facilities. The commonest response was resigned acceptance, with little pressure to make children attend school. But one alternative was self-help, either by establishing facilities under the control of a caste or community, or side-stepping the issue by using private commercial schools. In some respects, even the dominant castes followed this route. But while the leading castes moved on beyond government schooling, Muslims (especially girls) were moved into Islamic alternatives rather than enrolled into government schools or private 'secular' alternatives.

Most private provisions were in the towns. In addition to numerous private primary schools there were two Christian secondary schools in Bijnor (one Catholic, one Church of North India), a private boys Inter-

College and the Bijnor Inter-College (a Muslim foundation for boys only, following the state curriculum, with additional instruction in Islamic subjects). Most students came from the town, but wealthier families from surrounding villages sent their children to private schools and colleges. Most private schools, of course, charged fees (usually about Rs 15 per month for younger children, up to a day's wage for a male labourer) and required a clean uniform in good repair (adding up to maybe Rs 80 a year) as well as school-books (another Rs 50 or so a year for junior schools). For the poor and landless, these costs were beyond their pockets; even the Harijans, who usually faced lower fees (Rs 8 per month), were severely under-represented. Muslim girls were almost totally absent from private secular schools, even when they were run by Muslims. There was only one private school near Qaziwala, at Rahimpur: it was run by three Muslim brothers from Begawala, but of the 219 pupils just 33 were girls, only nine of whom were Muslim (and only one a Sheikh from Qaziwala). Six Qaziwala Sheikh boys attended the school.

Muslims have developed a complex network of Islamic schooling for their children. The *madrasā* run by Sheikhs at Begawala, 1 km from Qaziwala, was established in 1959. It grew rapidly in the 1980s, and had 800 students on its books in 1991. The fees were nominal because funding was provided by donations. The largest contribution to the total annual revenue of Rs 250,000 a year came from the post-harvest gifts from Muslim landholders in the surrounding villages. The *madrasā* staff taught Urdu and a full range of Islamic studies up to the level which allows admission to the Deoband seminary in Saharanpur District (for more details, see Metcalf 1984). Successful graduates from the Deoband four-year course gained a qualification as a *maulvī*. In the Begawala *madrasā*, the main Islamic classes were restricted to boys, and girls were taught only to read the Qur'an Sharīf, unless they attended the Urdu or Hindi classes.

The relationship of the *madrasā* to the formal government system was ambivalent. Only in 1989 did the *madrasā* begin to teach Hindi, which might open up access to government or other public sector employment. Hindi was also required for negotiating the public sphere of offices, shops, transport and so on. In 1989 the *madrasā* committee also decided to apply for government recognition, which would bring some assistance with equipment for the higher classes. After the 1991 elections which brought the BJP to power in UP, however, the manager of the *madrasā* abandoned this attempt, because he feared that the government would not permit the *madrasā* to provide the kind of education that Muslims wanted to give their children.

In the *madrasā*, there are more girls than boys in the elementary classes for learning to read the Qur'an and in the Hindi classes alike, but this was hardly a result of policy. Whereas the boys' classes are held in several large airy halls, the girls are restricted to cramped classrooms in one corner of the large courtyard, and the three women teachers hardly have room to turn around. Furthermore, the *madrasā* operates a policy of excluding all girls who are *jawān*, (i.e. who have started to menstruate) so all the children in the higher religious classes are boys. The staff explain the larger numbers of girls in the lower classes by saying that the boys are involved in farm work from the age of eight or nine, whereas the girls' involvement in housework was less incompatible with going to school. In addition to the *madrasā*, *maulvīs* teach young children to read the Qur'an Sharīf in the mosques or at their homes. In Qaziwala, despite the proximity of the *madrasā*, some girls and young children visited literate women at home in order to learn to read the Qur'an Sharīf.

In Nangal, a committee of Brahman members of the Rashtriya Swayamsevak Sangh (RSS) manages a Montessori primary school with 86 students in five classes, 18 of whom are girls. The RSS is a militant Hindu organization; in 1948 one of its members assassinated Mahatma Gandhi, apparently because Gandhi was perceived as being 'soft' on Muslims. In independent India the RSS has played a prominent role in many anti-Muslim riots. Not surprisingly, no Muslim children attended the RSS school. A private junior secondary school, recognized by the government, and with about 150 students and five teachers, was established on land controlled by Jats, who put up the initial money and who dominated the school management committee. In 1989 the teachers opened a Montessori primary school, to allow them to teach English from the first class and not just from class 6.[10] Most students were Jats. Partly in response to the Jat school, the Chamars established a secondary school in their own neighbourhood in 1986. With only 50 children in the three classes, and only two teachers in 1990, it was not successful. Only one Muslim boy attended the Scheduled Caste school; none attended the Jat school. The *maulvī* at the mosque in Nangal was supposed to take classes, but at any sign of communal tension he stayed away. In 1990–91, no Islamic schooling was taking place in Nangal.

[10] Jat attitudes towards education seem to have changed dramatically in the past forty years. A number of local sayings (along with many others reported in the colonial attempts to essentialize caste identities) suggest that Jats are inherently stupid: one example we heard was *parhā lykhā Jāt, sol' duni āth* ('Even an educated Jat thinks that sixteen times two equals eight').

Schooling for boys

Sheikh boys in Qaziwala

Of the Sheikh men in Qaziwala who began cohabiting between 1950 and 1989, only 16 per cent could read or write in Hindi in 1991. A further 19 per cent could read or write some Urdu or Arabic. In our sample, eleven men had no schooling at all; four had learned to read the Qur'an Sharīf; and seven had some schooling in Hindi. Yet literacy was widely respected by Sheikh men, and, like the Jats, the unschooled Sheikhs were defensive about their inability to read and write. They frequently commented that they had been damaged in every way (*sārā nuqsān*) by their illiteracy, sometimes describing themselves as 'thumbprint people' (*angūthā-wāle*, referring to their inability to sign their names on official forms), or as 'blind'. Some said that others treated them as if they were animals. When Roger interviewed two Sheikh men from Qaziwala who worked as labourers at the sugar mill in Bijnor, they were squatting in a gateway, sheltering from the rain. One said:

It's like this, being illiterate (*an-parh*) is why we are sitting around on straw like animals, why other people can kick us like dogs and call us *tu* [the disrespectful form of 'you']. People with jobs show us no respect. (Ali, S1, poor peasant, no schooling)

Illiterate men, and those only haltingly literate in Urdu or Arabic, talked about two main problems. Without school certificates they were ineligible for most kinds of stable, well-paid employment, and they had to pay or rely on others to read official documents, bus destinations, cane passes, payment slips and so on for them, all of which were produced only in Hindi. The charge made by lawyers for reading an official letter or other document could be as much as Rs 15, or between half a day and a day's wage. Relying on kin or other people from the village had its own problems, since they could not always be around to deal with, for example, the clerks at the electricity supply office, who might demand extra payments or not give a proper receipt for money paid in.

The unschooled Sheikh men expected their sons to do no better than they had done themselves. If they had the money, they said, they would send their sons to school to whatever level they were capable of reaching, preferably to the private school at Rahimpur. But if their sons left school early or refused to study, there was little they felt they could do: after all, they themselves had, as many of them put it, started playing around and ignoring their parents' wishes, and they would have difficulty stopping their sons from copying their own bad examples.

Those Sheikhs with government or Islamic schooling were unhappy that they had been unable to turn their schooling into employment, and that it did not seem to provide them with any other benefits. Thus Nasim (S12), who had been schooled to the eighth class, said that he could now read little more Hindi than was necessary to read the cane passes. None the less, the men with more schooling themselves had higher aspirations for their sons.

I was educated to fifth class in Hindi at Begawala. The benefit is that I can read passes and receipts from the sugar mill. My sons want to be doctors, but the expense is too much. I'd like them to do tenth class and then get some jobs as mechanics – farming is much too hard work. I've been up since 3 in the morning and now I have to go back to the fields. I'm just staying back to talk to you. (Usman, S19, middle peasant)

Jat boys in Nangal

Among the Jats in Nangal, the men's experience of schooling was extensive. Of the men who started cohabiting between 1950 and 1989, only forty (17 per cent) did not complete primary schooling; thirty-one (13 per cent) completed primary schooling, sixty-seven (28 per cent) completed junior high school (up to eighth class) and ninety-one (38 per cent) had at least two years of schooling beyond that. In our sample, only seven men were totally unschooled, or had so little schooling that they could no longer read and write Hindi. These men were defensive about their lack of schooling, and blamed a combination of their own lack of interest and their family's needs for labour to explain why their schooling was so brief:

I am the second son and I went only to third class; basically I can't read. At that time the position of my household was low and I was needed to work on the land. I also had no interest in study, but my elder brother went to twelfth class. (Rishipal, J19, middle peasant, born 1961.)

The remaining seventeen men in our sample had been to higher secondary school or beyond, usually in the hopes that they would then be able to compete for Government jobs. Even though they had all failed in this attempt, they generally still saw some value in their schooling, and were hoping their sons could succeed where they had failed:

I failed English in twelfth class and couldn't take the supplementary exam because my younger brother committed suicide and I was needed in the house. I liked Geography and English, and the English was necessary if I wanted service, but I wasn't much good at it. Education was good for my mind (dimāg) and general knowledge jānkārī) but not much else; I sometimes read the paper, but not regularly: I had a subscription for three to four months but no more. But there is no loss from my education. There are more benefits than costs. (Ajay, J5, rich peasant, born 1959.)

I have two sons, and we will educate them both as far as possible. I'd like one to have employment and one to do farming or to help me in my tailoring business. I don't mind if one son goes out of Nangal. It's difficult because my wife is uneducated: she can't help with their homework and I don't have time, so we have to pay for tuition in the village. (Jas Vir, J15, ten years of schooling, middle peasant, born 1954)

Some men did additional training in the hopes of employment; for example, Surinder (J11) took an apprenticeship in electrical engineering and worked as a trainee with the UP State Electricity Board for two years. When it became clear that no permanent jobs would be available for many years he came back to Nangal and turned to farming. The issue of acquiring enough schooling to get a good job was paramount in men's view of schooling, though they acknowledged that schooling alone was not enough: men also need influence *(sifārish)* or the money to pay substantial bribes. None of the men in our sample had been successful, and all had returned to the family business of farming for a living. But this did not diminish their beliefs in the value of schooling for themselves or their sons. Several had brothers who had managed to gain some form of government employment or were professionally qualified and working outside of Nangal. Locally, it was accepted that over-schooling could make men unfit for farming. Most book knowledge had no relevance to local agriculture, and while children were at school they were not learning farming skills. Furthermore, some men with secondary schooling felt that farming was beneath their dignity.

I have one son and I want no more – though some people think there is strength in having many children. We'll see what comes in future for him. I'll educate him as far as possible. If he's educated he'll be able to get a good job and do other things – the educated can do anything. Nowadays farming's a business with lots of writing work and you need to do things on time. All the educated men in Nangal can do farming. But there's a danger that men like that will sit around doing nothing, just getting money from their parents. (Rishipal, J19, three years' schooling, middle peasant)

Sheikh and Jat men compared

There were, then, marked differences between the Jat and the Sheikh men in terms of the amount of schooling they had received, and their commitment to schooling for their own sons. The Jat men were clearly more exposed to 'modern' influences than the Sheikh men. For example, all those schooled beyond higher secondary school had had to go regularly to one of the local towns. They also expressed a greater belief in the value of schooling. So might this be the key to fertility differences? Or is the issue one of girls' autonomy? We will first discuss the meaning of schooling for the Sheikh and Jat wives, and the implications of boys' and girls' schooling for fertility, and return to some explanations of what might account for these differences in schooling experiences in Chapter 6.

Schooling for girls

Indian government policy has increasingly drawn attention to the low enrolments of girls, and many separate government girls' primary schools have been established, usually in the same villages as existing schools, and often on adjacent plots. Girls, especially as they approached puberty, found moving in public space a risk. Their freedom of movement was much more limited than that of their brothers, and their reputations (and thus their marriageability) were threatened if they appeared too self-confident about dealing with boys. All parents were concerned about the sexual harassment of a daughter. Unless she had a brother as chaperon, a girl might be regarded as fair game by boys from her own caste and community as well as others. At primary level, parents preferred to send daughters to girls' schools, or to ones with female teachers. As girls got older, even those from locally dominant castes were believed to be vulnerable, though serious cases of sexual harassment were not very common. Few girls continued their schooling beyond fifth class, since this usually involved travel beyond the village, and even fewer rural parents let girls aged 14 or over study at the higher secondary schools and inter-colleges in towns. The few who did so might ask a close relative in town to act as chaperon, try to establish an urban base themselves, insist on a reliable adult accompanying them to school, or restrict their daughters to studying 'privately' at home. Only a narrow band of the wealthiest landowners schooled their daughters beyond eighth class.

Several women described differences in style and demeanour between an illiterate person and one who had been educated: some of the uneducated women described themselves as just like a beast, with connotations of being brutish or simple (*pashu ke samān*). One common and colourful assertion was that an uneducated person given their death sentence written on a piece of paper would wander around happily with it because of ignorance of its contents. Most women agreed, then, that education had a value in itself, a unique value for any individual who has been educated. As one woman put it, 'Education is not something that another person can snatch away, but all other things can be taken away or divided.' Beyond that, women often found it difficult to articulate the benefits of education; whereas non-literacy had many drawbacks (*sārā nuqsān*) literacy gave 'just every advantage' (*sārā fāydā*). But not all accepted that education might greatly improve a woman's lot: as several women said, even those with a lot of schooling still had to cook and make dung cakes, so it was hard to see direct benefits.

Sheikhs and Qur'anic schooling for girls

Among the Sheikhs in Qaziwala, there was less pressure for girls to marry 'up' in status. If close-kin marriages were arranged, such status concerns had little significance, since such marriages might involve an exchange of brides, sometimes across two generations. None the less, brides were expected to have less schooling than their husbands, or at most an equal amount. This was the dominant pattern for the 233 Sheikh women who began cohabiting between 1950 and 1989. In 68 marriages the husband had more schooling, and in 119 marriages the partners had equal schooling experience. None the less, in 39 cases the wife could read the Qur'an (and possibly Urdu) while her husband was illiterate. Of our sample women, 14 had learnt to read at least part of the Qur'an Sharīf or the Urdu script; only one of them had received any secular education, but she did not complete even one year and could not read Hindi. None of the sample women was married to men less-educated than they were.

Those women whose parents had sent them to learn described a situation where neither of their parents were strong supporters of learning, nor were they themselves interested in learning. Although parents would often beat their children to make them go to school, several girls would hide, lose their books, or refuse to continue when they were beaten by the teacher.

There was a mosque in Qaziwala during my childhood, but I didn't go there to study. I went to women in the village. I didn't complete reading the Qur'an Sharif. I got involved in play. My parents tried a lot to get me to study, and they beat both me and my sister a lot. Over there [in the house they were sent to] the [woman] teacher used to beat us and here in the house our parents used to. But even so I didn't study. Then I thought that rather than "eat" beatings from both directions it was better just to be beaten by my parents. Now I think that if I had studied, it would have been good. My sister also didn't study. Both of us read *sipāre* (sections) but now we don't remember. (Amna, 51, born and married within Qaziwala, poor peasant)

There was no school or *madrasā* in my village during my childhood. A school is now being built. There was a *madrasā* in the next village. I went to study Qur'an

Sharīf in the mosque but I read only one section because my parents didn't pay attention to my education. No one in my parents' home is educated. (Nur Jahan, S12, born 42 km from Qaziwala, unschooled, poor peasant)

Women pointed out that even if they did want to learn, 'protecting a girl's honour' (and thus the honour of her family) made it very hard for girls to go to school. Of the women born in Qaziwala itself, by no means all were able to take advantage of the proximity of the *madrasā* after it was built in 1959, one km away at Begawala:

We are nine siblings. Eight were educated, and the youngest goes to Begawala to study. One sister and two brothers are older than me. I'm the fourth child. There's no school or *madrasā* in Qaziwala. Those who studied went to Begawala or learnt to read Arabic with an educated woman. Or if any young woman in the house is more educated, then she will teach children. I and my older sister studied only in Qaziwala. All the rest went to Begawala. Previously, people didn't send girls there, so we also weren't sent. Neither of my parents told me to study, I myself studied. There is one woman who teaches children, five or seven children go to her and she also teaches Urdu. She also taught me Urdu, but I've forgotten. I continued to go for study after my marriage. Then four years later was the *gaunā* (cohabitation), and I didn't go any more. (Hasina, S6, rich peasant)

I'm uneducated but all my sisters are educated. They've studied the Qur'an Sharīf in Begawala. When I was small, I sometimes went and sometimes didn't. When I got big I gained some sense – but then my parents wouldn't send me! I read two to four sections (*sipāre*) after becoming big [reaching puberty] but then my marriage was settled here, and I was kept indoors in case I met my future husband on the path. I myself am capable of praying and fasting (*namāz-rozā lāyaq*) and that's fine. Because the children are always around me, I don't say my prayers more than once or twice a day. He [her husband] does the household accounts. The accounts do not stay in the hands of those women who are educated. What's the benefit from being educated or uneducated, since I'm not responsible for my own affairs (*ikhtiyār*)? (Farmudan, S3, middle peasant)

The remaining woman from our sample who was taught to read Arabic was brought up in Bijnor town.

I can read only the Qur'an Sharīf, and nothing else. I studied at home, my mother alone taught me. Previously the general opinion was not in favour of education. Who thought about education? But now people do, and I think children should be educated. If a girl can study a bit, it can only be good, if it's in her fate (*nasīb*). My aunt's (FBW) daughters went to school. My aunt was good-hearted, and whatever the children wanted to do, they could do it. Those children studied only because it was their wish to do so. (Rasheeda, S16, middle peasant)

The ten women who did not even start any schooling blamed their parents and the absence of schools in their village when they were growing up for their inability to read and write. Girls might be kept at home because they were needed to do housework, or because of poverty:

Among us sisters none is educated, because there was no school in my parents' village. There was a mosque but no *maulvī* to teach the children. With *maulvīs* it was like this, that one would come for two days and having taught for a bit would go away and not return within a month. I myself went to study occasionally, but on the way I would stop and begin playing and eating. (Parveen, S14, middle peasant)

One of my sisters read the Qur'an Sharīf, not at the *madrasā*, but at the house of someone who had learned the Qur'an by heart. It's hard to rear children in poor houses. That's why my brothers were put to work. Neither my mother nor my father are educated either. If there had been money, they would have educated the children, but otherwise, how could they be educated? (Wakila, S21, landless)

Even the uneducated women, however, were now trying to ensure that their children have at least a basic schooling.

We both, husband and wife, want the children to study. It's also his [her husband's] wish. We sent Fatima to several places, in the village as well as Begawala, but Fatima didn't study. One should educate one's children, even if you [parents] eat less. If the children become capable of reading and writing that's fine. It's not necessary that they should get service, that's a matter of destiny *(qismat)*. But however much they study that's fine. Whoever studies is not useless. (Usmana, S19, middle peasant)

In Qaziwala, though, most parents' ambitions for their children did not extend much beyond completing a few years at the *madrasā* in Begawala. If that was the most they expected, they seemed happy for their sons and daughters to receive a similar level of schooling. If they had greater ambitions, however, a different set of views applied to the schooling of boys and of girls.

I have one boy and two girls and I want the girls and boy alike to study. The boy goes to Begawala and he will go again after *Eid*. The older girl is still little and not capable of going to Begawala. I will just educate my son and daughters to whatever level they can study in Begawala. We would need money for sending them to Bijnor to study. Where would such money come from, that we could educate them very much? In any case, after studying in the *madrasā* the boy too will end up as a labourer. I want to educate the girls to read the Qur'an Sharīf and some Urdu. Then my children will become competent *(durust)* to do their religious duties. Now, when marriages are being arranged, boys ask if the girl's a bit educated or not. That's why a little education is necessary. If I myself had read the Qur'an Sharīf, it would have been good. I've had no benefit or damage from not being educated. I'm OK, but these days everyone looks at education [when arranging marriages]. (Gulshan, S5, landless)

My older daughter goes to Begawala to study. The second [a boy, Azam Ali] goes to Rahimpur school. The younger girl reads Qur'an Sharīf at home. We'll educate the boy but not the girl. Azam Ali is studying Hindi and reading the Qur'an Sharīf at home, so that he can be capable of doing his prayers and fasts properly. For girls, it's a separate calculation. Once girls reach puberty they're stopped. That girl standing over there now isn't going to study any more. I want to put my boys into service. There are too many of us doing farming. There's plenty of money for educating children, but we shan't educate the girls. (Farmudan, S3, middle peasant)

Thus girls were educated (if at all) not for careers or employment, but for marriage. Even a minimum of schooling for girls may not lead to the desired marriage. As one Sheikh woman put it, few girls get husbands in service (implying that there was no point in educating them).

The meaning of girls' schooling for Jats in Nangal

The conventional perspective on schooling for girls – mainly held by the older generation, and increasingly on the decline in Nangal – was that lengthy education for girls was costly and rather pointless. Schooling was valued primarily as a route to employment, but girls were not going to be sent out to 'service' and they would do the same work in the house after marriage, whether educated or not.

What would have been the advantage of being educated? I suppose that if I were educated, I might have been married into a better house or to a man in service. But beyond education is destiny. Even some educated girls are not getting men in service or good houses, and some uneducated girls are going into good houses. That's a matter of one's own destiny. In any case, whether you're educated or not, there's no difference in the housework. (Shivani w/o Som Pal, J12, uneducated, middle peasant)

Only a few young women in Nangal indicated that they intended to educate their daughter with employment in mind, in marked contrast to their own and their husbands' views on schooling for their sons. For daughters, employment was simply not a consideration (as it had not been for the women themselves). In Nangal, one of the two Jat women with an MA decided not to pursue her own studies further because she would not be permitted to work outside the home:

After doing my BA, I was married. Then I did my MA alongside my husband. I wanted to study even further, but my husband does not like service. He said that even if I studied further I would have to take charge of the house and would not be sent out for service. So what is the point of studying any more since I shall have to stay in the house? (Shamo w/o Shiv Singh, J1, MA Hindi, rich peasant)

Employment for a woman was a possibility to be activated only in dire circumstances, a residual ambition at most: 'in a calamity [i.e. widow-hood], an educated daughter could live in her in-laws' house without being a burden on anyone. She will stand on her own feet.' (Nirdosh, J3, tenth class pass, middle peasant).

The alternative view was that schooling was a benefit for all, but that for girls, schooling was necessary in order for them to be married to an educated man. These days, schooling for girls was widely seen as a key factor in the marriage market. People often talked about the responsibility of trying to marry one's daughter into a 'good house' (*achchhā ghar*). This was something of a catch-all term, for people in different economic circumstances have different expectations and options. Apart from pertaining to the physical structure of the house and to its social atmosphere, the term implies a family that was at least moderately well to do (preferably owning a lot of land or in a flourishing business, public sector employment or professional occupation). Such economic security can usually be taken to mean that the women of the house need not work outside, be it in the family fields or in paid employment. Sustaining such an economic position requires the young men of the family to be educated if they are to have any hope of obtaining employment that will reduce the drain they make on the family land, and ensure that they will comfortably be able to support their parents and also their wife and children in the future. And these days, an educated groom was likely to insist on being married to an educated bride.

The marriage system has, of course, long been competitive; recently the main changes have been a rise in dowry demands and the increasing significance of the girl's schooling in the issues which parents consider, alongside landholding, sub-caste or family (*khandān*), and appearance. The Jat marriage system – as in much of north India – was hypergamous, in that brides are expected to marry 'up'. While a bride may be married to someone of equal education, it was far more common for a bride to be married to a man with some years more education than herself: in Nangal, for instance, that gap was anywhere up to a dozen years. Only 5 of the 240 women who began cohabiting between 1950 and 1989 had more than one year's more schooling than their husbands, and 38 had the same level of schooling. The parents of grooms with many years of schooling usually expected substantial dowries to accompany a bride. They regarded this demand as a legitimate recompense for their expenditures in schooling their son, and in recognition of the fact that their daughter-in-law could expect a relatively affluent lifestyle. The high dowries demanded by the parents of potential grooms with even more schooling meant that only very wealthy parents were willing to educate a girl very far. Even though the overall sex ratio was highly adverse to women, parents of girls with a wide range of educational achievement were in competition for matches with smaller numbers of highly educated men. Clearly, everyone cannot succeed in marrying their daughter into a 'good house'. Parents of girls have to look in places where they think they will be accepted:

> Everybody wants a good boy and a good house for their girl. My father wanted there to be land. The boy should be a little bit educated, and there should be no demands [for dowry]. The boy's people should be straightforward, and they shouldn't live too far away. He didn't want a boy in service because I'm not educated. My brother had wanted me to be married to an educated boy, but my father said, 'What sort of education has our girl got that we should go looking for an educated boy? This boy is straightforward, what else is necessary?' (Dholi w/o Dharmpal, J20, third class pass, middle peasant, husband second class pass)

The key advantage educated girls were considered to enjoy, and the reason most women gave for wanting their daughters to be schooled, was precisely this enhancement of their marriage chances: unschooled girls, they feared, would be hard to marry into a good house:

> It would be good if my son could stand on his own feet – I'd like him to get service. The girls will study just a little – what service do farmers' girls do? But I do want them to study. Everyone wants an educated girl, so if they aren't educated there'll be worries over getting them married. (Jagvati, J15, uneducated, middle peasant)

> My father-in-law says that my daughter should just be sent to school until she is capable of some work (*kām lāyaq,* i.e. housework), say to eighth or tenth class, for she is to be married and not sent out for service. But I want to get her properly educated, because boys generally want to be married to an educated girl. (Asha, J5, tenth class pass, rich peasant)

Chance elements were important in affecting which girls went to school and for how long. This can be seen in the wide range of experiences within the sibling groups of the Nangal women, schooled and unschooled alike. There were uneducated sisters alongside educated ones, and women who had never been to school with brothers who had completed tertiary education. Sometimes the building of a school in the village enabled younger sisters to become more educated than older ones. But, equally, girls attending school were not always encouraged to continue if they wavered, preferred to play or feared the teacher's beatings; and older sisters were sometimes more educated than younger ones. There seems no clear trend even within families. Parents who were otherwise in favour of giving their daughters a good schooling might none the less stop one daughter from going to school to meet some pressing immediate need, whereas the girl's sisters may have been able to continue for much longer.

Something of these shifting sands can be captured in our sample women's experiences of schooling. Several had faced obstacles in being educated. Some never went to school, or had their schooling stopped because their labour was needed at home, especially if they were the oldest daughter or if their mother was ill. Others were spoiled by their grandparents and kept at home (rather than exposed to the harsh discipline of school life) because of the special love felt for them. Some had been prevented from attending school because there was no school in their natal village. But the more general picture was one of parents' not exerting much pressure on their daughters: the uneducated women often looked back regretfully, commenting, 'What parents paid attention to girls' schooling in those days?' Even some women whose parents had attended to their schooling found their education curtailed because relatives considered no more was necessary for marriage:

My parents stopped my education in order to get me married. I'd come to an age to be married and they said that I had enough education for marriage. They said my in-laws could let me study further if they wished, but my parents had fulfilled their own wishes on that. (Shamo w/o Shiv Singh, Jı, MA Hindi completed after marriage, rich peasant)

Then again, the importance of marriage was linked to a range of tactics as parents weighed up the importance of educating a girl against the problems of doing so. Many villages with primary schools do not boast secondary ones and girls often stop attending school after completing fifth class. Partly this was because parents will not allow their near pubertal daughters to travel beyond their village. In addition, girls were often taken out of school because their parents judged them sufficiently educated for marriage and now in need of being taught domestic skills without the distractions of school work. In villages with schools just up to eighth class, similar considerations come into play at that stage. Girls living in peri-urban villages have more chance of being educated to higher levels because schools are more accessible. Moreover, girls who have completed eighth class can continue their studies by enrolling as 'private' rather than 'regular' students. The private student studies at home and from private tutors, a neat way of ensuring that she acquires the desired accreditation while both learning domestic skills and being protected from gossip that might affect her marriage chances. Unlike the 'regular' student, she rarely faces challenges to her self-confidence from negotiating the vagaries of travelling alone or meeting people outside her kin network. (This kind of complication is rarely considered by those who focus on simple measures of 'years of schooling' and extrapolate to the kinds of experiences they assume this involves.)

Not surprisingly, parents who feel they have misjudged the effort they should have put into educating their daughters may resort to deceit in order to achieve a successful marriage for them.[11] Sometimes this involved showing falsified school certificates; in other cases parents just asserted that their daughter was educated when she was not.

When my marriage was being arranged, my brother lied and said I was fifth class pass. My husband found out afterwards and was very angry. He wouldn't speak to me properly. Then he went to my parents' house and asked why he hadn't been told in the first place, for then he could have married me or not as he pleased. Then my brother asked my husband what service he was doing, and if he was planning to send me out for service [to work in a white-collar job]. What can I tell you about what I have had to endure because of being uneducated? (Vinod, J16, uneducated, middle peasant)

Her husband put a brave face on the situation:

If the boy is educated, the girl also should be educated. An uneducated girl can't remember things so well. She can't make sure the children go to school properly. It wasn't my choice to have an uneducated bride, but we had to take what we could get. I didn't have any service, so what could we expect? (Vijay, J16, tenth class, middle peasant)

Schooling was not simply an important factor in marriage negotiations, however. Most of the women considered that schooling had some important practical benefits within marriage, even for those women who would not be in employment or be compelled to deal with bank officials and the like.

Previously I thought, what, would I get a job after being educated? Now I realize that being able to read is also essential for all household affairs. But what can I do now? (Shalu, J22, uneducated, middle peasant)

Discussions with the men about why they wanted educated brides indicated considerable consonance between men's and women's views of the importance of schooling for a woman's domestic roles. One asset was that a schooled wife had good manners and was no longer a rustic:

Writing-reading is never useless, because it increases your knowledge. Your education stays with you. If I need to make a calculation, then I can do so. I can also read books. And an educated person looks different, their style of dress is different. An unlettered person is uncouth (ganwār) and doesn't even know how to make conversation properly. (Asha, J5, tenth class pass, rich peasant)

Consequently, educated women were considered better able to fulfil the 'status production' aspects of their domestic obligations.[12] While this

---

[11] Deceit on the boy's side also occurs, of course, about his employment and income as well as his schooling, driven by attempts to maximize the dowry that was offered. In marriage negotiations, in general the boy's side has more freedom of action.

[12] The 'status production' work done by Indian women in maintaining and enhancing the status of the family is discussed in Papanek 1979 and Sharma 1986.

includes being socially competent and knowing how to treat guests properly, it most especially concerns child-rearing (*pālan-poshan*). An educated mother will be able to teach her children good manners and good habits: as one man put it, 'If the wife is educated, the children will turn out all right' (*agar gharwāli ki talīm hai, bachche sahe ho jāenge*). Central to the child-rearing roles of educated women was the task of supervising children's school work, ensuring that the children apply themselves to their studies (rather than running around the village out of control) and saving money that might otherwise be spent on tuition fees. Uneducated women not only cannot help with their children's school work but have to contend with their children's querulous and disrespectful comments: as one women put it, 'If I were educated, my child wouldn't call me stupid (*bāvli*).'

If I'd been educated, I would have to do the same housework. But being educated is another matter. If I'd studied, it would have been good – I realize that now. I'm very upset that my parents didn't compel me. A human being without education is just like a beast. I can't teach the children, nor can I do accounts. There's nothing but damage from being uneducated. (Sheela, J23, uneducated, middle peasant)

I don't get any great benefit from being educated. I'm tenth class pass and have to cook *rotī* (food, bread). If I were more educated, I would still have to cook *rotī*. And if I were completely uneducated, there would still be this very housework to do. It's not that my in-laws send me out for service or don't make me cook *rotī* because I'm educated. But there's this benefit, that I can teach my children, or deal with essential papers, and I can read books if I ever have spare time. There's never any disadvantage in being educated. (Madho, J6, tenth class pass, rich peasant)

Some women also talked of being able to help with household accounts (*hisāb-kitāb*) and keeping records of gift exchanges in the wider kinship network. Men also welcomed those social skills of educated women that might save them time or effort. An educated woman can go shopping or visit her natal village without difficulty. The one certain disadvantage of a totally uneducated wife was that she cannot read or write letters; but, then, as a few men cheerfully acknowledged, this might usefully keep a man's parents-in-law ignorant of their daughter's domestic disputes. The only man who considered his wife's education had economic benefits outside the domestic sphere was Satish, whose wife Sudeshwala managed the farming while he earned a small income as the time-keeper at a local bus stand. According to Satish, Sudeshwala's education has helped not only with the child care and the general atmosphere of the house, but it has made her able to think carefully and make the right decisions in the farm work (see further below).

While some men said that an uneducated wife was not necessarily unintelligent, and was just as likely to see to the housework and the children properly, most would concur with one uneducated woman's comment, 'This is not an era to be without education'. Women's education was thus valued, but not for any increase in autonomy which education might give a woman. The motivation was to get her better married, and make her a better wife and mother. The crucial point here is that – barring Satish – those who advocated female education, just as much as those who considered it unnecessary, were framing their arguments within the same idiom. Whether a woman should be primarily a wife and mother was not at issue. What was being contested was whether and to what extent schooling can enhance a girl's marriage chances and make her a better mother.

Jat and Sheikh schooling strategies compared

The perception of girls' schooling as a factor in the marriage market, not the employment market, applies to Jats and Sheikhs alike. Yet there were major differences between the patterns of Jat and Sheikh schooling. Jat girls and boys were sent to the most convenient state schools, or (if their parents could afford it) to the private schools in the larger villages or towns. There they were taught largely (or completely) by Hindu teachers, and many of the stories they read involved characters from Hindu mythology. They learnt Hindi, the official language of the UP State. Until the students reached Inter-Colleges in the larger towns (in classes nine to twelve) boys and girls mostly followed the same formal curriculum. The main difference between boys and girls was thus in the length of schooling. At the higher levels, girls and boys tended to choose different subjects, and girls were more likely to complete their formal education as 'private' students (not attending classes at the college). None the less, they participated in similar kinds of schooling for the most part. The content of the schooling, and the manner in which it was transmitted, placed considerable stress on obedience, rote learning, and (for the girls) offered little in the way of overt messages that might encourage them to criticize their positions. Girls were schooled in order to get a 'good' husband, and, once married and with children, to be able to help get their own children through school.

Partly to avoid the Hindu atmosphere of the government schools, many Sheikh parents sent their children – boys and girls – for a *madrasā* education. Here they learnt how to fast and pray correctly. Beyond learning to read the Qur'an, Sheikh children (like Jat children) listened to moral tales and learnt to read a series of texts with uplifting messages.[13] Since the interpretations of Islam which predominate in rural north India stress the need for mothers and daughters to be dutiful and pious, there was little scope here either for the formal content of this kind of schooling to raise women's consciousness. Parents want their daughters to be able to fulfil their religious obligations. A girl should have no 'lack', for she was going to her in-laws, and should give them no reason to complain about her ability to raise her children correctly. Sheikh girls in the *madrasā* or taking Islamic lessons from *maulvīs* or women in their homes received a very different form of schooling from that offered to their brothers. A boy's religious schooling, however, was rarely described as a benefit in the marriage market, though the parents of girls might look for an educated son-in-law in the belief that he would treat his wife better than an illiterate man would do. Sheikh boys were more likely to have no schooling at all or to receive a secular schooling than were Sheikh girls, and this was a major difference from the situation among the Jats. Among the Jats, boys were primarily schooled to improve their chances in the job market, but even if that strategy failed, they could still command better dowries than comparable unschooled men.

Schooling, fertility and child mortality

At a gross level, Jat fertility was much lower than Sheikh fertility. Jat women also had more schooling than Sheikh women. *A priori* there is a case that because the Jat women had more schooling, they wanted fewer children on average and they were more able to act to limit their fertility than were Sheikh women. Here we want to investigate further the significance of schooling in helping to understand the differences in fertility behaviour of the two populations. In this discussion we regard Qur'anic schooling as potentially on a par with government schooling, even though much of the demographic literature is concerned only with western or secular education.[14] We do so because many of the hypothesized ways in which schooling and fertility (or mortality) are said to be linked could also apply to Qur'anic schooling: the experience of being out of the home and mixing with one's peers, the discipline of

---

[13] One example of the kind of text used is *Bahishti Zewar*, a late-nineteenth-century set of discussions of appropriate behaviour for women; see Metcalf 1992.

[14] Terminology is a problem here: as we have suggested on p. 192, there is a set of Hindu assumptions built into government schooling. Some teachers may elaborate on these Hindu elements, others may downplay their significance. In the schools run by the RSS, Hindu elements are undoubtedly stressed in many ways. (For a discussion of similar points with respect to Scheduled Caste children, see Nambissan 1996.) It is thus invidious to pick out Qur'anic schooling and label it 'religious', as is commonly done.

time-keeping, or the significance of schooling within family strategies for raising their social status, for example, rather than the formal content of the curriculum *per se*.

Direct comparisons between the unschooled and the schooled women are likely to be misleading, because access to schooling was relatively recent. Of the women who began cohabiting between 1950 and 1989, forty Jat women were schooled to class six or above. In 1990 they had been married for an average of only nine years, whereas the unschooled had been married for an average of sixteen years. Similarly, in Qaziwala, women with Qur'anic education had also been married for an average of nine years and uneducated women for fourteen years. Comparisons must thus be between women married for roughly the same lengths of time, and, as in Chapters 3 and 4, we compare age-specific marital fertility rates for three cohorts of women: those born up to 1945, 1946–1955, and 1956–1965. First, for both villages, we look briefly at the relationships between the schooling of the husband and fertility, contraception, child mortality and ages at marriage. We then consider the differences between the schooled and unschooled Jat and Sheikh women, considering the same variables. Finally, we discuss the extent to which the schooled women differ from the unschooled ones in terms of their autonomy, both in their household patterns and in their reproductive lives.

Male schooling and fertility

Among the Jats, male schooling has an inconsistent relationship with fertility. In the first cohort, the men with the lowest fertility rates were those with between one and eight years of schooling (most of whom completed primary school, or five years). In the second cohort, men with nine or more years of schooling have the lowest fertility; and in the third cohort, the small number of unschooled men have the lowest fertility rate (see Table 5.2). In the first cohort (those whose wives were born before 1946) child mortality differences are relatively small, but in the second cohort, the average numbers of children surviving to the age of five are virtually the same for all men with any number of years of schooling (3.6 children for men with between one and eight years of schooling, and 3.7 for men with nine or more years of schooling), whereas the unschooled men have on average 4.1 surviving children. Links between men's schooling and child mortality seem to be stronger than the links with fertility, but even this does not apply for the first cohort, where the differentials are very small. In general, our data are consistent with the wider demographic literature, in finding weak

Table 5.2. *Total marital fertility rates, and percentage of children surviving to age five, of couples by schooling of husband and year of birth of wife, up to 1965, Nangal Jats*

Wife's year of birth	Schooling of husband				
	None	1–8 years	9+ years	Unknown	All
Pre-1946	7.60	6.69	7.28	6.88	7.08
Children surviving to age 5	78%	75%	77%	70%	75%
Number of husbands	23	33	17	20	93
1946–1955	5.73	5.46	4.59	3.60	4.97
Children surviving to age 5	80%	80%	87%	100%	83%
Number of husbands	8	19	31	3	61
1956–1965	1.59	3.46	2.63	–	2.71
Children surviving to age 5	71%	79%	80%	–	79%
Number of husbands	6	22	44	–	72

Source: Maternity histories and village census carried out by authors, September–December 1990.

Note: For women born pre-1946, the figures are for children born at mother's age 15–44; for those born 1946–1955, the mother's age group is 15–34; for women born 1956–1965 the mother's age group is 15–24. Survival rates are calculated for children born up to 1985.

Table 5.3. *Percentage of couples contracepting, and their mean number of living children, by schooling of husband, and wife's year of birth up to 1965, Nangal Jats*

Wife's year of birth	Contraceptive status	Years of schooling of husband				
		None	1–5 years	6–8 years	9+ years	All current couples
Pre-1946	% Contracepting	9%	nil	29%	35%	20%
	Average number of living children	4.0	–	5.0	4.5	4.64
	Total number of couples	**23**	**14**	**20**	**17**	**75**
1946–1955	% Contracepting	44%	55%	55%	63%	59%
	Average number of living children	4.75	4.2	3.67	3.84	3.97
	Total number of couples	**9**	**9**	**11**	**30**	**59**
1956–1965	% Contracepting	33%	43%	53%	40%	42%
	Average number of living children	2.5	3.67	3.13	2.24	2.63
	Total number of couples	**6**	**7**	**15**	**44**	**72**

Note: In calculating these figures, we have omitted 17 widowed, divorced and separated women for the pre-1946 cohort, and 2 widowed women from the 1946–1955 cohort. Totals include living men whose schooling is unknown.

relationships between husband's schooling and wife's fertility. But men who have been to school longer are more likely to have wives who are using a modern contraceptive or to be sterilized themselves. Furthermore, they do so, usually, at smaller family sizes than men with less schooling, who seem to be limiting their families by different means, since they end up with much the same number of children (see Table 5.3).[15]

Among the Sheikhs, we can distinguish between government and Islamic schooling, but once again the relationships are inconsistent between cohorts. In the first cohort, men who had been to government schools had the lowest fertility rates. In the second cohort, those with an Islamic schooling have the lowest rate; and in the third cohort, the unschooled men have the lowest rate (see Table 5.4). Schooling of both kinds does seem to have had a relationship to child mortality for men whose wives were born before 1956, however, with those who have been to any kind of school experiencing smaller numbers of their children dying. As a result, on average, the men with schooling have had more children surviving beyond the age of five, even though their wives have given birth to fewer children.[16] Since there are so few Sheikh couples practising contraception, we cannot analyse any possible relationships between male schooling and contraceptive use.

Jat fertility and female schooling

Jat women in the first cohort who have been to school gave birth to fewer children, but their completed family sizes are only slightly below those of unschooled women (4.67 compared to 4.84), because they have had fewer children die (see Table 5.5). In the second cohort there is a clear inverse statistical relationship between schooling and number of children ever born, which remains when current family sizes are considered. In the third cohort, women who have been to school have very similar numbers of children surviving to age 5 as have unschooled women. There is a more consistent relationship between the schooling of the mother and the survival of her children, with the unschooled women in each cohort experiencing higher mortality rates for their children.

Further, when either husband or wife has been sterilized, schooled women have in general as many living children as unschooled women

---

[15] Surprisingly, Jat men with more schooling get married, on average, considerably younger than men with less schooling: we will return to why this might be so in Chapter 6, but here it is worth pointing out that there is no reason to expect this to have any effect on the couple's fertility, since it is the woman's age at marriage which normally affects this.

[16] The anomalous case is men whose wives were born in 1956–65; it is not clear why men with government schooling should have seen so many of their children die.

Table 5.4. *Total marital fertility rates, and percentage of children surviving to age five, of women by year of birth up to 1965, and by schooling of husband, Qaziwala Sheikhs*

Wife's year of birth	Schooling of husband				
	None	Islamic	1 or more	Unknown	All
Pre-1946	9.12	8.37	7.21	7.31	9.06
Children surviving to age 5	64%	75%	71%	74%	69%
Number of husbands	41	13	4	18	76
1946–1955	7.26	6.67	6.80	5.71	7.07
Children surviving to age 5	71%	83%	83%	75%	75%
Number of husbands	35	10	8	1	54
1956–1965	3.73	3.78	4.08	–	3.78
Children surviving to age 5	78%	82%	65%	–	78%
Number of husbands	54	15	11	–	80

Source: Maternity histories and village census carried out by authors, Qaziwala, February–April 1991.
Missing cases: nil
Note: For women born pre-1946, the figures are for children born at mother's age 15–44; for those born 1946–1955, the mother's age group is 15–34; for women born 1956–1965 the mother's age group is 15–24. Survival rates are calculated for children born up to 1985.

(see Table 5.6). Proportionately more schooled women are using contraception than are the unschooled women. Of the men and women married after 1959, fifty-four have been sterilized. The mean number of living children of the seven women with secondary schooling (class six or above) is 3.7 children; of the thirteen women with one to five years schooling it is 3.2 children; and of the thirty-four uneducated women it is 3.8 children. What these figures hide, however, is that educated women who have been sterilized have had fewer children die: 7 per cent of the children of the sterilized women schooled to class six or above, compared with nearly 15 per cent of the children of sterilized women with less than five years of schooling, died before they reached their fifth birthday. There are also differences in the kind of contraception being used: the unschooled women were more likely to be sterilized, if they are contracepting, and less likely to be using a Copper-T or a contraceptive pill than are women who had been to school.

At an overall level, then, the tables suggest relatively small and inconsistent differences between the fertility experiences of schooled and unschooled Jat women. This is surprising, since so many studies have shown much clearer and stronger statistical relationships. Part of the reason for this lack of clear differences may be because, for women born

Table 5.5. *Total marital fertility rates, and percentage of children surviving to age five, of women by schooling and year of birth, up to 1965, Nangal Jats*

	Years of schooling of woman			
Woman's year of birth	None	1–5	6+	All
Pre-1946	7.30	6.46	6.67	7.08
Children surviving to age 5	74%	82%	100%	75%
Number of women	74	18	1	93
1946–1955	5.22	4.81	3.49	4.97
Children surviving to age 5	82%	85%	100%	84%
Number of women	39	17	5	61
1956–1965	2.45	3.29	2.52	2.61
Children surviving to age 5	75%	85%	83%	79%
Number of women	36	15	21	72

Source: Maternity histories and village census carried out by authors, Nangal, September–December 1990.

Missing cases: nil

Note: for women born pre 1946, the figures are for children born at mother's age 15–44; for those born 1946–1955, the mother's age group is 15–34; for women born 1956–1965 the mother's age group is 15–24. Survival rates are calculated for children born up to 1985.

Table 5.6. *Percentage of couples contracepting, and their mean number of living children, by schooling of wife, and her year of birth, up to 1965, Nangal Jats*

		Years of schooling of woman			
Woman's year of birth	Contraceptive Status	None	1–5	6 +	All current couples
Pre-1946	% Contracepting	13%	40%	100%	20%
	Average number of living children	4.25	4.67	6.00	4.64
	Total number of couples	**59**	**15**	**1**	**75**
1946–1955	% Contracepting	59%	53%	80%	59%
	Average number of living children	4.36	3.22	3.00	3.97
	Total number of couples	**37**	**17**	**5**	**59**
1956–1965	% Contracepting	42%	40%	43%	42%
	Average number of living children	2.60	2.67	2.67	2.63
	Total number of couples	**36**	**15**	**21**	**72**

Note: In calculating these figures, we have omitted 17 widowed, divorced and separated women for the pre-1946 cohort, and 2 widowed women from the 1946–55 cohort.

Table 5.7. *Average age at marriage for men and women by wife's schooling and year of cohabitation, Jat women born up to 1965, Nangal*

Wife's year of birth	Average age at marriage	Schooling of wife			
		None	1–5 years	6+	All
Pre-1946	Wife's age	17.4	17.2	16.5	17.3
	Husband's age	21.5	20.3	35.5	20.5
	Number of couples	74	16	1	91
1946–1955	Wife's age	17.5	18.0	17.7	17.7
	Husband's age	21.7	20.6	18.9	21.2
	Number of couples	39	17	5	61
1956–1965	Wife's age	17.8	19.3	20.2	18.8
	Husband's age	23.4	21.8	22.3	22.7
	Number of couples	26	14	12	52
All	Wife's age	17.5	18.1	19.3	17.8
	Husband's age	21.9	20.9	22.1	21.7
	Number of couples	139	47	18	204

Source: Maternity histories and village census carried out by authors, Nangal, September–December 1990.
Missing cases: 4

up to 1955, schooling had little impact on a woman's age at marriage (see Table 5.7). The indicator we have used – age-specific marital fertility – controls for age at marriage. But even were we to use other indicators (like age-specific total fertility) there would be no reason to change our conclusion.

In our sample, women schooled beyond the age of thirteen or fourteen were married 2.5 years older than the unschooled, but that reflects the fact that we chose the most schooled women in the village as key informants. The sample of educated women were also slightly younger (twenty-seven on average, versus twenty-nine) and had thus been married for shorter periods (8 years as against 12). Only two of the women (both uneducated) had as many as four children; four had three children, 13 had two children, and four had one child. Six (five of them uneducated) had already been sterilized and a further seven (two uneducated) were using the contraceptive pill or an IUD. The most clear-cut difference between the schooled and unschooled women in their use of contraception, then, was in the choice of contraceptive method. The unschooled were more likely to choose – or have foisted on them – methods (such as sterilization or an IUD) which did not depend on regular action on their part. To this extent, at least, schooling might have tended to increase Jat women's sense of being able to cope with contraceptive technologies which leave some power in the woman's hands.

Sheikh women, Qur'anic schooling and fertility

The statistical relationships between schooling and fertility are weak for Jats, but even weaker for the Sheikhs. As we have seen, whether or not Sheikh girls were schooled at all, very few are now able to do more than read their prayer books. Even Urdu literature is beyond most of them. The number of women born before 1946 who received an Islamic schooling is too small for any generalization. Those born between 1946 and 1955 who were taught to read the Qur'an have higher fertility rates than those who did not receive an Islamic education (see Table 5.8). But for those born between 1956 and 1965, the reverse is true. There was also only a weak relationship between Qur'anic education and the age at which women were married – not surprisingly, since girls have to leave the *madrasā* once they reach puberty. Only for the third cohort, those born between 1956 and 1965, are the differences in the predicted direction, with the women receiving an Islamic education marrying on average six months older than unschooled women; but by itself, this amount of difference would have little effect on completed family sizes (see Table 5.9).

The evidence from the maternity histories of the ever-married Jat and Sheikh women of any relationship between schooling and fertility is thus equivocal at best. Schooling could be having an impact in ways that are not captured by the maternity histories, however. We now turn to consider whether the women with more schooling differ systematically in other ways, by looking in more detail at the experiences of our sample women when their marriages were being arranged, and at their ability to affect their domestic living arrangements. In other words, even if schooling seems to have little impact on Jat and Sheikh women's fertility, does it none the less enhance their autonomy?

Schooling and autonomy

Marriage decisions

No unschooled Jat woman said that she had been asked for her opinion about her marriage: 'Who asked girls in those days?' was a common retort. When they were married – between 1970 and 1985 – arranging marriages was the responsibility of parents and their parents had simply done as they pleased in the matter.

Table 5.8. *Total marital fertility rates, and percentage of children surviving to age five, of women by schooling and year of birth up to 1965, Qaziwala Sheikhs*

	Schooling of woman		
Woman's year of birth	None	Islamic	All
Pre-1946	9.10	8.18	9.06
Children surviving to age 5	68%	75%	69%
Number of women	73	3	76
1946–1955	6.78	7.64	7.07
Children surviving to age 5	77%	72%	75%
Number of women	36	18	54
1956–1965	3.89	3.48	3.78
Children surviving to age 5	75%	87%	78%
Number of women	58	22*	80

Source: Maternity histories and village census carried out by authors, February–April 1991.
* The total of mothers born 1956–65 includes one woman with class 8 schooling.
Note: For women born pre-1946, the figures are for children born at mother's age 15–44; for those born 1946–1955, the mother's age group is 15–34; for women born 1956–1965 the mother's age group is 15–24. Survival rates are calculated for children born up to 1985.

Table 5.9. *Average age at marriage for men and women by wife's schooling and wife's year of birth, of women born up to 1965, Qaziwala Sheikhs*

		Wife's schooling		
Wife's year of birth	Average age at marriage	None	Islamic	All
Pre-1946	Wife's age	15.5	15.5	15.5
	Husband's age	18.7	17.8	18.6
	Number of couples	71	4	75
1946–1955	Wife's age	16.5	16.6	16.5
	Husband's age	20.0	20.8	20.2
	Number of couples	36	17	53
1956–1965	Wife's age	16.6	17.1	16.7
	Husband's age	20.8	19.8	20.5
	Number of couples	58	22	80
Pre-1966	Wife's age	16.1	16.7	16.2
	Husband's age	19.7	20.0	19.7
	Number of couples	165	43	208

Source: Maternity histories and village census carried out by authors, February–April 1991.
Missing cases: Three widows for whose husbands we have no age at marriage.

Previously who asked a girl's opinion? I couldn't even have uttered a word about it – I was too embarrassed. I just silently overheard discussions about my marriage. (Sheela w/o Sushil, J23, uneducated, middle peasant)

With us, no one asks a girl's opinion – and I was a girl and also uneducated. My brother with a BA was not even asked about his own marriage and he was very angry about that. But with us, the parents do everything – they arrange their children's marriages just as they wish. (Shalu w/o Sher Singh, J22, uneducated, middle peasant)

Shalu's comments might suggest that educated girls have more influence over their own marriages, but according to the educated women in Nangal, this was not so:

My opinion wasn't asked and nor did I say anything to anyone about my marriage. Since my parents themselves were looking for a good house to send me to, what need was there for me to speak? (Madho w/o Mahavir, J6, 10th class pass, rich peasant)

Neither was my opinion asked about this boy, nor did anyone take any notice of any opinion of mine. If I'd expressed my own wishes, my father wouldn't have been able to stand the shock. When my aunt forbade one possible match, he said that it was wrong of her to give that boy a bad reputation. So for that reason I stayed silent. My father's very old-fashioned, and in this matter he considers it very bad for a girl to speak. (Ujala w/o Uday, J4, 10th class pass, middle peasant)

Most of the Jat women had been aware that their marriage was being arranged, but only one had voiced her opinion to her parents:

I was able to continue at school until eighth class as I was still small but then my father stopped my schooling. He began talking about getting me married but when I heard that I said I would first study some more and then get married. My schooling was stopped for a year, but then (as a result of my obstinacy) my father filled out the forms and I studied up to tenth class at home privately. I still wanted to study some more but my parents got me married. I managed to study because of my obstinacy, otherwise who would have educated me? My marriage was delayed for just one to two years – otherwise I would have been married at sixteen or seventeen. As it was I was married at 17, which is one year earlier than the law permits. My parents looked for a boy in one other place – he was my sister's husband's younger brother. I myself said I didn't want that match – it isn't right to have two sisters married into one house. Then my parents looked here in Nangal. (Nirdosh w/o Navid, J3, tenth class pass, middle peasant)

In general, the married Jat women – whether educated or not – had played no part in the arrangement of their own marriages. Although there are some signs that the situation was beginning to change, there was little prospect of women having a substantial say in the choice of their husbands. So far, even educated girls in towns are only being given the opportunity to offer general opinions; for example, not to go to the same house as their sister, or to ask for a husband with a job, rather than a farmer.

I wasn't asked for my opinion, but my younger sister [with an MA] is being married now and they asked her what she thinks, because we have now understood that a girl's opinion should be asked. (Shamo w/o Shiv Singh, J1, BA, rich peasant)

The picture among the Sheikhs was little different, even though formal education for married women in Qaziwala has been exclusively Qur'anic and a much smaller proportion of our Sheikh sample had any education than of our Jat sample. In practice, Qur'anic education does not entitle a girl to be consulted over her marriage, although educated girls are more likely to be aware that the Islamic marriage contract requires that the bride give her consent during the wedding ceremony.

People here don't ask a girl's opinion about her marriage and nor would my parents have listened if I'd said anything. Whatever the parents have done is correct. And my parents have done everything properly for all three of us married sisters. All three boys are good – they're all educated. (Hasina w/o Hasan, S6, Qur'an Sharīf, middle peasant)

I was fourteen or fifteen when I was married. I don't know whose decision it was. In those days it was like that, if anyone had asked I wouldn't have been able to say what marriage was. Now everyone has become aware. No one asked my opinion about my marriage. At the nikāh (formal consent) my parents gave the permission, not me. (Parveen w/o Parvez, S16, uneducated, middle peasant)

The one Sheikh woman who did speak up was Mehsar (see Chapter 4), an uneducated woman from Qaziwala itself. In general, then, as for the Jats, a Sheikh girl's own educational level had little apparent effect on whether she was consulted either about when or to whom she would be married. This is not to say that the educational levels of the girl and her potential groom were irrelevant in weighing up the suitability of potential matches; indeed they were generally very salient (and we shall return to this important question in the next chapter). Schooled women could hope for a better home, and a more pleasant married life. But we have no evidence that they had more voice in the marriage negotiations, or additional ways of indirectly influencing the decision about who they are to marry.

Household patterns

What of the impact of schooling on living arrangements after marriage? Are schooled women more likely to be living in separate households from their mothers-in-law, and so more able to influence their everyday lives? Of Jat women who began cohabiting between 1970 and 1989 (and therefore most likely to be 'joint'), 45 per cent of those with no schooling, 62 per cent of those with primary education, and 66 per cent of those with more than primary schooling, were 'joint'. Among the Sheikhs, 26 per cent of the unschooled, but 48 per cent of those who learnt to read the Qur'an Sharīf, were 'joint'. Again, as we showed in Chapter 4, class is the first explanation for these patterns: schooled women were more likely to be from the middle and rich peasant group. Since the total numbers are small, any more refined analysis must be approached very cautiously. None the less, of these relatively young women (aged between twenty and forty) more educated women are more likely to be in joint households. Among the rich and middle peasant Jats, 49 per cent of uneducated women are living jointly, compared with 65 per cent of women with some schooling. Similar patterns hold for the much smaller numbers of poor peasant and landless Jats. Among the Sheikhs, the figures for the small number of rich and middle peasant women living jointly are 34 per cent of unschooled women, and 55 per cent of those with a Qur'anic education; again, similar patterns hold for poor peasant and landless households, in which 22 per cent of uneducated women, and 42 per cent of educated women are in joint households. In all classes and in both caste groups, then, educated women are more likely to live in a joint household, even after taking into account the length of marriage.

On the face of it, then, the women who we would have predicted to have more 'autonomy' seem to be living in domestic arrangements that normally allow women less autonomy. But these patterns tell us nothing about relationships within households. Education may increase a woman's autonomy by raising the respect in which she is held. It may be that such women enjoy more autonomy within a joint household than unschooled women, and do not feel the same urge to separate. Is it the case that an educated woman can reduce her subordination to her mother-in-law or her husband, by comparison with her uneducated sister, whether she was living jointly with her mother-in-law or in a separate household?

In our sample of households in Nangal, 13 of the 23 women were living in a joint household of some kind; the mothers-in-law of eight of the 23 were dead; and only two women were living separately from their mothers-in-law. One of the educated women was living separately from her mother-in-law: this was Shamo (Ji) who described her mother-in-law as 'free' (*āzād*) because she lived apart from her husband and stayed sometimes with Shamo and sometimes with her sister-in-law. For two of the remaining educated women, the issue did not arise because their mother-in-law was dead. Seven educated women were living with their mothers-in-law, in five cases also with at least one sister-in-law. In such households, there is little evidence that schooling has helped the women to negotiate better terms.

Now the entire housework, cleaning, sweeping, wiping floors, washing clothes, all this is done by me. Though my mother-in-law does any additional work that there is. But the responsibility for getting it done is mine. No one helps me with my work, I have to do it all myself. In the village no one helps anyone else. Whatever has to be done must be done as my mother-in-law wishes. My own wishes don't prevail. For instance, with food, I do the cooking but I first have to ask my mother-in-law what is to be cooked. I can't just cook whatever I wish. (Poonam w/o Pankaj, J8, landlord, eighth class pass, joint with mother-in-law)

I don't want to be separate, because on becoming separate you get many responsibilities. But just now I only have to do the cooking and water jobs, the work is done by one or the other of us; my mother-in-law cares for the children, and I am also joint with a sister-in-law. Sometimes one makes the *roti*, sometimes one scours the dishes. And I can visit my parents whenever I wish and stay however long I want. I have nothing to worry about except cooking and housework. All the other responsibilities for gift-giving and social calls is with my mother-in-law. And nor have we fought about any matter, nor is there fighting about work. (Madho w/o Mahavir, J6, rich peasant, tenth class pass, joint with mother-in-law and sister-in-law.)

For schooled and unschooled women alike, the issues of domination and responsibility recurred. They expressed their ambivalence about establishing separate households. In a separate household they would no longer be under their mother-in-law's thumb. On the negative side of the equation, however, they would have to worry about social and economic concerns, and face greater difficulty in coming and going, especially to visit their parents.

In Qaziwala, nine of the twenty-two sample women were living in a joint household, the mothers-in-law of five of the twenty-two were dead, and eight women were living separately from their mothers-in-law. As in Nangal, many women stated that they preferred to live in a joint household because they had no responsibilities.

While you're in a joint household you can go anywhere without being worried, but when you live separately you have to ask someone to help you, and whoever it is will only be able to cook. She can't take any responsibility off your shoulders. There's no benefit in living separately. When you live separately you also have to keep control over the children all by yourself. Living separately means you have complete responsibility, but when you live in a joint household all the responsibility for food and clothing is on your mother-in-law. (Usmana w/o Usman, S19, uneducated, middle peasant, five sons and two daughters)

We separated when there was too little room to live in and the roof of the building we were living in was falling down. That was why we separated. The farming is still joint. When everyone else comes over to join us in the new house then we will be joint again. Even now all the food and so on come only from my parents-in-law because the farming is joint. I am just cooking separately. It's like this, if I cook here first the food goes there, and if food is cooked there first it is sent to me here. Being joint keeps life *mazā* (tasty) though in joint households one has to work the whole day. And while I am separate, I get up very early and do my work and then have a holiday all day. But they [the rest of her in-laws] will come over here to live and then I will live in a joint household again. (Farmudan w/o Fida Husain, Qur'anic schooling, middle peasant, born and married in Qaziwala)

If there are differences in the extent to which women are able to negotiate pleasant working and living arrangements within joint households, local wisdom explains this solely in terms of the personal characteristics of the mother-in-law. Some schooled women are fortunate in their mother-in-law, but others are not. In other words, we have no evidence to suggest that schooled women have been more able to use their schooling as a 'weapon of the weak' to bargain better relationships with their mothers-in-law than have unschooled women.

Fertility processes

Earlier in this chapter we noted that schooling seemed to affect Jat women less through their completed family sizes (which were much the same, or even larger than those of unschooled women) than through their ability to limit the mortality of their children. At an overall level, then, there is little reason to suppose that Jat women with more schooling are better able to influence their fertility than are those with less schooling, or none at all. How do the women themselves perceive the situation?

As we have seen in Chapter 4, the one Jat woman who reported a completely independent set of decisions about contraception was uneducated (Sudha, J11); and the one woman whose contraception was decided by her husband without consulting her (Shivani, J12) was also uneducated. Apart from these extreme cases, educated and uneducated women alike described situations in which discussions about fertility control were on-going between the couple and the husband's kin, with occasional interventions from the woman's natal kin. But the women who had been to school also seemed more likely than unschooled women to use modern contraception to stop having children. Even more clearly, among the women using contraception, the women with more schooling were much more likely to use spacing methods – the pill or IUD – whereas the unschooled were more likely to be sterilized. Women with more schooling spoke more confidently about managing the temporary contraceptive methods:

I'm taking pills at present and I don't have any damage from taking pills. So it may be that I won't have the operation, for as long as the job is done by the pills what is the need for the operation? If the pills cause some damage, I'll leave off taking them and have the operation – but I don't want any more children. (Lalita w/o Lokender, J9, eighth class, landlord, one son and one daughter)

I'm taking pills to stop having more children. As long as the pills do the work that's all right. If not, then I'll have to have the operation. My husband also doesn't want me to have the operation. He says that the pills are right for as long as they do the work. But if not, then the operation will have to be done. My mother-in-law (HFBW) has had the operation, so how could she forbid me? I and my husband prevail about family planning. There's a woman from Bijnor who knows some medicine to prevent children altogether. I may take that medicine, but if I can't obtain it I'll have the operation. (Anjali w/o Anil, J10, joint with her husband's aunts, rich peasant, eighth class pass, two sons)

I don't want any more children and nor does my mother-in-law, for both my children were born by Caesarean and I had a lot of trouble. And so having seen the troubles I had with my deliveries, that alone made my mother-in-law say that there should be no more children, saying that if I died then who would look after the children? My husband also doesn't want more children. My father-in-law says nothing, he would be embarrassed. In our family everyone is having just two children. After my son was born I took pills and used the condom too; when the boy was 3 years old I stopped taking pills and my daughter was born, and now I have got a Copper-T. My mother-in-law doesn't know about the Copper-T, she does not like all these things; so I went to Bijnor with my husband and got the lady doctor to insert a Copper-T. At first, for a couple of months I had some trouble but later I got better after taking some medicine. We're getting on fine with the Copper-T, and if any trouble arises I can also have the operation. But no more children must be made. (Poonam w/o Pankaj, J8, landlord, eighth class, joint with mother-in-law, one son and one daughter)

There was evidence, then, that Jat women in Nangal with at least secondary schooling were better able to handle medical personnel, and to understand and control the use of temporary contraceptive methods. The similarities in fertility outcomes between educated and uneducated women have disguised real differences in how they achieved small families. But educated women's own reports also made it clear that they were using these methods with the full and active support of their husbands: indeed, condom use requires a husband's collaboration on a regular basis. Educated women usually reported that their parents-in-law were involved in the discussions as well. In Nangal, then, female schooling was linked to low fertility among Jats less because indepen-dent-minded women were insisting against the views of their in-laws that they wanted small families, and more because their in-laws had already reached that conclusion. These households were actively engaged in implementing a collective strategy in which an educated daughter-in-law and wife was expected to have a small number of children, who would in their turn be educated to an advanced level. In Qaziwala, by contrast, schooling was not a dominant feature of household strategies. Whether or not a woman had received schooling herself, couples were still very uncertain about how and when they might begin to space or limit their families. If girls' schooling made a difference to fertility, then, it was less because of its impact on the individual woman when she grew up, and more as an indicator of family-building strategies within the caste group of which she was a part. We return to this argument in Chapter 6.

Conclusion

The motor behind girls' education was the place of young educated men in a rapidly changing economic situation; as more boys were educated to higher and higher levels, girls' education was dragged up behind them. With increasing problems of obtaining employment, the stakes for young men were rising all the time. The dilemma besetting parents was that the marriage market was very fluid, and a seemingly sensible strategy during the girl's childhood might be out of kilter with the marriage market by the time she reached marriageable age. Levels of education for girls that would have been considered more than adequate just a few years ago now seemed incapable of ensuring a good match for them. How could they calculate what was best for their daughter? How much could they afford to spend on educating her? How much education would she need to ensure a good match? What was the pool of well-educated young men from whom her husband could be chosen? Could she be over-educated and unmarriageable?

In discussing girls' schooling with Sheikhs and Jats, the idea that a schooled woman was of benefit to her husband – in terms of status production work, or the management of the household, for example – was the most common response. But the possibility that schooling might make a woman speak up more, or expect to be consulted over key aspects of her life, was also occasionally mentioned. The assumption that women who have been to school may be more able to be assertive seems to have entered into everyday discussions about women and what they could do. But few people in Bijnor could point to individual rural women who might be exemplars of the changes that are said to flow from schooling. Schooled and unschooled women could hardly be differentiated in this regard. Schooling did not necessarily seem to increase a woman's ability or inclination to act or think rebelliously. (If anything, perhaps, the reverse was the case, since schooled women are more likely to be living in a joint household, and to have been presented with norms of respectable behaviour at school.) There was, then, a general unwillingness to express independent views, or to attempt to achieve them, which was common to the Jat and the Sheikh women.

An alternative orientation would focus on women's positions if their current situations 'break down' in some way, through divorce, separation, or widowhood. There are very few jobs for educated women, and those there are (such as teachers in the private schools beginning to spread in the larger villages) pay very poorly – Rs 300 or so a month, compared to an average of Rs 600 for manual farm or factory labour. In this sense, Jat and Sheikh educated and uneducated women alike are vulnerable. Only one woman in our sample demonstrated behaviour which suggests that she would be able to manage on her own in such circumstances.

Sudeshwala (J2) was from a village near Bijnor town, and went to school and Inter-College there. After failing her seventh class exams she wanted to stop, but her parents insisted that she continue. She finally passed her tenth class exams. When she was married to Satish in Nangal, he was a clerk in a government ration shop in a neighbouring village, and his father had already died. Soon afterwards, he was accused of embezzlement and suspended. He was thrown into jail, and his brother refused to bribe the police to get him out. Money was lent by Satish's married sister, and given by Sudeshwala's parents and by Sudeshwala herself from savings.

Satish and Sudeshwala became financially separate from his brother at that point. But Satish had had a 'fit' over his brother's attitude, and was said to be incapable of working their land. He earned a small income by acting as clerk for the local bus-owners' union. He said it was up to Sudeshwala whether they kept the land or sold it, and Sudeshwala decided to farm the land herself. As a woman, she could not plough, so she hired a servant; and Satish helped with some of the heaviest labour – lifting and loading cane for example. But she managed all the farm income herself, which she said would have been impossible if she were not educated.

Even so, she remained unusually dependent upon her parents. They gave to her partly out of love and partly because she was living in straitened circumstances. They told her not to bother Satish with financial worries but to turn to them instead if she needed anything. This she did. She had never bought clothing for herself and her children in all the time she had been married and her father had given her quite substantial sums of money on several occasions, not just the token Rs 20 or Rs 50 that a visiting daughter would normally expect to receive. She intended to send her son to live with her parents, as pressure of work prevented her from delivering him to school in Nangal. She was keen to see him educated and taught him a little at home when she had time. She left her baby daughter asleep at home while she collected fodder and did other farm work. She also wanted the girl to be educated: at least a little solid education was necessary, though beyond that (she said) it was a matter of destiny.

Even though the educated don't get jobs either these days, I still want my children to be able to do their own household accounts. Education never causes damage. I now think I should have gone further in school. Education's good for everyone, whether they get a white-collar job or not. My own education was at least of this much benefit, that I can teach my children something and I can keep my accounts. (Sudeshwala w/o Satish, J2, 10th class pass, middle peasant)

We should not, therefore, romanticize Sudeshwala, nor see her as a role model for other women. Her solution to the situation was the only plausible way of averting the financial disaster of leaving the farm untended or selling the land. She was coping but only with considerable financial help from her parents. And she felt overburdened by her responsibilities. Unlike other women who listed in loving detail the jewellery and other items they had received when they married, Sudeshwala could not recall anything. Her mind was filled with her work around the home and the farm. Since her cohabitation, she had never been to stay long at her parents' home – not even when her younger sister was married – because of her work in Nangal. She went only for the day or at most overnight. She compared herself unfavourably with her mother, whom she described as 'never having seen what direction my father's fields are in'. In relation to family planning, she was adamant:

I absolutely don't want any more children. For one thing I have a son and a daughter. We have both 'things' so what else needs to be done? Secondly, all the work is on my shoulders. No one comes to help me out, so who could I make responsible for the care of my children?

Even Sudeshwala's rather extraordinary situation, then, lends little support to the notion that education was a route to autonomy for women. In general, indeed, our discussions with women in both Nangal and Qaziwala did not point to any differences between women who had many years of schooling and the unschooled with respect to their attitudes towards independent work, or the norms they articulated about joint and separate living, and the financial implications that those living arrangements entailed.

In the next chapter we will suggest, none the less, that Jat and Sheikh women were implicated in different forms of patriarchal domination, in which the schooling of Jat women definitely played a role. We contrast their position with that of Sheikh women in terms largely of the wider political economy in which they and their husbands were located.

6   Fighting with numbers

I have three sons – the third came in the foolishness of looking for a girl. I will try to educate them all to MA level in the hopes they will get service. It doesn't matter if they all go away to work, I can always employ someone to do the farm work. Unless they get a good job, what benefit will there be from the education? Fortunately, my wife can supervise the children's study; I myself don't have the time.

(ROGER:) Why did you want a girl?)

First to help her mother in the house, before she is married; secondly because if there is any work to be done (like getting a glass of water or some food) a girl will never refuse but a son will; also a daughter is needed for me to get the merit of giving a daughter in marriage.

(ROGER:) Why not have only one son, then he would get all the land?)

Like I said, I need more than one in case that one son is bad.

(ROGER:) Why not have many more sons?)

Yes, that would be good for making the country strong; and would be important, for example in fighting, like against the Muslims, because their population is growing faster. But children are too expensive: the everyday costs are so high I couldn't afford any more. (Charan h/o Chitra, J24, middle peasant)

Questions of population size enter into political discussions in various ways in India. At the state government level, arguments are made about whether resources should flow from the central government in proportion to the relative population sizes of the States, or whether faster-growing States should be penalized. The numbers in different religious or caste groups are routinely discussed in the news media, with reference to their electoral significance. Politicians active in all arenas, from the village to the nation, are likely to have their own explanations for why the population control programme has not been more successful in reducing fertility (Pai Panandikar and Umashankar 1994). But, compared to the interest shown in the economic causes of demographic change (or the lack of it), relatively little attention has been paid to the *politics* of fertility and mortality in the demographic literature on the Indian sub-continent. In little more than an aside, for example, Wyon and Gordon (1971: 231) note that in Punjab people say that, 'Fights are won by men, not by contraceptives', but they do not follow this up with more discussion. The contention of this chapter, however, is that economics and politics are inevitably intertwined, and that an analysis of economic motives for fertility control makes sense only in a context of job opportunities and landholding which is structured communally as well as by class. In other words, classes and castes which have moved to lower levels of fertility have done so because they are able to defend their economic positions through access to urban opportunities and political dominance. It therefore makes sense for them to invest in the schooling of a small number of sons rather than in numbers *per se*. In the specific case of the Jats of Nangal, we suggest that they have limited their population as part of a semi-conscious strategy of population limitation in response to local political and economic conditions.

By contrast, Sheikhs do not have either the political or economic security to make such calculations meaningful for them.[1] *Pace* the BJP and its supporters, there is no evidence that the Sheikhs have collectively attempted to increase their population: rather, as a result of Sheikh exclusion from the benefits of local social changes, their fertility has remained high longer than might otherwise have been expected. Hindu chauvinists – the BJP and its supporters, before them the Jan Sangh and the RSS – justify their hostility in part on the grounds that Muslims are 'anti-national' in their failure to adopt contraception. But this hostility is itself part of the reason for the Sheikhs' continued slowness in adopting family planning.

A useful starting point is the work of Mead Cain (1981, 1983), who portrayed high fertility as an insurance against risk. Many of these risks were environmental – to do with fear of famine, or the unpredictable mortality of young children or of adults – but some were social in origin. Cain's account also deals with gender politics – the risks of an unsupported old age, and the particularly parlous position of widows without adult sons to look after them. In addition, he discusses the political risks posed (especially in Bangladesh) by the absence of reliable forces of law and order. As a result, the physical and economic security of a household may depend heavily on its political clout. Households need to build and maintain tactical alliances with other households, and to retain the ability to call on men to fight to defend field boundaries or houses. In this context, Cain suggests, the failure of national-level politics has tended to add a political dimension to the advantages for Bangladeshi villagers in having large families, with a considerable demographic impact at village and household level. Where the environ-

---

[1] Feelings of insecurity do not necessarily lead couples to avoid family limitation: in some circumstances the reverse may be the case. We return to this point later in this chapter.

ment of risk is less adverse – as in the State of Maharashtra, in western India – Cain argues that sons cease to be such a political necessity, and households can think of family limitation as a strategy.

As with Mamdani's analysis of Punjab, with hindsight we can raise several questions about Cain's analysis of Bangladesh, where, despite little or no evidence of improvement in the micro-politics Cain describes, fertility dropped dramatically in the latter part of the 1980s. A further problem with accepting Cain's analysis is the question of whether or not the mechanisms he is describing have entered into people's consciousness. Few of the north Indian village studies provide any evidence that households, classes or castes have consciously striven to keep fertility high for political reasons.[2] One exception is the study by John Marshall of a village in Meerut District (just 50 km or so west of Bijnor). Marshall reported that the Chamars there were keenly aware of the possibility that their growing numbers of voters would begin to provide political strength, despite the continuing poverty of the Chamars vis-à-vis the land-owning castes. As a result, Chamar leaders rarely passed on contraceptive information since they believed that this might reduce their political influence (Marshall 1972: 28). No other studies provide such clear evidence. For example, Mamdani briefly discussed how large families gave farmers some security in disputes with other farmers over land, and how Jat landowners as a whole benefited from their numbers in disputes with the agricultural labourers, but he seemed to think that this was not as important as the economic benefits that large families provided. When he considered the impact of mechanization on relationships between Jats (the dominant caste, owning almost all the land in his study) and the service castes, he wrote about the demand for labour, not about any political calculations of how their relative numbers might impact on intercaste relationships.

Deriving strength from brute numbers is more likely to be the strategy (implicit or explicit) of the relatively powerless. Those who own land or have education, urban links or the cash to buy protection (from the police or from armed guards) will not need many sons or cousins to maintain or better their positions. But just because families with large numbers of sons can call upon physical force in their disputes with neighbours or other groups in village politics, does not necessarily mean that couples have large families in order to be well protected in such

---

[2] Fargues 1993:13 argues that Muslims in Gaza and on the West Bank 'bet on the size of their family group' and have exceptionally high fertility, despite high urbanism and literacy. But he cites no micro-level data in support of this claim, and ignores the highly insecure setting of the refugee camps.

disputes. As with the economic arguments we considered in Chapter 3, there is a risk in confusing what many sons do after they are born with reasons why they were born in the first place. Furthermore, Cain's analysis, as an attempt to explain continuing high fertility, is vulnerable to Tim Dyson's argument that continuing high fertility in an area of generally high fertility rates is not what needs to be explained: reasons must rather be sought for why some groups move earlier to lower their fertility rates than do others (Dyson 1991).[3]

There is also little evidence that caste groups note the effects of the population growth of other castes. One exception is the work of Monica Das Gupta (1981). In her study of Rampur, a Jat-dominated village close to Delhi, she states that demand for agricultural labour began to fall in the 1950s, as Jat landholdings were fragmented to a size small enough for individual households to farm themselves. Chamars perceived this change as a significant reason why they needed to educate their sons and look for new sources of income. The decline in annual wage contracts with Jat farmers also probably contributed to rising political militancy among the Chamars, as they tried to avoid paying rent for house-plots to the Jat landowners, for example. In the past, in a dispute over land, the physical strength of the two parties had been crucial: memories of a particular fight continued to structure the attitudes of the grandson of the man who had been successful because he could muster more men to fight on his side (Das Gupta, 1988: 94). But by 1975, when she collected her data, most of the young couples – Jats and Chamars alike – seemed to perceive small families as beneficial. She suggests this was a result of falling child mortality rates and the spread of new ideas and new education and job opportunities from Delhi.

Taking the village-level sources as a whole, though, we have little reason to believe that individual households take intercaste or inter-communal disputes seriously into account as reasons for having additional children. None the less, political leaders often accuse their opponents of encouraging high fertility as a conscious strategy to increase the size of their 'vote-bank', or their natural constituency. Mamdani (1972) provides a village-level example of this. In Manupur, prosperous farmers, and men from outside the farm economy, saw the growing numbers of the poor as a threat to their traditional dominance. But in village, *panchāyat* or constituency politics, intercaste and

---

[3] This may not be always the case: it may be necessary to explain why some occupational groups (such as miners and crofters in Scotland at some periods) have higher fertility than the surrounding population (Michael Anderson, personal communication). But in a situation where the norm is high fertility (as in rural Bijnor) the Jats stand out as an exceptional case.

intercommunal balances are usually more significant than interclass differentials: after all, there are nearly always more poor than rich. Because caste and class groupings often overlap, though, it is sometimes difficult to disentangle which is more important.

In order to assess the plausibility of the claims that religion determines fertility, we shall first consider the available national data on religious differentials. We shall then discuss the relevance of these views to our data from Bijnor.

Religion and fertility at the national level

Most of the recent public discussion of the political consequences of differential fertility patterns is concerned with comparing rates for Muslim and Hindu Indians. Since 1970, but with increasing vigour since 1985, claims about Muslim hostility towards family planning have been a prominent feature of propaganda put out by the *Sangh Parivār*, (which is the collection of organizations embracing the Bharatiya Janata Party (BJP), the Vishwa Hindu Parishad (VHP), the Bajrang Dal (the VHP's youth wing) and the Rashtriya Swayamsevak Sangh (RSS)), and by other organizations which have a similar perspective, such as the Shiv Sena.[4] They make three linked claims: Muslim men are more 'hot' (for example, as meat-eaters) and sexually active than Hindu men, and thus threaten to rape Hindu women and 'plant Muslim children' in them; they have more children from their own wives, aided by their right to have up to four wives; and they plan to use Muslim money to convert poor Hindus, and to bring in Muslims from Pakistan and Bangladesh to aid their project of outnumbering Hindus as soon as possible (Basu et al. 1993: 74–5).

Shorn of their wilder excesses, the BJP claims that religious group identities have an impact on fertility do have something of an academic pedigree. Particularly since the Princeton European Fertility Project seemed to show the weakness of economic explanations for fertility differentials, 'culture' in a generalized sense and often 'religion' very specifically, have been brought in to explain differences in fertility levels or in the timing of fertility declines, in Europe and in Africa as well as in Asia (Kertzer 1995; Caldwell and Caldwell 1987; Mazrui 1994). In India itself, few demographers give religion a prominent role in explaining fertility differences (for an exception, see Davies 1976).

We have a principled objection to using religion as an explanatory variable in understanding demographic change. In general, comparing

---

[4] See, for example, Hendre 1971; Prakash 1979.

Muslim and Hindu fertility (or mortality) is a form of essentialism, presuming that Muslims (as a whole) and Hindus (as a whole) share common features which make them appropriate units for comparison. Simple observation suggests the fallacy of such an approach. Caste differences amongst Hindus are only the most obvious, with major differences in social indicators for Brahmans at one extreme, and Scheduled Tribes at the other. Even the categories of Scheduled Tribe or Scheduled Caste are hardly meaningful social groupings, though they are treated as such for some aspects of Government policy. Class-based, regional and urban–rural differences are also clearly considerable and highly significant. Such variability is also true for Muslims: Keralan Muslim traders from Cochi town in south India speak a different language, have different social expectations, and live in very different ways from the rural Sheikhs of Qaziwala one thousand miles to the north. Caste-like differences among Muslims, while not marked by the same concerns of purity and pollution as among Hindus, none the less reflect different life-chances and structural positions. *A priori* variability within the categories 'Hindu' and 'Muslim' is likely to be more significant than variations between the two categories.

Furthermore, the communalization of population discussions is part of the BJP's political strategy: to argue on the grounds it has chosen is to concede the plausibility of the claim that 'the philosophical postulates of a particular religion ... constitute the exclusive, unchanging organisational principle for an entire people across all kinds of spaces, times and historical change' (Basu et al. 1993: 74). Creating a unitary 'other' is a way in which the BJP strengthens its claims to represent all those who regard themselves as Hindus. None the less, in order to deal with arguments which do stress the differences, we will begin by using the data which seem to show that Muslim Indians have higher fertility rates than Hindus (Table 6.1) and ask whether this can be said to result from particular features of Islamic social thought and doctrine, which affect Muslims *as Muslims.*

The demographic arguments can be divided into two sets: those concerned with intentional behaviour; and those that relate to the unintended consequences of patterns of behaviour which differ between members of the two religious communities. In the first set, we consider arguments about the Islamic teachings about birth control and the use of population size as a political weapon. In the second set, we include arguments about the effects of polygamy, and of attitudes towards the desirability of marriage *per se.*

Table 6.1. *General marital fertility rates for Hindus, Scheduled Castes and Muslims, by place of residence, India, 1972 and 1978*

General marital fertility rate:	1972		1978		
	Hindus	Muslims	Hindus	Scheduled Castes	Muslims
Rural	173	191	169	174	185
Urban	131	149	138	159	172

Sources: 1972 figures: Registrar-General, India 1976; 1978 figures: Registrar-General, India, 1982
Note: These figures are age standardized.

Manifest effects of Islamic doctrines

Hindu as well as Muslim religious leaders in India have argued in favour of population growth as part of political strategies. For example, David Mandelbaum (1974: 105) lists a number of Hindu leaders who opposed family planning, with support from communal political parties (Shiv Sena and the Jana Sangh, now the BJP). They drew on a common-sense understanding among Hindus that Hinduism was threatened by falling numbers, either absolutely or in relation to other groups. Pradip Datta has captured the 'taken-for-granted' nature of much Hindu thinking on the subject, tracing back the origins of this view in Hindu communalist writings to the early 20th century. By the 1980s and 1990s, he argues, an authoritative understanding of this potential for decline was part of the 'common truth, a product of social "good sense"'' (Datta 1993: 1305). Middle-class Indians have often repeated some version of this common-sense argument to us. In the past, Sikhs and Christians, as well as Muslims have been accused of using religious conversions as well as faster population growth rates to undermine Hinduism, for example in early 20th century Bengal (Datta 1993). Nowadays, however, Muslims have been the target of most claims of this kind (Krishnakumar 1991; Wright 1983; van der Veer 1994).[5]

Amongst Muslim Indian positions, family planning has been attacked

[5] A recent summary concludes that 'several intermediate and backward castes ... are unenthusiastic about the family planning programme. In addition, neither the Muslim minority nor its leadership is supportive of family planning' (Pai Panandikar and Umashankar 1994: 102). The emphasis on Muslim lack of enthusiasm for population control is thus exaggerated for political reasons: the population growth of Scheduled Castes and Tribes, from 23.6 per cent of the Indian population in 1981 to 24.7 per cent in 1991 (probably faster than that of the Muslim population) is ignored in the discussion of comparative population totals. The most likely explanation is that the BJP and its supporters hope to gain the political support of those who represent the SCs and STs, and hence refrain from highlighting their population growth.

in the pages of *Radiance*, the journal of the Jama'at-i-Islami. Maulana Maudoodi (the founder of the party, who moved to Pakistan but retained influence in India) argued that birth control produces sexual anarchy (Wright 1983). Muslim leaders in Bijnor have certainly succeeded in persuading many Sheikhs that sterilization is unIslamic, and would cause the sterilized person to be excluded from Paradise. But in Pakistan, Maudoodi's position is not so widespread, and other Islamic leaders have not denounced sterilization in particular, despite their generalized opposition to the Pakistani Government family planning programmes. The recent demographic history of Bangladesh, with a rise in contraceptive use rates from 3 per cent in 1970 to 40 per cent in 1991, suggests little support for any claim that South Asian Muslims are doctrinally opposed to contraception (Kabeer 1995).

The widespread assumption that Islam is hostile to family planning draws on (and feeds into) a much wider pattern of portraying Muslim societies as dominated by Islam (in ways which are not usually paralleled by discussions of other religions). Such classically Orientalist arguments are usually assumed to have particular consequences for women (Obermeyer 1992; Said 1978). In many cases, this involves extrapolation from the writings of a small number of Islamic theologians, with little thought being given to their social locations, to divisions and disputes among different schools of Islamic thought, or to changes through time, let alone to any evidence that these views are heeded or followed by any particular identifiable group of Muslims.[6] In other cases this assessment is based on demographic indicators. Caldwell (1986) noted that, until the 1980s, Islamic countries in the Middle East were poor health achievers (relative to their wealth) and also, despite relatively high levels of female literacy, continued to have high levels of fertility.

Fargues (1993) provides a recent example of an Orientalist argument when he links Islamic fundamentalism, dreams of world conquest, and high fertility rates. In the Middle East, there are both high levels of fertility and pro-natalist statements by religious or political leaders. Fargues assumes (without any evidence) that individual couples (or at least, husbands) respond to these calls out of a sense of religious or national duty. But some data directly contradict the assumption of 'patriotic' or 'religious' child-bearing, and others are open to alternative interpretations. Thus Fargues claims that 'the oil monarchies of the

---

[6] As Cassen (1978: 56) argues, 'Even if we could state what is the full net impact of encouragements and discouragements to procreation in scripture and teachings, we would not know how influential they are, and whether that influence is waning.' Despite this, Mazrui (1994: 125) has no hesitation in saying that 'fundamentalist Muslim families in Africa and elsewhere may resort to having more and more children as a strategy of "multiplying in the name of Allah" '.

Peninsula ... form the last bastion of Arab resistance to family planning programmes' (1993: 3), yet Obermeyer produces figures which show that Bahrain, Kuwait and the United Arab Emirates (and to a lesser extent, Qatar) have seen dramatic declines in fertility since 1950, with high levels of contraceptive use. Similarly, Fargues claims that in Gaza, total fertility rates have stayed high (and have perhaps even increased) because Muslim Palestinians have adopted a strategy to improve their chances for a better future through large families, to give them political power despite their poverty (1993: 13). He also blames the UN relief agency for providing free schooling, on the grounds that this removes the link between increasing costs of child-bearing and fertility decline. Yet the high levels of fertility in Gaza (by comparison, for example, with Israeli Arab Druze and Muslims, or even the West Bank Arabs) are at least as plausibly a reflection of the high levels of insecurity faced by Gaza residents (Fargues 1993: 12).

In general, then, it is relatively easy to challenge the cruder arguments that Islam and high fertility are linked through conscious religious and political strategies, by citing evidence of the variety of theological positions within Islam, the very varied social, economic and political institutions to be found in countries with Muslim populations, and very varied demographic experiences. One can point to the tensions in Islamic doctrines between egalitarian and inegalitarian views, and to the 'tremendous complexity and diversity that is found in the Muslim world' (Obermeyer 1994: 60; see also Ahmed 1982). Omran (1992) focuses on the lack of clarity in Islamic texts over the acceptability of different forms of contraception, noting that some sources condone *coitus interruptus*, suggesting (by extension) that all forms of non-terminal family planning are acceptable. Some theologians have argued that abortion is acceptable before 'ensoulment', which is believed to take place after the third month of pregnancy. The motivation for contraception is also a factor which can change the way it is viewed by some authorities: a wish to avoid poverty or raise family living standards is an unacceptable motive, whereas a desire to avoid danger to the health of the mother or the transmission of a major disease can be morally justified. Sterilization, as a permanent interference with divine will, and a sign of lack of faith in God's ability to care for all those who are born, is not apparently supported by any school of Islamic jurisprudence (Khan 1979: 184–191). But even the theological objection to sterilization has apparently not prevented large numbers of men and women undergoing these operations in a number of Islamic countries, including Iran, where sterilization was banned after the Revolution of 1979, but made available again after 1989 (Obermeyer 1994).

Thus high levels of Muslim fertility cannot be explained with reference to supposed universal Islamic condemnation of contraception in general, nor of sterilization in particular. We must ask instead why some Muslims, at some times and in some places, are more receptive to attempts by some of their religious leaders to condemn contraception, than are other groups. Until the late 1980s, as far as most people in Bijnor were concerned, family planning and sterilization were regarded as synonymous. Throughout our research in Bijnor we have been confronted by women asking for alternative methods, and denying that the government family planning staff had anything other than sterilization to offer. Clearly this was not factually the case, since some women had Copper-Ts inserted, and the contraceptive pill was available in some health centres in Bijnor. But we heard many stories of family planning workers refusing to provide anything but sterilization to women who expressed an interest in family limitation. Peripheral health workers face financial incentives and pressures to achieve their sterilization targets, and have often resorted to bribery and falsifying their records in attempts to do so.[7] As a result, the population as a whole have felt they were being coerced too rapidly into final decisions about their fertility; the Muslim population have felt cornered, in that they could not use the only method of contraception that they believed was on offer.

Community membership and customary practices

In most versions of Islamic law, Muslim men are allowed to have up to four wives (if they can treat them all equally) and this, it is sometimes claimed, produces higher fertility rates among Muslims. *A priori* this might sound persuasive, when (for example) it is produced as a slogan comparing a man with one wife and two children with a man with four wives and twenty-five children.[8] But the argument is clearly fallacious. For every Muslim man with four wives, other things being equal, there will be three unmarried Muslim men. The Muslim population could grow faster by this means only if women were converting to Islam in large numbers, and marrying Muslim men, for fertility is a matter of how many children each *woman* bears.[9] Furthermore, women in polygamous marriages usually have fewer children than comparable

---

[7] In our own research, we discovered how unreliable the records for temporary methods at the Dharmnagri health centre were. Narayana and Kantner (1992) provide more detail on the national picture.

[8] *Ham do, hamāre do, vah pānch, uske pachchīs* ('We two, our two' [an official slogan of the Indian family planning programme], 'those five, their twenty-five'.)

[9] There is no evidence to support the BJP claims of mass conversions of women, neither forced abductions nor voluntary shifts of religious allegiance, though it was an issue for

women in monogamous unions.[10] But even if polygamous marriages led to faster population increase, this would not explain differential fertility rates among Hindus and Muslims. Polygamy is in practice a strategy for wealthy men, not just in Islamic settings but among members of other religious groups in Eurasia as well (Goody and Tambiah 1974). Thus, for example, the proportion of Muslim men with more than one wife (as reported in the censuses of 1931, 1941, 1951 and 1961) was small, and much the same as that of Hindus (GOI, 1974: 66–67). In our study, this picture is confirmed: polygamy is very rare in both caste groups. Two Jat men (out of 268 married men of all ages) and three Sheikh men (out of 281) had two wives or more.[11]

Other aspects of the social organization of South Asian Muslims might contribute to higher levels of fertility. For example, the proportions of women who marry, the ages at which they marry, and whether they can remarry if they are widowed before the end of their potential child-bearing years all have potential implications for fertility. In India, estimates of the proportions of women who marry actually suggest a higher figure for Hindu women aged 15–49 than for Muslim women, according to 1988 data (National Sample Survey 1990). This is slightly surprising, since Sheikhs in Bijnor were more likely to stress what they saw as a religious requirement for all adults to be married than did Jats. The NSS and Census data also suggest a higher average age at marriage for Muslims, which is not reflected in our Bijnor data, but is probably due to the inclusion in the Hindu figure of the Scheduled Castes, whose age at marriage is often below that of Muslims.

The effect of widow remarriage on comparative fertility rates is a complex one. A few Hindu upper castes forbid a widow from remarrying, whereas no Muslim *jāti* do. Since women in these Hindu castes are sometimes married to men considerably older than them, the ban on their remarriage could make a difference to the number of children they bear: the chances are quite high that they could be widowed before the menopause. Kingsley Davis estimated that bans on widow remarriage reduced overall Hindu fertility rates by some 16 per cent between 1901 and 1941. Quite possibly, however, the extent of the

---

the new Indian and Pakistani Governments during and immediately after Partition in 1947: see, for example, Menon and Bhasin 1993.

[10] There are several possible reasons for this finding. One is that men often take second and third wives as a result of the infertility of their first wives; but since infertility is often a male problem, these later wives may also have difficulty in having children. Men also tend to be older by the time they acquire second, third or fourth wives, so these women are more likely to be widowed before menopause.

[11] In Qaziwala and Nangal as a whole, as many Hindu men had two wives as did Muslim men (five in each village), despite the fact that polygamy is illegal for Hindus.

ban on widow remarriage has been exaggerated. Many Hindu *jāti* are inclined to ignore the ban in practice, even if they are committed to it in their claims for moral precedence over other castes who allow it. Life expectancies have risen steadily since the Second World War, and the age differential between husbands and wives has declined, so the proportion of Indian women widowed while still in their child-bearing years has dropped considerably. Mandelbaum concluded that 'the taboo on widow remarriage seems to have become quite a minor factor in contemporary fertility rates' (1974: 35). Our own data suggest that most young widows – Jat and Sheikh alike – are remarried within one or two years.

Regional issues in differential fertility

Further compelling evidence against the idea that Islamic belief is universally hostile to family planning comes from the finding that Muslim fertility rates in India show the same kinds of variation by region and residence as do those of Hindus. For India as a whole, in 1972 and 1978 alike, urban general marital fertility rates for Muslims were below rural rates (see Table 6.1). Data for 1978 by State show that although Muslim fertility rates were always above Hindu ones, and usually above those of the Scheduled Castes, they varied in similar ways, with urban rates being below rural rates, and rates in the Large North Indian States being above those in central, east and south India (see Table 6.2). One implication is that fertility rates for Hindus in much of north India are higher than those for Muslims in many parts of the rest of the country. Part of the explanation for 'high Muslim fertility' in India as a whole, then, merely reflects the fact that Muslims are a larger proportion of the population in north India (where the fertility rates are relatively high) than they are in the rest of India (where the fertility rates are relatively low).

What does not emerge from these figures, however, is that across India, in town and countryside alike, Muslims are in weaker economic positions than Hindus. More than half the urban Muslims are reported to have incomes below the poverty line, compared to 35 per cent of urban Hindus; 79 per cent of rural Muslim households own less than one hectare, compared to 68 per cent of rural Hindu households (Krishnakumar 1991; Shariff 1995). Similarly, indicators of schooling show Muslims to be less well-educated than Hindus, reflecting their weaker economic position. Both schooling and economic position have very strong relationships with fertility – much stronger than the relationships with religion. Unfortunately, there are few good multivariate analyses

Table 6.2. *Age-standardized total marital fertility rates by religion, and residence, major States, India, 1978*

States	Rural			Urban		
	Hindus	Scheduled Castes	Muslims	Hindus	Scheduled Castes	Muslims
Large North Indian:						
Bihar	4.78	4.72	4.91	3.95	3.25	5.04
Madhya Pradesh	5.92	6.44	6.24	5.06	4.79	5.43
Rajasthan	5.98	6.01	6.80	4.55	5.03	5.34
Uttar Pradesh	6.55	6.60	7.35	5.17	5.53	6.77
Central and Eastern:						
Andhra Pradesh	4.78	4.56	5.93	3.64	4.06	4.13
Gujarat	5.71	5.52	5.50	4.82	5.32	5.80
Karnataka	5.05	4.65	5.16	4.30	4.55	5.10
Maharashtra	4.22	5.61	5.51	4.11	3.90	5.38
Orissa	5.58	4.91	8.58	5.04	5.20	6.00
West Bengal	4.62	5.12	5.73	4.06	5.75	4.95
Southern:						
Kerala	4.60	4.61	5.63	4.50	4.53	5.23
Tamil Nadu	4.75	4.85	4.99	4.15	4.26	4.75
North-western:						
Haryana	5.05	5.33	6.14	4.53	5.04	4.28
Punjab	5.72	6.04	N/A	4.90	5.62	N/A

Source: Registrar-General, India 1982. But note that some of these figures show inconsistencies, only some of which can be corrected from the data provided.

which put all these factors together to see the net relationships between religion and fertility and mortality. One, conducted in the rural area of Koil Tahsil, in Aligarh District 160 km south of Bijnor, demonstrates that the fertility differentials of caste Hindus, Scheduled Castes and Muslims can be understood as outcomes of the impacts of income, education, child mortality, and age at marriage (Khan 1991: 110–15). Not surprisingly, then, orthodox demographers give religion a very small part in the overall explanation of fertility differences.[12] For example, Cassen (1978: 57) suggests that, 'The difference between the fertility of educated, well-off, urban Muslims and Hindus is relatively small; but

[12] This has not always been so: Davies (1976) assembles a wide range of sources which, he argues, show that higher Muslim fertility is 'not a mere reflection of some other underlying social or economic differences between the two communities' (p. 2) but his work has generally been ignored, not least because he operates with an essentialist notion of 'community' and cites evidence which suggests that this residual impact can at best be only very small (see Table II, p. 2). See also Anker 1977.

the average socio-economic and educational status of Muslims is lower than that of Hindus.'

In similar vein, Dyson and Moore conclude that religious identification has relatively little influence on the degree of female autonomy (1983: 53). Their treatment of religion is relatively brief and unsatisfactory, but the key point they make is that in terms of the variables in which they are interested, regional factors seem to outweigh religious ones. Hindus and Muslims within the regional demographic regimes show far more similarities with each other (in terms of patterns of kinship exogamy, age at marriage, post-marital residence patterns etc.) than they do with co-religionists elsewhere in the sub-continent.

In other words, most demographers seem to believe that most of the differences in fertility rates between Hindus and Muslims in India are the result of differences in region, residence, class and schooling, rather than any supposed differences in religious orientation.[13] Demographic differences reflect the different economic and regional distributions of the two communities. Muslims are more numerous in northern towns, where they occupy worse housing and have lower-paid jobs than do clean-caste Hindus; in the north generally, child death rates are higher than in south India. The contribution of religion *per se,* after taking account of these economic and regional differences, is very small. Cassen puts it this way: other things being equal, the decline in Muslim fertility rates is about 10 years behind the decline in Hindu rates (Cassen 1978: 57).

Even if the causes of higher Muslim fertility have little to do with religion (in a narrow sense), nevertheless the Muslim population is growing slightly faster than that of Hindus. On a range of indicators, Muslim fertility rates in 1978 were about 10–12 per cent above those of Hindus, at the all-India level, with a Muslim crude birth rate in 1978 of about 32.5 compared to a Hindu rate of about 29.5 (Registrar-General, India 1982). But growth in the population by religion is also an outcome of mortality.[14] The rather limited available evidence suggests that infant mortality among rural Muslims in 1978 was below that of rural Hindus, but the rate for urban Muslims was above that of urban Hindus. Overall, Muslim infant mortality rates were about 109 per 1,000 live births in 1978, compared with about 121 per 1,000 live births for Hindus, a

[13] This conclusion holds after various standardizing procedures have been followed, for example taking into account differences in the proportions who marry, and the different age distributions of the different religious groups, as well as the major social and economic variables.

[14] Migration and conversions are also theoretical possibilities, but in the 1970s at least, the net effect of conversions and migrations seems to have been minimal, and there is no evidence that they were more important in the 1980s.

difference of 11–12 per cent (Registrar-General, India 1981), reflecting the greater concentration of Muslims in urban areas. Putting together fertility (Muslim rates 10–12 per cent higher than Hindu rates) and mortality (Muslim rates 11–12 per cent lower than Hindu rates), leads to a predicted Muslim growth rate in the 1970s of about 30 per cent, compared to a predicted Hindu growth of 24 per cent. The observed pattern was exactly that, leading to a rise in the Muslim share of the total population of India from 11.2 per cent to 11.4 per cent.[15]

As far as we can tell, then, the difference in Muslim and Hindu population growth rates can be explained mostly by the socio-economic differences between the two populations, not by any supposed religious determinism. In terms of the future, the growth rate differences are not large enough to have significant effects on the population balance of India as a whole. Demographic crystal ball-gazing is an extremely inexact art, and comparisons of future growth rates involve assumptions about shifts in fertility and mortality which become increasingly unreliable. But even assuming that Muslim birth rates remain above Hindu birth rates, it is unlikely that the Muslim proportion of the Indian population will rise to as much as 15 per cent of the total by the year 2021 (Cassen 1978: 57).

Clearly, then, there is no substance in the scaremongering propaganda predicting that Hindus will be outnumbered in the foreseeable future. But far from challenging this assumption head on, the Government of India tries hard to avoid releasing population figures for the different religious categories, and the 1991 Census figures giving a religious breakdown had not been published by the end of 1995. Mandelbaum notes that in some of her political statements, Indira Gandhi stood out against the communalized politicization of population issues. On one occasion she argued that the claim that 'the family planning programme will upset the relative population ratios of the various groups in our society and thus weaken the political power or bargaining position of these groups' was a 'pernicious fallacy' (Mandelbaum 1974:105), the fallacy that political power flows from brute numbers, not from affluence or the use of any other political resource. She did not directly challenge the other fallacy, that differential population growth rates would make a significant difference to the balance of the population in the foreseeable future. Indeed, neither point has been spelt out with much conviction by any political leader of substance.

Since Muslim and Hindu fertility in general seem to respond to the same kinds of social and economic influences, the causes of higher

---

[15] These calculations exclude Assam, where the Census could not be held in 1981.

Muslim fertility are to be looked for in the positions Muslims hold within local social situations. After we control for some of the most obviously 'independent' differences between Muslims and Hindus, such as region of residence and urban or rural location, Muslims tend to be poorer and less well-educated. Does their poverty help account for their lower schooling achievements, or vice versa? According to all-India figures, age for age, in rural and urban areas alike, fewer Muslim than Hindu boys and girls are currently attending schools of any kind (Krishnakumar 1991). In urban areas and in rural areas up to the age of nine, approximately equal percentages of Hindu and Muslim boys are attending school. Fewer girls attend school, from both communities, and again, there is little difference between the situation for Hindu and Muslim girls. But in rural areas, after the age of nine, Muslim girls are much less likely to be attending school, compared to Hindu girls, than are Muslim boys compared to Hindu boys. This is partly a result of the relative concentration of Muslims in north India, where overall school enrolment rates are anyway lower than in the rest of the country. But even within north India, as our Bijnor data confirm, Muslim schooling rates are below those of Hindus in the same class position, especially for schooling beyond primary level. Why should this be so?

One possibility is that Muslims place a lower value on schooling than do Hindus. Our comparison of Jats and Sheikhs would support such a conclusion, but we should not end the enquiry there. Far more importantly, if it is true, is why this should be so. Why might Muslim parents spend less money on schooling for their children, or place less pressure on them to attend school? There are two radically opposed and potentially plausible explanations of why schooling levels are lower among Muslims. One would start from the 'attitude towards schooling' and argue that this leads to worse job prospects and economic decline. This is the explanation favoured by the BJP: Muslims, according to such an account, are irrational and ignorant and therefore responsible for their lack of success in business and careers. An alternative explanation starts from Muslim experiences of exclusion from the job market, which gives schooling a lower value for Muslims than for comparable Hindus. It is very hard to think what kind of data would allow us to analyse the relative contributions of these two possible processes. None the less, several pointers lead us to prefer the second version of events.

In Bijnor, for Hindus and Muslims alike, schooling for boys is seen largely as a resource in the job market, and secondarily as an element in marriage arrangements. Schooling for girls is seen largely in terms of its contribution to a girl's marriageability, and therefore it tends to follow behind the schooling of boys.[16] Parents will educate a girl up to a level just below that of the kind of boy they expect her to marry. So the key question is the extent to which boys' schooling leads to jobs. And as we have seen in Bijnor, Sheikhs do not believe that their sons will get good jobs, no matter how far they are schooled, whereas the chances for Jat boys (while still not guaranteed) are better. Elsewhere in India too, Muslims are less well represented in senior positions than their schooling might suggest (Krishnakumar 1991).

Muslims benefit from no job reservations in the government services, as many Sheikhs pointed out. The changes brought about by implementing the Mandal proposals in UP are unlikely to improve matters for Muslims. Secondly, job appointments – in the private sector and except at the very highest levels of the public sector – are believed to be strongly influenced by social origins and personal considerations. Being hired and promoted in the police, in schools and for male health workers, for example, are highly competitive, and most Jats and Sheikhs claimed that influence or a bribe was necessary even to ensure that one was considered at the final stages. The eventual appointments often owe a great deal to the caste, religious background or region of origin of those making the appointment, if other things (like qualifications and bribes) were similar. Thus the Uttar Pradesh police is known to have very few Muslims; the Provincial Armed Constabulary (used in riot situations and intercommunal violence) has almost none. When Mulayam Singh Yadav was Chief Minister of UP, it was reported that large numbers of Yadavs were recruited to the public service on temporary contracts, or Yadavs on temporary contracts found their positions regularized. When the BSP leader, Mayavati, became Chief Minister briefly, some government positions were reclassified as restricted to Scheduled Castes, and Muslims who had already spent money on bribes to improve their chances in these posts found their payments were wasted. Firm evidence for all these claims is hard to come by, but the fact that they are *believed* is a significant element in people's calculations about whether schooling will lead to jobs. There is thus a circularity: the absence of Muslims from key positions (perceived and/or real) damages further the chances of Muslims getting appointments in the future, both directly (through their ability to influence appointments) and indirectly (by disheartening students and their parents at crucial stages of their progress through schooling).

In addition, of course, schooling itself is not a standardized commodity. Private schools, relatively well-resourced and teaching

[16] For further discussion of similar points for south India, see Caldwell et al. 1988: Ch. 7.

many subjects through the medium of English, give their pupils many advantages over pupils at ill-equipped and understaffed state schools. The quality of schooling or people's ability to make use of the schooling which is offered, is also heavily affected by the economic and social background of the student. Poor rural children get a poorer quality of schooling, and may not be able to make the best use of it.[17] Urban families may pay considerable sums to send their children to private schools, and to hire tutors – often teachers from the same school, or from state schools – to coach their children after school hours. Children from the Scheduled Castes and Tribes have scholarships and fee waivers, and the promise of a better chance of a job at the end of the road. Muslims, generally coming from poorer backgrounds, are differentially disadvantaged, and do not have official government support in attempting to overcome the limitation of their backgrounds. These problems may then be exacerbated by *maulvīs* and others who use this sense of exclusion to argue for even greater withdrawal from the Indian mainstream.

In sum, then, there is no reason to suppose that Muslim Indians want more children because of specific Islamic injunctions to 'go forth and multiply'. Nor do Muslims have higher fertility as a result of indirect influences of Islamic ideology *per se*. None the less, fertility differences between the Sheikhs and the Jats still need to be explained. In looking at whether religious identities play a part in explaining these differences, we shall first consider the reasons for low Jat fertility, because (as Dyson 1991 argues) the reasons for a fall in Jat fertility are much more in need of explanation than the reasons why fertility has not fallen so fast among the Sheikhs or among many other groups in rural Bijnor. Crucially, too, there are many ways in which Jats are not typical north Indian Hindus, in demographic terms, and we must also discuss here the long-standing and consistent patterns which set them off from many other Hindu groups. We shall then argue that the fertility of the Sheikhs can be understood much more in terms of their marginalized position as part of a minority group within Indian society, rather than as a response to any 'essential' feature of Islam.

Jat marriage and fertility

The crucial considerations which contribute to understanding why Jats have controlled their fertility are specific kinship practices that have

---

[17] Urban, middle-class students find their schooling makes more sense to them, because they can call on more developed 'cultural capital', in Bourdieu's terms (Bourdieu and Passeron 1977)

affected inheritance patterns for at least 100 years; and a local dominance at the District level (and more widely) that has allowed them to manipulate political resources (schools, clinics, employment and advancement) in their own interests. Two linked aspects of Jat behaviour have resulted in small family sizes, in Bijnor and elsewhere in north India. The first is excess female mortality (female infanticide up to the latter part of the nineteenth century, and the relative neglect of girl children since then); the second is the presence of a sizeable number of adult Jat men who remain unmarried.

Female infanticide was common among many land-owning castes in north India in the nineteenth century, and possibly before that. There are well-documented cases where the highest status lineage within a caste systematically killed most of its baby girls. The Jats, however, were generally not in this category: most of the notorious cases in the North-Western Provinces were of Rajputs or Gujjars. Evidence for female infanticide among the Jats of Bijnor was largely indirect, derived from the abnormal ratios of boys and girls which were discovered in the early censuses, along with anecdotal evidence about families who had killed all their daughters. The 1872 Census of India reported sex ratios by adults and 'minors', for the whole population and separately by caste, as part of the campaign to eradicate female infanticide.[18] The reported sex ratios for Bijnor were among the most masculine in north India. For Hindus as a whole, Bijnor had the fourth lowest female/male sex ratio in the North-Western Provinces (Miller, 1981: 62). In part this just reflects the fact that reported sex ratios were (and still are) most masculine amongst the rural (or agricultural) populations; figures for the towns show a much less unbalanced picture, so Districts like Bijnor (with a small urban population) tended to have more masculine sex ratios (see Table 6.3). But even after taking account of these factors, the Provincial authorities in the 1870s believed that Bijnor was in need of close attention to explain the adverse figures and to implement an anti-infanticide campaign.

In practice, the administration had good grounds for being somewhat sceptical about the precise figures: the enumeration in Bijnor in 1871 threw up so many anomalies that it had to be repeated in 1873 before the Provincial Government was happy with the result. Even after the corrections, however, some young married 'minor' girls still living in their parents' homes may have been missed from the count, being

---

[18] The figures for 'minors' relates to children under the age of 14 or so. This age was chosen because the census authorities tried to distinguish between children born before and after the events of 1857–8, since that was the most prominent event in recent memory. For more on this, see R. Jeffery et al. 1984.

Table 6.3. *Sex ratios by main castes, adults and minors, 1872, Bijnor District*

Caste	Sex ratio:		Total population:		Child–woman ratio*
	Adult	Minor	Adult	Minor	
Hindus:					
Brahman	800	830	20,356	8,414	0.93
Rajput	875	801	45,083	21,610	1.03
Bania	879	816	11,883	5,231	0.94
Chamar	965	903	74,306	42,604	1.17
Jat	698	573	46,213	20,728	1.09
Other Hindus	862	816	129,180	67,993	1.14
Muslims:					
Sheikh	1,016	885	29,944	15,230	1.01
Other Muslims	938	859	129,182	69,099	1.11

Source: Census of the North-West Provinces and Oudh, 1872
* The child–woman ratio is 'minors' per 'adult female'

omitted not only by their fathers but also by their fathers-in-law
(R. Jeffery et al. 1984). The ratios may well also have been biased by
the general underenumeration of females (a major problem over much
of India until the 1901 census); and by the differing male migration
patterns (large numbers of men from some castes were attached to the
army and so might have been missed from the census). The adult
figures are most likely to be distorted by underenumeration of females
and by the effects of migration, but the figures for 'minors' are less
affected by migration and underenumeration, and are therefore a better
guide to the extent of excess female mortality. These figures suggested
that Bijnor was, for female infanticide, among the worst Districts in
north India.

Within Bijnor, the Jats were the only caste accused by the British
authorities of killing their daughters. After female infanticide was
outlawed in 1870 they were subject to official surveillance in an attempt
to stop the practice continuing. The Jats themselves strenuously denied
the charges and resented the policing mechanisms introduced (a
requirement that all births be registered, and a detailed enquiry into the
cause of every girl's death). After 1870, recorded numbers of girls rose
steadily. The authorities interpreted this as evidence of the success of
their campaigns, and as evidence that Jats were not as 'committed' to
female infanticide as were (say) Rajputs in other parts of north India. By
1900 the numbers of Jat girls enumerated had risen to 'acceptable'
levels, and the British authorities believed there was no further need to

keep a special watch on any villages.[19] In our own research, we have heard no accusations that, either now or in the past, Jats practised female infanticide. None the less, Jat sex ratios were radically out of line with other Hindu castes at least until 1931 (the last Census when separate tabulations are available by caste) (see Table 6.4).

Much higher proportions of men also remain unmarried among the Jats than amongst other castes (see Table 6.5). Clearly, this may in part be a reflection of the shortage of Jat girls for them to marry, but the pattern of a substantial proportion of Jat men remaining unmarried into late adulthood can be seen in the four censuses in which age and caste were tabulated (1901, 1911, 1921 and 1931), despite rises in the Jat sex ratio. The 1931 census for Bijnor shows that there were still only 787 Jat females for every 1,000 Jat males. In the United Provinces as a whole, nearly 19 per cent of Jat men in the age group 25–44 were unmarried, but fewer than 10 per cent of Sheikh men were unmarried at these ages. Put together, these two statistics suggest that there were 10 per cent fewer married Jat women (per 1,000 Jat population) than married Sheikh women. Thus Jat crude birth rates were likely to be substantially below those of the Sheikhs, even if (as the 1872 census child–woman ratios suggest) married Jat women had more children on average than did Sheikh women.

Whether or not Jats as a caste planned to limit their numbers, that certainly seems to have been the outcome. For the years in which the census gives caste-based figures by Districts (1872–1931) it appears that the total number of Jats declined from 66,900 to 55,200, whereas numbers of Sheikhs nearly doubled from 45,100 to 89,400.[20] Sheikh figures may be affected by other Muslims newly claiming to be Sheikhs over this period (especially in 1931), but the figures for Chamars (unlikely to be boosted in this way) also show a rise of 15 per cent, despite the fact that they were among the poorest groups in the District.

Excess deaths of girl children, and relatively large numbers of unmarried adult Jat men, still characterized the demographic picture in Nangal in 1990. The maternity histories of the Jat women show an excess of female child deaths, though the numbers (particularly in the recent past) are too small to give a very reliable picture (see Tables 6.6 and 6.7). The sex ratios at birth for the Jats, at 792 girls per 1000 boys

---

[19] At least two other possibilities exist. Jats may have become more skilled in manipulating the returns, recording some boys as girls in order to avoid further policing; or the whole matter may have been one of underenumeration, and once fewer Jat girls were missed from the count, the figures improved without any necessary change in Jat behaviour.

[20] We have no clear explanation for this decline: the period included the heavy mortality from influenza in 1919–21, but there is no reason why Jats should have suffered more than other castes.

Table 6.4. *Census sex ratios for selected castes, Bijnor District, 1872–1931*

Year	Jats	Sheikhs	Chamars
1872	657	970	942
1911	747	937	932
1921	802	905	953
1931	787	858	938

Source: Census of the North-West Provinces and Oudh (1872 and 1911); Census of the United Provinces of Agra and Oudh (1921 and 1931).

Table 6.5. *Marital status of Jat, Sheikh and Chamar men and women aged 24–43, 1931, United Provinces*

	Jats:		Sheikhs:		Chamars:	
	Men	Women	Men	Women	Men	Women
Single	18.6%	1.3%	9.7%	3.2%	5.2%	1.0%
Married	69.7	86.6	81.4	84.8	86.7	85.8
Widowed	11.6	12.0	8.9	12.0	8.1	13.2

Source: Census of the United Provinces of Agra and Oudh, 1931.

are suspiciously low, since the 'normal' figure is between about 900 and 950. Try as we might, we could find no evidence of girl babies who had been 'forgotten' or left out for some other reason (such as a death in suspicious circumstances). If the figures for births and deaths from our maternity histories are reasonably accurate, row 8 in Table 6.6 suggests that the ratio of under five female mortality rates to male mortality rates is higher for Jat children (1.88) than among the Sheikhs (1.37). In other words, girls have died in much larger numbers (proportionately to boy deaths) among the Jats than among the Sheikhs. Of course, if we have failed to discover more girl births (and suspicious deaths) among the Jats than among the Sheikhs (as the sex ratios at birth suggest) then the 'real' differential could be even greater than this.

As completed family sizes have fallen in Nangal, and more mothers are educated, one might expect excess female mortality to fall. For children born in the 1970s and 1980s, the gap between the life chances for girls and those for boys has increased slightly compared to the gap for those born in the 1950s and 1960s. This is mainly because the mortality rate for boys has dropped faster than that of girls, among the rich and middle peasants who form the bulk of the Jat population in Nangal (Table 6.7). By contrast, among the poor peasant and landless

Table 6.6. *Sex ratios of reported live births, and proportions surviving to age five, born before 1986 to ever-married Jat women in Nangal and Sheikh women in Qaziwala, who started cohabiting between 1950 and 1985*

	Jat	Sheikh
Sex ratios: at birth	792	991
Sex ratios: of those surviving to age 5	684	886
Number of births	733	852
Number of mothers	175	171
Number of child deaths	127	226
% girls dying before age 5	25.3%	30.7%
% boys dying before age 5	13.4%	22.4%
Ratio of female under-5 mortality to male	1.88	1.37

Source: Maternity histories, 1990–91.
Note: These figures relate only to children born up to the end of 1985, to women whose cohabitation began between 1950 and 1985. Sex ratios are females per 1,000 males.

Table 6.7. *Child mortality of children born 1950–1985 to ever-married women who began cohabiting between 1950 and 1985, by class and year of birth, Nangal Jats*

		Boys	Girls	Girl/Boy U5MR ratio
Children born 1950–69				
Upper class	U5MR	14	21	1.54
	Child deaths	3	4	
Middle class	U5MR	13	22	1.77
	Child deaths	11	17	
Lower class	U5MR	15	52	3.51
	Child deaths	4	13	
All classes	U5MR	13	28	2.14
	Child deaths	18	34	
Children born 1970–85				
Upper class	U5MR	11	21	1.83
	Child deaths	5	5	
Middle class	U5MR	13	24	1.83
	Child deaths	22	32	
Lower class	U5MR	17	29	1.68
	Child deaths	10	13	
All classes	U5MR	14	25	1.80
	Child deaths	37	50	

Source: Maternity histories, 1990–1.
Notes: U5MR is the under-5 mortality rate, expressed as a percentage of live births. The class categories used are landlords and rich peasants in the upper class; middle peasants in the middle class; and poor peasants and the landless in the lower class.

Table 6.8. *Under-five mortality rates per 1,000 births 1965–84, by presence of living siblings, Nangal Jats and Qaziwala Sheikhs*

	Female births			Male births		
	Number of sisters			Number of brothers		
	0	1 or more	All births	0	1 or more	All births
Nangal Jats	224	240	233	109	119	115
Qaziwala Sheikhs	327	287	303	181	261	233

Source: Maternity histories, 1990–91

Jats, the ratio of female to male mortality rates has dropped considerably, leaving the overall picture fairly stable. In her restudy of the villages included in the Khanna Study, Monica Das Gupta has shown that second or third daughters are still vulnerable to neglect by families whose commitment to a small family is matched by the requirement that at least one child be a son (Das Gupta 1989). In Nangal, however, the presence of a sister does not seem to reduce a girl's chance of survival: first children (whether boys or girls) seem to have had only slightly better chances of survival than second or later births of children of the same sex (see Table 6.8)

Jat men in Nangal remain unmarried in much higher proportions than men from other castes. Of all Jat men aged 25 or more, 17 per cent were single, compared to 5 per cent of Sheikh men in the same age category in Qaziwala. Men in the youngest cohort were even more likely to be unmarried: of Jat men aged 25–34, nearly 25 per cent were still single in 1990, compared to 8 per cent of 25–34 year-old Sheikh men in Qaziwala. We would expect that poorer men are less likely to receive an offer of a Jat girl by conventional means. They are also less likely to be able to afford to 'buy' a bride from an impoverished man from elsewhere. Two features of the situation of Jats in Nangal suggest that Jats were conscious of the effects of these patterns on population dynamics and land fragmentation, and not just unable to find a Jat bride. Crucially, some single men were relatively affluent, and therefore capable of 'buying' a non-Jat bride if they wished (see Table 6.9).

Furthermore, men with several brothers were more likely to remain single than were only sons or men with one brother. No only sons among the Jats in Nangal remained unmarried, and the more brothers there were, the greater the likelihood of one or more of them remaining unmarried. Some local sayings also support the idea that Jats recognized that if one or two brothers remained unmarried, a household's position

Table 6.9. *Numbers of single Jat men aged 25 or above by father's landholding and number of brothers, Nangal, 1990*

Number of brothers:	Father's land holding					Married and single men	Percent of all men single
	>10 acres	5–10 acres	2–5 acres	0–2 acres	All landholdings		
0	0	0	0	0	0	22	0
1	2	6	2	3	13	75	17.3
2	3	7	3	6	19	94	20.2
3	7	1	0	0	8	47	17.0
4	4	2	0	0	6	28	21.4
6	0	0	3	0	3	10	30.0
Unknown					2	29	6.8
All single men aged 25+	16	16	8	9	49		
All men aged 25+	180	76	31	18	305	305	16.1
Single men as % of men aged 25+ in each landholding group	8.9	21.1	25.8	50.0	16.1		

Source: Census and landholding records, Nangal, 1990; for 2 single men, information on their siblings or their father's landholding is missing.

might improve. For example, *'Vah ghar to māldār hī nahīn, jis ghar main ek randuā na ho'* ('A house is not wealthy unless it has an elderly widower' – here meaning an unmarried brother or father's brother). In order to follow this argument through further, we need to remember that amongst the Jats, the first move in a marriage negotiation is usually made by the family of a girl, who approach the family of a potential groom, usually through intermediaries. In these discussions, the parents of a Jat girl are careful to avoid the possibility of downward mobility which would result from marrying her into a family with many sons, unless they have alternative sources of income. A young man may remain unmarried, then, because no offer is made for him. Even if his father is relatively well-to-do, his pride may make him unwilling to accept as a daughter-in-law a bride from distinctly lower-class families, yet these may be the only ones willing to make an offer. As in other castes, a man may 'inherit' a wife if his brother or a cousin dies; or he may search for a woman to 'buy'. Thus, if a man none the less remains single, it is unlikely that he was unable to find a bride, but probably that he did not make strenuous efforts to 'buy' one: the frequency with which this happens is what makes Jats stand out from the other castes. A young unmarried man may have sexual relations with the wife of one of his brothers, particularly if he is fed from their hearth: again, at least according to gossip, this *de facto* fraternal polyandry happens more frequently amongst Jats than among other castes.

The effects of sons remaining unmarried can be illustrated through a case study. Baldev Singh was born around 1900–10, and inherited a secure tenancy of about 30 acres. He had five sons who lived to maturity. The eldest son married and died leaving a widow with one son; she sold all his land and her son, a watchman in a pottery factory, was unable to look after her well.[21] Baldev's second and fourth sons remained single; in 1990 they lived in the same household as his fifth son, who married and himself had one son, aged 19 and a student in Bijnor. He expected to inherit about 20 acres of land from his father and his two unmarried uncles. Baldev's third son also married; he had only one son (and three daughters) and this son's son expected to inherit his five acres. If each of Baldev's sons had married, and had two or three sons living to maturity, Baldev's land would have been inherited by maybe ten to fifteen grandsons, each of whose share (in the absence of large-scale land purchases) would have been only two or three acres. In fact, only three

---

[21] This is the typical fate of widows who cannot support themselves. Since she is no longer in Nangal we could not find out why she did not get remarried to one of her late husband's unmarried brothers.

sons married; 80 per cent of Baldev's land is intact, and will be inherited by two of his three grandsons.

Not all Jat families were able to keep their landholdings together in this way. Moka Singh, for example, born around 1890, also controlled about 30 acres. He had four sons, and only the eldest, Hardev Singh, married. Hardev, however, had eight sons (one of whom died in infancy) and six of them (all but the youngest) have now married. The three younger married sons each house one of the unmarried uncles, and have a larger share of the land as a result. But there are already twelve great-grandsons: only three of them are likely to inherit as much as five acres, two will inherit about two-and-a-half acres each, and the rest will inherit less than an acre. There are also eleven great-granddaughters to be married. Not surprisingly, perhaps, each of the six married couples who have at least one son is using contraception: three women and one man are sterilized, and the woman with a young son after four daughters is using a Copper-T.

Jat demographic patterns, then, are more consistent with the view that at least some families have a conscious strategy to reduce land fragmentation, than that the high number of unmarried men is a simple response to a shortage of potential brides. Jat men are said (locally) to be quite willing to marry women from other castes, and their wives then become Jats by marriage – something unheard of among the other castes. This again seems to be a well-established pattern: according to Crooke, as a result of infanticide 'Jats are much addicted to purchasing girls of low caste and passing them off among their friends as genuine girls of the tribe and then marrying them' (Crooke 1896 Vol. III: 29). Pradhan (1966: 84) suggested that this pattern of 'buying' a wife from another caste was uncommon among the Jats of Muzaffarnagar, Meerut and Saharanpur (the three Districts immediately west of Bijnor) whereas marriages by 'elopement' were more frequent. We did not hear of any 'elopements' among the Jats of Nangal, but there is plenty of evidence of 'buying a wife'. In Nangal, 32 Jat married women (11 per cent) were said to have come from 'the hills' or 'the east' (eastern UP, or even Bihar), or from some distance away to the south or west. Younger sons and widowed or separated men have gone out and looked for a bride themselves, in some cases buying a woman who had already been married.

However, if that were the whole story, we would expect unmarried Jat men and those who took brides from a distance in 'unorthodox' marriages to be predominantly from the poorer families, as it is for men from other caste groups. In the north Indian hypergamous marriage system, 'unattractive' men – in this context, men with physical disabilities or from the bottom of any endogamous group – face real difficulties in arranging a marriage. While this clearly accounts for some of the cases of never-married men, Table 6.9 shows that nearly one-third of unmarried Jat men had fathers owning at least 10 acres.

Furthermore, Jat landlord, middle or rich peasant men who were the eldest brother or had no brothers or who had no sons by their first wives or were widowed at an early age, apparently found it relatively easy to marry for a second or even a third time. Nine men in Nangal had married more than once, of whom four contracted their second marriage while their first wife was still living. These four made 'respectable' second marriages with local Jat women, because they had no children from their first wife, and were marrying again in order to provide themselves with a male heir. By contrast, four of the five widowed men 'bought' their second bride from a distance.

We would argue, then, that the restriction of marriage for a substantial minority of Jat men, and female infanticide (and female neglect) were ways of regulating population growth in the interests of conserving the resources of the lineage (see Das Gupta 1993 for a similar argument with respect to Punjabi Jats). We have no totally compelling way of assessing whether such actions were the result of conscious planning in the past, but one clue suggests that it might have been. The leading Bijnor Jat family at Sahanpur, near Najibabad, some thirty kilometres from Nangal, operated a policy of primogeniture until the mid-1930s. Under this arrangement only the marriage of the eldest son was recognized as legitimate: any younger sons could take a 'wife' but their children would have no claim on the estate. By this measure the estate was kept undivided. These Jats seem to have been the only local *zamindārs* to operate in such a way. While this rule – and the reasons for it – would obviously have been known throughout all the Jats in the District, we have no means of knowing whether they entered into the decisions made by less prominent Jats. But such an attempt to avoid land fragmentation is at least consistent with the current demographic practice among Jats in Nangal. We can trace continuities between the historical pattern (reduced fertility in the economic interests of the joint family) with the current pattern of heavy use of contraceptives and near universal adoption of a small family norm, in the economic interests of the nuclear or stem household.

These high and nearly uniform patterns of family limitation may be partly a result of village characteristics. In Nangal, the Chamars (relative to Chamars elsewhere) also had high levels of contraceptive use, which might reflect the fact that Nangal is a relatively large village, with good communications and above-average provision of government facilities (schools, health sub-centre etc.). This may contribute to relatively low child mortality levels, for example. But the influence of village size and the Jats' dominant position reinforce each other. Here the contrast with the Sheikhs of Qaziwala is instructive.

Sheikh marriage and fertility

While the Jat demographic pattern has been unusual in several respects, the Sheikh demographic regime is statistically much more familiar. As we have already seen (see Tables 6.3 and 6.4), Sheikh sex ratios have historically been much closer to 'normality'. Sheikhs had one of the least 'masculine' sex ratios in the District in 1870, perhaps reflecting the fact that a higher proportion of people who called themselves Sheikhs lived in urban areas at the time. None the less, the figures do suggest some neglect of girls (and possibly high maternal death rates), since the recorded sex ratios were adverse to women in 1872, and worsened over the succeeding 60 years. With a child–woman ratio of 1.01 in 1872, compared to a Jat figure of 1.09, Sheikh fertility rates were probably lower than those of Jats in the 1870s. None the less, as a community, the Sheikh population was more likely to grow since Sheikh men married earlier, and fewer Sheikh adult men remained single or widowed (see Table 6.5).

Our own figures from Qaziwala suggest that Sheikhs there have had a more balanced set of mortality rates by sex in the past, but that this situation seems to be changing (see Table 6.10). For children born in 1950–69, the under-5 mortality rates for Sheikh girls were 10 per cent below those for boys, but for children born 1970–85, under-5 mortality rates for Sheikh girls were over 65 per cent above those for Sheikh boys. The probable reason for this shift can be seen from the figures for the different classes. (Because of the small numbers of landlord and rich peasant Sheikh couples, we have combined them with the middle peasant category.) Mortality rates for boys in the wealthier groups have dropped sharply, but rates for girls have stayed much the same. As with the Jats, families able to afford better standards of nutrition and the new medical treatments that have become available since the mid-1960s seem to have used them to keep their sons alive, whereas the conditions for girls have changed much less. Mortality rates for girls will probably eventually decline, but until that happens, girls are relatively much more heavily discriminated against than in previous years – though still by not so much as are Jat girls in Nangal. Among the Jats of Nangal, girl/boy under-5 mortality ratios were around 1.9 from 1945–1990; among the Sheikhs the ratio had risen to only 1.66 in the 1980s.

Only 13 Sheikh men aged 25 and over were still single in 1991, less

Table 6.10. *Child mortality of children born 1950–1985 to ever-married women who began cohabiting between 1950 and 1985, by class and year of birth, Qaziwala Sheikhs*

		Boys	Girls	Girl/Boy U5MR ratio
Children born 1950–1969				
Upper and middle class	U5MR	30	24	0.80
	Child deaths	9	11	
Lower class	U5MR	33	30	0.91
	Child deaths	18	20	
All classes	U5MR	32	28	0.86
	Child deaths	27	31	
Children born 1970–85				
Upper and middle class	U5MR	17	34	1.97
	Child deaths	23	42	
Lower class	U5MR	21	30	1.41
	Child deaths	45	57	
All classes	U5MR	19	32	1.66
	Child deaths	66	99	

Source: Maternity histories, 1991.
Notes: U5MR is the under-5 mortality rate, expressed as a percentage of live births. The class categories used are landlords, rich peasants and middle peasants in the upper and middle class; and poor peasants and the landless in the lower class.

than 5 per cent of all the men in this age category. Far more Sheikh men aged 25 and over were married (at 87 per cent) than were Jat men in Nangal (at 77 per cent). While this may in part have been a result of the more equal sex ratios among the Sheikhs, it may also reflect the general preference among most Hindu and Muslim castes (except for the Jats) for all men to marry. The system of marriage arrangements may also have played a part. As we showed in Chapter 4, the initiative in Sheikh marriages lies with a boy's kin, whereas among the Jats the initiative lies with a girl's kin. There is thus more scope for Sheikh men and their kin to search actively for a bride before they grow too old, whereas Jat men and their kin may be inhibited about being so active in search of a bride until they are much older. Whatever the causes, however, the Sheikh marriage patterns are much more normal for north India in general, whereas the Jat patterns are unusual.

The demographic implications of the marriage patterns and fertility and mortality rates common in Bijnor until recently can provide a stark contrast to those of the Jats described above. Proportionately more Sheikh girls survive and marry (and do so at an earlier age) than do Jat girls. As a result, even if each Sheikh woman were to have the same number of children as Jat women, the growth rate of Sheikhs in Qaziwala would still be about 10 per cent above that of the Jats in Nangal. In fact, as we saw in Chapter 2, Sheikh women have between one and two more children than their Jat counterparts. This difference is slightly reduced by the effect of the higher child mortality rates. As Tables 6.7 and 6.10 together show, 25 per cent of Qaziwala Sheikh children born between 1970 and 1985 died under the age of 5, compared with 18 per cent of children born in the same period among the Jats of Nangal. But since Sheikh women still have more children who live to maturity than do their Jat equivalents, population growth and land fragmentation is much more noticeable in Qaziwala.

One dramatic example which encapsulates some of these effects is that of Abdul Razaq. He was born in about 1910, and inherited (and purchased from an ex-*zamindār*) about 20 acres. His wife had six sons who lived to maturity (three more died in infancy and a fourth died from tetanus aged 15; and two of her four daughters have also died). All six sons married and have had children. When Abdul Razaq died in 1991 his land was still being operated as a single unit. The six brothers were 'progressive' farmers, jointly owning a tractor, an electric engine and two diesel pumping sets. But they all depend on the land, and have inherited only just over three acres each. Abdul Razaq's youngest son married in 1989, so the third generation is not yet complete, but already there are eleven granddaughters and nineteen grandsons. Only one of the grandsons (a non-commissioned officer in the army) has off-farm employment which might generate a surplus to allow him to purchase more land or acquire higher-quality education for his own children. Forty-three people are currently in the households supported by these 20 acres; forty years ago the land was supporting only four or five people.

Other men have inherited land undivided since their grandfather's time, but this cannot be seen as the result of conscious policy. Niazuddin is the largest landholder in Qaziwala, with about 30 acres of land. His father Amir Hussein inherited only about 6 acres, but was able to buy another 20 acres or so in a neighbouring village. Niazuddin is the only son to have lived to maturity, and he still farms this land. His wife bore five sons and four daughters, but two of the sons died. The two elder surviving sons have married, but the eldest, after ten years of marriage, has no children, and the second married in 1990. In about 1950 the 30 acres were supporting four or five people; now (at much higher yields) they are still supporting only eight, including Niazuddin's widowed sister. Significantly, however, none of his three sons has a college education, and they all work on the land.

Even rich peasant Sheikhs, as we have seen in Chapter 3, show few signs of limiting their family sizes. In Chapter 4 we also noted that many Sheikh couples respond to questions about family size by saying that it is a subject which they leave to God to decide. But matters are not as simple as this might suggest. Many Sheikhs responded to questions about family planning (like those we asked to collect women's maternity histories) by asking us why we were asking such questions. As a result of considerable pressure from government servants of one kind or another (the nurse-midwife and the doctors in the health centres and hospitals, the land registrar and other revenue officials, for example) many Sheikhs see themselves as under threat on the issue of family planning, and raising the topic is very delicate. We found it hard to generate discussion of desired family size, even though we strenuously denied any link between ourselves and the State family planning services, and backed this up by refusing to offer contraceptive services when we were asked, instead providing only general advice.[22]

Sheikh men would often not answer direct questions about family planning or desired family size. When Roger asked Waheed (S21) if his four boys and a girl were more than enough, or if he wanted some more, he grinned and did not answer. Roger stopped the interview at that point, and was later warned that if he continued asking about family size, the message would get around, and men would refuse to be interviewed even about the other, less-sensitive topics such as economic issues and education. Women would usually answer, but even so, in Qaziwala, unlike in Nangal, we had a number of problems with women who were unwilling to tell us about their maternity histories. Some said that they were scared that their husband would beat them, because they had not been given permission to answer our questions. Others accused us of wanting to count Muslims so that they could be recruited to fight against the Americans in the Gulf War, and be killed. Some Sheikh women were openly hostile, apparently believing that we represented the (Hindu) government or were there to press them to be sterilized:

What benefit will we get from what you're writing? There's nothing for us Muslims. There's neither diesel nor education nor agriculture. This year half an acre of wheat has been spoilt as we didn't get fertilizer. Nor can we get diesel for the engine, so what can we do? In every place we're dying of poverty. You're writing down the children, give us some medicine to stop children being born. Who's asking why you're writing about our children? No matter how many children we have, what are you giving us? Yes, no matter how many educated people come, they all say, 'Yes, there are so many children.' But the children are ours and the expenses are ours, and what does it cost them?

[22] For further details, see P. Jeffery et al. 1989 and P. Jeffery and R. Jeffery 1996

Sheikhs believed they were targeted because of their religion, and they also said that Islam was the reason why they could not be sterilized as the government wants. Sheikhs often discussed family limitation in terms which suggested that, although small families were desirable, they were only offered sterilization. Some women told us that the nurse-midwife had denied that any other form of contraception existed. But most Sheikhs, like Wakila, and Parvez and his wife Parveen, believed that sterilization was contrary to Islam.

I don't want any more children but I haven't made any arrangements. Nor have I asked my husband or my mother-in-law their opinion. Among us Muslims, if having children becomes closed from Allah's side then that's what happens. But the operation can't be done. When God produces even some little grub, then He also provides its food. When I and my husband were just two people, even then there was food to eat – and today there are children and even now He is giving us bread. (Wakila w/o Waheed, S21, landless, lives separately from her mother-in-law and two sisters-in-law, four sons and one daughter)

PARVEZ: How can one feed, wash and clothe children properly? I have eight, no, nine children. You can send your girls to a good school – there are only two of them. It's a matter of money. Here no one can educate children properly. Whatever poverty there is in Qaziwala is due to having many children; however much any one may earn, that's too little. But there's no way to stop children except sterilization and we can't have the operation because afterwards we can't make our prayers.
PATRICIA: There are other ways; if you go to hospital why don't you get a doctor to tell you some other way?
PARVEEN: We are frightened to go to hospital. We'll take medicine from the *hakīm* in Inampura. (Parvez, S14, middle peasant, farms 25 acres with father and four brothers, can read the Qur'an Sharīf; lives with his wife Parveen, uneducated, separately from her mother-in-law and five sisters-in-law. They have seven sons and two daughters)

No-one can tell him [her husband] what to do. He's not eating his father's earnings, he depends on himself. I could do something without telling him, but he says that if anything goes wrong, what will happen? Who will do the work and who would pay the medical expenses? But we're afraid of sterilization. Also it's not in our religion. I have heard that some people get "hot" in their brain from pills and so I'm afraid of pills also. But I'm thinking of Copper-T. My sister-in-law had a Copper-T put in three days ago by the Qaziwala woman "doctor". She had pain for one day and had pills and is now OK. So I'm also thinking for myself. (Salma w/o Sultan, S17, lives separately from her two sisters-in-law, mother-in-law dead, no schooling, two sons and one daughter)

The number of Sheikhs in Qaziwala is growing, then, for a combination of reasons. Nearly all Sheikh men are married, and their wives marry at relatively young ages. None of the wives works outside the home, and few of them have received secular schooling. Although many young women and some young men express a desire for small families, very few use modern contraceptive techniques. On the one hand, they believe that Islam is opposed to sterilization; on the other hand, they perceive themselves as vulnerable to a Hindu government which is keen that they should be sterilized. But either way, in the light of their continuing high levels of child mortality, they do not wish to use terminal methods, in case any of their children (especially their sons) might die. None of these characteristics make them unusual, locally or in other pre-transitional settings: their specifically Islamic beliefs and norms of behaviour add very little to an explanation of their fertility patterns. We have no evidence that Muslims are intentionally trying to out-breed Hindus; or that features of Muslim women's domestic position make significant differences to their ability or desire to reduce the number of children they bear.[23]

A political economy of demography in Bijnor

Jats in Nangal and Sheikhs in Qaziwala display two very different demographic regimes: high fertility and high mortality among the Sheikhs, low fertility and lower mortality among Jats.[24] The explanation of these different patterns has to be sought not in the intrinsic messages of religion *per se*, but in the interactions between religion and political economy. Religion and caste are social markers which locate groups in positions of social and political dominance or subordination. At the top of the local political scale, because of their landholdings and their political skills, the Jats have created a situation of relative security, in which they can influence government activity to their benefit – ranging from state tubewells or access to bank credit on the one hand, to the location of schools and health centres on the other. This has been a long-term achievement. In this context, it has been feasible to operate a strategy of family limitation in the interest of preventing land fragmentation; and (more recently) to use schooling aimed at urban employment for second and third sons.

Sheikhs occupy a declining position, in which the state (especially in the last 40 years) and major sources of credit (since the mid-nineteenth century) have been in the hands of Hindus – Jats but also Brahmans and Banias. When it comes to allocating jobs and resources, politicians and

---

[23] Muslim women are more vulnerable than Hindu women to divorce in Indian family law, and their husband's right to have more than one wife at a time in theory puts them in a weaker legal position, but such notional legal rights seemed to make little difference to most women in Bijnor on an everyday basis.

[24] They are alike, however, in having excess female mortality, both among children and during the child-bearing ages.

bureaucrats look first to caste; when Hindu politicians and bureaucrats have to make a choice between Hindus from different castes and non-Hindus, Muslims claim that Hindus stick together. In response, Muslims have turned to their own institutions, feeling they cannot rely on the organs of the state. But this leaves them badly served with 'public' resources (schools and clinics, cheap loans and subsidized agricultural inputs). The turn to Islamic education perpetuates the poor job chances of their sons. Muslim poverty (personal and collective) and downward mobility thus helps to explain their higher mortality rates not as a consequence of Islam itself, but of being Muslim in a Hindu-dominated society (in Bijnor, a Jat-dominated local state). Where does that leave fertility? High fertility rates are both a cause and a consequence of the Sheikh situation. Clearly, there is no substantial evidence of fertility limitation in the past. Before the 1950s, this probably led to relatively slow population growth and land fragmentation. When rising agricultural productivity and improving health care led to population growth, so did the Sheikh sense of alienation. Now they are faced with the consequences of population growth, the results of land fragmentation and a pervasive sense of personal and collective insecurity.

Differences among the women or in gender roles and obligations are not crucial in grappling with contrasts between the Sheikhs and the Jats; for both caste groups, women are subordinated by powerful mechanisms. They are similarly excluded from the ownership and control of property, and similar ideas of *izzat* (or prestige) constrain their movements and limit their involvement in many public sphere activities. Better urban links among the Jats may enable Jat girls to achieve secondary or college schooling. In addition, the dominance wielded by their husbands may allow Jat women to overcome some of the restrictions on their mobility: they may be more protected in public space, and be more able to take advantage of the relative freedom which comes from urban residence after marriage. But in many respects they remain vulnerable to male power; the sex-ratio data and material presented in Chapter 5 support this viewpoint. Young Jat and Sheikh women alike are also subject to the age- or seniority-based hierarchies among women.

It is possible to trace back many aspects of the differences between the two castes to patterns which emerge from the Census and other inquiries of the British period. Many of the historical patterns for UP up to the 1930s could still be traced amongst members of the Sheikh and Jat *jāti* in Bijnor in 1990–91. By contrast to the Jats, then, what has to be explained for the Sheikhs is their lack of change. Their current high fertility is to be expected for a population which has not experienced radical social or economic changes in the past 30 years: the growing productivity of the land has only just kept pace with their expansion in numbers. The Sheikhs are not *demographically* unusual: but it does seem to be unusual for a land-owning group to have taken so little advantage of the social and economic changes that have swept across north India since the mid-1960s. The question we now want to consider is why this seems to have been the case. Two possibilities need to be addressed: is there something about their caste culture which has inhibited them from responding to opportunities (especially those offered by different levels of government, such as education, health services and cheap credit) or have they been systematically excluded from them?

The first possibility is very hard to assess. For example, Islam as a creed shows no signs of hostility to schooling in general. The first words in the Qur'an enjoin the believer 'Read!' Islam is as much a religion of the urban trader as of the desert tribesman, so it is hard to argue that Islam is in any way opposed to schooling. In UP itself, throughout the British period when the Census reported literacy by caste group, the Sheikhs were better educated than the Jats. This may reflect a higher proportion of Sheikhs than Jats living in the towns, but equally the Jat stereotype of stolidity, of having an 'upside-down coconut' for a brain would suggest that, if anything, it was more likely that there were internal barriers to schooling among the Jats than among the Sheikhs.

The current differences in literacy rates by religion, which show higher literacy rates for Hindus than for Muslims, can be mostly explained in terms of region, residence patterns and economic status: the independent effects of religion are small by comparison. And similar arguments can be made about Hinduism as for Islam: religious beliefs by themselves do not explain behaviour in fields such as education. There are highly educated castes (most obviously the Brahmans but also, among Muslims, the Saiyids) and those for whom lengthy schooling is rare. Hinduism shows more evidence of attempts to prevent some castes (the Harijans) from benefiting from education than does Islam. Although some Sheikhs blamed Muslim attitudes for the low levels of school enrolments and achievements in their caste, this is a contested view.

Similar problems arise in trying to understand patterns in the use made of health services. Sheikhs may have higher death rates for their children, but it is hard to explain this in terms, for example, of differences in beliefs held by members of the different religious communities. Certainly, a serious comparative analysis of 'degrees of fatalism' would be difficult to conduct and hard to interpret. The case for intrinsic differences in attitudes is, therefore, at best not proven.

What we would argue, however, is that it is not necessary to posit such differences, since the evidence of systematic exclusion is enough to explain the patterns we observed.

Government schooling in UP has several communal features, and indeed most Muslims regard government schools as increasingly communalized. The language in which they teach has been of crucial significance. A key educational conflict of the immediate post-Independence period in UP was over the position of Urdu, perceived by many to be a Muslim language because of its script (a form of Persian, introduced by the Mughals), and because much Urdu literature was written by Muslims. Once Urdu was downgraded in UP to an optional language available only in some secondary schools, many Muslims felt the state was attempting to undermine their religious allegiances, by making it harder for them to learn Arabic.[25] Not only is Urdu not taught in government schools in Bijnor district, but the village teachers are almost all Hindus or Christians. Some of them made clear their distaste for things Islamic by, for example, refusing to make any allowances for Muslim students during Ramzan. Muslim students described to us their belief that Hindu students would be given preference in marks or other privileges. Further, teachers supplement their incomes through tuition fees. They are accused of favouring their own community when accepting pupils for tuition, and favouring their tutees in class. We cannot evaluate these claims nor the extensiveness of such behaviour, but people's *belief* that it happens acts as a further disincentive for Muslim children and their parents to take state schooling seriously. Finally we can also note, more speculatively, that Hindu teachers would probably regard a posting to a school in a Muslim village as a punishment, to be avoided if possible. Teachers trying to arrange a transfer spend many days in Bijnor or even in Lucknow; while they are engaged in these negotiations they rarely turn up to teach.

School attendance rates owe a great deal to the politics of school location. We do not have any accounts of how most of the schools around Nangal and Qaziwala were established, but we can presume that such decisions are rarely, if ever, made on the principle of locating schools where they will serve the maximum number of pupils, or to equalize access for different groups. The few academic accounts of school location suggest that when schools are a scarce political resource, they are allocated and placed according to the outcome of political pressure. In the 1950s and 1960s, villages that wanted a primary or junior secondary school had to provide some *panchāyat* or private land

---

[25] Brass 1974; Farouqui 1994; see also Lelyveld 1993.

and lobby hard for a decision to favour their village over competitors. Small villages with wealthy and well-connected landlords might acquire schools despite their inaccessibility; large villages might be ignored. Within villages, schools have usually been sited at places easily accessible to the children of dominant castes, who have usually controlled the public space in the historical core of the village: children from subordinate groups have been admitted only on sufferance. Put together, these features of school locations have given the Jats in Bijnor many more chances of success than the Sheikhs. As one of the dominant castes in the District and region in the 1950s and 1960s, they were able to ensure that their villages were well served by new schools; and as the dominant caste within villages like Nangal, they ensured that their children have had prior claims on these new schools. Education has become more widespread, and the benefits of state schooling have paled in contrast to those offered by private schools, and the Jats have been well placed to move on, maintaining their relatively privileged positions.

Thus Jats have been much more successful than Sheikhs in using education as a strategy to lessen their dependence on agriculture. They did not adopt education earlier than other Hindu castes: indeed, they have a reputation of being 'backward', compared with Brahmans and Banias. But they have managed to get their caste-fellows into positions of influence – members of the UP State Assembly, for example – and used this influence to give them more than their share of public employment. Jats are well entrenched in the police and the military (as was the case for Jats from Ludhiana and in Rampur: see Wyon and Gordon 1971, and Das Gupta 1981: 92). In Nangal, of the 104 men over the age of 50 in 1990, eight had pensions from their time in the police or the army. Jats had also acquired posts as teachers, and three Jat men over the age of 50 were or had been teachers. Altogether, in 1990 seven Jat men from Nangal were in 'service', that is, they had secure employment in one or other branch of the public sector.

It is hard to exaggerate the significance of these positions. A permanent position in the public sector provided a regular cash income well above what could be earned in equivalent private sector jobs. In 1990 teachers in private schools were paid no more than Rs 300 per month, whereas a government teacher earned at least Rs 1,200. Furthermore, government employment usually allowed some scope for additional income, either legitimate or corrupt. Teachers were usually allowed to give private tuition in their houses after and/or before school hours; other government servants could usually sell their favours in some form or other to bring in an extra income. People who held junior positions could pass on their jobs to a child if they died or were forced to retire through ill-health.

Some higher grades of government staff were entitled to a pension or a substantial lump sum on retirement. Several Jat families had benefited considerably from one member gaining a government job, including the family of the current chairman of the Nangal *panchāyat*. His father was a government tubewell operator under the British, and his brother was also employed in the irrigation department.

By contrast, Sheikhs had lost their educational advantages by the inter-war period, and had very few political resources to mobilize when school locations were being decided during the expansionary 1950s and 1960s. This has led to a cycle of reproduced disadvantage. When the Qaziwala primary school was built it was not placed in the space controlled by the Sheikhs within the village. Despite serving 3 villages (and a primary school-aged population of 500 or more) it still has only 2 rooms and 2 teachers, and a total enrolment of only 94 in 5 classes. Both teachers are Hindu women who have travelled out from Bijnor town on a daily basis since 1982.

No Qaziwala residents are school-teachers themselves; a culture of attendance at and success in state schooling has yet to develop. Sheikh men have rarely been successful in gaining state employment. One man with a BA is employed as a Cane Officer in a neighbouring District and another, with an MComm, has a job in a government cane mill. No man over the age of fifty has any kind of government employment, let alone one which will provide a pension or other financial benefits. More Sheikhs have invested in religious education, and eight of them are employed as teachers in *madrasās* or as *imāms* at mosques elsewhere.

Qaziwala, after all, is nearly as large a village as Nangal, and has easier access to the facilities offered by Bijnor. It too has been provided with a primary school and a health sub-centre, but whereas in Nangal they work well, in Qaziwala they do not. The sub-centre in Qaziwala is rarely open, and offers very few services. The primary school in Qaziwala teaches few children (mainly Harijans) and has hardly grown in size since it was established. Both 'demand' and 'supply' factors seem likely to have been important in these differences. Teachers and health workers (mostly Hindu) are more willing to work in Nangal than in Qaziwala, and villagers in Nangal are more likely to demand the services they have to offer, as well as being better able to influence the District administration to maintain the quality of what is provided.

Conclusion

The Jats of Nangal experienced a different environment, with far less risk, from that of the Sheikhs of Qaziwala. 'Security' is caste-specific. As a caste which was dominant at the District or sub-District level, Jats could be secure in their ability to command resources when necessary. For them, security did not depend in any great measure on the number of their children, but on their ability to manipulate kinship and caste relationships. They were in a position to take advantage of state facilities and of growing urban employment and other economic opportunities (trade, professions, urban land) to a far greater extent than were members of other castes. Jat family building strategies were consonant with their aggressive pursuit of political power, of education for their children, and of economic advancement on several different fronts. They were investing in tractors, in *khandsārī* (small sugar factories), and in brick works; their sons were in the Army and the police, or were lawyers in Bijnor or teachers.

Most Jat families now try to send their sons as far as a degree or a Master's qualification: a few try for medical or engineering training. The same families usually try to educate their daughters at least to degree level, to improve their chances of marrying a well-educated young man. In doing so, they are committing themselves to a long period of considerable expenditure.

As we noted in Chapter 3, recent discussions of the Bangladesh case suggest that increasing poverty and landlessness may be generating a desire for smaller families, which, in the presence of (supposedly) relatively non-threatening contraceptive services, has been turned into a rapid decline in total fertility rates (Cleland 1993; Thomas 1993; Kabeer 1996). In Bijnor, this situation could be fast facing the Sheikhs, as they experience continuing land fragmentation in the absence of dramatic gains in land productivity.[26]

Jat fertility rates have fallen very fast whereas Sheikh fertility is much the same as it was twenty or more years ago. It is a gross error, however, to leap from different fertility rates to the argument that Muslims were having more children in order to try to outnumber Hindus *because of their Islamic beliefs*. Religion in itself did not cause these differences in fertility behaviour. Many other features differentiate the Jats and the Sheikhs, and their religious beliefs are far from the most important of these. But because religion as an ethnic marker does affect everyday aspects of the lives of the Sheikhs, their identities as Muslims do indirectly influence their fertility. As Hammel argues (1995: 225) 'where

[26] But note that a recent study of the Green Revolution in Uttar Pradesh suggests that two strategies which are open to the Sheikhs – dairying, and the cultivation of labour-intensive, high-value crops – could maintain living standards in the absence of off-farm employment opportunities, since Bijnor town provides such an accessible market; see Sharma and Poleman 1993.

ethnic labels are effective proxies [for demographic behaviour] they are useful largely because elites have employed ethnic criteria to allocate sub-populations to positions in political and economic structures.' These do not need to be religious in origin: in the case of Sicily between the two World Wars, it was an ethnic classification on the basis of occupation (as *bracciante*, or labourer) which conditioned an ethnic response of continuing high fertility when other social groups had moved to limit their family sizes (Schneider and Schneider 1995: 185).

In India, it may be that brute numbers are of declining political significance: the days of 'vote-banks', when political parties could count on a small number of influential leaders to deliver the votes of *jāti* and groups of *jāti*, are over. Despite the numerical majority of Scheduled Castes (21 per cent) and Muslims (40 per cent) in Bijnor District (see Table 6.11), the BJP still managed to win the seat in the national elections of 1991 and 1996, and to take five of the seven Bijnor seats in the UP State elections in 1991 and again in 1993.[27] With the decline of the Congress Party in UP, the opposition to the BJP is fragmented and unable to make its voting power count.

What then is the future for these two *jāti* in Bijnor? The outlook for the Jats is by no means all positive. As in many other parts of the country, they are educating their sons to college level but rarely seeing a direct return for this investment. But some of them are becoming establis¹ 1 in commerce or in self-employment as minor professionals of one kind or another. For their farm incomes, they are heavily dependent on the government to continue agricultural subsidies and guaranteed prices in order to maintain their living standards. But at least they have managed to reduce and limit the extent of land fragmentation and most farm units are big enough to provide a reasonable living standard in the current economic conditions.

For the Sheikhs, the next few years are likely to be increasingly difficult. As a result of past population growth, farm sizes are already too small to provide an adequate living for many of them, and this situation will be aggravated as more landholdings are fragmented. They have not yet shown an interest in alternative strategies, such as dairying and the cultivation of labour-intensive, high-value crops like fruits, spices or vegetables. Their sons have little chance of permanent white-collar

---

[27] In terms of the electorate, the share of SCs and Muslims is likely to be less than these numbers suggest, because they have more children under the voting age of 18. In 1996 the BJP won with only 37 per cent of the vote. For more detailed discussion of Muslim electoral politics see Engineer 1996; for more on voting patterns in UP in the 1996 elections, see Shankar 1996; Misra 1996; Hantal 1996.

Table 6.11. *Percentage distribution of total population by 'religion', Bijnor District, 1921–1991*

	1921	1931	1951	1961	1971	1981	1991
Hindus	63.8	61.6	62.1	62.3	62.0	59.2	(57.8)
Scheduled Caste	(18)	(18)	18.8	20.2	20.3	20.3	20.7
non-Scheduled Caste	(46)	(44)	43.3	42.1	41.7	38.9	(37.1)
Muslims	35.9	37.6	36.5	36.5	36.7	39.5	(40.4)
Others	0.3	0.8	2.2	1.2	1.4	1.4	(1.8)
Total (000s)	**740**	**835**	**984**	**1,191**	**1,490**	**1,939**	**2,455**
Caste Hindus per 100 Muslims	(128)	(115)	119	115	114	98	(92)

Source: Census of India volumes, relevant years. Note that the 1921 and 1931 Censuses do not identify 'Scheduled Castes' and these figures are estimates based on totals for individual castes which were subsequently 'Scheduled'. In the 1991 Census, 2,755 people returned themselves as Buddhists: these are probably 'neo-Buddhists' who would otherwise appear as Scheduled Castes.

urban employment, nor of establishing themselves in business or in independent professions. Their best chances for preventing further economic decline lies in developing technical trades where Muslims have traditionally been strong, as mechanics or in the building trades. As in Bangladesh, the increasing poverty and landlessness of the Sheikhs may generate an increasingly strong desire for smaller families, which, despite the presence of relatively threatening contraceptive services, could be turned into a rapid decline in total fertility rates (Cleland 1993; Thomas 1993; Kabeer 1996). But there is a danger that this will be too late to prevent their further economic decline. The tragedy of the Sheikh demographic regime, then, is that it epitomizes the position of Muslims in India generally: essentialized by others, they are increasingly becoming a scapegoat for the frustrations of others, when they – as a new underclass – are suffering already from their exclusion from mainstream social institutions. The strengthening social divisions we witnessed in Bijnor in 1990–91 are unlikely to weaken in the foreseeable future: the nightmare of 'riot after riot' is a reality which will not leave Bijnor alone.

7   Conclusion

So far we have deliberately kept very close to the detail of our case study of Jats and Sheikhs in Bijnor, but here we want to discuss the relevance of this small-scale study beyond the bounds of Nangal and Qaziwala, and Bijnor District. In brief, our study should provoke questions about the current so-called Cairo consensus that women's empowerment via schooling, and fertility and morality decline inevitably go hand-in-hand. Our criticisms of this consensus are highlighted by our approach, which stresses the need to contextualize, to specify the content of schooling as well as its meaning to those involved, in order to understand demographic change. Finally, our account can provide insights into the emergent political situation in India.

The Cairo consensus

The 1994 Cairo Conference on Population and Development accepted the argument that the ability of women to control their own sexuality is an important element in fertility decline. Indeed, this was the starting point for our research in 1990. At Cairo, direct attempts at reducing fertility were given less overt priority than women's empowerment. Feminist rhetorics were adopted, and some tantalizing shifts in vocabulary were adopted by the major donor agencies. Women's rights – broadly as well as in the sphere of reproduction – are now part of the official agenda. 'Empowerment' is a term much bandied about and used to legitimize inputs into the educational sector, while the notion of 'unmet needs' for contraception is brought in to support the case for empowering women so that they can achieve the small families they are said to want.

These shifts would apparently please those feminists who have stressed the centrality of sexuality and fertility to women worldwide. We ourselves remain convinced that empowering women is a desirable goal in its own right. But we would add our voices to those who caution against a too-rapid celebration of the use of feminist terminologies at

Cairo. Such talk still implies that women are victims – of male power, of state oppression – but victims who are contrariwise also key villains of the piece, because of their excessive child-bearing. Commitments to population control remain strong, and the implications for women may still be unpleasant. In India, for example, population programmes have targeted women, particularly since 1977, at least in part because women have less power to resist than men do. Such programmes have marginalized many aspects of women's reproductive health (pelvic inflammatory disease, infertility, or other gynaecological complaints) and their health status in general. Women have been stereotyped as mothers by not taking account of women's work, which may not only cause occupational morbidity but also undercut their ability to fulfil their 'mothering' roles. The population programmes have also ignored issues of the safety and control of the technologies of fertility limitation, and women have had little chance to make an informed choice about contraception, or to reverse their decision if they change their minds. In all these matters, let alone the stark issues of life and death for girl babies and female foetuses, there is clearly much cause for concern about the situations of many Indian women. These women deserve support in their efforts to overcome barriers to their fuller freedom. But that support must not be conditional on their reducing their fertility.

We may be wrong to be cynical about the use of feminist rhetorics by those who support the Cairo consensus. Nevertheless, we still need to enter some caveats to any endorsement of the views expressed there. The Cairo consensus is based on two questionable assumptions, for it is not clear that schooling always leads to empowerment, nor is women's empowerment necessarily a precondition for fertility to decline. Our own findings suggest that women who have been to school seem to have little more freedom, autonomy or scope for the exercise of agency than unschooled women, and that fertility reduction among the Jats cannot be explained by any greater empowerment of Jat women. This cannot be read, however, as an attempt to undermine those who wish to improve the quantity or quality of schooling for girls in UP, or to find other ways to empower women. On the contrary, our point is simply that we should not *assume* that girls' schooling leads to their empowerment, nor that schooling or empowerment will lead inevitably to lower fertility.

The general Cairo arguments fail to look closely at what is meant by schooling, and how its content and meaning can be dramatically different in different places and at different times. By extracting schooling from its context, they uncritically assume that schooling has characteristics that may not appear in real schools and for real pupils. Girls' schooling can lead to women's empowerment only when class, community and gender politics are changed to make this possible. The Cairo consensus produces an individualistic account, and fails to consider the structural contexts in which women find themselves. This means that in some settings and at some times, rising or falling school enrolments may take place alongside fertility stability, decline or even increase, and girls may find that, when they reach adulthood, their schooling is of little use to them as they negotiate their way through life.

In so far as these findings suggest that girls' schooling may not be a quick fix for fertility decline, we do not find this a worrying conclusion. Continuing high fertility, among the Sheikhs or other groups in north India may be a problem for these groups, and especially for women who find themselves bearing more children than their physical and psychological health can stand. But we do not see a rising population as a major threat to global survival or Indian development or those other benefits which are often said to be threatened by the relatively high fertility of poor people. We would rather hope that our findings might lead to more clarity in policy-making with respect to girls' schooling and women's empowerment. The problems of schooling for girls in India will not be solved by more schools that are much the same as the existing ones: we must argue for improved quality, for schools that open minds rather than close them – in the UK as much as in UP.

Our findings point to continuing gender inequalities that affect almost all women in Bijnor, and there is obviously a case for redoubled efforts to ameliorate the situation. Even the best schools will not lead to an immediate empowerment of women if girls are sent to school as part of a strategy to improve their positions in a marriage market, rather than as a route to economic independence. In any case, even if consciousness-raising occurs, it must not be confused with empowerment: women who have been to school will not be empowered by their schooling if they remain embedded in structures that limit their room for manoeuvre. It is not only in Bijnor that young married women who have been to school face much the same domestic structures as the unschooled, with arranged marriages, migration on marriage, and the prospect of residing in households where their older in-laws have a major say over their fertility and other aspects of their everyday lives.

In the current political and economic climate, in India and beyond, schooling and empowerment programmes have few supporters. If we criticize the schooling that is provided, we may play into the hands of those who favour retrenchment in the educational sector. In such circles – among the economists of the World Bank attempting to implement Structural Adjustment Programmes, the senior civil servants in Delhi and Lucknow, or the patriarchal politicians who dominate Indian political life – female schooling and empowerment are not issues worth fighting for, unless they bring with them the promise of lower fertility. Because these elite groups share Malthusian views on the future of the world they may be persuaded by arguments which emphasize the fertility-reducing benefits that education and empowerment pro- grammes seem to offer. But we should not support schooling and empowerment programmes on false premises: we do not want to see schools ranked by the number of children their graduates bear, nor rotating credit schemes evaluated in terms of contraceptive adoption.

Until we are convinced otherwise, then, we remain suspicious that the hijacking of feminist vocabulary merely masks an agenda that actually prioritizes fertility reduction and is prepared to engage with girls' schooling or women's empowerment solely as a means to that end.[1] We need more detailed local accounts of the bases of women's disempower- ment, and the scope of schooling and other strategies to enhance the opportunities which women have.

Micro-studies and demography

A major contribution can be made by demographic studies that are sensitive to the possibilities offered by ethnographic methods. In 1979, when John Caldwell, P. H. Reddy and Pat Caldwell began a research project on the origins of demographic change in south India, they surprised many demographic colleagues by challenging the almost exclusive reliance on large-scale social surveys and censuses that characterized most orthodox demography at the time. In their study of the area around a Primary Health Centre in Karnataka, the Caldwells and Reddy demonstrated how a detailed knowledge of a local setting could help in understanding family planning decision-making.

Since that research, a growing body of work testifies to the benefits of the kind of research we have employed in Bijnor: an attempt to understand the 'cultural and social diversity which really explains why fertility or mortality levels persist in one place rather than another' (Caldwell, Reddy and Caldwell, 1988: 34). In our study, class position, schooling and aspects of women's everyday situations all have an intimate relationship with the fertility and child mortality regimes of the Jats and the Sheikhs. Yet the relatively small differences which emerge within each caste group cannot help to explain the relatively large differences between them. Among Jats and Sheikhs alike, the landless and poor peasants tend to have more children, even after a larger

---

[1] For further discussions of this view, see Petchesky 1995 and Hartmann 1995.

proportion have died, than do wealthier peasants. Again, in general, women who have been to school have slightly smaller numbers of children than do the unschooled women – but the effect of child mortality means that their completed family sizes are not very different. In each case, the patterns for one cohort of women do not necessarily apply to women in other cohorts. The explanations offered by those who stress the economic rationality of large families, or the modernizing or empowering influence of schooling, are of limited value.

More applicable, for these groups in Bijnor at least, is the general approach of Mead Cain (1981, 1983), who stresses the importance of uncertainty – and, we would add, of opportunity structures these patterned uncertainties imply.[2] The lowest levels of fertility occur among those sectors of the population – the middle and rich peasant Jats – who have the most favourable physical, social, economic and political environments. Their opportunities, of course, are not unlimited, nor can they exclude uncertainty completely: unexpected child deaths are only the most obvious of the events that undermine their confidence. Nor does their local social dominance protect the Jats from vulnerability. A variety of threats, such as those posed by the numerically larger landless and poor peasant Chamars, or from the effects of economic liberalization in the Indian economy, all pose a challenge to the privileged access to government jobs and to the subsidies and protected markets on which Jat affluence is based. Conversely, the highest fertility is found among those groups with most reason to feel that they have little control over their futures – poor and middle peasant Sheikhs, but also poor Chamars and other members of the Scheduled Castes, as well as of the less numerous clean Hindu castes, who are outside the scope of this study.[3]

Communalism and politics in India

Uncertainty and fears for the future will not necessarily help us to understand fertility choices in all other settings, though it is plausible to look at some obvious fertility differentials in this light. The cases of the Catholic–Protestant fertility differences in Northern Ireland, or of Arab–Jewish differences in Israel, or of class-based differences in fertility elsewhere, are only the most obvious. In these examples, as in Bijnor, the possibility of fertility control, or of planning a family size, is

---

[2] Cain talks of risk environments, but this connotes calculable, forward-oriented chances. We prefer to talk of uncertainty, the individual and collective perception of those risks as they affect people and others regarded by them as in similar circumstances.

[3] We have discussed these groups in some of our earlier work: see, for example, P. Jeffery et al. 1989; Lyon 1988.

something of which most people are aware. The confidence to implement preferences for a family of a particular size, however, is not so widely shared. These everyday concerns of threats and opportunities, rather than the dictates of theological doctrines, help us to make sense of the observable fertility differentials.

The unfolding events which surrounded us during our research in 1990–1991 made us increasingly aware of the contribution that communal politics can make to people's sense of vulnerability and opportunity in all spheres of Indian life. Muslims were most adversely affected by these events. What has happened in India since 1991 suggests that we were witnessing not just a local phenomenon, but a process affecting more and more people, and one whose ramifications are growing rather than declining. In 1990, the attempt to demolish the Babri mosque in Ayodhya failed; in December 1992, with a BJP government in office in UP, the police and paramilitary forces stood back and allowed Hindu activists to destroy the mosque and to clear the site. Riots broke out all across India, as in 1990, although this time, not in Bijnor town. The BJP government in UP was suspended by the central government. After the State elections of 1993, the new UP government was formed by a coalition of the Bahujan Samaj Party (BSP), representing members of the Scheduled Castes, and Mulayam Singh Yadav's Samajwadi Party (SP), with support from Other Backward Castes, especially in eastern UP, and Muslims. This government was inherently unstable, and Mayavati, the leader of the BSP, eventually broke away and formed a new administration with the support of the Congress and the BJP. This arrangement also could not last long; when it collapsed, the Central Government took power again. The new State elections held in mid-1996 also failed to produce stability.

The national elections of May 1996 produced a hung Parliament, with no party able to rule on its own. The BJP, the largest single party, failed to win any others to its cause, and the National Front, a combination of Left parties (the two Communist parties and the Socialists) and low-caste- and regionally-based parties, formed a coalition with support from the Congress party. As we write, the signs are that the BJP will use their enhanced legitimacy to increase their pressure for avowedly Hindu policies. The polarization between the mainly high-caste, urban middle-class supporters of the BJP and the rural low-caste poor peasants and Muslims who are the electoral base of the National Front, seems bound to grow. None of the parties can expect a mandate for strong rule, and new national elections before the allotted five-year span seem inevitable.

In these circumstances we cannot feel confident that social changes will benefit the people we have described in these pages, nor those in comparable villages across north India. In broad terms, the UP State elections followed the pattern of results from the national elections of May 1996, and the new UP assembly is divided, with the BSP, BJP and SP alike unable to create a stable government. None of these parties is committed to changing the structures that generate class, gender or communal inequality. At best they want to redistribute the spoils of office to favour one group rather than another. Everyday sexism not only divides women one from another, but also makes it hard for men and women to act together in support of more equitable relationships; everyday communalism divides the poor who might in other circumstances come together to create more substantial changes.[4] Local riots and intercommunal discrimination do not disappear of their own accord, but require systematic social and political efforts to combat them and the social groups which benefit from them. An organized secular and socialist movement is required if the conditions for the average villager – woman or man, Hindu, Muslim or Scheduled Caste – are to improve materially in the foreseeable future. But as we write, such a prospect looks increasingly unlikely.

[4] We have discussed these aspects of Bijnor life in P. Jeffery and R. Jeffery forthcoming; and in P. Jeffery, forthcoming.

Bibliography

Adams, Alayne and Sarah Castle 1994. 'Gender Relations and Household Dynamics,' pp. 161–73 in Gita Sen et al. *Population Policies Reconsidered: Health, Empowerment, Rights,* Boston: Harvard School of Public Health

Agarwal, Bina 1994. *A Field of One's Own: Gender and Land Rights in South Asia,* Cambridge: Cambridge University Press

Agnihotri, S. B. 1995. 'Missing Females: A Disaggregated Analysis,' *Economic and Political Weekly,* Vol. 30, No. 33, pp. 2074–84

Ahmed, Leila 1982. 'Western Ethnocentrism and Perceptions of the Harem,' *Feminist Studies,* Vol. 8, Fall, pp. 521–34

Akbar, M. J. 1988. *Riot After Riot: Reports on Caste and Communal Violence in India,* New Delhi and Harmondsworth: Penguin Books

Anderson, Benedict 1983. *Imagined Communities: Reflections on the Origin and Spread of Nationalism,* New York and London: Verso

Anker, Richard 1977. 'The Effect of Group Level Variables on Fertility in a Rural Indian Sample,' *Journal of Development Studies,* Vol. 14, No. 1, pp. 63–76

Anker, Richard, Myra Buvinic and Nadia H. Youssef (eds.) 1982. *Women's Roles and Population Trends in the Third World,* London: Croom Helm

Appadorai, Arjun 1993. 'Number in the Colonial Imagination,' pp. 314–39 in Carol A. Breckenridge and Peter van der Veer (eds.). *Orientalism and the Postcolonial Predicament: Perspectives on South Asia,* Philadelphia: University of Pennsylvania Press

Attwood, D. W. 1992. *Raising Cane: The Political Economy of Sugar in Western India,* Boulder and London: Westview Press; New Delhi: Oxford University Press

Banerjee, Nirmala (ed.) 1990. *Indian Women in a Changing Industrial Scenario,* New Delhi: Sage

Baru, Sanjaya 1990. *The Political Economy of Indian Sugar: State Intervention and Structural Change,* Delhi: Oxford University Press

Basu, Alaka 1987. 'Household Influences on Childhood Mortality: Evidence from Historical and Recent Mortality Trends,' *Social Biology,* Vol. 34, Fall/Winter, pp. 187–205

1992. *Culture, the Status of Women, and Demographic Behaviour: Illustrated with the Case of India,* Oxford: Clarendon University Press

1996. 'Girls' Schooling, Autonomy and Fertility Change: What do These Words Mean in South Asia?,' pp. 48–71 in Roger Jeffery and Alaka Basu (eds.). *Girls' Schooling, Women's Autonomy and Fertility Change in South Asia*, New Delhi: Sage Publications

Basu, Tapan, Pradip Datta, Sumit Sarkar, Tanika Sarkar and Sambuddha Sen 1993. *Khaki Shorts, Saffron Flags*, Delhi, Orient Longman

Bayly, Christopher A. 1983. *Rulers, Townsmen and Bazaars: North Indian Society in the Age of British Expansion 1770–1870*, Cambridge: Cambridge University Press

Becker, Gary 1960. 'An Economic Analysis of Fertility,' in *Demographic and Economic Change in Developed Countries*, Universities-National Bureau Conference Series, No. 11, Princeton, NJ., Princeton University Press

Berer, Marge 1993. 'Population and family planning policies: women-centred perspectives,' *Reproductive Health Matters*, Vol. 1, No. 1, pp. 4–12

Bernstein, Henry, Ben Crow and Hazel Johnson, (eds.) 1992. *Rural Livelihoods: Crises and Responses*, Oxford: Oxford University Press

Beteille, André 1992. *The Backward Classes in Contemporary India*, Delhi: Oxford University Press

Binswanger, Hans P., Robert E. Evenson, Cecilia A. Florencio and Benjamin N. F. White (eds.) 1980. *Rural Household Studies in Asia*, Singapore: Singapore University Press

Bliss, Christopher and Nick Stern 1982. *Palanpur: The Economy of an Indian Village*, Oxford: Oxford University Press

Bok, Sissela 1994. 'Population and Ethics: Expanding the Moral Space,' pp. 15–26 in Gita Sen et al. (eds.). *Population Policies Reconsidered: Health, Empowerment, Rights*, Cambridge: Harvard University Press

Bose, Ashish 1991. *Demographic Diversity of India: 1991 Census*, Delhi: B. R. Publishing Corporation

Bourdieu, Pierre and Jean-Claude Passeron 1977. *Reproduction in Education, Culture and Society*, translated by Richard Nice, London and Beverly Hills: Sage

Bradley, Candice 1995. 'Women's Empowerment and Fertility Decline in Western Kenya,' pp. 157–78 in Susan Greenhalgh (ed.). *Situating Fertility: Anthropology and Demographic Inquiry*, Cambridge: Cambridge University Press

Brass, Paul Richard 1974. *Language, Religion and Politics in North India*, London and New York: Cambridge University Press

Briggs, George W. 1972. *The Chamārs*. Reprinted from Oxford University Press 1920, Delhi: Low Price Publications

Bruce, Judith and Daisy Dwyer (eds.) 1988. *A Home Divided: Women and Income in the Third World*, Stanford: Stanford University Press

Byres, Terence J. 1988. 'Charan Singh (1902–87): An Assessment,' *Journal of Peasant Studies*, Vol. 15, No. 2, January, pp. 139–89

Cain, Mead 1980. 'The Economic Activities of Children in a Village in Bangladesh,' pp. 218–47 in Hans P. Binswanger et al. (eds.). *Rural House-hold Studies in Asia*, Singapore: Singapore University Press

1981. 'Risk and Insurance: Perspectives on Fertility and Agrarian Change in India and Bangladesh,' *Population and Development Review*, Vol. 7, No. 3, pp. 435–74

1983. 'Landlessness in India and Bangladesh: A Critical Review of National

Data Sources,' *Economic Development and Cultural Change*, Vol. 32, October, pp. 149–67

1984. 'Women's Status and Fertility in Developing Countries: Son Preference and Economic Security,' World Bank Staff Working Papers No. 682, Population and Development Series No. 7

1986. 'The Consequences of Reproductive Failure: Dependence, Mobility and Mortality among the Elderly in South Asia,' *Population Studies*, Vol. 40, No. 3, pp. 375–88

1988. 'The Material Consequences of Reproductive Failure in Rural South Asia,' pp. 20–38 in Daisy Dwyer and Judith Bruce (eds.). *A Home Divided: Women and Income in the Third World*, Stanford: Stanford University Press

1990. 'Risk and Fertility in a Semi-Feudal Context: The Case of Rural Madhya Pradesh,' Research Division Working Papers No. 19, The Population Council, New York

Cain, Mead, S. K. Khonam and S. Nahar. 1979. 'Class, Patriarchy and the Structure of Women's Work in Rural Bangladesh,' *Population and Development Review*, Vol. 5, No. 3, pp. 405–38

Cain, Mead and Geoffrey McNicoll. 1986. 'Population Growth and Agrarian Outcomes,' Centre for Policy Studies Working Paper 128, Population Council, New York

Caldwell, John C. 1979. 'Education as a Factor in Mortality Decline: An Examination of Nigerian Data,' *Population Studies*, Vol. 33, No. 3, pp. 395–413

1980. 'Mass Education as a Determinant of the Timing of Fertility Decline,' *Population and Development Review*, Vol. 6, No. 2, pp. 225–55

1982. *A Theory of Fertility Decline*, New York: Academic Press

1985. 'Strengths and Limitations of the Survey Approach for Measuring and Understanding Fertility Change: Alternative Possibilities,' pp. 45–63 in John Cleland and John Hobcraft in collaboration with Betzy Dinesen (eds.). *Reproductive Change in Developing Countries: Insights from the World Fertility Survey*, Oxford: Oxford University Press

Caldwell, John C. and Pat Caldwell 1987. 'The Cultural Context of High Fertility in Sub-Saharan Africa,' *Population and Development Review*, Vol. 13, No. 3, pp. 409–37

Caldwell, John C., P. H. Reddy and Pat Caldwell 1988. *The Causes of Demographic Change: Experimental Research in South India*, Madison and London: The University of Wisconsin Press

Caplan, Lionel 1977. 'Social Mobility in Metropolitan Centres: Christians in Madras City,' *Contributions to Indian Sociology*, Vol. 11, pp. 193–218

Carter, Anthony T. 1985. 'Agency and Fertility: For an Ethnography of Practice,' pp. 55–85 in Susan Greenhalgh (ed.) *Situating Fertility: Anthropology and Demographic Inquiry*, Cambridge: Cambridge University Press

Cassen, Robert H. 1978. *India: Population, Economy, Society*, London: Macmillan

Census of India 1981, Occasional Paper No. 2 of 1989 *Child Mortality, Age at Marriage and Fertility in India*

Census of India 1981, Occasional Paper No. 5 of 1988 *Child Mortality Estimates of India*

Chaianov, A. V. 1966. *The Theory of Peasant Economy*, translated by Daniel Thorner, Basil Kerblay and Richard E. F. Smith, Homewood, Illinois: American Economic Association

Chakrabarty, Dipesh 1995. 'Modernity and Ethnicity in India: A History for the Present,' *Economic and Political Weekly*, Vol. 30, No. 52, pp. 3373–80

Chanana, Karuna (ed.) 1988. *Socialisation, Education and Women: Explorations in Gender Identity*, New Delhi: Orient Longman

  1988. 'Social Change or Social Reform: The Education of Women in Pre-Independence India,' pp. 96–128 in Karuna Chanana (ed.). *Socialisation, Education and Women: Explorations in Gender Identity*, New Delhi: Orient Longman

Chowdhry, Prem 1994. *The Veiled Women: Shifting Gender Equations in Rural Haryana 1880–1990*, Delhi: Oxford University Press

Clark, Alice (ed.) 1993. *Gender and Political Economy: Explorations of South Asian Systems*, New Delhi and Oxford: Oxford University Press

Cleland, John 1993. 'Equity, Security and Fertility: A Reaction to Thomas,' *Population Studies*, Vol. 47, No. 2, pp. 345–52

Cleland, John and John Hobcraft in collaboration with Betzy Dinesen (eds.) 1985. *Reproductive Change in Developing Countries: Insights from the World Fertility Survey*, Oxford: Oxford University Press

Cleland, John and Christopher Wilson 1987. 'Demand Theories of the Fertility Transition: An Iconoclastic View,' *Population Studies*, Vol. 41, No. 1, pp. 5–30

Cleland, John and Shireen Jejeebhoy 1996. 'Maternal Schooling and Fertility: Evidence from Censuses and Surveys,' pp. 72–106 in Roger Jeffery and Alaka Basu (eds.). *Girls' Schooling, Women's Autonomy and Fertility Change in South Asia*, New Delhi: Sage

Cleland, John, Nashid Kamal and Andrew Sloggett 1996. 'Links Between Fertility Regulation and the Schooling and Autonomy of Women in Bangladesh,' pp. 205–17 in Roger Jeffery and Alaka Basu (eds.). *Girls' Schooling, Women's Autonomy and Fertility Change in South Asia*, New Delhi: Sage

CMIE (Centre for Monitoring the Indian Economy) 1985. *Profiles of Districts, Part 1, A–K*, Bombay: CMIE

Cochrane, Susan 1979. *Fertility and Education: What Do We Really Know?*, Baltimore: Johns Hopkins University Press

Cohn, Bernard 1987. 'The Census, Social Structure, and Objectification in South Asia,' in his *An Anthropologist among the Historians and Other Essays*, New Delhi: Oxford University Press

Crooke, William 1897. *The North-Western Provinces of India: Their History, Ethnology and Administration*, London: Metheun, (second edition: Karachi: Oxford University Press, 1972)

Das, Veena (ed.) 1990. *Mirrors of Violence: Communities, Riots and Survivors in South Asia*, Delhi: Oxford University Press

Das Gupta, Monica 1978. 'Production Relations and Population: Rampur,' pp. 177–85 in Geoffrey Hawthorn (ed.) *Population and Development*, London: Cass

1987. 'Selective Discrimination against Female Children in Rural Punjab, India,' *Population and Development Review*, Vol. 13, pp. 77–100

1990. 'Death Clustering, Mothers' Education and the Determinants of Child Mortality in Rural Punjab, India,' *Population Studies*, Vol. 44, No. 3, pp. 489–505

1995. 'Fertility Decline in Punjab, India: Parallels with Historical Europe,' Population Studies, Vol. XLIX, November, pp. 481–500

Datta, Pradip Kumar 1993. ' "Dying Hindus": Production of Hindu communal common sense in early 20th century Bengal,' *Economic and Political Weekly*, Vol. 28, No. 25, pp. 1305–19

Datta, S. K. and John B. Nugent 1983. 'Are Old Age Security and the Utility of Children in Rural India Really Unimportant?,' *Population Studies*, Vol. 38, No. 4, pp. 507–12

Davies, Christie 1976. 'Hindu and Muslim Fertility in India,' *Quest*, Vol. 99, No. 1, pp. 1–20

de Haan, H. H 1988. *Alternatives in Industrial Development: Sugarcane Processing in India*, New Delhi: Sage Publications

de Tray, Denis 1980. 'On the Microeconomics of Family Behaviour in Developing Societies,' pp. 69–97 in Hans P. Binswanger et al. (eds.). *Rural Household Studies in Asia*, Singapore: Singapore University Press

Dixon-Mueller, Ruth 1993. *Population Policy and Women's Rights: Transforming Reproductive Choice*, London: Praeger

Dube, Leela 1988. 'Socialisation of Hindu Girls in Patrilineal India,' pp. 166–92 in Karuna Chanana (ed.). *Socialisation, Education and Women: Explorations in Gender Identity*, New Delhi: Orient Longman

Dumont, Louis 1970. *Homo Hierarchicus: The Caste System and its Implications*, translated by Mark Sainsbury, Chicago: University of Chicago Press

Durrenberger, E. Paul (ed.) 1984. *Chayanov, Peasants and Economic Anthropology*, New York: Academic Press

Dyer, Caroline 1993. 'Operation Blackboard: Policy Implementation in Indian Elementary Education,' unpublished PhD thesis, University of Edinburgh

Dyson, Tim and Mick P. Moore 1983. 'On Kinship Structure, Female Autonomy and Demographic Behaviour in India,' *Population and Development Review*, Vol. 9, No. 1, pp. 35–60

Dyson, Tim 1991. 'Child Labour and Fertility: An Overview, an Assessment and an Alternative Framework,' pp. 81–100 in Ramesh Kanbargi (ed.). *Child Labour in the Indian Sub-continent: Dimensions and Applications*, New Delhi: Sage

1992. 'An Assessment of Recent Demographic Trends in India,' in Barbara Harris, S. Guhan and Robert H. Cassen (eds.). *Poverty in India: Research and Policy*, Delhi: Oxford University Press

Easterlin, Richard A. 1983. 'Modernisation and Fertility: A Critical Essay,' in Richard A. Bulatao and R. D. Lee (eds.). *Determinants of Fertility in Developing Countries*, Washington D. C. : National Academic Press

Ehrlich, Paul R. 1968. *The Population Bomb*, New York: Balantine

Engineer, Asghar Ali (ed.) 1984. *Communal Riots in Post-Independence India*, London: Sangam

1991. 'Press on Ayodhya "Kar Seva",' *Economic and Political Weekly*, Vol. 26, No. 20, pp. 1263–65

(ed.) 1991. *Mandal Commission Controversy*, Delhi: Ajanta Publications

1995. 'Bhagalpur Riot Inquiry Commission Report,' *Economic and Political Weekly*, Vol. 30, No. 28, pp. 1729–31

1996. 'How Muslims Voted,' *Economic and Political Weekly*, Vol. 31, No. 21, pp. 1239–41

EPW Research Foundation 1994. 'Social Indicators of Development for India II: Inter-State Disparities,' *Economic and Political Weekly*, Vol. 29, No. 21, pp. 1300–08

Fargues, Philippe 1993. 'Demography and Politics in the Arab World,' *Population: an English Selection*, Vol. 5, pp. 1–20

Farouqui, Ather 1994. 'The Emerging Dilemma of the Urdu Press in India,' *The American Journal of Economics and Sociology*, Vol. 53, July, pp. 360–2

Federici, Nora, Karen Oppenheim Mason and Solvi Sogner (eds.) 1993. *Women's Position and Demographic Change*, Oxford: Clarendon Press

Folbre, Nancy 1988. 'The Black Four of Hearts: Towards a New Paradigm of Household Economics,' pp. 248–62 in Judith Bruce and Daisy Dwyer (eds.). *A Home Divided: Women and Income in the Third World*, Stanford: Stanford University Press,

Freire, Paolo 1972. *Cultural Action for Freedom*, Harmondsworth: Penguin,

Galanter, Marc and Rajeev Dhavan 1989. *Law and Society in Modern India*, Delhi: Oxford University Press

Goody, Jack and Stanley J. Tambiah 1974. *Bridewealth and Dowry*, London and New York: Cambridge University Press

Gopal, Sarvepalli (ed.) 1991. *Anatomy of a Confrontation: The Babri Masjid-Ramjanmabhumi Issue*, New Delhi: Penguin

Gold, Ann Grodzins 1994. 'Gender Violence and Power: Rajasthani Stories of Shakti,' pp. 26–48 in Nita Kumar (ed.). *Women as Subjects: South Asian Histories*, Calcutta: Stree

Government of India 1974. *Towards Equality: Report of the Committee on the Status of Women in India*, New Delhi: Department of Social Welfare, Ministry of Education and Social Welfare

Government of Uttar Pradesh 1990. *Statistical Diary, Uttar Pradesh 1989*, Lucknow: Economic and Statistics Division, State Planning Institute

Greenhalgh, Susan 1990. 'Toward a Political Economy of Fertility: Anthropological Contributions,' *Population and Development Review*, Vol. 16, No. 1, pp. 85–106

1994. 'Anthropological Contributions to Fertility Theory,' Population Council Research Division Working Papers No. 64, New York

1995. 'Anthropology Theorises Reproduction,' pp. 3–28 in Susan Greenhalgh (ed.). *Situating Fertility: Anthropology and Demographic Inquiry*, Cambridge: Cambridge University Press

Greenhalgh, Susan (ed.) 1995. *Situating Fertility: Anthropology and Demographic Inquiry*, Cambridge: Cambridge University Press

Gupta, Jyotsna 1993. ' "People Like You Never Agree to Get it": Visit to an

Indian Family Planning Clinic,' *Reproductive Health Matters*, Vol. 1, No. 1, pp. 39–43

Hammel, Eugene 1995. 'Economics 1, Culture 0: Fertility Change and Differences in the Northwest Balkans, 1700–1900,' pp. 225–58 in Susan Greenhalgh (ed.). *Situating Fertility: Anthropology and Demographic Inquiry*, Cambridge: Cambridge University Press

Hantal, Bhimasen 1996. 'BSP: Gaining Strength,' *Economic and Political Weekly*, Vol. 31, No. 21, pp. 1242–43

Hardin, Garrett 1995. *Living within Limits: Ecology, Economics and Population Taboos*, New York: Oxford University Press

Harrison, Paul 1992. 'Battle of the Bulge,' *The Guardian* (London) 1 May, p. 25

Hart, Gillian 1991. 'Engendering Everyday Resistance: Gender, Patronage and Production Policies in Rural Malaysia,' *Journal of Peasant Studies*, Vol. 19, No. 1, pp. 93–121

Hartmann, Betsy 1987. *Reproductive Rights and Wrongs: The Global Politics of Population Control and Contraceptive Choice*, New York: Harper and Row

Hartmann, Betsy and Hilary Standing 1985. *Food, Saris and Sterilisation: Population Control in Bangladesh*, London: Bangladesh International Action Group

Harvey, David 1989. *The Condition of Postmodernity: An Enquiry into the Origins of Cultural Change*, Oxford: Basil Blackwell

Haynes, Douglas and Gyan Prakash (eds.) 1991. *Contesting Power: Resistance and Everyday Social Relations in South Asia*, New Delhi: Oxford University Press

Hendre, Sudhir 1971. *Hindus and Family Planning*, Bombay, Supraja Prakashan

Hobsbawm, Eric 1973. 'Peasants and Politics,' *Journal of Peasant Studies*, Vol. 1, No. 1, pp. 3–22

Illich, Ivan 1976. *Deschooling Society*, Harmondsworth: Penguin

Inden, Ronald B 1990. *Imagining India*, Oxford: Blackwell

Inkeles, Alex 1974. 'The School as a Context for Modernization,' in Alex Inkeles and D. B. Holsinger (eds.). *Education and Individual Modernity in Developing Countries, International Studies in Sociology and Social Anthropology*, Vol. 14, Leiden: Brill

Inkeles, Alex, and David H. Smith 1974. *Becoming Modern: Individual Change in Six Developing Countries*, London: Heinemann Educational

Jackson, Cecile 1993. 'Questioning Synergism: Win-win with Women in Population and Environment Policies?,' *Journal of International Development*, Vol. 5, No. 6, pp. 651–68

Jackson, Monica 1976. 'Caste Cultures and Fertility in South Karnataka,' unpublished PhD thesis, University of Edinburgh

Jain, Anrudh K. and Moni Nag 1986. 'Importance of Female Primary Education for Fertility Reduction in India,' *Economic and Political Weekly*, Vol. 21, No. 36, pp. 1602–7

Jain, Devaki and Nirmala Banerjee (eds.) 1985. *The Tyranny of the Household: Investigative Essays on Women's Work*, New Delhi: Shakti Books

Jeffery, Patricia 1979. *Frogs in a Well: Indian Women in Purdah*, London: Zed Press forthcoming 'Religious Identity, Gender Politics and Community,' in Julia Leslie (ed.). *Gender, Religion and Social Definition*, New Delhi: Oxford University Press

Jeffery, Patricia and Amrita Basu (eds.) 1997. *Appropriating Gender: Comparative*

Perspectives on Women's Agency and Politicized Religion in South Asia, New York and London: Routledge

Jeffery, Patricia and Roger Jeffery 1994. 'Killing my Heart's Desire: Education and Female Autonomy in Rural North India,' pp. 125–71 in Nita Kumar (ed.). *Women as Subjects: South Asian Histories*, Calcutta: Stree

1996. *Don't Marry me to a Plowman! Women's Everyday Lives in Rural North India*, Boulder: Westview

forthcoming 'Silver Bullet or Passing Fancy? Girls' Schooling and Population Policy,' in Ruth Pearson and Cecile Jackson (eds.). *Gender Research and Development: An Agenda for the 1990s*, London: Routledge

Jeffery, Patricia, Roger Jeffery and Andrew Lyon 1988. 'When Did You Last See Your Mother? Aspects of Female Autonomy in Rural North India,' in John Caldwell, Allan Hill and Valerie Hull (eds.). *Micro-Approaches to Demographic Research*, London: Kogan Page International

1988. 'Conundrums of Child Survival: Class, Ethnicity and Sex Differentials in Child Mortality in Rural North India,' mimeo

1989. *Labour Pains and Labour Power: Women and Childbearing in India*, London: Zed Books

Jeffery, Roger and Alaka M. Basu (eds.) 1996. *Girls' Schooling, Women's Autonomy, and Fertility Change in South Asia*, New Delhi: Sage

Jeffery, Roger and Patricia Jeffery 1992. 'A Woman Belongs to Her Husband: Female Autonomy, Women's Work and Childbearing in Bijnor,' in Alice Clark (ed.). *Gender and Political Economy*, New Delhi: Oxford University Press

1994. 'The Bijnor Riots, October 1990: Collapse of a Mythical Special Relationship?,' *Economic and Political Weekly*, Vol. 29, pp. 551–8

Jeffery, Roger, Patricia Jeffery and Andrew Lyon 1984. 'Female Infanticide and Amniocentesis,' *Social Science and Medicine*, Vol. 19, No. 11, pp. 1207–12

1989. 'Taking Dung-Work Seriously: Women's Work and Rural Development in North India,' *Economic and Political Weekly*, Vol. 24, pp. WS 32–7

Jeffrey, Robin 1993. *Politics, Women and Well Being: How Kerala Became a Model*, New Delhi: Oxford University Press

Jejeebhoy, Shireen 1991. 'Women's Roles: Health and Reproductive Behaviour,' pp. 114–48 in J. K. Satia and Shireen Jejeebhoy (eds.). *The Demographic Challenge: A Study of Four Large North Indian States*, Delhi: Oxford University Press

Jodha, N. S. and R. P. Singh 1991, 'Child Labour in Dryland Agriculture in India,' pp. 63–77 in Ramesh Kanbargi (ed.). *Child Labour in the Indian Sub-continent: Dimensions and Applications*, New Delhi: Sage

Kabeer, Naila 1995. 'Ideas, Economics and the Sociology of Supply,' mimeo

Kanbargi, Ramesh (ed.) 1991. *Child Labour in the Indian Sub-continent: Dimensions and Applications*, New Delhi: Sage

Kandiyoti, Deniz 1988. 'Bargaining with Patriarchy,' *Gender and Society*, Vol. 2, No. 3, pp. 274–90

Kertzer, David I. 1995. 'Political-economic and Cultural Explanations of Demographic Behaviour,' pp. 29–52 in Susan Greenhalgh (ed.). *Situating Fertility: Anthropology and Demographic Inquiry*, Cambridge: Cambridge University Press

Khan, M. E. 1972. *An Analysis of Family Planning Practices in India*, Baroda: Operations Research Group

1979. *Family Planning Among Muslims in India: A Study of the Reproductive Behaviour of Muslims in an Urban Setting*, Delhi: Manohar

Khan, Mohammed Firoz 1991. *Human Fertility in Northern India*, Delhi: Manak Publications

Kiely, Ray 1995. *Sociology and Development: The Impasse and Beyond*, London: UCL Press

King, Elizabeth M. and M. Anne Hill (eds.) 1993. *Women's Education in Developing Countries: Barriers, Benefits and Policies*, Baltimore and London: Johns Hopkins University Press

Kocher, James 1980. 'Population Policy in India: Recent Developments and Current Prospects,' *Population and Development Review*, Vol. 6, No. 2, pp. 299–310

Krishnakumar, Asha 1991. 'Canards on Muslims: Calling the Bluff on Communal Propaganda,' *Frontline*, Vol. 8, No. 21, pp. 93–8

Kumar, Krishan 1995. *From Post-Industrial to Post-Modern Society*, Oxford: Blackwell

Kumari, Ranjana 1989. *Brides are not for Burning: Dowry Victims in India*, London: Sangam Books

Lambert, Helen 1996. 'Caste, Gender and Locality in Rural Rajasthan,' pp. 93–123 in Christopher J. Fuller (ed.). *Caste Today*, Delhi, Oxford University Press

Lelyveld, David 1993. 'The Fate of Hindustani: Colonial Knowledge and the Project of a National Language,' pp. 189–214 in Carol A. Breckenridge and Peter van der Veer (eds.). *Orientalism and the Postcolonial Predicament: Perspectives on South Asia*, Philadelphia: University of Pennsylvania Press

Lerner, David 1968. 'Modernisation: Social Aspects,' pp. 386–95 in David L. Sills (ed.). *International Encyclopedia of the Social Sciences*, Vol. 9 and 10, London: Collier-Macmillan Publishers

LeVine, Robert A. 1980. 'Influences of Women's Schooling on Maternal Behaviour in the Third World,' *Comparative Education Review*, Vol. 24, No. 2/2, pp. 53–105

LeVine, Robert A., S. E. Levine, A. Richman, F. Medardo Tapia Uribe, C. Sunderland Correa and P. M. Miller 1991. 'Women's Schooling and Child Care in the Demographic Transition: A Mexican Case Study,' *Population and Development Review*, Vol. 17, No. 3, September, pp. 459–96

Lindenbaum, Shirley 1990. 'The Education of Women and the Mortality of Children in Bangladesh,' pp. 353–70 in Alan C. Swedlund and George J. Armelagos (eds.). *Disease in Populations in Transition: Anthropological and Epidemiological Perspectives*, New York: Bergin and Garvey

Lockwood, Matthew and Paul Collier 1988. 'Maternal Education and the Vicious Cycle of High Fertility and Malnutrition,' Policy, Planning and Research Working Papers (WPS 130) in Women in Development, Population and Human Resources Department, The World Bank, Washington D.C.

Lukes, Steven 1972. *Power: A Radical View*, London: Macmillan

Lyon, Andrew 1988. 'One or Two Sons: Class, Gender and Fertility in North India,' unpublished PhD thesis, University of Edinburgh

Mahmud, Simeen and Anne M. Johnson 1994. 'Women's Status, Empowerment and Reproductive Outcomes,' pp. 151–59 in Gita Sen et al. (eds.). *Population Policies Reconsidered: Health, Empowerment, Rights*, Boston: Harvard School of Public Health

Mamdani, Mahmood 1972. *The Myth of Population Control: Family, Caste, and Class in an Indian Village*, New York: Monthly Review Press

Mandelbaum, David G. 1974. *Human Fertility in India: Social Components and Policy Perspectives*, Berkeley: University of California Press
   1988. *Women's Seclusion and Men's Honor: Sex Roles in Northern India, Bangladesh and Pakistan*, Tucson: University of Arizona Press

Mani, Lata 1990. 'Multiple Mediations: Feminist Scholarship in the Age of Multinational Reception,' *Feminist Review* No. 35, pp. 24–41

Mason, Karen O. 1984. *The Status of Women: A Review of its Relationships to Mortality and Fertility*, New York: Rockefeller Foundation
   1993. 'The Impact of Women's Position on Demographic Change During the Course of Development,' pp. 19–42 in Nora Federici, Karen Oppenheim Mason and Solvi Sogner (eds.). *Women's Position and Demographic Change*, Oxford: Clarendon Press

May, D. A. and D. M. Heer. 1968. 'Son Survivorship Motivation and Family Size in India: A Computer Simulation,' *Population Studies*, Vol. 22, No. 2

Mazrui, Ali A. 1994. 'Islamic Doctrine and the Politics of Induced Fertility Change: An African Perspective,' pp. 121–34 in Jason L. Finkle and A. Alison McIntosh (eds.). *The New Politics of Reproduction*, supplement to *Population and Development Review*, Vol. 20, New York: Oxford University Press

McGregor, Robert S. 1993. *The Oxford Hindi–English Dictionary*, Delhi: Oxford University Press

McNicoll, Geoffrey 1992. 'Changing Fertility Patterns and Policies in the Third World,' *Annual Review of Sociology*, Vol. 18, pp. 85–108
   1994. 'Institutional analysis of fertility,' Research Division Working Papers No. 62, The Population Council, New York

Menon, Ritu and Kamla Bhasin 1993. 'Recovery, Rupture, Resistance: Indian State and Abduction of Women during Partition,' *Economic and Political Weekly*, Vol. 28, No. 17, pp. WS2–11

Metcalf, Barbara D. 1982. *Islamic Revival in British India: Deoband, 1860–1900*, Princeton: Princeton University Press
   1992. *Perfecting Women: Maulana Ashraf Ali Thanwi's Bahishti Zewar*, Delhi: Oxford University Press

Miller, Barbara 1981. *The Endangered Sex: Neglect of Female Children in Rural North India*, Ithaca, New York: Cornell University Press

Minkler, Meredith 1977. 'Consultants or Colleagues? The Role of US Population Advisers in India,' *Population and Development Review*, Vol. 3, No. 4, pp. 403–19

Mintz, Sidney W. 1985. *Sweetness and Power: the Place of Sugar in Modern History*, New York: Viking

Misra, Amaresh 1996. 'Politics in Flux,' *Economic and Political Weekly*, Vol. 31, No. 22, pp. 1300–2

Misra, Bhaskar D. 1982. 'Social Cultural Aspects of Population Growth,' pp. 255–67 in *Population of India*, Country Monograph Series No. 10, New York: United Nations

Mitra, Asok 1978. *India's Population: Aspects of Quality and Control*, New Delhi: Abhinav Publications

Mody, Nawaz B. 1987. 'The Press in India: The Shah Bano Judgement and its Aftermath,' *Asian Survey*, Vol. 27, August, pp. 935–53

Mukhopadhyay, Nilanjan 1994. *The Demolition: India at the Crossroads*, New Delhi: Indus

Murthi, Mamta, Anne-Catherine Guio and Jean Drèze 1995. 'Demographic Outcomes, Economic Development and Women's Agency,' Discussion Paper 61, The Development Economics Research Programme, London, London School of Economics

Nag, Moni 1982. 'Modernisation and its impact on fertility: the Indian scene,' Centre for Policy Studies, Working Papers No. 84, New York: The Population Council

Nag, Moni and Neeraj Kak 1984. 'Demographic Transition in a Punjab Village,' *Population and Development Review*, Vol. 10, No. 4, December, pp. 661–78

Nambissan, Geetha B. 1996. 'Equity in Education? Schooling of Dalit Children in India,' *Economic and Political Weekly*, Vol. 31, No. 16–17, pp. 1011–24

Narayana, G. and John Kantner 1992. *Doing the Needful: The Dilemma of India's Population Policy*, Boulder: Westview Press

Nevill, H. R. 1908 (1928). *Bijnor: A Gazetteer*, Allahabad: Superintendent, Government Press

Obermeyer, Carla Makhlouf 1992. 'Islam, Women and Politics: The Demography of the Arab Countries,' *Population and Development Review*, Vol. 18, No. 1, pp. 33–60

1994. 'Religious Doctrine, State Ideology and Reproductive Options in Islam,' pp. 59–75 in Gita Sen and Rachel C. Snow (eds.). *Power and Decision: the Social Control of Reproduction*, Boston: Harvard School of Public Health

O'Hanlon, Rosalind and David Washbrook 1992. 'After Orientalism: Culture, Criticism and Politics in the Third World,' *Comparative Studies in Society and History*, Vol. 34, No. 1, pp. 141–67

Okely, Judith 1991. 'Defiant Moments: Gender, Resistance and Individuals,' *Man*, Vol. 26, No. 1, pp. 3–22

Okely, Judith and Helen Callaway (eds.) 1992. *Anthropology and Autobiography*, London: Routledge

Omran, A. R. 1992. *Family Planning in the Legacy of Islam*, London and New York: Routledge

Operations Research Group 1990. *Family Planning Practices in India: Third All-India Survey*, Baroda: Operations Research Group

Overall, Christine 1987. *Ethics and Human Reproduction: A Feminist Analysis*, Boston and London: Allen and Unwin

Pahl, Jan 1983. 'The allocation of money and the structuring of inequality within marriage,' *Sociological Review*, Vol. 31, pp. 237–62

Pai Panandikar, V. A. and P. K. Umashankar 1994. 'Fertility Control and Politics in India,' pp. 89–104 in Jason L. Finkle and A. Alison McIntosh, (eds.). *The New Politics of Reproduction*, Supplement to *Population and Development Review*, Vol. 20, New York: Oxford University Press

Pandey, Gyanendra 1991. 'In Defence of the Fragment: Writing about Hindu–Muslim Riots in India Today,' *Economic and Political Weekly*, Vol. 26, Nos. 11 and 12, pp. 559–72

Pandey, Gyanendra (ed.) 1993. *Hindus and Others*, New Delhi: Viking

Pant, Rashmi 1987. 'The Cognitive Status of Caste in Colonial Ethnography: A Review of Some Literature of the North-West Provinces and Oudh,' *Indian Economic and Social History Review*, Vol. 24, No. 2, pp. 145–62

Papanek, Hanna 1979. 'Family Status Production: The "Work" and "Non-work" of Women,' *Signs*, Vol. 4, pp. 775–81

Patnaik, Utsa 1976. 'Class Differentiation Among the Peasantry,' *Economic and Political Weekly*, Vol. 11, No. 39, pp. A82–A108

Petchesky, Rosalind 1995. 'From Population Control to Reproductive Rights: Feminist Fault Lines,' *Reproductive Health Matters*, Vol. 6, No. 1, pp. 152–61

Pradhan, M. C. 1966. *The Political System of the Jats of Northern India*, Bombay: Oxford University Press

Prakash, Gyan 1992. 'Can the "Subaltern" Ride? A reply to O'Hanlon and Washbrook,' *Comparative Studies in Society and History*, Vol. 34, No. 1, pp. 168–84

Prakash, Indra 1979. *They Count Their Gains–We Calculate Our Losses*, New Delhi: Akhil Bharat Hindu Mahasabha

Raheja, Gloria G. 1994. 'Women's Speech Genres, Kinship and Contradiction,' pp. 49–80 in Nita Kumar (ed.). *Women as Subject: South Asian Histories*, Calcutta: Stree

Raheja, Gloria G. and Ann Grodzins Gold 1994. *Listen to the Heron's Words*, Berkeley and London: University of California Press

Rajan, Rajeswari Sunder 1993. *Real and Imagined Women: Gender, Culture, and Postcolonialism*, London: Routledge

Rajan, S. Irudaya, Mala Ramanathan and U. S. Mishra 1996. 'Female Autonomy and Reproductive Behaviour in Kerala: New Evidence from the Recent Kerala Fertility Survey,' pp. 269–87 in Roger Jeffery and Alaka M. Basu (eds.). *Girls' Schooling, Women's Autonomy and Fertility Change in South Asia*, New Delhi: Sage

Ramaseshan R. 1990. 'The Press on Ayodhya,' *Economic and Political Weekly*, Vol. 25, pp. 2701–5

Ravindran, T. N. Sundari 1993. 'The Politics of Women, Population and Development in India,' *Reproductive Health Matters*, Vol. 1, No. 1, pp. 26–38

Registrar-General, India 1976. *Fertility Differentials in India*, New Delhi: Ministry of Home Affairs, Government of India

    1981 *Survey of Infant and Child Mortality, 1979*, New Delhi: Ministry of Home Affairs, Government of India

    1982 *Survey Report on Level, Trends and Differentials in Fertility, 1979*, New Delhi: Ministry of Home Affairs, Government of India

Report of the UP Zamindari Abolition Committee 1948. Allahabad: Superintendent, Government Printing

Robb, Peter (ed.) 1995. *The Concept of Race in South Asia*, Delhi: Oxford University Press

Rostow, Walt Whitman (ed.) 1963. *The Economics of Take-off into Sustained Growth*, London: Macmillan

Rudolph, Lloyd I. and Susanne Hoeber Rudolph 1987. *In Pursuit of Lakshmi: The Political Economy of the Indian State*, Hyderabad: Orient Longman

Saberwal, Satish and Mushirul Hasan 1984. 'Moradabad Riots 1980: Causes and Meanings,' *Economic and Political Weekly*, Vol. 19, pp. 208–27

Said, Edward W. 1978. *Orientalism*, London: Routledge and Kegan Paul

Safilios-Rothschild, Constantina 1982. 'Female Power, Autonomy and Demographic Change in the Third World,' pp. 117–32 in Richard Anker, Myra Buvinic and Nadia H. Youssef (eds.). *Women's Roles and Population Trends in the Third World*, London: Croom Helm

Sathar, Zeba, Nigel Crook, Christine Callum and Shahnaz Kazi 1988. 'Women's Status and Fertility Change in Pakistan,' *Population and Development Review*, Vol. 14, No. 3, pp. 415–32

Satia, J. K. and Shireen Jejeebhoy (eds.) 1991. *The Demographic Challenge: A Study of Four Large North Indian States*, Delhi: Oxford University Press

Savitri, R. 1994. 'Fertility rate decline in Tamil Nadu: some issues,' *Economic and Political Weekly*, Vol. 29, No. 29, pp. 1850–2

Schneider, Peter and Jane Schneider 1995. 'High Fertility and Poverty in Sicily: Beyond the Culture vs. Rationality Debate,' pp. 179–201 in Susan Greenhalgh (ed.). *Situating Fertility: Anthropology and Demographic Inquiry*, Cambridge: Cambridge University Press

Scott, John 1990. *Weapons of the Weak: Everyday Forms of Peasant Resistance* Delhi: Oxford University Press

Sen, Amartya 1990. 'Gender and Co-operative Conflicts,' pp. 123–49 in Irene Tinker (ed.). *Persistent Inequalities: Women and World Development*, New York: Oxford University Press

 1995. 'Population Policy: Authoritarianism versus Co-operation,' mimeo, MacArthur lecture given in New Delhi, August

Sen, Gita 1995. 'Women, Poverty and Population: Issues for the Concerned Environmentalist,' pp. 67–86 in Lourdes Arizpe, M. Priscilla Stone and David C. Major (eds.). *Population and Environment: Rethinking the Debate*, Boulder: Boulder

Sen, Gita, Adrienne Germain and Lincoln Chen (eds.) 1994. *Population Policies Reconsidered: Health, Empowerment, Rights*, Cambridge: Harvard University Press

Sen, Gita and Rachel Snow (eds.) 1994. *Power and Decision: The Social Control of Reproduction*, Boston: Harvard School of Public Health

Shah Commission Inquiry 1978. *Report of the Shah Commission of Inquiry: Third and Final Report*, Delhi: Government of India, Controller of Publications

Shankar, Kripa 1996. 'Lok Sabha Elections: Balance Sheet,' *Economic and Political Weekly*, Vol. 31, No. 21, pp. 1243–44

Shariff, Abusaleh 1995. 'Socio-Economic and Demographic Differentials between Hindus and Muslims in India,' *Economic and Political Weekly*, Vol. 31, No. 46, pp. 2947–53

Sharma, Rita and Thomas T. Poleman 1993. *The New Economics of India's Green Revolution: Income and Employment Diffusion in Uttar Pradesh*, Ithaca and London: Cornell University Press

Sharma, Ursula 1980. *Women, Work and Property in North-West India*, London: Tavistock

1981. 'Male Bias in Anthropology,' *South Asia Research*, Vol. 1, No. 2, pp. 34–8

1986. *Women's Work, Class and the Urban Household*, London: Tavistock

Simmons, Ozzie G. 1988. *Perspectives on Development and Population Growth in the Third World*, New York: Plenum Press

Simon, Herbert 1976. *Administrative Behavior*, New York: The Free Press

Singh, Ajit Kumar 1987. *Agricultural Development and Rural Poverty*, New Delhi: Ashish Publishing House

Sofat R. 1991. 'Aligarh Hospital "Massacre": Fact and Fiction,' *Economic and Political Weekly*, Vol. 26, pp. 1205–6

Sridhar, V. 1991. 'Fiction and Fact: The Real Plight of the Minorities,' *Frontline*, Vol. 8, No. 21, pp. 99–101

Srinivas, Mysore Narasimha 1962. *Caste in Modern India*, Bombay and London: Asia Publishing House

Standing, Hilary 1991. *Dependence and Autonomy: Women's Employment and the Family in Calcutta*, London: Routledge

Stone, Ian 1984. *Canal Irrigation in British India*, Cambridge: Cambridge University Press

Summers, Lawrence, H. 1993. 'Foreword,' pp. vii–ix in Elizabeth M. King and M. Anne Hill (eds.). *Women's Education in Developing Countries: Barriers, Benefits and Policies*, Baltimore and London: Johns Hopkins University Press

Swedlund, Alan C. and George J. Armelagos (eds.) 1990. *Disease in Populations in Transition: Anthropological and Epidemiological Perspectives*, New York: Bergin and Garvey

Szreter, Simon 1996. *Fertility, Class and Gender in Britain 1860–1940*, Cambridge: Cambridge University Press

Tambiah, Stanley Jeyaraja 1989. 'Bridewealth and Dowry Revisited: The Position of Women in Sub-Saharan Africa and North India,' *Current Anthropology*, Vol. 30, August/October, pp. 413–27

Tarlo, Emma 1995. 'Body and Space in a Time of Crisis,' mimeo, paper presented to the meeting of the South Asian Anthropologists Group, London, September

Tinker, Irene (ed.) 1990. *Persistent Inequalities: Women and World Development*, New York: Oxford University Press

Tilly, Charles 1986. *The Contentious French*, Cambridge, Mass., London: Belknap Press

Thomas, Neil. 'Land, Fertility, and the Population Establishment,' *Population Studies*, Vol. XLV, November 1991, pp. 379–97

1993. 'Economic Security, Culture and Fertility: A Reply to Cleland,' *Population Studies*, Vol. 47, No. 2, pp. 353–9

Thompson, Catherine S. 1985. 'The Power to Pollute and the Power to Preserve: Perceptions of Female Power in a Hindu Village,' *Social Science and Medicine*, Vol. 21, pp. 707–11

van der Veer, Peter 1987. 'God must be Liberated: A Hindu Liberation Movement in Ayodhya,' *Modern Asian Studies*, Vol. 21, No. 2, pp. 283–301

1994. *Religious Nationalism: Hindus and Muslims in India*, Berkeley and London: University of California Press

Vatuk, Sylvia J. 1969. 'A Structural Analysis of the Hindi Kinship Terminology,' *Contributions to Indian Sociology*, Vol. 3, No. 1, pp. 94–115

ViczZiany, Marika 1982. 'Coercion in a Soft-state: The Family Planning Programme of India,' *Pacific Affairs*, Vol. 55, Fall, pp. 373–402

Visaria, Leela 1985. 'Infant Mortality in India: Level, Trends and Determinants,' *Economic and Political Weekly*, Vol. XX, Nos. 32–34, pp. 1352–59, 1399–405, and 1447–50

1996. 'Regional Variations in Female Autonomy and Fertility and Contraception in India,' pp. 235–60 in Roger Jeffery and Alaka M. Basu (eds.). *Girls' Schooling, Women's Autonomy and Fertility Change in South Asia*, New Delhi: Sage

Visaria, Pravin 1975. 'The Myth of Population Control by Mahmood Mamdani (book review),' *Population Studies*, Vol. 29, No. 2, July, pp. 323–7

Visaria, Pravin and Leela Visaria 1994. 'Demographic transition: Accelerating Fertility Decline in 1980s,' *Economic and Political Weekly*, Vol. XXIX, Nos. 51–52, pp. 3281–92

Vlassoff, Carol 1992. 'Progress and Stagnation: Changes in Fertility and Women's Position in an Indian Village,' *Population Studies*, Vol. 46, No. 2, pp. 195–212

Vlassoff, Michael 1991. 'An Assessment of Studies Linking Child Labour and Fertility Behaviour in Less Developed Countries,' pp. 101–22 in Ramesh Kanbargi (ed.). *Child Labour in the Indian Sub-continent: Dimensions and Applications*, New Delhi: Sage

Vlassoff, Michael and Carol Vlassoff 1980. 'Old Age Security and the Utility of Children in Rural India,' *Population Studies*, Vol. 34, pp. 487–99

Watkins, Susan C. 1993. 'If All Ae Knew About Women Was What We Read in Demography, What Would We Know?,' *Demography*, Vol. 30, No. 4, pp. 551–77

Weiner, Myron 1991. *The Child and the State in India: Child Labor and Education Policy in Comparative Perspective*, Princeton: Princeton University Press

Webster, Andrew 1990. *Introduction to the Sociology of Development*, Basingstoke and London: Macmillan

Wiser, Charlotte Viall and William Henricks Wiser 1971. *Behind Mud Walls, 1930–1960*, Berkeley: University of California Press

Wiser, William Hendricks 1936. *The Hindu Jajmani System*. Lucknow: Lucknow Publishing House

World Bank 1989. *India: Poverty, Employment and Social Services*, Two volumes, New Delhi: World Bank

1991. *Gender and Poverty in India: A World Bank Country Study*, Washington, D.C. World Bank

Wright, Theodore P. Jr. 1983. 'The Ethnic Numbers Game in India: Hindu–
Muslim Conflicts over Conversion, Family Planning, Migration and the
Census,' pp. 405–27 in William C. McCready (ed.). *Culture, Ethnicity and
Identity: Current Issues in Research*, New York: Academic Press

Wyon, John and John Gordon 1971. *The Khanna Study: Population Problems in
the Rural Punjab*, Cambridge, MA: Harvard University Press

Yadava, K. N. S. 1995. *Status and Fertility of Women in Rural India*, Delhi:
Manak

Zachariah, K. C. 1984. *The Anomaly of the Fertility Decline in India's Kerala State:
A Field Investigation. Staff Working Paper No. 700*, Washington D.C., The
World Bank

Index